Understanding Cognition

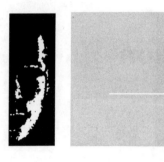

Basic Psychology

This series offers those new to the study of psychology comprehensive, systematic and accessible introductions to the core areas of the subject. Written by specialists in their fields, they are designed to convey something of the flavour and excitement of psychological research today.

Understanding Children's Development
Second Edition
Peter K. Smith and Helen Cowie

Understanding Neuropsychology
J. Graham Beaumont

Understanding Cognition
Peter J. Hampson and Peter E. Morris

Forthcoming

Understanding Abnormal Psychology
Neil Frude

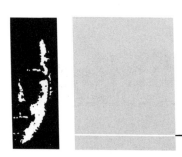

Understanding Cognition

Peter J. Hampson
and
Peter E. Morris

WITHDRAWN
FROM
STOCK

BLACKWELL
Oxford UK & Cambridge USA

Copyright © Peter J. Hampson and Peter E. Morris 1996

The right of Peter J. Hampson and Peter E. Morris to be identified as authors of this work has been asserted in accordance with the Copyright, Designs and Patents Act 1988.

First published 1996
2 4 6 8 10 9 7 5 3 1

Blackwell Publishers Ltd
108 Cowley Road
Oxford OX4 1JF
UK

Blackwell Publishers Inc.
238 Main Street
Cambridge, Massachusetts 02142
USA

British Library Cataloguing in Publication Data

A CIP catalogue record for this book is available from the British Library.

Library of Congress Cataloging-in-Publication Data

Hampson, Peter J.
    Understanding cognition / Peter J. Hampson and Peter E. Morris.
        p.   cm. – (Basic psychology.)
    Includes bibliographical references and index.
    ISBN 0–631–15749–2. — ISBN 0–631–15751–4 (pbk.)
    1. Cognition.   I. Morris, P. E. (Peter Edwin)
  II. Title.   III. Series: Basic psychology (Oxford, England)
    BF311.H332   1995   153–dc20   95–6421
                                                        CIP

ISBN 0–631–15749–2; 0–631–15751–4

Commissioning Editor: Alison Mudditt
Desk Editor: Hazel Coleman
Production Manager: Lisa Eaton
Text Designer: Ian Foulis
Picture Researcher: Ginny Stroud-Lewis

Typeset in 10 on 12pt Palatino by Photoprint, Torquay, S. Devon
Printed in Great Britain by Alden Press, Oxford

This book is printed on acid-free paper.

This book is dedicated to

Margaret and Joseph
and
Lucy and Susan

Contents

Figures

Tables

Series Editor's Preface

Psychology is a relatively new science which has already made notable achievements; yet its methods are constantly being questioned and re-defined. This book is one of a series of introductory psychology texts, designed to convey the fast-moving and relevant nature of contemporary research while at the same time encouraging the reader to develop a critical perspective on the methodology and data presented. The format of the book is intended to aid such independent inquiry, as is shown in particular by the boxes at the end of each chapter that concentrate on individual studies as 'worked examples'.

The books in the Basic Psychology series should be accessible to those with no previous knowledge of the discipline. *Understanding Cognition* can profitably be used by students on their own without a teacher, but resources aimed at groupwork are also included: a further reading section, discussion points and practical exercises follow each chapter.

Peter K. Smith

Preface

This book has been a long time in gestation and has gone through various drafts before reaching its final state. Our aims have been to provide a basic, but reasonably thorough introduction to contemporary cognitive psychology. These are not easy aims to reconcile, and throughout the production of this book we have felt torn between wishing, as researchers, to do full justice to this or that area, and producing a text, as teachers, that could be read and understood by someone with little formal background in psychology. We hope we have succeeded in steering a middle course. The text is intended primarily for first year undergraduates, and for those A-level students, guided by their tutors, who seek a deeper appreciation of contemporary cognitive psychology. As reasonably experienced teachers of psychology we feel that the boundary between the A-level curriculum and that typically offered for first year undergraduates is necessarily blurred, since not all psychology undergraduates have taken, or have had the opportunity to take, psychology at A-level, and some A-level students may wish for a more satisfying coverage of an issue or area than that typically offered by a standard introductory text. Our text is an attempt to straddle this divide, and is designed to support either the A-level or early part of the degree curriculum.

Books on cognition often follow a common format, working through the intake, maintenance, transformation, elaboration and use of information, typically starting with pattern recognition and ending with thinking. We have chosen to depart from this structure, and have divided our book into three parts. In the first, we consider the major elements of cognition, focusing on the basic structures, processes and mental operations involved in memory, perception, attention, skills and language. In the second part we examine cognition in action and consider a variety of cognitive activities particularly, though not exclusively, from a real-world perspective. The third part then reviews three approaches to modelling cognition. This structure may not be to everyone's taste, but we already know that others find it refreshing. We believe that it lays out three complementary strands of contemporary cognitive psychology in a clear and accessible way, and provides a welcome alternative to the standard 'linear' treatment.

Psychology is an exciting and fast-moving discipline, and cognitive psychology is one of its most vibrant parts. As we read through our final draft before its despatch to the publishers we were struck by just how much research has been conducted during the (comparatively short!) time in which we have been working as university researchers and teachers of psychology. Tales of 'when we were students' aside, there simply was not such a range of issues discussed when we were undergraduates, and the extension of the 'cognitive approach' outside its original range has been staggering. Has this explosion of research been accompanied by real progress in our understanding of the mind, or have there simply been new problems raised with little prospect of their solution? On the whole we are optimistic that progress has been made. To take just a few examples, we are surer now than we were, say, 20 years ago, of the importance of both structural and functional levels of explanation in cognition. We now see clearly, in a way that was only dimly perceived earlier, the challenge of the ecological approach, and we are beginning to grasp how the relationships between everyday and laboratory approaches to mind might be studied. We now understand the possibility of extending cognitive methods and findings to other areas and issues as diverse as neuropsychology, police interrogation procedures, learning to learn and clinical psychology. We also know (or at least have strong evidence to support the view) that people are not strictly rational rule-following systems. Cognition probably relies more on good matching, perceptual and memory skills than it does on thinking, understood as a rational activity, or on rule following. Of course, there are some new problems which we did not anticipate a generation ago, and some old ones which still need to be resolved. The new debate between symbolism and connectionism looks set to drag on, while attention and the even thornier problems of consciousness are still with us. The path between cognition and emotion is starting to be cleared, but more needs to be done to establish the true nature of the linkage.

Two names appear on the front of this book, but behind them are a large support group of individuals whose help we must acknowledge. They include the various people who have helped in the writing and production of the book, and others who, sometimes simply by their presence, have helped the process along. We would therefore like to take this opportunity to thank Fiona Lyddy for invaluable and conscientious help in the final preparation of the text, John McCarthy for various timely references, several groups of students for reading and commenting on earlier drafts, Alison Mudditt for her unending patience and skill as a commissioning editor, and Peter Smith, the series editor, for helping us to a successful conclusion. We also wish to thank secretaries Jo Rose and Noreen Moyhihan in Cork and Sheila Whalley and Anne Hayton in Lancaster. There are, as well, a number of other individuals who have wittingly or otherwise helped to bring this project to fruition, too numerous to mention by name, but to whom we are also grateful. Thanks also to our departmental fax machines, and to the inventors of electronic mail!

We would also like to single out for special mention the various anonymous reviewers who commented on earlier drafts of the manuscript: both those who advised on individual chapters, and those who assessed the entire product. Their comments were extremely helpful and always perspicacious. Not least because they calmly steered us away from making too many substantive errors, and gently indicated the occasional typographical challenges which might otherwise have led us to lapse into 'grateful degradation'! No doubt we have been unable to satisfy them all with our redrafts, but we can assure them that where we have chosen stubbornly to pursue our own path it was not without pausing and carefully discussing the alternatives on offer. Needless to say, any errors which remain are most certainly our fault, not theirs.

Our respective Departments of Psychology must by now be used to the absence of book-writing colleagues, but thanks to ours anyway. Families have a less obvious, though no less onerous burden to shoulder. Thanks to Margaret and Joseph and Lucy and Susan for patiently waiting for their names to appear in print, and to our book-widows, Shelagh and Priscilla, for their constant support.

Peter J. Hampson
Peter E. Morris

Acknowledgements

The following have been reprinted from other sources:

Figure 4.3 from *To See But Not To See: A Case Study of Visual Agnosia*, by Humphreys, G.W., and Riddoch, M.J., 1987. Reprinted by permission of Lawrence Erlbaum Associates Ltd., Hove, UK.

Picture of a cow – an example of a hard to discern object, p.22, *The Listener*, 8 December.1988.

Satellite image of earth taken from space, p.46, *The Guardian*, 25 April 1989.

Every effort has been made by the publishers to trace copyright-holders. If any have been inadvertently overlooked, the publishers will be glad to rectify this situation in future reprints.

1 Introduction

In the sequel to his book *2001: A Space Odyssey*, Arthur C. Clarke describes the activities of advanced, extra-terrestrial beings who journey through the void searching for signs of intelligent life. They roamed the vast expanses of space, writes Clarke, because '. . . in all the Galaxy they had found nothing more precious than mind, (and) they encouraged its dawning everywhere' (p. 291, 1983).

Clarke is surely right to recognize the uniqueness and importance of mind, but suppose for the moment that we are the advanced life forms roving space who chance across the planet Earth. Recognizing that intelligent life exists on this planet is perfectly straightforward. Evidence for it is everywhere: radio and television signals pour into space and signal its presence, roads and railway tracks criss-cross the land, fields are ploughed, houses and other great structures litter the landscape, and medium-sized, bipedal, sexually dimorphic creatures carry out a bewildering range of constructive and destructive activities. But having found intelligent life, or at least detected its presence, how shall we describe it? What sort of minds do these creatures have? Are they like ours? Do they work in the same way? How shall we start to find out?

To answer these questions our space friends would need to turn to psychology. Psychology, as they would soon discover, is a broad enterprise spanning the vast chasm between the biological and the social sciences. Cognitive psychology is that part of psychology which concerns itself with the structure and functions of the mind. It is this branch of psychology which will be examined in this book. The word *cognitive* comes from the Latin word *cognoscere*, meaning *to know*, and this indicates what cognitive psychology is all about. Cognitive psychology tries to explain how the human mind comes to know things about the world around it, about other people, and about itself, and how it uses this knowledge to perform an impressive range of tasks such as remembering, speaking, performing skilled actions, solving problems and reasoning. Like most modern psychologists, cognitive psychologists adopt a scientific perspective toward the working of the mind. That is, they assume that mind is a natural phenomenon which can be studied using the same systematic techniques that have worked so well in other disciplines. They also assume that mind is better described as a set of processes, which rely on the brain, rather than as a separate, mysterious 'thing', and that these processes are lawfully related to what a person does or says. The assumption that mental processes are linked with observable behaviour is very important. It allows the cognitive psychologist to perform controlled experiments which test theories about inner mental processes by observing their effects on outward measurable behaviour. We will explore and illustrate this key idea in more detail later on. For now, we merely note that although minds cannot be directly externally observed, their effects can, and these can be studied using scientific experiments. Cognitive psychology, therefore, can be defined as that branch of experimental psychology concerned with explaining mental processes. A second characteristic of contemporary cognitive psychology is its emphasis on clear and coherent theories, and a growing interest in constructing models or simulations of theories which are then mimicked using artificial information-processing devices such as computers. As we shall also discover, a close neighbour of cognitive psychology, cognitive science, combines the experimental techniques of cognitive psychology with the computer modelling methods of research into artificial intelligence to prise open and explore the secrets of the mind.

However, this is to anticipate much of what comes later. First, some background. Cognitive psychology is a relatively new branch of psychology, and by putting cognitive research into its wider scientific and historical context, we will be in a better position to understand how it is possible to study mind at all, and why psychologists study mind in the way they do.

Some Historical and Cultural Background

For various cultural reasons it took scientists a long time to get round to studying mind, and once they did so, they still had to develop the right sort of language and explanations to tackle it properly.

It often surprises people to learn that although people have speculated on the nature of mind, thinking and consciousness for over 2,000 years, the scientific study of human mental activity is quite recent. Psychology itself is only just over a hundred years old and cognitive psychology, that branch of the discipline which concerns itself with mind and thinking, is much younger. Many psychologists would agree that cognitive psychology only really got going in the past 40 or 50 years, though there were some important psychologists working in the early years of the twentieth century whose concerns were broadly cognitive. Why then has it taken so long even to begin to understand mind? If psychology is the scientific study of behaviour and mental life, why have psychologists been so slow in addressing half of their subject matter? To see why, it helps if we stand back and look at the development and history of psychology in relation to other sciences.

Viewed from a wider perspective, the youthful nature of psychology contrasts markedly with other more established sciences like physics, chemistry and biology. Physics, in particular, has had a remarkable 500 years, enjoying a continued success from the time of Newton and Galileo. In the twentieth century we now have the first theories which attempt to explain all aspects of the physical universe within the one framework. These so-called grand unification theories are magnificent achievements which link our understanding of previously separate areas such as subatomic physics, electromagnetism and gravity. Nowadays, few would deny the right or competence of physics to offer such accounts, but this was not always the case. In Galileo's time, the medieval church took it upon itself to offer complete cosmological theories of how the world and the universe were created, how they worked, and what their ultimate fate would be. In short, rather than confining itself to matters spiritual and ethical, the church and its theologians offered alternative accounts of the universe to science. Hardly any modern philosophers of religion would now maintain that this is what theology should be doing, but in Galileo's time such opinions held sway and their political and cultural influence was immense. The clash between the accepted version of the universe and the newer scientific theories is well known. Astronomers such as Copernicus and Galileo proposed accounts of mankind's position in the universe at odds with the approved version. By claiming that the sun, not the earth, was the centre of the known universe, they displaced humans from their previously central position in a universe designed solely for their convenience. Later astronomers completed this removal by showing that our solar system was only one among many, and relegated humanity to a relatively insignificant and lonely spot: a small planet (by astronomical standards) spinning around a relatively small star in one out of thousands of galaxies.

It was gradually accepted that this scientific view of the physical world was essentially correct, but life in general, and human life in particular, was still thought to be special and somehow beyond the reach of full scientific explanation. Living beings were believed to be endowed with a special quality known as *élan vital*, or the stuff of life, but to inhabit an essentially inert universe. The situation changed slowly. It was eventually recognized that living things too, or at least their parts, could be thought of as mechanical systems subject to simple physical laws. The discovery of the principles governing the circulation of the blood, the way in which muscles act on bones as levers, and the reflex responses of animals to certain stimuli all illustrate this trend. But mind was still seen as special and beyond the reach of mechanistic explanation. The philosopher Descartes (1596–1650) developed these ideas. He argued that it was conscious mental activity that separated humans from animals and endowed people with the gift of voluntary action and thinking.

By the seventeenth century, the consensus among many educated people, as well as those actively engaged in science, was that the physical universe was inert, that this inert universe was inhabited by living things whose bodies worked as complex mechanisms, that life itself was mysteriously different from non-life, and that conscious mind, the most mysterious substance of all in the universe, was a non-physical entity which, possessed by humans alone, separated man from animals and allowed the voluntary control of action.

Such a view prevailed until the biological sciences really got going in the nineteenth century and, it should be acknowledged, is still tacitly held by many non-scientific people today. Developments in biology, however, have made this simple view untenable. To begin with, Charles Darwin (1809–82) showed how the principles of natural selection could explain the wide variety of living systems that inhabit our planet. His Theory of Evolution accounted for the wide variation between living things without any appeal to purpose or an initial creator. The theory was important for two reasons. First, it demonstrated how quite complex physiological and biological systems could emerge through the interaction of a changing environment with small variations in an organism. Second, like the earlier discoveries of Copernicus and Galileo it dethroned people and changed their place in the scheme of things. This time it toppled humans from the summit of the ladder of life, and placed them as one admittedly very clever species amongst all the others. The Theory of Evolution implied that people and animals were more closely related than had previously been thought and that evolution was not necessarily leading in any particular direction. Nor could it be claimed that humans were better designed or equipped than their fellow animals. They had certain skills, for sure, but like all living things they were merely adapted to the environment, or, as we would now say, the ecological niche, in which they lived.

It has taken us over a hundred years to begin to appreciate the full meaning of the Theory of Evolution. Other developments in the biological sciences have sharpened this understanding and shown the essential continuity of all life. Among these, one of the most notable is the discovery of the structure of the DNA molecule, the basis of all living things, and the consequent growth in our understanding of the biochemical nature of living systems. Another is the great advance in genetics and our understanding of the inheritance of general characteristics of living things which has occurred during this time.

So, a number of shifts in our scientific and cultural viewpoint have taken place during the past 400 years: from a person-centred, person-sized universe, to an immense, empty, largely inert one; from a world in which people and animals were biologically distinct, to one in which living things were essentially related. We have come a long way, the journey has taken a long time, and it is hardly surprising that we have only just arrived at the most intriguing problem of all, the nature of mind. A problem made doubly difficult by the enormous influence of Descartes' philosophy on Western culture, which effectively separated human minds from the rest of the physical and biological world. Minds were off limits or at least hard to grasp.

Inside or outside views?

There is a danger in writing a brief history of the development of ideas like this that the reader will think that the progress from physics to biology to psychology has been regular and predictable. To some extent we have smoothed over many of the bumps along the way! Ideas were often developed early on, but only fully exploited later. In biology, for instance, although the Theory of Evolution was proposed in the nineteenth century, its full impact has been appreciated in the twentieth in the wake of developments in molecular biology and genetics. In psychology too, the general intellectual climate was suitable for studying mind at the end of the nineteenth century, but conditions within the discipline were not then right. One problem was that the dominant method used within psychology at the time, introspection, proved unsuitable for exploring mental processes.

Introspection is the process whereby one looks into one's own mind and reports the contents. At first glance, this might seem an obvious and foolproof way of studying mind. Surely the fact that we can all introspect or notice ourselves seeing, thinking, remembering and making decisions should be a great help in discovering how mental processes work. Psychologists tried hard to use introspection to study mental activity when the discipline first emerged. By carefully examining themselves carrying out a range of tasks, they hoped to build up a list of the major mental states, ideas or building blocks of mental life. Influenced by advances in chemistry, where John Dalton had shown that all substances were formed from different arrangements of a limited number of elements listed in his Periodic Table, the first psychologists wanted to discover the mental atoms used in thinking which, they thought, would combine, in different ways, to form complex ideas or mental molecules.

A great deal of work went into training student introspectionists to analyse their mental states, but, with the benefit of hindsight, it is easy to see that the approach was doomed to failure. For one thing mental activity is private. I may be able to observe and report what I am thinking, but there is no easy way for you to check whether what I experience is the same as that experienced by another person. Silly debates then result about, say, whether my experience of the colour 'red' is the same as yours. Not surprisingly, with more complex phenomena, different introspectors often produced different reports of what was supposedly the same event. A second difficulty is that when we introspect we may alter or perturb what we are introspecting. Suppose you are trying to introspect on the normally effortless process of looking at an object. It is quite likely that your usual smooth pattern of eye movements is disrupted by looking at yourself looking. The fact is, we are never in a position, through introspection, to know what the unobserved mental activity would have been like. A third, and possibly more serious problem is that the introspective method assumes all important mental activities to be conscious, or open to introspection in the first place. This we now know to be false. A great deal of human cognition takes place without the person concerned being aware that it is happening. If you doubt this, perhaps a little introspection might help! You are undoubtedly a skilled reader. Consider how you read this book. As your eyes scan this page they periodically fixate or stop at various points in the text. When they do so information about the words in front of you is taken in and processed. As a given word is read, it makes contact with a vast store of information about itself and related words. Some of this information is made available to allow you to understand the word and combine it with others in the sentence. Having read a paragraph or two you will have some memory, however sketchy, of what you have read. You will, of course, be aware of some of these activities and be able to report them, but a great deal of what goes on will not be conscious. Think about how a word is perceived, makes contact with its meaning in memory, and is then read aloud. Can you really observe all this happening? We doubt it. The entire process of reading a word aloud takes place in less than a second, and many of its component operations take far less time than that. What is consciously available to you is only a limited subset of all the cognitive operations that take place. Or consider speaking to someone. You are aware roughly of what you want to say and how to say it, but you need not and often cannot consciously concern yourself with the exact details of how words are selected from memory, arranged into reasonably grammatical sequences, checked and edited for appropriateness, and the speech apparatus controlled. The process of introspection suggests that there must be more going on than can be introspected, but the process of introspection cannot be used to investigate it.

Psychologists soon became aware of these and other problems with introspection and a possible solution was offered by J.B. Watson. Watson's suggestion was quite radical. If the introspective method was so error-prone, it should be abandoned. Furthermore, Watson argued that the subject matter as well as the methods of psychology should also change. Psychology should no longer concern itself with mind, consciousness, feelings and other subjective phenomena, but should examine only what was observable and external, namely behaviour. The advantages of Watson's behaviourist programme over introspection are easy to see. By making behaviour rather than mind the central concern of psychology he replaced something subjective, private and inaccessible with something objective, public, easy to access and record. To be a true science, Watson claimed, psychology must study only that which is observable and checkable. Three things were observable in principle: what had happened to a person in the past, what the present environmental conditions were and how the person reacted as a result. Behaviour depended on one's learning history and present stimuli, not inner subjective forces.

According to Watson, such a science could study the behaviours of children as well as adults, and animals as well as people. The approach also covered clinical and pathological states. For instance, in a famous study, Watson and colleagues showed how the fears of babies and the phobias of adults could be understood in terms of their behavioural experiences with noxious or unpleasant stimuli rather than deep-seated, psychic conflicts.

Behaviourism brought a number of benefits to psychology. Its methods meant that psychologists were able to perform objective experiments which could be checked and, if necessary, repeated by other psychologists. Its insistence that only the publicly observable was suitable for discussion stopped wild speculation, but in the process, mind was banished.

Changing times: the rise of cognitive psychology

For over 50 years the behaviourist approach dominated academic, Anglo-American psychology and thousands of students were taught that at last the discipline had thrown off its mentalist trappings and really become a science. However, after the Second World War, the behaviourist influence began to wane. There are several reasons for this. To begin with, the sorts of accounts proposed by several prominent behaviourists, such as Tolman and Hull, began to refer increasingly to the role of internal factors in controlling behaviour, something which non-behaviourists such as Sigmund Freud had been doing for many years. Another reason is that the type of problems considered by psychologists began to change. Instead of studying the responses of volunteers in experiments (known as 'participants') to simple stimuli, psychologists started to examine human perception and perform-ance in more complex environments. During the War, military personnel had to learn to use complex machines such as large tanks, anti-aircraft guns and bombers. Lots of these machines had several controls and presented the operator with multiple sources of information. For example, when flying even the simplest aircraft, pilots had to monitor the skies for enemy fighters, check their altimeter, air speed indicator, fuel gauge and other instruments, navigate, control the throttle, keep the aircraft at the appro-priate orientation, and respond to messages over their radio. Situations such as flying an aeroplane seemed to involve intelligent, skilful actions rather than simple responses to simple stimuli. Indeed, the best pilots, and those who survived the conflict, were those who could anticipate future trouble and plan accordingly rather than just automatically respond to the present situation. Anticipation and planning were concepts absent from the behaviourists' armoury. Shortly after the War other difficulties in using the new technology became apparent. Air traffic control operators began to use the new radar systems to guide aeroplanes through the increasingly crowded skies. Their job was described as one of long periods of excruciating boredom, waiting for a small blip to appear on a radar screen, interspersed with short periods of intense panic when too many blips appeared at once! Air traffic controllers had to concentrate and maintain vigilance during the long waiting periods, and then selectively attend to the correct signals during the busy ones, but again, behaviourism had little to say about concentration, vigilance and attention.

Very soon a number of new concepts arose in psychology. Several of these followed directly from work on attention and skill needed to understand how people could operate complex machinery, but there were other changes too. During the 1950s, a branch of mathematics known as Information Theory emerged. This abstract approach to the mathematics underlying all information was eagerly taken up by psychologists in the belief that the formal measures of information it offered would be useful in explaining how people as well as machines could act as information transmission devices. At first, it seemed that Information Theory could be easily applied to people as well as machines. Early successes, such as the finding that human choice reaction time was affected more by the amount of information in a situation rather than by the number of stimuli present, encouraged the use of formal measures of information, but this abstract approach to information diminished when it became apparent that the meaning of the stimuli was important too. Gradually, the formal application of Information Theory declined, but its legacy was a general belief that, although complex, people were basically processors of information and meaning. Other concepts also established themselves. For example, the notion that cognitive processes rely heavily on feedback and control came from studying how complex machinery worked, and from developing disciplines such as control engineering. Yet others came from studying the rules and grammar which underlay language in the hope that these linguistic rules would be found to have psychological validity too. Important work by the linguist Chomsky stimulated psychologists to consider how so open-ended and creative an activity as language could be produced by finite rules and processes. Chomsky also showed, in his devastating criticism of B.F. Skinner's book *Verbal Behavior*, how a purely behavioural account of language based on a simple application of reinforcement theory could not succeed, by pointing out that people are capable of understanding and producing novel, well-structured utterances for which they have never been rewarded in the past.

Finally, the advent of the digital computer showed how a suitably programmed mechanical device could perform tasks that previously it was thought could only be done by people. Even as early as the end of the 1950s there were computers that could play a creditable game of chess and solve geometry problems. The computer finally liberated psychologists from old-fashioned ways of thinking about mind and showed them how a complex machine like a computer could use a set of instructions to do intelligent things. Gradually the suspicion emerged that this might be a good way of thinking about mind. If the brain was a little bit like a computer then the mind could be likened to its programs. Mind was no longer construed as a 'thing' but as a set of processes or procedures for operating on symbols.

These new ideas were, as we shall see, what cognitive psychology really needed to get going. For many centuries, there was little or no scientific work on the mind; at the end of the nineteenth century, when the intellectual climate improved, the methods were wrong; but at last a new way of talking about mind – as an intelligent, symbol-processing system – emerged. Such changes and new concepts meant that many psychologists gradually abandoned the more extreme versions of behaviourism to argue instead that some account of the internal workings of the mind was needed. Perception, attention, memory, language and thinking were back on the agenda, and information processing began to seem far more important than responding to stimuli. However, we would not like to leave the reader with the impression that with the return of the old problems came an uncritical return to the old methods. The behaviourist revolution had not been in vain. The new cognitive psychologists were in no hurry to return to the earlier subjective techniques such as introspection. Instead, they claimed that it was possible to collect behavioural data from well-designed experiments in which people were presented with carefully controlled stimuli and their responses recorded. In doing this they were acting as good methodological behaviourists. Where they differed from behaviourists was in proceeding to make inferences from the behavioural data about the internal mental activities of their participants. An example will illustrate this more clearly. Imagine that an experimenter found that participants remember more words from different categories such as fruit, furniture and animals when the words are arranged into ordered lists than when they are jumbled together. A strict behaviourist would be content with the finding and conclude that ordered verbal material simply produces better subsequent memory than unorganized material. A cognitive psychologist, on the other hand, would be likely to infer from this that the human memory system itself is internally organized, and the full power of the system can be exploited when its internal structure is supported by the organization of the material to be remembered. Our cognitive psychologist would feel more confident in this claim if he or she then went on to show that participants impose their own, idiosyncratic order on what to an external observer looks like a completely disordered set of stimuli. By making inferences from behaviour about unobservable events, the cognitive psychologist acts like the physicist who observes and measures various (behavioural) phenomena and effects and infers the existence of entities and forces such as fundamental particles, magnetism and gravity which can never be directly observed.

What is Mind and How Shall We Study It?

Suppose we admit that we can make inferences about mental activity from behaviour. What sort of a thing is a mind? In fact, as you are probably gathering, and as we indicated earlier, psychologists are generally agreed that mind is not a thing at all. Instead, they regard mind as a set of processes or activities for operating on symbolic representations of the world which cooperate to form a mental or cognitive system rather than an entity of some sort. These ideas sound complicated, but as we hope to show they make good sense. We will spend a short time considering them before moving on.

It is a pity that the word 'mind' is frequently used as a noun in English. A noun, as all primary school children know, is a naming word often used to refer to persons, places or things. If mind is a noun we tend to think that it must refer to a thing, but then the trouble begins. If it is a thing it is a strange one, to be sure. It is non-physical, has no weight, colour or extension. How on earth can such a 'thing' exist, and how can it affect and be affected by the brain? These questions are made easier if we drop the idea that mind is a thing, and conceive of it instead as a set of activities. Think about digestion: the word 'digestion' refers not to a single thing or entity, but rather to a complex set of biochemical and physiological activities starting with the ingestion of food into the mouth, continuing with the absorption of substances by the stomach, gut and muscles and the storage of energy in the liver, and ending with the excretion of waste products. These digestive activities can only take place because there exist a set of physiological organs, such as the mouth, gut and stomach, which support them. Also, when we look at each activity in more detail we see that it is made up of a myriad of interacting biochemical processes. The digestive system as a whole involves the organs and their associated biochemical processes acting in concert.

In a similar way we can think of there being a set of mental processes carried out by a mental organ, the brain, which are needed to carry out activities such as memory, perception, language and thinking. These processes make use of what are known as internal representations of the world: images, words, concepts and other symbolic structures. This is why cognitive psychologists often speak of the mind as a symbol-processing system. The entire set of activities, of processes operating on symbolic structures, reflects the working of the cognitive system. The phrase 'cognitive system' will occur frequently in this book, so it is worth exploring in turn exactly what we mean by system. The word 'system' comes from the Greek meaning 'organized whole' and has a long entry in the *Shorter Oxford English Dictionary* where, among other things, it is defined as '. . . a set or assemblage of things, connected, associated or interdependent, so as to form a complex unity: a whole composed of parts in orderly arrangement according to some scheme or plan . . .' (p. 227). Typical examples of systems are the solar system with its planets orbiting in an orderly fashion around the sun; the circulatory system with heart, blood vessels, lungs and other structures cooperating to transport blood and food to different parts of the body; the motorway system with its carriageways, slip-roads, service stations, roundabouts and traffic jams. So, a system is something which is complex, ordered, with many interrelated parts. To this we can add that biological and many man-made systems seem to work in a controlled and often self-controlled fashion towards a common end.

Parts of a system are often systems in their own right, in which case we call them subsystems. For example, a domestic house can be considered to be a system with complex parts designed to provide comfort and shelter, but in fact a house contains several potentially separable subsystems for dealing with heating, lighting, plumbing, refuse disposal and so on, each of which is a complex entity made up of interacting components. Breaking a system down into a relatively small number of simpler subsystems often allows us to understand it more easily.

Some systems are fixed or at least slowly moving, while others are dynamic and constantly changing. Road or rail networks are good examples of fairly static or fixed systems; their parts, once constructed, do not move around much, nor do their basic components change. On the other hand, biological systems often develop and increase in complexity. One has only to consider how any biological creature grows and changes to see that this is the case.

We can now see why it makes sense to refer to human cognition as a system. It goes without saying that mind is a complex entity. However, this does not mean that it cannot be explained. Like all systems, the cognitive system can be split into a series of highly connected, but nevertheless potentially separable subsystems. These are the major components or parts of the cognitive system, and correspond to the major sets of operations that the human mind performs. In Part I of this book, entitled 'Elements of Cognition', we shall explore these major subsystems of human cognition. First we look at the memory system and show how this in turn can be split into simpler processes and subsystems. In chapter 3 we turn to vision, one of the major perceptual systems through which we learn about and keep in touch with the world around us. There are, of course, other ways of perceiving the world, through touch, hearing, taste and smell, but the visual system is arguably the most important of these and one of the most extensively studied by psychologists. Language is the focus of chapter 4. Like perception and memory the human language system is itself composed of several interacting subsystems. Finally, in chapters 5 and 6 we examine attention, the way in which we direct our perceptual systems when dealing with several sources of information, and skilled actions.

While it is possible to tease out the major cognitive subsystems in this way and to examine them separately, we would not like the reader to think that their operations are completely separate. In practice these elements of cognition work smoothly together for the benefit of the system as a whole. Without perception, no new information could enter memory; without memory, things seen could not be interpreted in terms of familiar categories. Similarly, language might sharpen material in memory and perhaps alter how we perceive things, but without memory and perception, the ability to use language would never develop in the first place. In examining the elements of cognition, we shall come across several other features which further illustrate their systemic character. For instance, their dynamic and changing nature will be obvious at several points, but perhaps most clearly when we discuss memory, perception and skill. Memory is the quintessential changing system in that, like a good library, new material is continually entering and being classified. Moreover, but unlike a library, it seems that retrieving material from memory, the act of remembering itself, can sometimes result in changes to stored information. Memory is always in a process of flux; we cannot hold it still nor stop it from altering. Perception is constantly changing too. The more we see, the more we learn to see. Human skills develop and improve with time; they are rarely static. Human cognition is a dynamic system.

What then are the essential aspects of cognition which cut across our chapter headings of Part I? What makes human cognition as a whole so distinctive? This is not an easy question to answer, but if we had to choose only three aspects of human cognition they would be these: first, its powerful, though not perfect memory subsystems, which support virtually all cognitive activities from perceiving to thinking; second, its remarkable pattern recognition abilities which arise not just in perception, but are used in memory, language, thinking, problem solving and skills; third, its flexible ability to interact and communicate with a changing world. Memory, pattern recognition and (perceptual–motor, cognitive and communicative) skills lie at the heart of cognition, and although there are chapters devoted to these as separate entities, these key aspects of cognition are represented in different degrees throughout.

In Part II, the emphasis changes from studying the cognitive system itself to what can be done with it. Part II is entitled 'Using Cognition' and describes just some of the ways in which the mind can be used for remembering (chapter 7), planning and acting (chapter 8), reading (chapter 9) and problem solving and decision making (chapter 10). Two points are worth making here. Our list of cognitive activities is selective but broad. The number of possible applications of the human mind is of course potentially infinite. We could have included, for example, learning a foreign language, thinking creatively, appreciating music, doing arithmetic, proposing marriage, planning a garden . . . but to look at each task that the mind can do is often less interesting than using a range of related tasks to draw conclusions about its general operating characteristics, or the sorts of typical jobs we can do with the cognitive system. Even so, our range of cognitive activities is incomplete, but we hope it is reasonably representative. In selecting those to discuss we were guided by three main principles. We have chosen areas, such as remembering, where contemporary research has shifted from narrow laboratory studies to wider naturalistic work, a shift which has often coincided with a more applied focus to cognitive research. We also wished to give the reader some flavour of areas in which human cognition is error-prone, as in our discussion of action. Finally, we have selected issues, such as reading, in which there is an important interaction between cognitive subsystems.

A second point is that although separately partitioned in our book, the topics raised in Part II are not independent from those covered in Part I. For example, the sorts of errors people make when reasoning are linked in part to certain limitations of the memory system, attentional constraints affect reading, and the ways in which people perceive and label situations influence the ease with which they can solve problems. Using cognition is heavily dependent on the elements of cognition, and, in evolutionary terms, the cognitive system is the way it is because of the sorts of things that people need to do with it. Nevertheless, just as we can study different sorts of vehicles on the one hand, and the journeys made with them on the other, so we can look separately at the cognitive system itself in semi-isolation from its uses.

In Part III the emphasis changes again. As well as studying the mind through direct experimentation and in everyday situations, cognitive psychologists also try to model or mimic the operations of the cognitive system in various ways. To some extent this can be seen as an extension of the concerns of the earlier sections. Cognitive modellers, like all cognitive psychologists, want to understand how the mind is structured and how it is used. Hence, when planning this book, we did consider integrating the material in Part III into Parts I and II. However, after reflection, we opted for a separate section. In our opinion, work on cognitive modelling is sufficiently distinct and its methods sufficiently specialized to merit its own discussion. Part III consists of three chapters. The first, chapter 11, examines work on artificial intelligence (AI). Here, the idea that computer programs offer a good analogy for the mind is taken very seriously indeed and the goal is to get computer programs to mimic the human mind, as closely as possible, when performing certain tasks. A key issue in AI research is how the mind represents external reality, and, whatever their differences, traditional AI researchers are united in their agreement that such representations are highly symbolic in character. Chapter 12 is a somewhat different approach to modelling the mind. In the past 20 years, cognitive psychologists have become increasingly interested in abnormal as well as normal cognition. By studying people unfortunate enough to have suffered brain injury, it is possible to learn a lot about the cognitive system by seeing how it performs when damaged. Cognitive neuropsychologists use existing models of cognitive function to interpret the performance of the brain-injured and, in turn, use data gathered from studies of the effects of brain injury to refine and modify cognitive models. This vibrant area of research reminds us of how dependent all cognitive processes are on underlying neural structures, a theme which is echoed in the final chapter on connectionism. Connectionism unites the concern with computer modelling of AI research with the insight, from neuropsychology, that ultimately all cognitive processes are grounded in neural architectures. Connectionist models are still in their infancy, but the approach is so important that we have given it a complete chapter. Connectionism challenges many traditional assumptions of conventional AI and cognitive psychology, particularly the need for mind to be thought of as a symbol-processing system, and the notion that mental activity can be carried out without worrying about how the brain is involved.

Taken together, the three chapters in Part III represent important strands of the interdisciplinary enterprise that has become known as cognitive science, which is another good reason for giving them special consideration. Cognitive science combines aspects of cognitive psychology, artificial intelligence, neuropsychology, linguistics and the philosophy of mind, on the assumption that all these disciplines are dealing with similar problems but with different tools. The hope is that by combining techniques solutions will be produced more rapidly. As well as being interdisciplinary, cognitive science is also marked by its insistence that its models shall be as clear and internally consistent and coherent as possible. If anything, it is more concerned with coherence than with the models' correspondence with reality, a task that tends to be left to cognitive psychology to check.

Cognitive psychology and cognitive science are currently among the fastest developing research areas in psychology, and look set to grow for some time to come. It appears, at last, that psychology is now on the right track towards a fuller understanding of human cognition, despite many earlier false starts and many unsolved problems.

And so, having hopefully understood where we have come from, and made our future travel plans, we are now ready to begin our own exploration of human cognition, turning first to one of the most central elements of the mind: the memory system.

Further reading

You can learn about the emergence of cognitive psychology by reading two of its classics: G.A. Miller, E. Galanter and K. Pribram 1960: *Plans and the Structure of Behavior*. New York: Holt, and D.E. Broadbent 1958: *Perception and Communication*. Oxford: Pergamon. The first major 'text' in cognitive psychology, however, was U. Neisser 1967: *Cognitive Psychology*. New York: Appleton-Century-Crofts, published at the end of the 1960s. This was a state of the art review of the area at the time, and has been very influential since.

However, if you are interested in delving further into the history of the cognitive approach, you could look at K. Craik 1943: *The Nature of*

Explanation. Cambridge: Cambridge University Press, for an early view on the idea of mind as a symbol-processing system.

A review of methods used to research human cognition can be found in W. Kintsch, J.R. Miller and P.G. Polson (eds) 1984: *Methods and Tactics in Cognitive Science*. Hillsdale, New Jersey: Lawrence Erlbaum.

Discussion points

1   Why do you think it took psychology so long to develop, compared, say, with physics or chemistry?
2   What is meant by the term 'cognitive psychology' and how did this approach emerge?
3   If minds are such private and personal entities, how can they ever be studied scientifically?
4   What advantages are there in treating cognition as a system? What are the major elements or subsystems of cognition?
5   In what ways might mental processes be modelled?

Part I

Elements of Cognition

2 Memory

In recent years most of us have become familiar with a vast range of new ways of recording information and making it available in the future. Video tapes, audio cassettes and CD players have become part of the furniture of the living room, while it has become normal for most office desks and many shops and homes to sport a computer. The popularity of such information technology has emphasized the value that we place on storing, retaining and retrieving information. Rather than downgrading the importance of the human memory system, these products of late twentieth century technology both rely upon and supplement the human memory systems that have evolved through millions of years. The strengths and weaknesses of these information storage and retrieval systems can help to highlight the properties of our human system.

It is important to remember that the success of these information systems lies in their superiority, in certain ways, over our own memories. If our memories enabled us to relive the full richness of a musical performance there would be far less need for audio tapes and CDs. If we could remember in great detail exactly what we had seen while on holiday, there would be little need for cameras, and home videos would be less entertaining. Many of the modern aids to remembering are popular because of the way in which they record the past, exactly as it happens.

While there are times when it would be very nice to have a built-in mental video recorder, it would be quite wrong to denigrate our memory system for failing to match the accuracy of reproduction of video recordings and CD discs. To do so would be to miss the essential fact that our memories have evolved to solve a far more pressing set of problems than the need to replay the past in times of boredom or tranquillity.

We must begin by asking what human beings use their past experience for? The answer is for just about everything that they do. All our words, thoughts and actions have developed and been shaped through our past experience. From birth until death our lives involve the continuous learning from our current situation and the modification of all that we do in the future as a result. The importance of learning is not, of course, restricted to human beings. Virtually all animals modify their behaviour through experience. What is, however, less common to the rest of the animal kingdom is the human ability to control and modify behaviour. More than any other animal, human beings analyse, plan and choose their actions. Their behaviour reflects not merely learning through past experience but also the evaluation of that past experience on many occasions throughout each day as they attempt to plan their actions to lead to the most successful outcomes.

It is to serve this capacity for consideration, flexibility and the planned control of behaviour that the processes that we normally refer to as memory have evolved. It is essential to the whole process of planning our actions that we should be able to comprehend what is happening to us, to make sense of what is going on, to imagine likely alternatives of our actions, and to reuse and re-evaluate experiences from our past. Our perceptual systems supply us with information about what is currently happening around us. Our memory systems allow us to interpret this in concepts with which we are familiar, and supply expectations about what is likely to happen next. The challenge to our memory systems is a continuous one of supplying any useful information from our past that will help our current understanding of what is happening to us now and likely to happen to us in the future.

It may now be becoming clear why a memory system that resembled a video recording would not, in itself, meet the needs of the human memory system. If we had a memory system which, rather passively, recorded in great detail everything that had happened to us in the past, the problem of using that information would remain. Among all the many thousands of hours of recording, how would the appropriate moments for understanding and predicting what would happen in the current, perhaps very dangerous situation be located? What is required is a system that is organized, classified and selected to meet the probable requirements upon it. The biggest challenge to any large-scale information storage system is to be able to locate the relevant information quickly. In this and the later chapter on Remembering (chapter 7) we will discuss how our human memory system has developed in response to these problems.

Minute by minute, day by day, year by year, new information is being entered in your memory. If you think back to what you did when you got up and had breakfast this morning, and if you give yourself time to recall and reconstruct what you did, you will find that you can remember a great deal. At least that much new information has been stored just from one ordinary morning of your life. There were probably many other things from this morning that you did store in memory but you cannot recall. Vast amounts of information are stored continuously in our memories. The question for this chapter is what determines how well things are entered, how long they remain and how easily they can be remembered again later.

There are, as the last sentence implies, three logically distinct stages that we must consider. For you to remember something, you must have stored some record of it in memory when it occurred. This storing is called encoding. Then that record must have remained adequately intact over the intervening time, and finally you must have found it again and retrieved the memory. In this chapter we will discuss these three stages of encoding, storage and retrieval separately, but it is important to emphasize all the time that this does not mean that the processes are independent. In fact we begin our examination with some general problems of retrieval, but as will quickly become apparent, what can be retrieved at any time depends upon what was encoded and how the original encoding took place.

As well as examining the major functions of memory, we will also consider some of the ways in which psychologists have discussed the division or partition of the memory system into separate stores and subsystems in this chapter. Historically speaking, research on memory examined many of these structural distinctions before moving to consider functions such as encoding and retrieval, and many excellent textbooks on memory (cf. Parkin, 1993) reflect this, and deal first with structural issues. We have chosen not to do this. Instead, we wish initially to show what is essential for memory as a whole and to concentrate on how memory works in general, often with reference to quite recent research, and only then to explore finer subdivisions within the system. So we begin with a problem for all memory systems: retrieval.

The Problem of Retrieval

Any large store of information brings with it the problem of how that information can be made available again at the appropriate time. The easiest storage system is to pile in the information as it comes, whether it be books, notes that we have taken, audio and video recordings or memories. We all are tempted to store things by merely putting them away. The problems arise when we need them again. To find them we have to search through the pile, the drawer, the shelf, the tape or whatever, until we find the thing that we are looking for. As we add more and more to our store, this search takes longer. On average we will have to look through half our stored items each time. Eventually we are forced into a system of classifying and categorizing. This takes time and effort at the point of putting away a new item, but is repaid by the speed of finding it again later. So, we may shelve our own books by topics, file notes in special books and so on. Libraries use a mixture of methods to make the location of books easier. They shelve books on the same topic together, but they also provide indexes based on the author and the participant.

Thus, for any large information storage system, it is necessary at the time of entering new information to code it in ways that make it easy to retrieve when the information is needed. Two very important factors are that the accessibility of an item depends upon the ways it has been coded and that the more ways of coding, the greater the likelihood of retrieval. To continue the library analogy, it is easy to retrieve a book in most libraries if we know the name of the author, since libraries classify new books in that way.

However, if you know many things about the book, but not its exact title and author, you may be in a hopeless position. It is of no help to know that it is a small blue book with a picture of a Gothic mansion on the front, that it has 231 pages and was published by Pulp Publishers. None of this was used by the library when classifying the book and it will not help its retrieval. Obviously, at the expense of more time and effort at the time of purchase, such details could have been recorded and the book found.

The point of this analogy is that with any system that stores as much information as does the human memory system, what is recoverable depends upon what details are stored and are then available at the time that the information must be retrieved. In many ways, though, the human memory is not like a library. For example, it is probably wrong to assume that memories are stored in particular locations. It is also likely that the actual content of the memory can help in its retrieval, which is not so for books.

Encoding ► ►

However important learning and memory may be, and without them all our skills, our thought and our language would be impossible, it is still the case that our memories exist to serve the more central function of making sense of our experience, and for carrying out and planning future actions. It is therefore not surprising that what we remember is also very much a by-product of the cognitive processes that take place as we deal with the world. Some tasks demand more processing than others, or require more distinctive or elaborate processing, and what is stored in memory seems to be a copy and result of this processing, so that what is remembered is determined by what we were doing at the time.

The point that memory depends upon the situation and the task that we are undertaking is demonstrated by two contrasting memory phenomena. One is our very poor memory for some things that we have encountered daily, the other is the vivid memories that we can have of important events in our lives. The first was well illustrated by Nickerson and Adams (1979) who tested the recognition and recall of the details of an American penny. They found that only one of their 20 participants could correctly draw in the main details and writing on the face of the coin – and that participant was a coin collector! On average only three of the eight features could be correctly recalled. Given a recognition test, almost 60 per cent of their participants selected an incorrect drawing. Try the test yourself for the ten pence coin illustrated in figure 2.1. Which one of them is the correct drawing? Most British people select the wrong drawing. Morris (1988) found that only 15 out of the 100 students that he tested selected the correct representation, while half the students got even the direction that the head was facing the wrong way round.

Many of us will have held and seen a 10p coin on most days of our lives. However, when we select coins from our loose change, we do so only in comparison to other coins that are very different in design, so there is no need to look carefully at the details on the coin. The daily task of handling coins does not require us to process the details of the coin face, rather we are often under pressure to select the right coins quickly, for example when giving change. The consequence is that we never do learn the layout of the coins, but learn to discriminate rapidly between them on the basis of their distinguishing features of size, colour, weight, edges, and so on.

On the other hand, if you think of some particularly important moment in your life, especially one that was not foreseen, then you will often have a very vivid memory of it that extends to remembering who you were with, where you were, and so on. This phenomenon, known as vivid or 'flashbulb' memory since it resembles a flash photograph recording all the details of the moment, was first described by Colegrove (1899) who, years after the event, recorded the memories of people on hearing of the assassination of Abraham Lincoln. It came to the notice of modern psychologists following the murder of President Kennedy, when many people found that they had vivid memories of hearing the news. Brown and Kulik (1977) collected many accounts of such memories for other dramatic news stories. Rubin and Kozin (1984) examined the situations that led to the four most vivid memories of a group of participants. They found that the personal importance of the event was a major feature.

Why we have vivid autobiographical memories is not fully understood. It may be that the situation is especially distinctive so that it is easy to retrieve from memory; it may be that frequently thinking about the event helps to keep it available for recall. We will discuss both of these possibilities later. One interesting possibility is that when an important event occurs, our

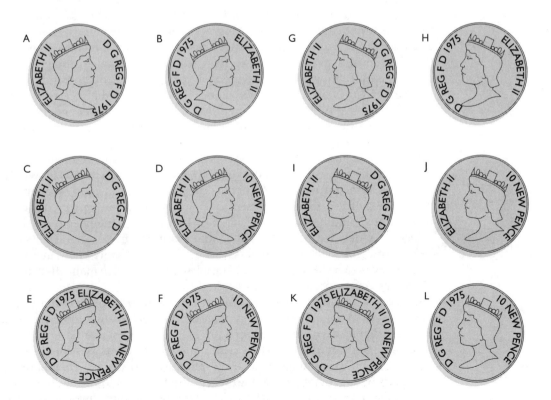

Figure 2.1   Drawings of a 10p coin. The reader is invited to decide which one is correct from memory

memory systems may be designed to record all the details possible to help us cope with the dangers that would have accompanied many such events (see Brown and Kulik, 1977 and Neisser, 1982 and chapter 7 for a discussion). Even if no danger is involved, the storing of apparently irrelevant details could be a useful property of our memories when the normal routine of life is broken. Schank (1982) has argued that when the complex knowledge representations known as schemata (more fully discussed in chapters 7 and 8) that help guide our actions fail to predict what actually happens, it is in this situation that we lay down detailed memories so that, in the future, new schemata can be developed from the stored details. Whatever the reason for flashbulb memories, they do illustrate that what we remember is very much determined by the situation in which the information is acquired and by what we do with it.

Levels of processing

In a famous paper, Craik and Lockhart (1972) tried to capture in a general framework the way in which what we remember is determined by the activities that go on at the time of encoding. They argued that the strength and persistence of a memory trace was a by-product of the perceptual processes that had occurred. They conceived of perceptual processing as varying in 'depth'. For them, shallow processing would involve just the superficial details of what was encountered, for example just the shape of the letters of a word. Deeper processing would involve the sound of the word, and deeper still would be processing of the meaning of the word. The deeper the processing the better the memory, while merely repeating the same level of processing of an item would not improve storage.

Craik and Tulving (1975) provided several powerful demonstrations in support of Craik and Lockhart's claim. They showed that the ease with which words were recognized or recalled was very much dependent upon the task that the participants had been given to carry out upon them. If asked to classify the words according to whether or not they were in capitals, recall and recognition were very poor. They improved markedly if the words had to be classified as rhyming with a given word. However, there was far better recall, and, for example, four times as good recognition, for words that had to be processed for their meaning, perhaps by deciding if they fitted into a given sentence or if they were a member of a given category. A detailed account of this study is given in box 2.1. This same pattern of results was obtained even when the participants knew that their memory was to be tested. It was the task itself that had the main effect upon what was remembered.

Craik and Tulving themselves did not favour the idea of a continuum of depth of encoding. They argued instead that processing took place in distinguishable domains dealing with the physical, semantic and other aspects of the stimulus, and that within a domain it was possible to have varying amounts, or degrees of elaboration, of processing. They showed that even with semantic encoding, where the task was to decide if a word did or did not fit a given sentence, the more elaborate the sentence, the better the subsequent recall, especially if the sentence was given as a memory cue. Thus amount as well as type of processing could be an important predictor of subsequent memory.

One aspect of the levels of processing theory was that merely maintaining an item without further processing should not improve its memorability. An experiment by Craik and Watkins (1973) suggested this was so. It was found that getting participants to repeat out loud the last four words from a longer word list for 20 seconds (the earlier words had been shown for only three seconds each) did not improve the long-term memory of the repeated words.

While the levels of processing theory was an important step forward with its emphasis upon the tasks and type of processing that are undertaken, it was not long before the problems and flaws attracted considerable criticism. To begin with, the whole idea of depth of processing was attacked from two angles. First, it did not fit with more recent theories of perceptual processing which have suggested that analysis does not proceed simply from structure to meaning, but that 'top-down' predictions of the likely meaning can aid perception, and that analysis may go on at all levels simultaneously. Second, perhaps the heaviest criticisms were directed at the problem of measuring independently the depth or level of processing that had been achieved (Nelson, 1977; Baddeley, 1976). In the original theory, it was argued that the poor performance in some tasks was used both as proof that only superficial encoding had occurred, and as evidence that superficial encoding leads to poor recall. Without an independent measure of the level of processing the argument was circular.

The criticism that levels of processing is a circular explanation may be too harsh, since it can be applied to many other theories of psychology. The possibility always remains in a psychological experiment that other variables, apart from the one the experimenter has manipulated, have caused whatever effect is discovered. For any experiment, several independent indications of the effect of the experimental manipulation could then be demanded, just as they were by the critics of levels of processing. Perhaps such evidence, were it available, would be very useful and reassuring, but it is rare for experimenters to take more than one measure of the change in the state of the participant. It is therefore hard upon proponents of levels of processing to single them out for criticism in this way.

Nevertheless, Parkin (1979) did take up the criticism that there was no independent measure of the level to which an item was processed. He was able to show that the task of deciding on the pleasantness of words, or whether they named living things, led to interference in the processing of later words. Judgements on more superficial levels, however, had no such effect. This gave an indication that these tasks differed on the type and extent of processing that had taken place. He also found the normal 'levels of processing' result, that the semantic processing for pleasantness and the living/non-living judgement led to better recall at an unexpected test than did the judgements on the numbers of syllables. In this way he was able to provide independent evidence for the influence of the type of processing that took place upon subsequent recall (see Parkin, 1993 for a further discussion).

Perhaps a fairer criticism of the levels of processing theory is that it overemphasizes encoding without recognizing the importance of both the specific nature of the encoding process and the conditions that are available at retrieval. To predict retrieval effectively it is necessary to know in more detail than just the level or depth the type of encoding that has taken place and the information available at retrieval. This was illustrated by Morris et al. (1977). Their participants first answered questions about the meaning or rhymes for a set of words. Recognition memory was then tested in two ways. In the first test the participants had to pick out the old words from a mixed list of old and new words. In the second test they had to identify words that rhymed with the ones that had been presented (which were not shown at this stage). On the first test, the semantic task produced the better recognition; however, on the rhyming test, the initial requirement to judge whether the presented item rhymed with a given word led to better recognition than did the semantic task. Clearly, therefore, a general claim that semantic (deep) encoding results in better memory has to be qualified by the way the memory is tested.

While the original depth of processing theory has not been completely successful as an explanation, it has succeeded in advancing our understanding. It does, as Baddeley (1982) has commented, give us a useful rule of thumb for predicting how effective an encoding task will be. It was also the first approach to memory that properly addressed the flexibility of encoding processes and illustrated how varied and variable these can be.

Reasons for Forgetting

The other side of the coin concerned with how we remember is why do we forget, and what mechanisms are responsible for forgetting? There are many possible reasons, and it is likely that all of them play some part. Perhaps the reason that first suggests itself is that the memory decays while it is stored, so that it is not available at the time when retrieval is required. It is hard to doubt that memory does decay. Whatever the actual storage mechanism may be, it will depend upon the physiology and biochemistry of the nervous system and this, like all biological systems, is subject to change and decay. Early research on memory by Ebbinghaus (1885) revealed that if memory was tested over differing periods of time, there was at first a rapid loss, then a gradually slowing decline. Most memory studies have found similar decline, whether it is for nonsense words (Woodworth, 1938) or for memories of salient events from the individual's life (Linton, 1982). Nevertheless, when Loftus and Loftus (1980) questioned a sample of psychologists on whether or not they thought that information, once entered into memory, remained there permanently, many said it *was* permanent. The reason is that, as psychologists have studied the conditions under which forgetting takes place, it has become obvious that although some information may be lost from memory through decay, the most dramatic reason for its failure to be recalled is often the influence of the cues for recall and the interfering effect of other material that has been learned. A failure to remember can thus be as (or more) likely to result from the inadequate cueing of the memory as from its loss through decay of a memory trace. As more work on retrieval processes has been carried out, the sensitivity of memory to cueing has been increasingly demonstrated, and confidence in the cueing explanation has increased. Having said this, however, we should make it clear that forgetting due to loss of information – to storage rather than retrieval problems – cannot be definitely ruled out. It is just that storage failure is hard to show conclusively in psychological experiments on memory since it can always be argued that a more powerful or appropriate retrieval cue would have done the trick and unlocked previously inaccessible information.

More recent research has shown how some information can be retrieved, though under special conditions in which the rememberer is not necessarily aware that remembering is taking place. This important phenomenon is known as implicit memory (Schacter, 1987; see also Parkin, 1993, for a good review), and we devote a much fuller discussion to this important topic at the end of this chapter. Although implicit memory phenomena are perhaps most apparent in amnesic participants (patients with severe memory disorders), they can also be observed under special conditions, using normal participants in memory experiments. We shall also discuss some of the retrieval methods used to explore these effects later in this chapter.

Encoding specificity

Returning to explicit memory for now, that is, situations in which people are aware that memory is being used, we wish to consider further the relation between encoding and retrieval, and their link with remembering and forgetting. The psychologist who has emphasized most specifically the relationship between what was originally encoded and the situation at retrieval is Endel Tulving (1983). Tulving argued, as we have done above, that what is encoded into memory depends upon the particular conditions pertaining at the time. For example, every time that we encounter a cat we do not store as part of the memory of that particular event all that we know about cats. Rather, the entry in memory will reflect the particular encounter with the cat in question. We might remember that it was soft, warm and furry and lay on our lap and purred, or, in another instance, we would particularly encode the tendency of cats to rush across roads if one had just forced us into an emergency stop. For the information that has been encoded on a specific occasion to be retrieved, it is necessary for there to be sufficient overlap between what is currently being processed by the cognitive system and the details of the original event encoded in memory. So, to continue our cat example, the later sight of a dog nearly knocked down by a car may re-evoke the memory of the cat with poor road sense, while a soft toy, or the feel of velvet, or the sound of purring might possibly remind us of the lap-top cat.

The processing of current events interacts with stored memory traces in a process called 'ecphory' by Tulving (1983). While the precise way in which this interaction occurs is still not fully understood, it is clear that the likelihood of retrieval does depend upon the similarity between the current processing of the cognitive system at retrieval and the encoded record of the original memory. The more similar the two are, the more 'overlap' there is between the information that specifies them. As informational overlap increases so does the likelihood of successful retrieval.

A further idea is that the contribution of retrieval and the memory record, or trace, to the act of remembering can vary. Particularly rich and elaborate encoding may require relatively little and unspecific information to cue its recall, while poorly encoded or very specific memories may require current processing that is very specific to the original events. For example, suppose you were the first person at the scene of a road accident and had to deal with a seriously injured person; it is likely that the decisions and actions required of you, and the emotions and thoughts aroused by the interaction, would be sufficient to ensure easy, and perhaps even unwanted, retrieval of the incident in a wide variety of situations. On the other hand, a superficial encounter with a person while in a queue to buy a train ticket may require that you return to the precise location again, and see the person waiting for the same train, for the original memory to be re-evoked.

Tulving's account of the relationship between encoding and retrieval is supported by many research findings. Research that has manipulated the context in which learning takes place has often demonstrated that restoring the original context will lead to better recall. For example, Smith (1979) found that when participants were given an unexpected test of their memory of a list of words learned 24 hours earlier, recall was approx-imately 50 per cent higher when tested in the same room than in a very different room. Smith was able to improve recall by the people who had changed rooms by first getting them to think about the room in which they did the learning, listing objects that they had seen. In a similar way, Malpass and Devine (1981) were able to improve the identification of the 'criminal' in a staged robbery by having the witnesses recall what they had been doing and the details of the room at the time. This has been developed by Geiselman (1988) into a very successful technique for helping eye-witnesses maximize their recall of crimes. The technique, known as the Cognitive Interview, encourages witnesses to mentally reinstate the context in which the event took place, to recall everything, and to try to recall from different perspectives and in differing orders. The Cognitive Interview was found to lead to 35 per cent better recall than the standard interviewing techniques used by the law officers who took part.

It is not just the external context that is important. Eich (1980) has reviewed what is known as state-dependent retrieval, showing that recall under the influence of drugs that change one's conscious state, such as alcohol or marijuana, is better when the recall condition matches that at learning, and the person is or is not under the influence of drugs at both times.

Similar results have been found with changes in mood. Bower (1981) manipulated the mood of his participants in several experiments, some-times by hypnosis, sometimes by getting them to read material that would create the different states. A switch in mood from, say, happy to sad, or vice versa, made a massive difference to recall, with performance declining if the mood changed between learning and recall, irrespective of the direction of change. Teasdale (1983) has looked at the memorizing of depressed patients. He finds, like Bower, that what a depressed person tends to remember is memories from times when they were depressed previously.

The result is then a vicious circle of more depression and more depressing memories. The effects of a wide range of contexts have now been investigated, and are reviewed by Davies (1979).

Even the reoccurrence of the same words at encoding and retrieval may not be sufficiently similar to cue recall, if the meaning of the word is used differently on the two occasions, or if a different aspect of the word is emphasized. For example, Light and Carter-Sobell (1970) required participants to remember words that have more than one meaning, and primed the meanings with qualifying adjectives. For example, the word JAM might be qualified with either 'traffic' or 'strawberry'. In the experiment the participants had to recognize these words. If they were paired with the same adjective at presentation and at testing, then 67 per cent were recognized, but when the adjective was switched to change the meaning, only 27 per cent were recognized. Barclay et al. (1974) showed that similar results would occur if unambiguous words had been encoded so that different properties were emphasized at learning and recall. Their participants read ten sentences. Different groups received different sets of sentences that emphasized alternative aspects of the thing that was the object of that sentence. So, some participants saw, as one of their sentences, *The student spilled the ink* while the other groups saw *The student picked up the ink*. These sentences emphasized the different properties of ink: that it comes in a bottle and that it is messy if spilled. Recall was tested by giving 20 cues, ten of which would be appropriate cues, and ten were related to the meaning emphasized to the other group, and called the inappropriate cues. For the sentences above, the cues were: *Something in a bottle* and *Something messy*. Barclay et al. found that more than three times as many of the objects were recalled to appropriate than to inappropriate cues.

When encoding takes place, therefore, what is stored is the particular sense of the sentences. At recall, that specific sense must be recalled by the cues available. Tulving (1979, 1983) has emphasized this relationship with his 'encoding specificity principle' which states that: 'The probability of successful retrieval of the target item is a monotonically increasing function of informational overlap between the information present at retrieval and the information stored in memory' (Tulving, 1979, p. 408). Forbidding though this may sound, the principle is actually quite easy to grasp: the more the overlap between stored information and information provided by the retrieval situation, the more likely we are remember successfully.

Interference effects

One reason for forgetting is, then, that the cues to recall do not sufficiently match any entry in memory to make it retrievable. Another alternative is that there are too many entries in memory activated by the retrieval cues, and none of them is sufficiently distinct to be selected. Much research has been carried out upon the way that the learning of information similar to that to be remembered hampers subsequent recall. This problem of forgetting caused by other learned material is called 'interference'. Some interference is caused by the learning of similar information after the memorizing of the items to be recalled, and this is termed 'retroactive interference'; other interference, 'proactive interference', is the result of similar information learned prior to the acquisition of the items in question. So, if someone is asked to learn word list A, is then presented with a similar list B to be learned, and then tested on list A, retroactive interference can arise through the effects of learning list B on memory for list A. Likewise, if, having learned list A and then list B, the person is then required to remember list B, proactive interference from the memory of list A can affect the learning of list B.

McGeoch and MacDonald (1931) provided an early illustration of retroactive interference. They had their participants learn a list of adjectives and then carry out some other activity before a further test. Recall was best if this time was filled by an activity other than learning new lists, but for those participants who did memorize new lists, the nature of the material presented was crucial. The most damaging to the memory of the original list was the learning of synonyms of the original adjectives. Other adjectives also led to poor performance. Lists of numbers had far less effect, and when tested again on the original list, those participants who had memorized lists of three-digit numbers could recall three times as many of the original list of adjectives as those who had memorized synonyms in the intervening period. Subsequently, others have demonstrated retroactive interference with more realistic materials; for example, Crouse (1971) used very similar short stories.

The influence of proactive interference was shown by Underwood (1957) who reviewed a number of studies in which participants had been taught a list of items and then tested 24 hours later. He showed that the rate of forgetting was dramatically related to the number of lists previously learned. If no lists had been memorized before, then, after 24 hours, about 75 per cent of the list could normally be remembered; if 20 lists had been memorized previously then only about 20 per cent of the 21st list would be recallable after 24 hours. However, not all of this drastic change can be attributed to forgetting through interference. Warr (1964) pointed out that as people learn more lists they become quicker at memorizing. A consequence of this is that participants have more exposure to the items on their first few lists, since they had to rehearse them longer to memorize them in the first place. When this is taken into account and the items are equated for their number of learning trials, the size of the decline with previous lists is much less than Underwood (1957) estimated, though it is still quite substantial, as Keppel et al. (1968) showed.

Modification of old by new memories

So far we have argued that much forgetting is the result of retrieval cues not sufficiently specifying the entry in memory to make its retrieval possible. Other earlier evidence from studies of electrical brain stimulation during brain operations, in which patients seemed to report long 'forgotten' memories, also suggested that vast amounts of material could be stored without necessarily being easily retrieved (Penfield, 1958). It was this sort of evidence that led the psychologists surveyed by Loftus and Loftus (1980) to conclude that the entries in memory are permanent. It is actually very difficult to contradict such a view since, whatever attempts at recall have failed in the past, the possibility will always remain that at some future time an apparently forgotten item will be suddenly recalled. Nevertheless, over the years, some psychologists have disputed the permanence of memory and have presented evidence that suggests that the entry in memory has been modified by new learning and the old memory eliminated. The most recent proponents of this view have been Elizabeth Loftus and her associates, although the idea that new learning causes the 'unlearning' of old memories has a long history (e.g. Melton and Irwin, 1940; Barnes and Underwood, 1959).

Loftus and Loftus (1980) review a series of studies they made on the memory participants had for details from a short sequence of slides. The slides showed the build-up to a road accident. At one point a car is seen by a Stop sign. If in the questioning afterwards about this scene, the question mentioned not a Stop sign but a Yield sign (the American equivalent of Give Way) then, when two slides are shown simultaneously to the participants later (one the original and the other with the Stop sign replaced by a Yield sign), 80 per cent of the participants chose the Yield sign as the one they had seen. Further experiments showed that this was not because they could remember both signs but chose the one mentioned, nor that they gave what seemed to be the answer the experimenter wanted. Even the offer of $20 for a correct answer did not change the proportion selecting the information inserted in the questioning. There was no evidence for the retention of the original information. Loftus and Loftus (1980) concluded that the original memory had been updated and deleted by the information supplied in the questions.

The Loftus research has stimulated many attempts to demonstrate that the information is still in memory but just not easily accessible. It does appear that under certain circumstances involving the ordering of the questioning about the incident and the slides that test recall, the original information can be retrieved (Bekerian and Bowers, 1983; Bowers and Bekerian, 1984). Nevertheless, even if the belief in permanence of memory has not been finally disproved by the Loftus research, the ease with which leading questions can bias memory and the difficulty of overcoming such a bias has been well demonstrated. More recently, the development of connectionist models (see chapter 13) has increased the plausibility of the continuous modification of memory. In connectionist models the 'memory' is seen not as a thing stored away like a book in a library, but as a dynamic property of the state of the network. The network is constantly having its weights modified and this may change the form of the output from the system.

Summary on forgetting and note on retrieval tests

To summarize this section on forgetting, we have identified several reasons why our memories may let us down. It is probable that the encoded information decays with time, but more important may be that the information available from the current processing in the cognitive system does not match the stored information and, as a result, fails to cue the stored memory. Other problems can be caused by the similarity of stored entries for other items. Finally, it is possible that subsequent entries in memory may modify and delete older memories, although this claim has yet to be substantiated by convincing evidence.

It is worth noting again, however, that all these failures to remember discussed so far are difficulties with explicit memory. Although recall or recognition fails in these circumstances, implicit retrieval might still be possible, as we shall show shortly.

The Structure of Memory

Thus far we have discussed memory as if it were a single system. However, over the century of research on memory, findings have accumulated that have led many psychologists to argue that the memory system is in fact composed of many, specialized, subsystems. These subsystems can be roughly classified into three types: those responsible for holding information for a very brief period of time, known as sensory memories; those holding information for several seconds, that is, short-term memories; and those that retain information indefinitely, that is, long-term memories. We will consider the evidence for these types of memories separately.

Sensory memories

The classical demonstration of the existence of a visual sensory memory, sometimes called an iconic memory, was reported by Sperling (1960). Using a tachistoscope, which allows the very brief presentation of visual information, he showed the participants in his experiments three rows of four letters for 50 milliseconds. After the presentation of the letters, the task was to write down the letters shown in their correct positions. On average, people can report only about four or five of these letters. In the next part of Sperling's experiments, a high, medium or low tone was sounded just after the letters were presented. The tone indicated whether the top, middle or bottom line was to be reported. In this case, the participants could usually report about three of the four letters in the appropriate line. They had not known, in advance, which line to report so that the results suggested that, at the moment when the letters were shown, the participants were capable of reporting about three from any of the three lines, that is, about nine letters rather than the four or five suggested by Sperling's first experiment. Sperling argued that the discrepancy between the apparent ability to report nine letters in his second experiment and the four or five in his first experiment came about because the participants possessed a sensory memory with a large capacity but one which lost information very quickly. Immediately after the presentation of the twelve letters, it was likely that all twelve would be retained within this sensory memory. However, as the participants attempted to retrieve the letters from this memory and write them down, the sensory, iconic memory rapidly decayed so that they could recall only those letters that could be retrieved from the sensory memory in the first fraction of a second.

Following the publishing of Sperling's research there was considerable interest in the properties of iconic memory. Many studies involved following the initial stimulus with a second stimulus intended to disrupt the processing of the iconic memory. For example, a set of letters might be followed by a pattern-mask a few milliseconds later. The pattern-mask typically was formed from broken fragments of letters in a random pattern. Using techniques such as these, Turvey (1973), for example, explored many properties of iconic memory and argued that it was not a simple passive store but rather the outcome of storage at a series of stages in the process of visual perception. Some researchers (e.g. Haber, 1983) came to doubt the importance of iconic memory and the research that it had engendered. Others (e.g. Coltheart, 1983) argued that iconic memory ensured that the perceptual system had a minimum time in which to process incoming stimuli.

Analogous to the iconic memory, there is a sensory memory for auditory information, sometimes known as the echoic memory. One illustration of this comes from studies of dichotic listening (see chapter 5) where participants are presented with two different messages, one to each ear, and have to repeat aloud one of the messages. At any point, the participant can usually report the last word or so from the other message, but this is rapidly forgotten. Glucksberg and Cowan (1970) showed that information in the second message was lost within five seconds. A simulation of the Sperling experiment for auditory information has been used (e.g. Darwin et al., 1972) in which consonants are simultaneously presented from several different locations and the participant's task is to report either all the consonants heard or just those from a particular location. As with Sperling's experiments on vision, these results suggest that, because the partial reports for a particular location give better results than would be expected from the total recall, there is, probably, an echoic memory that can be drawn upon to retrieve auditory information. Like the iconic memory, this echoic memory loses information rapidly.

Short-term memory

As early as 1890, William James drew a distinction between primary memory and secondary memory. James associated primary memory with the current contents of consciousness while secondary memory referred to information that was not currently consciously available but could be retrieved in appropriate circumstances. From the earliest days of the experimental study of memory (Jacobs, 1887), it has been recognized that there is a limited number of items (for example, letters or numbers) that can be recalled correctly in order after only one presentation. Holding in memory items up to this memory span is relatively easy, but the correct recall of numbers of items beyond the memory span requires several learning trails. The learning of more items than are held in the memory span seems to call upon different memory processes.

These hints about possible subdivisions of memory drawn from William James and from studies of memory span developed into a widely held acceptance of the existence of two memory systems, one short-term and one long-term, during the 1960s. Several sources of evidence converged to support the distinction. For example, Peterson and Peterson (1959) showed that even three words or letters were forgotten over a few seconds if participants were prevented from rehearsing the items to themselves. Studies of the recall of lists of words showed that participants preferred to recall the last few items from the list first and that this recall was not affected by factors that influenced the recall of the majority of words in the list, such as word frequency or the rate of presentation. More intriguing was the evidence that the short-term memory held information in a different form from long-term memory. Conrad and Hull (1964), for example, showed that when the memory span for lists of letters was tested with the letters being presented visually, the errors that were made involved confusing and forgetting letters that sounded similar rather than ones that were visually similar. Similarly, Baddeley (1966) showed that words which were phonologically similar (e.g. man, mad, cap, can, map) led to much poorer immediate recall than words that sounded differently from one another or that were similar in meaning but different in sound (e.g. big, huge, broad, long, tall). It looked as if short-term memory used some form of coding based on the sound of what was to be remembered while long-term memory depended upon the meaning of the item. Studies of brain-damaged patients with severe amnesia are also relevant here (e.g. Baddeley and Warrington, 1970). Patients suffering from amnesia typically have great difficulty in retaining newly acquired information for longer than a few seconds or minutes. They also frequently have problems in remembering information acquired before the onset of their amnesia (see also chapter 12). Baddeley and Warrington managed to show that despite their severe problems such patients had relatively normal memory spans. This finding suggested that it was possible to have an intact short-term memory together with an impaired long-term memory, and was used as further support for the short-term/long-term memory distinction.

The above, and related research, led to the development of models of memory that assumed that information first entered sensory memories specific to the modality in which the information was received. From there, the information was read out into a short-term store that had a limited capacity that was reflected in the memory span. The retention of the information in this short-term store was believed to be phonemic in nature and rapidly lost over a period of a few seconds, unless it was re-entered by the person rehearsing, that is, repeating, the items over again to themselves. From short-term store, it was assumed that information was selectively transferred to the long-term store, primarily as a function of the amount of time the item spent in the short-term store and the number of times that it was rehearsed or repeated. A well-known version of this model was presented by Atkinson and Shiffrin (1968).

Other studies conducted around this time appeared to support this model. Shallice and Warrington (1970), for example, reported a patient, KF, who had normal long-term learning ability but who was very poor at tests of memory span. At first this looked like evidence for separate, and separately damageable, short- and long-term memories. Together with the data from Baddeley and Warrington (1970), Shallice and Warrington's patient seemed to illustrate neatly what is known as a double dissociation of function. A double dissociation of function arises when performance on one of two tasks, say A or B, can be independently impaired, usually through brain injury, without affecting performance on the other. In practice this requires that at least one person is found who has difficulty with task A but not B, while at least one other person is found who has difficulties with task B but not with task A. It can then be argued that performance on tasks A and B is supported by separate brain areas and cognitive subsystems, particularly if it can be also shown that damage to different brain areas did in fact occur (see chapter 12). In the present case, Baddeley and Warrington showed that it was possible to have difficulty with long-term remembering while having no difficulties with a typical short-term remembering task, while Warrington and Shallice appeared to show the reverse. This dissociation of long- and short-term *remembering* could then be used to infer a separation between long- and short-term *stores*. A moment's reflection, however, should convince the reader that the matter is not quite so simple. In the standard multi-store model, information must first pass through short-term memory *en route* to long-term memory. If this is the case, it is hard to see why damage to short-term memory does not also affect the amount and possibly the quality of information reaching long-term memory. Thus, according to the model but contrary to Warrington and Shallice's data, patients with short-term memory impairments should also have problems with long-term memory. One solution to this problem is to argue that information need not pass through short-term memory to get into long-term memory. However, this explanation in turn has been overtaken by research, and nowadays data from the Shallice and Warrington study would not be used to support the short-term/long-term memory distinction. Instead it is usually discussed within the working memory framework which we consider below.

Other problems with the simple structural model of memory also arose. The link between rehearsal in short-term memory and strength of encoding in long-term memory was severely questioned by studies in which considerable amounts of rehearsal of some items failed to improve their subsequent recall (e.g. Craik and Watkins, 1973). The idea that the form of coding in short-term memory was essentially phonemic was also questioned (Morris, 1977).

Baddeley's model of working memory

While the details of the initial models of short- and long-term memory turned out to be incorrect, the original observations that had led to the postulation of the distinction remained, and were elaborated by further research.

In recent years, Alan Baddeley (1986, 1990) has proposed a very influential development of the original short-term/long-term memory model. Baddeley and co-workers, particularly Graham Hitch, wished not only to do justice to the large mass of data suggesting differences between short- and long-term remembering, but also to acknowledge that short-term memory can be used in a wide range of cognitive tasks which involve the active manipulation of information, such as mental arithmetic, reading and comprehension as well as in standard laboratory memory tasks. Another of their aims was to find out more, if possible, about the internal operations and functions of short-term memory. In particular, was short-term memory a simple single memory store, or was it subdivisible into a number of simpler components? Because they were interested in the active nature of this part of memory, and its internal dynamics, they prefer to use the term *working* memory rather than short-term memory to refer to the system responsible for the temporary storage and manipulation of information.

Baddeley's approach assumes that working memory has at least three components: a central executive, a visuo-spatial sketch pad and an articulatory or phonological loop (see figure 2.2). We will consider these in turn.

The central executive   In Baddeley's model, the central executive is the most important component of the system and also, unfortunately, the one that is least well understood. Baddeley sees the central executive as the part of working memory that controls the rest of the working memory system. He sees it as responsible for the organization and planning of the cognitive activities of the individual, and, as such, it closely resembles the BOSS component of our BOSS–Employee model (Morris and Hampson, 1983; Hampson and Morris, 1990). The central executive will be involved in comprehension, planning and the control of actions. As such, it underlies the processes of attention and planning that we describe in chapters 5 and 8. Baddeley (1990) argues that the frontal lobes of the brain support much of the functioning of the central executive and that this explains the dysexecutive syndrome or frontal lobe syndrome that is observed in patients with damage to their frontal lobes. Such patients have particular problems in controlling and structuring their actions.

Visuo-spatial sketch pad   Imagery is a non-verbal way of representing knowledge about the world, and, although it is possible to have images of smells, tastes, sounds and so on, it is visual imagery that has been most thoroughly investigated. In Baddeley's model, the visuo-spatial sketch pad is the system underlying visual mental imagery. It is the part of the

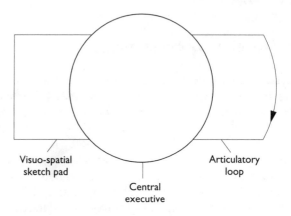

Figure 2.2 The working memory system, showing the central executive, the articulatory loop and the visuo-spatial sketch pad

cognitive system that we use when we imagine a scene or create a novel mental image that draws on our imagination rather than our memories.

The 1970s and early 1980s were a popular time for research on mental imagery among cognitive psychologists who were keen to explore the way in which images were represented in the cognitive system and the part that they played in cognition. Much of this research is discussed in Morris and Hampson (1983) and Hampson et al. (1989). Here we wish to draw attention to just one aspect of a very large research area, namely the way in which images are represented in the sketch pad. Objects and scenes in the real world have both visual and spatial aspects. Roughly speaking, we can see what things look like, where they are and how their parts are arranged. The question then arises whether mental images are visual or spatial entities or both. Baddeley and Lieberman (1980) pointed out that the basis of storage in the visuo-spatial sketch pad might be spatial coding rather than visual coding. They devised a task that required spatial but not visual information by requiring their participants, who were blindfold, to follow a swinging pendulum with the beam of a flashlight. This would involve using spatial but, obviously, not visual information. They found that this 'Pit and Pendulum Test' interfered with performance on some standard imagery tests, illustrating the importance of the spatial component in these tests. Further research, however, has demonstrated that visual as well as spatial coding is used by the visuo-spatial sketch pad (Logie and Baddeley, 1990).

The phonological loop The most extensively studied component of Baddeley's working memory model is the phonological loop. The model assumes that this is a slave system that can be used by the central executive to hold a small amount of phonological information for a short time. Rather like a continuous tape recording, the phonological loop can be used to keep speech-based information alive for extended periods of time. The findings of Conrad and Hull (1964) and Baddeley (1966) are attributed to this phonological loop. One piece of evidence for the limited size of the loop is that the memory span is sensitive to the speed with which words can be spoken. Baddeley et al. (1975) showed that the more syllables there were in the words to be recalled, the poorer was the performance, and that this relationship was closely matched by the speed with which the words could be read. Furthermore, words that have the same number of syllables but could be read quickly (e.g. *bishop* and *wicket*) are better remembered in immediate memory tests than words that are spoken more slowly (e.g. *Friday* and *harpoon*). Naveh-Benjamin and Ayres (1986) have shown that the memory span for digits spoken in different languages is closely related to the speed with which those digits can be read within those languages.

A very widely used technique to study the phonological loop is known as articulatory suppression. This simply involves requiring the participants in the experiment to repeat aloud a word such as 'the' while performing another task thought to require the loop. It is assumed that articulatory suppression will occupy the articulatory control processes and feed the spoken material into the phonological loop. Experiments using articulatory suppression have shown that, when to-be-remembered words are presented visually, there is no longer a word length effect nor does the similarity of the words influence recall.

Gathercole and Baddeley (1990) have been exploring the role of the phonological loop in children's learning of language. They tested over one hundred children before they had acquired any reading skills, and looked at the child's development of vocabulary during the first year at school. They found that their measure of the adequacy of functioning of the child's phonological loop, which they assessed from the child's ability to repeat back lists of non-word sounds, was a good predictor of the child's vocabulary even when measures of non-verbal intelligence were taken into account. They believe that the phonological loop is very important to children at the stage when they are acquiring new words (see box 2.2).

A final useful aspect of the phonological loop is that it can be used to explain the poor performance of the patient studied by Shallice and Warrington (1970) which we mentioned above. Instead of suggesting that this patient, and others like him, have damage to short-term memory as a whole, it now seems likely that their poor memory span is the result of more specific damage to the phonological loop.

Long-term memory

If the more complex working memory has largely replaced our earlier undifferentiated short-term memory, a similar fate has befallen long-term memory. No longer do psychologists think of long-term memory as a single system dealing with just one type of information. Tulving (1983), in particular, argued that long-term memory involved two sorts of knowledge: procedural and propositional. Procedural knowledge is knowing how to carry out skilled actions such as riding a bicycle or typing. We discuss the acquisition and use of such knowledge in chapter 6.

Propositional knowledge on the other hand is knowledge of facts. It is knowing that certain things have happened or are true, rather than knowing how to carry out skilled actions which is the basis of procedural knowledge. Tulving argued that propositional knowledge should be further seen as involving two types of knowledge: episodic and semantic. Episodic knowledge is information about events that have occurred within the rememberer's own life and experience. Semantic memory involves the store of knowledge about the world that is remembered independently of the time and place at which it was acquired. So, for example, my episodic memory of buying a puppy involves details of the particular kennels, the sights and sounds on that particular day, etc. On the other hand, my memory of what puppies are like is a generalized one involving them having four legs, being young dogs, needing house training and so on. One may remember much of such general knowledge without it being associated with any particular events from one's life.

Many psychologists would probably accept that some sort of distinction between the various classes of knowledge and information, procedural and propositional, and then episodic and semantic, makes good sense. What is less clear is whether separate subsystems of long-term memory are needed to deal with these different sorts of information, and if so how these subsystems are related. During the early 1980s a widely held view was that there were independent procedural and propositional subsystems, and that propositional long-term memory in turn was divided into separate episodic and semantic memories. Nowadays, those who still support the idea of different subsystems are less likely to claim that such subsystems are functionally independent. One view advanced by Tulving (1985) is that, like an onion, the three memory systems build on top of one another. Procedural memory is seen as the most basic subsystem, out of this semantic memory arises, and finally episodic memory out of semantic. This approach, which has still to be properly evaluated, has implications for the order in which the memory systems have evolved and develop, suggesting that procedural memory comes first. It also attempts to deal with the different levels of awareness or consciousness associated with the different forms of memory: procedural memory, it is suggested, can be used with little or no awareness while higher and more complex levels of awareness are associated with semantic and, in particular, episodic memory, as we shall see later. Finally, it tries to account for data from the brain-injured by suggesting that the evolutionarily and developmentally later and episodic subsystem may be more prone to damage than the more basic procedural subsystem.

Whatever the outcome of the debates on the architecture of long-term memory, in recent years there has been a considerable interest in studying episodic memory in its own right, which has come to be known as autobiographical memory, and we will discuss this in detail in chapter 7. In this chapter we wish to introduce some basic ideas about semantic memory.

Semantic memory

During the 1970s there was much theorizing about the possible basis and nature of semantic memory. Research explored the speed with which decisions could be made by drawing upon information in semantic memory. A common paradigm was to require participants to answer as quickly as possible questions such as 'Is a robin a bird?', 'Is an ostrich a bird?', 'Is a bat a bird?', 'Is a table a bird?'. Participants were relatively quick in answering that typical members of a category were indeed members of that category and in rejecting instances where the item involved (e.g. table) was very different from the category (e.g. birds). However, people were slower in confirming that members of categories that were atypical in either their features or the frequency with which they were associated with the category (e.g. ostrich as an example of birds) were members of the category. People also took relatively long to reject instances where the item under consideration shared features with common members of a category although not, in fact, a member of that category. So, in our example, when asked whether a bat is a bird, participants typically took longer to reject the statement than they did the question of whether a table is a bird.

One type of theory to account for these decisions argues that the comparisons are made by matching stored lists of the features of each instance. The more similar the features between the instance (e.g. robin) and the category (e.g. birds) the quicker a positive response. A very clear disparity of the features leads to a quick negative response. Overlap of features (e.g. bats and birds), or a less positive feature match than for typical items (e.g. for ostriches and birds), required a more detailed comparison. Such feature models (e.g. Smith et al., 1974) accounted for the reaction-time data but they were limited in their ability to generalize. For example, a simple feature comparison cannot cope with the difference between the questions 'Is a robin a bird?' and 'Is a bird a robin?'. Feature models also fall foul of the philosophical criticisms of Wittgenstein (1953) who argued that the definition of words could not be understood in terms of lists of properties that all exemplars of the category possess, but rather category membership depends upon what he described as 'family resemblance'. Just as different members of a family may share similar bodily features with one another (e.g. colour of eyes, colour of hair, etc.) but there is no set of bodily features that is possessed by all members of the family, so Wittgenstein argued, members of verbal categories share similarities but do not have defining features possessed by all members of the class.

A more successful approach to understanding the nature of semantic memory has been semantic network theories. These assume that instances and categories are represented as nodes in a network that interconnects the items and their properties. Collins and Loftus (1975) proposed an elaborate network model. The model involved various types of links. Class membership was indicated by IS A links (e.g. a robin is a bird). Negative links were allowed in the network to indicate special relationships (e.g. a bat is not a bird). The properties of the items were indicated by HAS links (e.g. a bird has feathers).

Figure 2.3, from Collins and Loftus (1975), represents a fragment of human memory, with the nodes standing for concepts and the lines between them indicating their conceptual relations. The shorter the line the greater the relatedness.

Collins and Loftus assumed that when a question was asked, the two concepts involved had their appropriate nodes within the network stimulated and activation spread from these nodes throughout the network. They also assumed that the strength of the connections in the network varied with the frequency with which the links were used. Answers to questions could be drawn from the information that was so activated. Positive and negative evidence was summed to explain the semantic relatedness data that we described above. Typical items from the category quickly accumulated enough shared links in the network to lead to a yes answer while untypical ones required the accumulation of more evidence and took longer.

While network models such as that of Collins and Loftus are inherently powerful they are difficult to test. They have also been criticized (Johnson-Laird et al., 1984) for neglecting the link between the concepts in the network and the world outside.

Another approach to semantic memory has been particularly associated with the work of Rosch. She argued that categories are represented by prototypes. Rosch (1978) argued that natural categories are determined by the perceived structure in the world. We experience the world as structured by the frequency with which some perceptual and functional attributes occur together. Thus, we experience feathers, wings and beaks together. Secondly, she argued that there is cognitive economy in categorization. In developing categories there is a compromise between the specificity of categories and the generality of instances that they cover. Rosch argued that there is a basic level of categorization that is the most useful one in normal talking and thinking. 'Chair' and 'car' are examples of basic-level categories. There are also superordinate levels that are less specific (furniture and vehicles) and subordinate levels that are more specific (kitchen chair, sports car). If people are asked to write down the attributes from each of

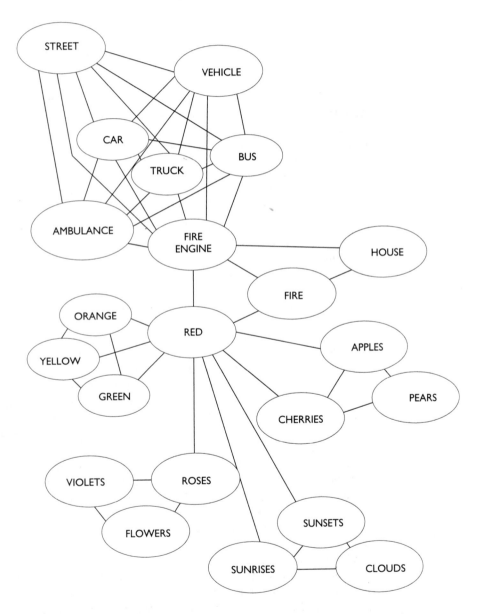

Figure 2.3   A schematic representation of concept relatedness in memory. Shorter lines represent greater relatedness. (Based on figure 1, Collins and Loftus, 1975)

these three levels, Rosch et al. (1976) found that people produce few attributes for the superordinate categories, a large number for the base-level categories and the same categories with one or two extras for the subordinate-level categories.

Implicit and Explicit Memories

So far we have discussed memory in terms of the conscious recollection or retrieval of previously acquired information. Most memory experiments involve asking the participants to remember information that they recollect having encountered before. The participants may not remember all the details of the material learned, but they normally remember encountering the material in the earlier stages of the experiment. It is easy to come to associate this conscious awareness with the learning itself, and assume that we will remember only what we recollect having experienced in the past. However, a little thought soon suggests that this connection between awareness of the original learning and the effect of the original encounter with the material upon the current state of our cognitive systems is by no means necessary. After all, even some of the simplest organisms have their behaviour modified through learning, and it is not necessary to assume that they will have conscious memories associated with these changes. We ourselves have developed all sorts of learned skills, reading, walking, driving and so on, without retaining awareness of the situations under which our behaviour was being modified, or even being aware of any modification taking place at all! In chapter 8 we give an account of the place of consciousness in relation to the cognitive system (the BOSS model), and this model implies that many of the subsystems that underlie cognition will be regularly modified without our conscious awareness.

Nevertheless, the relationship between conscious awareness of learning and our memory abilities have come to interest psychologists in recent years. One reason for this interest has been that it can be shown that experiences of which we have no recollection can still affect our performance on related tasks. Another reason is that amnesic patients who were once believed to have no ability to acquire new information can show changes as a result of experience that are identical with those of normals, yet patients with amnesia have no recollection of the original learning conditions.

A good example experiment from this area is by Jacoby (1983). He had participants study words (e.g. COLD) under one of three conditions. First, in the No-context condition, the words were presented in the form XXX–COLD. Next, in the Context condition, the words were paired with an antonym (e.g. hot–COLD). In both of these conditions the participants read the word aloud. Finally, in the Generate condition, they were given 'hot' and had to generate an antonym, normally, of course, generating COLD. Different groups of participants were tested in two different ways. One group took part in a conventional recognition test, being shown the words intermixed with new words, and being required to identify which were which. In this test, recognition was best for the Generate condition, next best for the Context condition, and worst for the No-context condition.

However, when the words were used in a perceptual identification task in which the words (and new words) were shown very briefly in a tachistoscope and had to be identified, the result was a complete reversal of this pattern. Now the better recognition came with the No-context condition, with the Context condition next, and the Generate condition being the poorest. Participants in the perceptual identification conditions are not aware that their performance has been affected by the earlier study of the word pairs; not only has this happened, but the residual effect of that earlier study is exactly the opposite from that in the recognition test, where the conscious recollection of the words is integral in the testing.

The fact that previously acquired information can affect subsequent performance without the person being aware that this is happening is an example of implicit memory. Implicit memory occurs when previously learned material is used without conscious or explicit recollection. Warrington and Weiskrantz (1970) provide an example of implicit memory in sufferers from amnesia. Four patients recognized only half as many items as 16 control patients without brain damage. However, when tested on the influence of words seen earlier on both the ease of identifying the words when each letter was degraded, and the generation of the words in a word stem completion task, where the first three letters of each word were given, the amnesic patients and the controls performed equally well, both being influenced by the prior exposure. Another example is a study in which amnesic patients were asked trivial questions, with the patients choosing from alternative answers and being told the correct answer. Where the patients made an initial mistake, they were retested a few minutes later. Now they were quite likely to be correct, but they were consistently unable to say why, that is, to recall having been told the answer a few minutes earlier. In a rather similar study with Korsakoff patients, Johnson et al. (1985) played brief melodies to their participants and repeated some of them later. While the patients had no recollection of which tunes they had heard earlier, they preferred the tunes that they had heard before. This is in line with Zajonc's (1980) research on the exposure effect, where stimuli are judged as more likeable merely because they have been encountered before.

Memory without awareness has been demonstrated in a number of situations, some of which have now become paradigms for investigating the phenomenon further. For example, fragment completion, where spaces indicate the missing letters in words to be identified (e.g. t_bl_ for table), lexical decision, where participants decide which letter strings (such as CAKE, or KECA) are words, as well as the perceptual identification technique used by Jacoby (1983) have been widely used to demonstrate better subsequent performance following earlier presentation of the critical items, with no awareness of the link by the participants. An early study involving fragment completion by Tulving et al. (1982) illustrated how implicit and explicit memory tasks can lead to different rates of forgetting. Figure 2.4 shows the accuracy of recognition of 96 words after either an hour or seven days, and the comparable priming effects on fragment completion after seeing those same words. While recognition of the words declined sharply over the time interval, the priming effect remained as strong, suggesting that different processes were involved in the two cases.

There are a number of competing theoretical accounts of such types of remembering that are still under test. One account, developed by Tulving and his colleagues (e.g. Tulving and Schacter, 1990), develops Tulving's (1983) earlier proposal of the existence of separate episodic, semantic and procedural memory systems by now adding a perceptual representational system to account for the dissociations between implicit and explicit tasks. In Tulving's classification of the memory systems, implicit memory can also come about through the functioning of the semantic memory system, since it is only the episodic system that provides recollections of the personal encounters with the stimulus material.

Alternative accounts do not require the division of the memory system but emphasize processing differences. Jacoby and Dallas (1981) introduced the concept of perceptual fluency. They suggested that implicit memory performance comes about because the perceptual processes that underlie the processing of the stimuli used in the experiments are made more fluent by the initial exposure. The words, melodies etc., are processed more quickly and easily having been processed once recently. They are not remembered explicitly, but may still 'feel special' to the participant. This

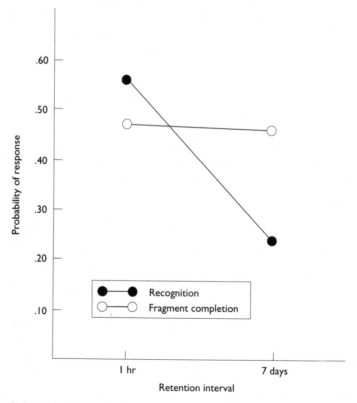

Figure 2.4 The effect of prior exposure to words on their recognition and on fragment completion after one hour and seven days. (Based on figure I, Tulving et al., 1982)

feeling special can lead to interesting errors if it is wrongly attributed by the participant. So, for example, Jacoby et al. (1989) found that participants who had rated lists of names on the basis of the fame of the person were likely to rate as famous made-up names that they had seen in the first part of the experiment 24 hours previously. The assumption is that the names were familiar but the source of the familiarity was no longer retrievable, so the participants attributed it to genuine fame.

Roediger and his colleagues (e.g. Roediger, 1990; Roediger et al., 1989) have developed the argument of Jacoby (1983) that the differences between implicit and explicit memory occur because of variations in conceptual and data-driven processing. Data-driven processing is relatively effortless, relying on the processes automatically triggered in the perceptual system when the stimulus is encountered. Concept-driven processes draw upon knowledge, expectations and strategies to enrich this basic coding. (This distinction can be seen as resembling the levels of processing distinction between physical and semantic analyses.) Roediger argues that differences in memory performance are found where the original data- or concept-driven processing is or is not transfer appropriate between the encoding and the retrieval conditions. According to this view, in the original Jacoby (1983) experiment the No-context condition was essentially data-driven, and led to good priming when the same stimuli were processed again in the perceptual identification task, which is also heavily dependent upon perceptual processes and has little scope for conceptual contributions. On the other hand, the Generate condition is essentially concept-driven, since the critical word is not presented. This generation can improve performance on subsequent tests that also involve conceptual processing (explicit recall or recognition), but does not add to the ease of perceptual processing of the critical word and so does not improve perceptual identification.

One interesting line of research on memory and awareness has been pursued by Gardiner and his colleagues (e.g. Gardiner and Java, 1993; Gardiner, 1988). Using a distinction originally made by Tulving, Gardiner's technique is to require participants to indicate for each item in a recognition test whether they (a) 'remember' (R), that is, consciously recollect seeing the item in the earlier part of the experiment, or (b) if they 'know' (K) that they have encountered the item before because it is familiar, but do not have any recollective experience of its occurrence. By manipulating the encoding conditions and measuring recognition in these two ways, Gardiner and his colleagues have demonstrated several interesting dissociations in memory as measured by the two criteria. A levels of processing manipulation comparing semantic and acoustic processing affects the R responses (better recognition for semantic processing) but not the K responses (Gardiner, 1988). Intentional learning and word frequency similarly affect the memories for which the participants have conscious recollections, but not those that are merely familiar (Gardiner and Java,1993; Macken and Hampson, 1993). Also, R responses appear to be more affected by age than K (Fell, 1992). On the other hand, it is possible to have no differences in 'remember' reports, but big ones on the 'know' measure. Gregg and Gardiner (see Gardiner and Java, 1993) conducted an experiment that purported to be on visual perception. Lists of words were presented on a screen very briefly at a very rapid rate. Participants were looking for any that were blurred, but none actually were. In a subsequent recognition test the modality either remained visual or was switched to auditory. On the basis of the data/concept-driven accounts of implicit memory, the experimenters predicted the 'remember' responses would be unaffected by the change in modality but that there would be a big detrimental effect for the 'know' responses, and that was what was found. In other studies, such as the judging of whether a letter string is a meaningful word (lexical decision), Gardiner and Java (1990) found better recognition of words than non-words for the remember responses, but better recognition of non-words with the know responses.

It is tempting to link K responding in the above studies with implicit memory, but while the two may be strongly related, workers in this area would urge caution. Implicit memory can occur without the participant having any awareness that remembering has occurred. Participants who provide K responses, though, are fully aware that they are in an explicit memory experiment. They are simply unaware of the full circumstances surrounding the encoding of the remembered material. R responses, on the other hand, reflect the use of episodic memory with full recollective experience (see Parkin, 1993).

Research on implicit memory has isolated some strong effects and, as we have just seen, has helped to demonstrate where conscious awareness is and is not related to memory performance, and the underlying processes are becoming clearer. Perhaps, however, future generations of researchers on learning and memory will be less surprised at the findings than many memory researchers were when they first appeared in the 1980s. As we pointed out at the beginning of this section, there is no reason to assume that all the changes that past experience makes to our processing systems should be available to conscious recollection. Those psychologists who, earlier in the twentieth century, concentrated on learning rather than memory did not assume any conscious access to the processes by which learning takes place. One consequence of the reappearance of learning as a subject for study, largely as a result of the success of connectionist models (see chapter 13), will be that the processes underlying implicit memory will seem less strange to future students of learning and memory.

Conclusions

In this chapter we have outlined some of the main factors that influence memory and given a sketch of the memory system. The intimate relation between encoding and retrieval has been discussed, the structure of the memory system considered, and the possibility that remembering can occur without awareness examined. We will return to more specific issues concerning memory in our chapter on Remembering (chapter 7).

Further reading

The reader who wishes to follow up material in this chapter in more depth is recommended to consult A. Parkin 1993: *Memory: Phenomena, Experiment and Theory* (Oxford: Blackwell) for a well written and up-to-date review. Another solid review is A. Baddeley 1990: *Human Memory. Theory and Practice* (Hove, Lawrence Erlbaum Associates). The topic of working memory is covered in more detail in a monograph devoted to the subject: A. Baddeley 1986: *Working Memory* (Oxford, Oxford University Press).

A good account of work on encoding can be found in V.N. Gregg 1986: *Introduction to Human Memory* (London: Routledge), and the classic work on reconstructive retrieval is F.C. Bartlett 1932: *Remembering* (Cambridge, Cambridge University Press). A thorough account of encoding–retrieval interactions and a full statement of his original views on memory systems can be found in E. Tulving 1983: *Elements of Episodic Memory* (Oxford: Oxford University Press).

Discussion points

1   Why is it more useful for human memory not to retain literal copies of all experiences?
2   Do we ever forget anything?
3   What effects does context have on memory?
4   What is meant by working memory? Why does working memory appear to be divided into separate subsystems?
5   Need we always know that we are remembering when we remember?

Practical exercises

1   The power of cueing is easy to demonstrate with the following experiment. Create a list of sentences, say around 20, of the form 'An x can be used as a y' (e.g. 'A newspaper can be used to swat flies'; 'A record can be used to serve chips'). Make sure each described relation is easy to image. Ask four or five people to participate in the experiment. Read the sentences aloud to them, and ask them to try to visualize the relationships described. After reading the sentences, give your participants a short arithmetic task to do for 30 seconds, then ask them to write down as many sentences as possible. They will probably remember around eight or nine. Now give them the first item in each sentence, and see if they can remember the other one (e.g. you supply 'record', and they write down 'chips'. Their performance should now be nearly perfect.

2   Measure someone's memory span. Write out lists of random numbers of varying lengths from 4 to 15 items long. Make sure there are lists of each length. Read the lists out, one at a time, at a rate of one digit every half-second, starting with the shortest and moving to the longest. Ask your participant to repeat back each string after hearing it. When the person makes errors in two consecutive lists, stop; their memory span is one less than the length of this list. See what effect varying the presentation time has on memory span. How could you measure backward digit span?

3   Design a levels of processing experiment to test the idea that deeper encoding leads to better subsequent face recognition. Cut out photographs of people's faces from magazines, making sure that they have no distinctive features such as hats or jewellery. Then take two groups of participants, and ask one to make a semantic decision about the face (e.g. 'Is the person honest'), and the other to decide on a physical characteristic ('Does the person have bushy eyebrows?'). In the subsequent memory test mix the original photographs with others which the participants have not seen before, and ask them to pick out the old from the new faces. To guard against guessing,

at the recognition phase, subtract the number of new faces misidentified as old faces (false alarms) from the number of new faces correctly identified. Which group performs best?

Box 2.1
Depth of processing

Craik and Tulving (1975) reported ten experiments that were designed to explore the levels of processing framework. They argued that the episodic memory trace was an automatic by-product of operations carried out by the cognitive system. The greater the degree of semantic involvement, the 'deeper' the processing and the more durable the memory trace.

Participants were asked various questions about words, with these questions intended to produce either shallow, intermediate or deep levels of processing. Shallow processing was achieved by asking questions about the typescript

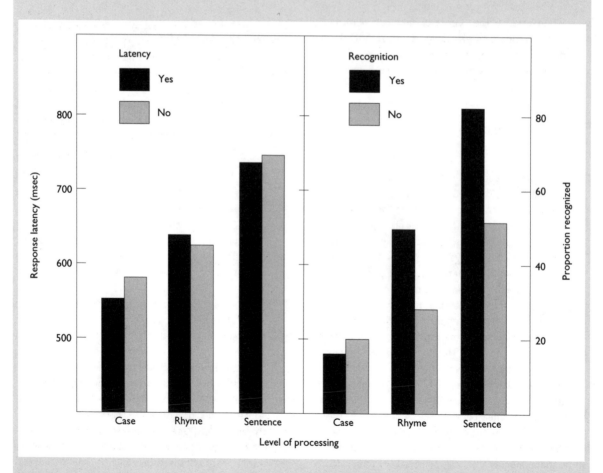

Box figure 2.1.1 The effects of depth of processing on latency of responding and accuracy of recognition. (Based on figure 1, Craik and Tulving, 1975)

of the words, intermediate processing by asking about rhymes, and deep processing by questioning whether the word would fit with a given category or into a sentence that was provided.

Method

The participants were tested individually. They were told the experiment was about perception and speed of reaction. The words were shown through a tachistoscope for 200 msec. Before the word was presented, the participant was asked a question. Three types of question were asked. In Craik and Tulving's second experiment the three questions were:

(a)   Is the word in capital letters?
(b)   Does the word rhyme with _____?
(c)   Would the word fit the sentence _____?

The latency of making the responses was recorded. Sixty questions were presented: ten Yes and ten No questions at each of the three levels. The questions were presented auditorily, followed two seconds later by the word on the tachistoscope. The participant responded as rapidly as possible by pressing one of two response keys. After the 60 trials, participants were given a list of 180 words which included the 60 original words and 120 distractors. They were told to indicate all the words that they had seen in the first phase. All the words used were five-letter common concrete nouns. Twenty-four participants were tested.

Results

The results of the latency of responding and accuracy of recognition are shown in box figure 2.1.1.

Craik and Tulving interpreted the longer latency for sentences than for rhymes and for rhymes than for case judgements as indicating a deeper level of processing. An analysis of variance (a mathematical technique for discovering whether observed differences are statistically significant at a given level of probability, p) on them for these latencies showed a significant effect of question type ($p < 0.001$), but there was no effect of response type of interaction.

There were very big differences in the recognition rates, ranging from 15 per cent for case decisions to 81 per cent for sentence decision. The improvement in performance was far greater for yes decisions than for no decisions. The analysis of variance showed a question type (level of processing) effect ($p < 0.001$), and a response type (yes–no) effect ($p < 0.001$).

Discussion

The results were interpreted by Craik and Tulving as demonstrating that different encoding questions lead to different response latencies, and that this is a reflection of the depth of analysis of the word. In further experiments in the paper they went on to explore the relationship between the speed of responding and the accuracy of memory, concluding that memory was not, necessarily, a consequence of processing time. They looked at recall as well as recognition and at incidental as well as intentional learning. In each case, the semantic processing led to far higher performance than the rhyme processing, which was, in turn, associated with much higher performance than the superficial encoding.

Based on F.I.M. Craik and E. Tulving 1975: Depth of processing and the retention of words in episodic memory. *Journal of Experimental Psychology: General,* 104, 268–94.

Box 2.2
Phonological memory deficits and language disorder

Gathercole and Baddeley explored the importance of the phonological component of working memory in the development of language skills in children. They hypothesized that it would be involved in vocabulary development and in learning to read.

The participants in their study were three groups of five children. The children in the Language Disordered Group (LDG) had been classified by educational psychologists and speech therapists as having disordered language development but normal intellectual abilities, and this was confirmed using standard tests of reading vocabulary and intelligence in the study. The children in the LDG group were matched with two groups of control children. The verbal control group were children with similar scores on the vocabulary test (the Short Form of the British Picture Vocabulary Scale) and the reading test (taken from the British Abilities Scales). These children were on average six-and-a-half years old, compared with the average chronological age of eight-and-a-half for the LDG group. The second control matched the LDG group in chronological age and were therefore superior in their reading and vocabulary.

In one test, the children tried to produce the same sounds as they heard on a cassette recording. The sounds were 40 non-words. They varied in length from one to four syllables and also in whether they contained single or clusters of consonant sounds.

Overall, there was far better performance by the verbal and non-verbal controls, both with 34 correct on average, compared with the LDG, who averaged only 21 correct. The performance of the LDG was at the level that Gathercole and Baddeley had previously found for normal 4–5 year olds.

When the length and complexity of the non-words was included in the analysis, the results were as shown in box figure 2.2.1. An analysis of variance showed that there were significant effects for groups of participants, non-word length and consonant type (p < 0.005), and an interaction between group and word length. Subsequent analyses showed that this resulted from the poorer performance of the LDG group on the longer length non-words.

Gathercole and Baddeley pointed to the very poor performance of the language-disordered children, who all scored lower than any of the control children. The matching of verbal controls on general language skills rules out the possibility that the repetition ability depends on such general skills. The authors concluded that the phonological working memory skills tapped by the non-word repetition play a central role in language development.

Based on S.E. Gathercole and A.D. Baddeley 1990: Phonological memory deficits in language disordered children: is there a causal connection? *Journal of Memory and Language*, 29, 336–60.

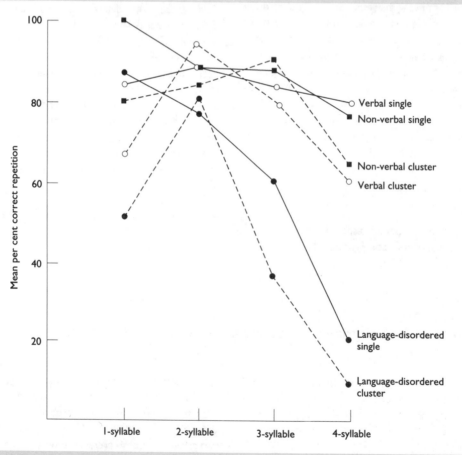

Box figure 2.2.1   Per cent correct repetition depending on group, word length and consonant type. (Based on figure 1, Gathercole and Baddeley, 1990)

3   Vision

Vision is one of the set of perceptual activities through which people learn about the world around them. We perceive by hearing, touching, tasting and smelling as well as by seeing, but vision is arguably the most important of these, and so we confine our attention to it here. (Various aspects of auditory perception will be examined in chapters 4 and 5.) Vision is clearly a vital cognitive function. If, without it, people do not necessarily perish, their lives are rendered quite difficult and sometimes perilous. Think back to the last time you got up during the night when in an unfamiliar house or hotel. Remember how hard it was to find the light switch? Perhaps you forgot where the door was positioned. Maybe you tripped and fell over a chair. When did you last experience a really severe fog? Recall how everyday objects looked unfamiliar. You mistook shadows for people and lampposts for trees. What do you think are the major problems experienced by blind people? It is easy to take vision for granted until it is destroyed or made difficult in some way or other.

But why precisely do we and most other animals need to see? What is it about vision that is so special? The above examples suggest one major reason for the evolution of visual abilities, namely that they provide the information needed to guide actions. Vision is sometimes called 'touch at a distance'. It allows us to keep one step ahead of the environment lest we literally step into it. Yet as well as guiding action, vision also indicates what is present in our surroundings, what things look like, how they are structured, where they are and where they are going. We see our world of organized scenes and moving objects by combining information from the light which reaches our eyes with knowledge stored in memory about the structure and identity of objects and scenes. We understand our surroundings partly by seeing them, but also by inferring what is there. Babies may well see, but, lacking any prior knowledge of the world, they do not understand what they see. Vision is therefore a genuine cognitive function, not merely a sensory one.

Psychologists interested in vision have traditionally asked how the visual system works, and, as we shall see in the course of this chapter, considerable progress has been made during the past 30 years in un-ravelling the basic mechanisms of visual perception. Important though this approach is, it has become clear of late that a broader perspective is needed to understand vision completely. If the link between vision and action is so crucial, then this must be systematically explored too. Understanding how visual information is processed is all very well, but the ways in which the visual system is dynamically used need to be examined.

Still another perspective acknowledges that humans and other animals occupy their own particular, special environments or ecological niches. The world of a frog or a house fly is a very different place from the world of a person. Frogs, flies and people live and act in quite distinct ways and need to perceive different things. The character of the information perceived by a particular creature, therefore, also needs to be analysed as well as the means by which it is processed.

Neisser (1976) offered a broad framework sufficient to accommodate these three aspects of vision which we will use to structure material in this chapter. Introducing the idea of the perceptual cycle, he argued that perceptual activity consists of

- information provided by the environment,
- which is picked up by schemata, cognitive structures concerned with our knowledge of the world around us,
- which, in turn guide exploratory actions, which then further sample the information available and so on.

Perception, as a whole, does not start with light in the world and end with ideas in the mind, it consists of endless sampling, processing and responding to the richness of our visual surroundings. Perception is a continuous cyclical activity. Animals only really stop visually perceiving when they are asleep, unconscious or dead.

As we pointed out in the introduction, human cognition is a unique blend of powerful memory systems, highly developed pattern recognition abilities and general purpose skills to interact with a changing environ-ment. All of these elements of cognition are important in the case of vision. Vision involves more than pattern recognition; it draws on memory, and drives and is informed by action.

Three major themes in this chapter reflect Neisser's approach. In the first section, we consider ways in which the visual world is structured, with particular reference to the important work of the psychologist J.J. Gibson, and to the Gestalt school; in the second, we review work on the internal mechanisms of visual perception; while in the third, we examine some of the uses to which the visual system is put.

The Structure of Visual Information

The visual world

The basic raw material with which vision works is light energy. Light, from sources such as the sun, candlelight or electric lamps, is reflected by objects and surfaces. This reflected light, picked up by the eyes and processed by the visual system, is structured in various ways. It varies in intensity, and in its frequency. Both the intensity and frequency of the light reaching the eyes depend on the relation between the light falling on objects and surfaces and the reflective qualities of objects and surfaces themselves, and both intensity and frequency provide vital clues to the nature of the visual world. Intensity, perceived as brightness, indicates a great deal about the structure of objects. For instance, an edge is usually a boundary between two areas differing in brightness, while light of different frequency produces the sensation of colour when picked up by special sensory cells. Unstructured light results in the perception of formless nothing (Metzger, 1930).

For a long time, students of perception thought that these basic physical facts, derived from classical optics, formed a sufficient starting point for perceptual theory. Light could be understood as a stream of rays with different qualities which the observer then analysed. Any further structure was provided by the observer's interpretation of the situation and was not inherent in the information itself. This situation has been radically altered by the work of J.J. Gibson (1966, 1979). Gibson argued that what was perceived could be described at a higher level than that offered by classical optics. Ecological optics, the higher level that Gibson had in mind, is a description of the geometry of surfaces, textures, moving objects and other relevant environmental phenomena from the point of view of a static or moving observer. In other words, Gibson realized that it was important to describe the layout of the environment from the viewer's vantage point. Perception, according to Gibson, depends on the structure in the light picked up by the observer, not simply on stimulation of the observer by the light.

To see how Gibson came to think in this way, it helps to know something about his early work. During the Second World War, Gibson was employed as a psychologist by the US military authorities. While thus employed, one of his jobs was to discover how to improve the performance of pilots who were experiencing difficulty in landing. Landing, one of the most danger-ous aspects of flying, involves the correct positioning of the aircraft in three dimensions and might be thought, therefore, to depend on good depth perception. Two obvious approaches to this problem, which Gibson tried, were to select those pilots who already had good depth perception, or to give those who had difficulty during landing special training in perceiving depth. These methods depended on the idea that some people have better perceptual systems than others, and that existing perceptual abilities can be improved. Unfortunately, neither method worked particularly well. Assum-ing the pilot had adequate perceptual abilities, happy landings seemed to depend as much on the richness of the cues in the environment as on the cleverness of the pilot's visual system. Not surprisingly, great care is now taken when constructing modern airports to ensure that the runway and approach path is suitably lit and appropriately marked. Structure in the light, or 'optical array', seems to be as important as structure in the head.

Another everyday example of Gibsonian principles is now frequently used by road traffic engineers to regulate the speed of vehicles approaching a traffic island (see figure 3.1). To make sure that cars reach the roundabout at a safe speed a series of parallel lines is painted on the road at right angles to the traffic flow. The spacing between these lines is made smaller and smaller the nearer one gets to the roundabout. The reader will appreciate, and may have experienced, the effect of trying to drive at constant speed across these lines. As the driver approaches the obstacle, it feels as if the vehicle's speed is increasing as more lines are traversed in a given time. Without having to be directly told, drivers automatically decelerate under these conditions. It takes an iron will not to do so! This traffic control technique, like the previous example, changes perception by changing the

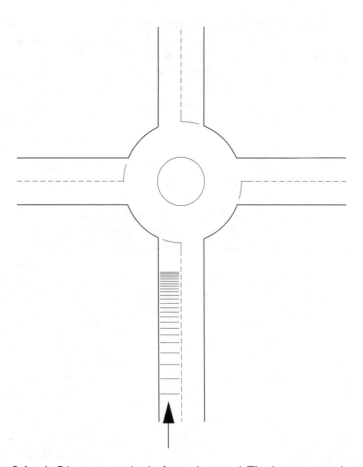

Figure 3.1 A Gibsonian method of speed control. The lines across the road get closer together as they near the roundabout. An impression of acceleration is created by driving across them at constant speed

structure of the perceived world, not by appealing to internal perceptual or cognitive mechanisms with a 'Reduce Speed' sign.

If structure in the light is so important, what form does this structure take? Gibson argued that the perceptual world is composed of surfaces of different textures, and that the texture of a surface can be directly used to perceive its orientation and depth. Some simple examples of textured surfaces are shown in figure 3.2.

Another obvious though important feature of the perceptual world for land-dwelling creatures is the horizon between land and sky. The horizon does not simply tell the animal where land ends and sky begins, it can also indicate the size and distance of an object. Objects which are the same size but different distances away from the observer are cut by the horizon in the same ratio, whereas objects of different sizes at the same distance have different horizon ratios (see figure 3.3).

Texture gradients and the horizon ratio are examples of what Gibson called perceptual invariants, unchanging aspects of the environment from

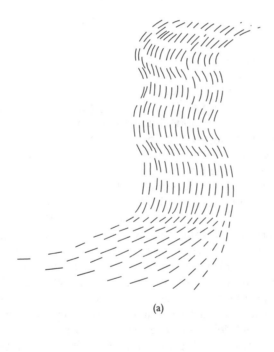

(a)

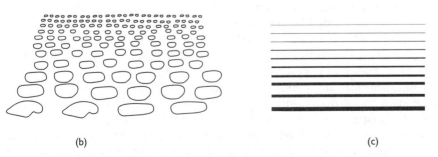

(b)   (c)

Figure 3.2 Texture gradients illustrating (a) shape and (b) and (c) depth

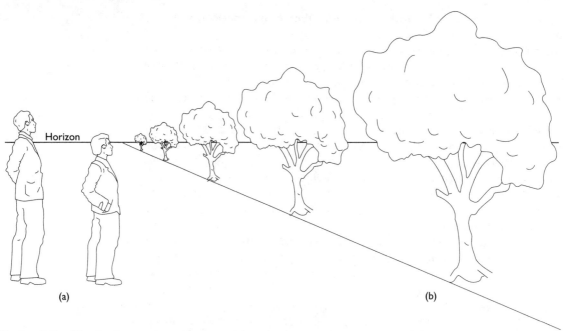

(a)   (b)

Figure 3.3   The horizon ratio: a perceptual invariant

the observer's viewpoint. A second and vital insight of Gibson is that animals move and as they do so, they sample the information around them. Motion results in the flow of optical information around the perceiver and the nature of this flow again provides important clues to position and depth. To understand what is meant by flow, consider the difference between looking out of the front and rear windows of a moving car on a long straight road. Looking through the front window, the perceiver is faced with an expanding optical field. Information which initially starts in the middle of the perceptual field eventually passes to the left, right, above or below the observer. A distant motorway footbridge, for example, which starts as a smudge on the horizon eventually passes over the roof of the car, while equally distant traffic cones pass eventually to the left or right. Looking through the rear window reverses this situation. Information moves from the periphery towards the centre of the field, producing a contracting flow. The stationary car immediately to my right shifts towards the centre of my visual field as it recedes into the distance. Thus, the mere presence of either an expanding or contracting flow field tells observers whether they are moving forwards or backwards. Moreover, the illusion of motion can be created by presenting viewers with such fields made up of very simple elements, as aficionados of space-travel films will attest.

A further important concept of Gibson's was that of 'affordance'. This is the idea that many perceived entities in the world have behavioural significance for the person or animal and permit, or afford, certain responses to be made with respect to them. For, instance, a door knob affords grasping, a level paved surface affords walking, a chair affords sitting. Thus the perceived array is linked with behaviour, or perception with action. Moreover, the affordance of an object or entity is not fixed but will vary according to the particular needs of the person or differ between species: a telegraph wire affords perching for a bird but not for a human.

Descriptions of the optical array and its affordances such as these form the central sources of information available to the perceiver. Where Gibson's theory departs even further from standard approaches is in asserting that perceptual variants and invariants are directly perceived, and that no complex series of information-processing operations is needed to analyse the visual world. In Gibson's account the person 'resonates' to the information in the optic array, but the nature of this resonance is left unexplained.

We disagree with this aspect of Gibson's account, since data from a number of sources, including neurophysiology, indicate that a large number of internal transformations, both analytic and constructive, are performed on the visual input before people are able to say that they perceive and recognize anything at all. Also, without recourse to some account of internal mechanisms, it is hard to see how Gibson can explain why members of different species pick up different aspects of the optic array. However, what Gibson has done is to indicate precisely what sorts of information these internal mechanisms might be expected to process. For instance, if texture is an important aspect of the human visual world, then, at some level, there must be internal systems which are sensitive to and can respond to textural information. Similarly, if information from moving objects and observers is frequently used, then systems for detecting the sorts of transformations described by Gibson might also be expected to exist. To date, however, it is fair to say that the full implications of Gibson's approach for the nature of internal mechanisms have yet to be realized.

Gestalt principles

An earlier, though in some ways complementary approach to Gibson's was taken by the Gestalt psychologists working in the 1930s. The Gestaltists differed from Gibson in emphasizing the active, organizing nature of mind and, in addition, they believed that perceptual abilities were largely inborn, unlike Gibson who stressed the importance of learning. However, like Gibson they concentrated on the appearance, or phenomenal qualities, of the perceptual world, rather than processing mechanisms, and showed how organization, or 'good form', can emerge from the relationship between simple perceptual elements.

It is difficult to do full justice to Gestalt psychology here, but we can select out some important themes, as we have just done for Gibson's work. One overriding principle is that the mind tries to structure incoming information in the simplest or most economical way. Certain perceptual shapes and arrangements were deemed by the Gestalt psychologists to be intrinsically good or coherent. These configurations were governed by the grouping principles of similarity, proximity and good continuation. So, elements that are alike will tend to be grouped together, as will those that are near together or seem to point in the same direction (see figure 3.4).

Although these grouping principles are important, to understand the Gestalt movement fully, it helps to see what it was designed to combat.

Prior to Gestalt psychology, the classical, associationist approach to perception, which had its roots in philosophy, suggested that our sensory receptors break down the perceived world into a number of separate sensations. Experience then teaches us to associate these sensations together in order to perceive integrated objects. In other words, we build up a picture of the whole from the individual parts. One difficulty with this is the fact that things are often perceived as having the same shape or form despite changes in the individual elements. As figure 3.5 shows, the same letter H is perceived despite changes in the elements that make it up.

To cope with this and similar demonstrations, the Gestaltists turned the traditional position around and argued that the perception of the whole, not the parts, came first. A famous adage of the Gestalt psychologist was that 'the whole is greater than the sum of the parts', meaning that pattern and organization often emerge directly from the relationship between discrete elements and cannot be deduced from a knowledge of the individual elements alone. Indeed, at times, elements can be missing or

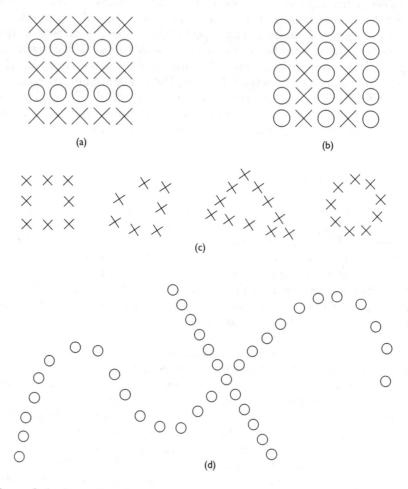

Figure 3.4 Some Gestalt grouping principles: (a) and (b) similarity, (c) proximity, (d) good continuation

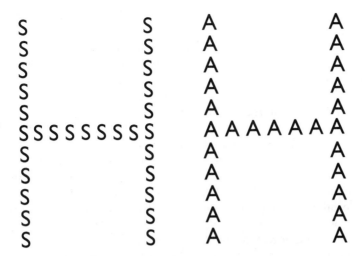

Figure 3.5 'The whole is greater than the sum of the parts.' Overall shape need not depend on the nature of the elements from which it is constructed

altered yet the overall shape can be perceived directly, so that for the Gestaltist, overall form is primary.

Examples of this are not hard to find. A circle still tends to be perceived in figure 3.6 despite the gaps in the line. A tune is still recognizably the same even when it is transposed into a different key. The same object can be seen as identical even though the distance and position from the observer are varied with consequent alteration in the views of its parts.

To explain how such holistic perception was realized in the brain, Gestalt psychologists offered a physiological theory to supplement their psychological account. Their suggestion, radical for its time, was that brain processes, or 'energy fields', directly reflect perceived objects in a similar holistic fashion. Brain fields, they argued, are isomorphic with the perceived world, and are formed by patterns of direct electrical current. Such brain processes were thought to pre-exist in the brain, to be activated by the

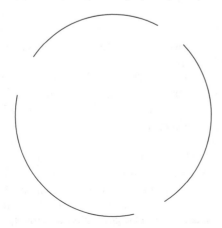

Figure 3.6   Shape can be perceived even when parts are missing

patterns of external stimulation, and to influence strongly the interpretation of perceptual elements.

The importance and immediacy of the perception of the whole and the holistic nature of the brain's response were thus both strongly emphasized by the Gestalt movement. As a result, the movement helped liberate psychology from the constrictions of associationism and, for many years, was the only real alternative to a rather sterile behaviourism, but few psychologists nowadays would accept all the details of the Gestalt approach. Certainly the idea that there exist brain fields isomorphic with the perceived objects is no longer taken very seriously. Views of a scene rarely take in the whole at once, so that it is hard to see how an overall brain field could be formed so directly. In addition, one of the central claims of the Gestaltist, namely that the whole always determines and therefore comes prior to the perception of the parts, can be shown to be inaccurate. There is now evidence that whole and part information can be processed separately (e.g. Humphreys and Riddoch, 1987b). Nevertheless most psychologists would accept that the Gestalt grouping principles accurately described many aspects of the organization of the visual world, and, as later work has shown, several of these principles, such as 'good form', seem to depend on the information content of the stimulus (e.g. Attneave, 1954).

To conclude this section, both Gibson's and the Gestalt approach are invaluable in reminding us of the inherent structure in the world. As such they are necessary for a full understanding of perception. Yet neither theory accounts sufficiently for how this structure is processed or perceived. Clearly, some such description is needed which discusses the perceptual mechanisms themselves, and which shows how these same mechanisms pick out precisely the visual qualities that the animal in question needs to see. Otherwise, if all the information and structure needed for perception is in the world, there should be no difference between the perceptual abilities of animals such as crabs, frogs or people. Since, as we shall see, such differences do exist, the visual systems of these animals must differ too, and must make a unique contribution to the act of perception.

Visual Information Processing: Visual Mechanisms

Having looked at the information available to the perceiver, it is now time to turn our attention to the second of our three aspects of vision: the mechanisms of visual perception.

A common experiment in school biology lessons involves the dissection of a bull's eye. During this experiment, students are invited to cut out part of the back of the eye, to cover the resulting hole with tissue paper and to point the eye at a window, illuminated light bulb or other light source. To the students' delight, a small inverted image of the window or bulb appears on the tissue paper. The eye, they are told, is rather like a camera and the picture which it takes is then simply relayed up to the brain.

As a simple account of the functional anatomy of the eye, the picture theory is reasonably adequate, but as a theory of visual perception it is wide of the mark. If the eye really does send a picture to the brain, what happens to it then? Is there some sort of inner screen on which the picture is projected? If this is the case, then who or what inhabits the inner cinema? The problem with the picture theory of perception is that it can easily lead to what philosophers call an infinite regress. If each time an object is pictured it has to be seen again, then there is a never-ending sequence of pictures and viewers (see figure 3.7)

Two further problems with the picture theory are, first, it implies that perception provides a literal copy of things in the world and, second, it implies that vision relies entirely on incoming information. Both implications are false. Optical illusions of various sorts show that perception does not always faithfully copy reality (see figure 3.8), while the fact that expectations, beliefs and motivation can all subtly affect the way things are perceived shows that internal information often combines with external during perception (Gregory, 1972).

The idea that vision can depend heavily on internal information as well as external information is an important one. Modern perceptual theories differ in the extent to which they emphasize what is known as bottom-up or data-driven processing with its reliance on the linear sequence of operations from sensory input to perception, as opposed to top-down or concept-driven processing which works in the other direction and uses knowledge to interpret incoming data. Gregory (1972), for example, claimed that

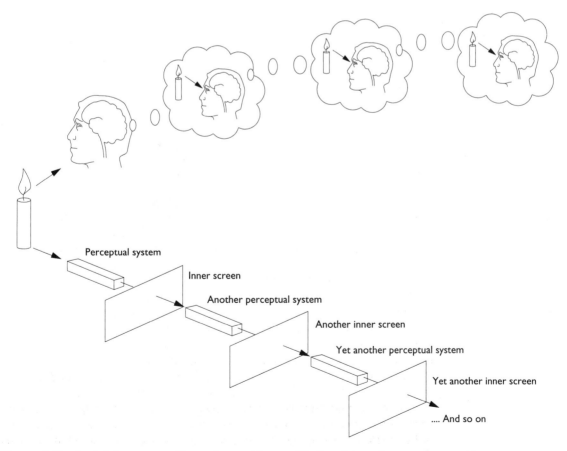

Figure 3.7 An infinite regress illustrating problems with the picture theory of perception

perception was a highly constructive act in which the perceiver continually made hypotheses about sensory information, and as such emphasized its top-down aspects. Gibson (1966), who, by contrast, stressed the sufficiency of the external information, would fall into the bottom-up group, as would Marr (1982) whose important model we shall describe shortly. To some extent, the preferences of perceptual theorists for one mode of processing

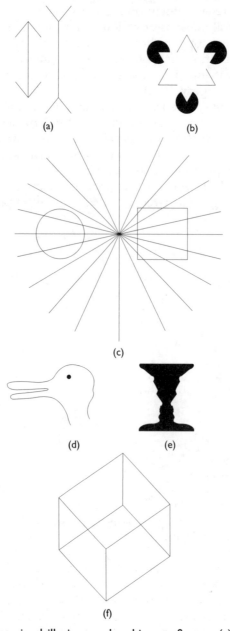

Figure 3.8 Some visual illusions and ambiguous figures. (a) Muller–Lyer illusion (the parallel lines are actually equal in lenth), (b) Kanizsa's illusory triangle, (c) distorted square and circle, (d) duck or rabbit? (e) vase or faces? (f) Necker cube (the 'front' and 'back' faces reverse)

over another may reflect the sorts of perceptual experiences they most often considered in their work. So, data-driven theorists have often considered what we might call 'trouble-free' perception, namely that which occurs with clear, unambiguous stimulus information and an unfatigued observer, while concept-driven workers, such as Gregory, have often studied 'problematic' perception involving illusions, poor stimulus information and poor viewing conditions. The study of concept-driven perception has shown that although perception may sometimes go wrong or be error-prone, it rarely fails or stops completely. Invariably the perceiver tries to make sense of the incoming information, but the sense which he or she makes may not correspond with reality. The philosopher Wittgenstein pointed out that all seeing involves seeing things as something or other, and the constructive and sometimes quite creative activities needed to do this have been well emphasized by psychologists such as Gregory.

Nowadays, the idea that both modes of processing are required to some degree would probably be accepted by most perceptual theorists, but, at present, the exact mix or balance between the two has not been established. What is clear is that the uncritical reliance of the picture theory on only one mode of processing is false.

The neurophysiology of vision

As an alternative to the picture theory, many psychologists assume that perception provides interpretations of the world around us, and does not merely re-present or transfer external reality into our heads. There is now good supporting evidence for this assumption. Studies of all sorts of creatures, from frogs and crabs to people, show that visual systems extract relevant information from light. The common frog, for example, seems to detect only four types of visual stimuli: static edges, moving edges, brightness changes, and small, roughly circular, moving objects. Studies show that frogs have exactly four different types of visual cells in their nervous systems which respond selectively to light energy. It is interesting to note, however, that the information which the frog detects is vital to its survival. Show a frog the Mona Lisa and it remains unmoved, but stimulate it with a small, circular, moving object and its visual system fires and its tongue lashes out to catch the supposed fly.

More complicated visual analyses are performed by humans and other vertebrates. Light-sensitive cells in the retina at the back of the eye together with other cells in the pathways leading up to the brain, and in the visual cortex of the brain itself, begin the job of coding the incoming information. Most of these neurophysiological systems respond more to changes in the light levels reaching the eyes than to stable light energy. The reason for this is simple. Differences in levels of illumination provide more information about external stimuli than do stable light levels. For instance, the edges of an object are often associated with a boundary between a light and a dark area, a place where illumination levels are changing quickly, and edges reveal a great deal about the structure and identity of objects.

There is, however, more to vision than detecting simple visual qualities such as features or edges. The combination and interpretation of such simple qualities into organized, meaningful representations is also necessary. Some quite remarkable evidence which supports this idea has recently emerged. For instance, it is known that certain cells in higher levels of the visual systems of mammals may respond selectively to quite specific classes of stimuli. Thus, Gross et al. (1972) reported that cells in the inferiotemporal cortex of a monkey responded most vigorously to the silhouette of a monkey's paw, while other cells responded vigorously to faces. Following up this work, Perret et al. (1988) have studied cells in an area of the macaque monkey brain known as the superior temporal sulcus which responds most strongly to faces. One of their major discoveries is that while these cells respond quite well to various examples of faces, they are often quite intolerant of alterations in face position, gaze direction and other facial characteristics. Thus, one sort of cell fires when a face is looking directly at the monkey, while another does so when the face is looking away (see box 3.1). This implies that these 'face detectors' not only signal information about the identity of the stimulus, but could also be providing information to help the animal in its social interactions.

Neurophysiologists are gradually beginning to discover how mammalian visual systems work, but their research cannot proceed in isolation. At the higher levels of perception, their explanations are often as concerned with the animal's overt behaviour and with the processing of meaningful stimuli, such as detecting and responding to a face, as they are with the internal mechanics of vision, such as detecting a variation in brightness. Neurophysiology tries to show how neuronal mechanisms work and are organized, but, particularly at the higher levels, the reason for these mechanisms and their functions are also psychological problems. For example, faces have an obvious psychological significance for primates and people, and so finding out what aspects of faces are likely to be perceived is as much a problem for psychology as it is for neurophysiology. Hence, some of the best work in neurophysiology now proceeds hand in hand with psychology. On its own, without further psychological explanation, neurophysiology cannot offer a complete theory of perception. Without knowing what psychological functions might be expected to exist, it is difficult to know precisely what neurophysiological mechanisms to look for.

Psychological levels of vision: Marr's theory

Moving beyond neurophysiology, psychologists have split the overall processes of vision into two major stages: low-level and high-level. Low-level visual processes, whose preliminary aspects neurophysiology has made some progress in unravelling, compute elementary analyses of the incoming data. At this stage, the presence or absence of objects is detected, objects and shapes are separated from their background and their basic structure worked out. High-level vision then uses these low-level analyses to sort out the shapes and objects we see into familiar categories such as trees, houses, dogs, pavements and so on. Thus, whereas roughly speaking, low-level vision deals with the shape, colour, structure and position of things in the world, high-level vision recognizes visual patterns and, as a result, produces the necessary information for objects to be identified, their functions determined, and their names retrieved.

Marr (1982) has offered a classic and detailed account of both high- and low-level vision, and parts of his theory have stimulated other work in perception and have been implemented as working computer programs (see chapter 11). Marr's account is important in that it is inspired by a wide range of theory and data. Unlike other researchers, he has drawn on several sources of knowledge in constructing his theory, including neurophysiology and neuroanatomy as well as psychology. This means that Marr's theory is more plausible than many of its competitors and, as a result, it has put the psychology of vision on a firm scientific footing. Marr was also very clear that the function of a particular aspect of perception should be specified first, before attempts were made to discover the details, in information-processing terms, of how it works. In fact, for Marr it was as important to ask what a psychological function was for, as it was to ask how it worked. Because of this, it is likely that many of the stages and processes in Marr's system which, at present, are part of his computational model will be found to have some psychological reality as well. Most subsequent work on the psychology of vision has been affected by Marr's theory, including our understanding of the effects of brain injury on visual perception (see chapter 11), which is why we have singled out his account for detailed examination, but we would like to make it clear that his account is only one example, albeit a good one, of modern theories of vision. Also, before describing Marr's (1982) theory in detail, we must emphasize that it is still a theory and its components only have a hypothetical status. Many of the stages and operations which Marr discusses have not yet been shown to have physiological or psychological validity, but because of the converging evidence which Marr used to deduce their necessity, it is likely that several of them will be shown to be important in the next few years, and his approach has already encouraged others to produce their own detailed theories of various aspects of vision which he identfied.

The theory reflects Marr's view that vision, like other important psychological functions, is modular. That is, it is a complex set of operations supported by potentially independent subsystems. Each subsystem or module has its own specialized job or operation to perform, which it does without interference from other modules, and communicates the results to neighbouring modules. An advantage of modular designs is that individual modules can be singled out, improved and worked on independently from the others. Thus evolution is likely to have favoured modular designs, since natural selection could work separately on individual modules. Also, damage to one module does not necessarily curtail the activity of the entire system (see chapter 12 for further discussion of modularity). The modular character of the approach is clearly illustrated by Marr's division of vision into a series of stages in which the sensory input is successively transformed into more highly interpreted and structured representations by computationally independent systems.

Before discussing these stages, two further general points about Marr's approach are worth noting. First, as we stated earlier, his theory provides an account of both low- and high-level vision, from sensory input to pattern recognition. Second, Marr maintained that large portions of perception were data-driven, and so he avoided building prior knowledge about specific situations, such as the shapes of particular objects, into his theory, though some general knowledge, such as the assumption that the world is made up of reasonably smooth surfaces and that most of the things we see are rigid objects, was included.

Turning now to the theory itself, the first major stage of vision results in the formation of what Marr (1982) called the raw primal sketch. This is a messy representation of the scene composed of short line-segments, bars and blobs. These merely show where the intensity of the light is changing most rapidly. Without further interpretation, the raw primal sketch does not denote how or where the image is organized nor even where simple features such as lines and angles can be found. It is simply a mathematical map of places where light energy, and hence information, is changing fastest.

The next stage is to construct what Marr calls the full primal sketch from the messy structures in the raw primal sketch. To do this, principles for grouping information together are used which resemble those discussed by the Gestalt school of psychology in the 1930s. Marr's system uses two important grouping principles and other more minor ones. Similar items such as blobs or bars which appear in a similar region are put together into higher-order units. Also, sets of segments that form continuous lines are joined up. These two principles have two important functions. Grouping similar items in the same area together allows regions or surfaces with similar properties to be detected. The second principle, finding continuous lines, is obviously important for detecting the boundaries of objects and their parts.

The full primal sketch thus formed is a useful but still limited representation. Although it gives some indications of the outline and boundaries of objects, and might perhaps allow the perceiver to draw or match objects, there are still a number of things it does not permit. Two important features not specified in the primal sketch are how the different surfaces in a scene are angled and how far away each surface is from the viewer. Knowledge of both of these is essential if the object is to be correctly interpreted and both are presented in what Marr calls the viewer-centred representation or 2-D sketch. This representation indicates what the object looks like but still only from the viewer's perspective. It specifies how the various parts are arranged as seen from a particular angle, but does not indicate how the object is structured in general terms.

The viewer-centred representation is built up by the processes which act on either the raw or full version of the primal sketch. These processes use a variety of cues to infer depth from the (visual) world itself and from the way the visual system works. These cues include the fact that, because people have two eyes, two slightly different views of the world are available (stereopsis), the fact that different views of themselves are revealed by moving objects, and the fact that shape can be deduced from shading and shadows. A full discussion of all of these is beyond the scope of this text, but we will briefly consider the nature of stereopsis.

To understand how binocular vision can give information about depth the reader might like to try the following. Hold a finger about 12 inches in front of your eyes. Now close your left eye. Notice where your finger is relative to the background. Now open your left and close your right eye. Note how your finger appears to move to the right relative to the background. Do the same again, but this time with your finger held further away. Your finger still appears to move, though not as much.

By finding the difference or 'disparity' between two views, the depth or distance of different objects, or parts of the same object, from the viewer can be worked out. While this sounds fairly easy, combining two views of the same object is, in fact, quite mathematically difficult. Nevertheless, Marr and Poggio (1976) have described a method for doing this, based on the primal sketch, which uses no prior knowledge of the object in question but is based on the stimulus information alone.

To recapitulate: so far we have described how the light energy is transformed into a raw primal sketch showing intensity changes, how neighbouring areas where intensity is changing fastest are grouped together, and how preliminary information about depth is built into the representation and the structure of the object or scene determined from one particular viewpoint.

The final stage of visual analysis, in Marr's scheme, is to work out how the object or scene is structured in general and then to recognize it and establish its meaning and function. To do this it is first necessary to deduce the full three-dimensional nature of the object independently from the viewer. In Marr's system this is known as forming the object-centred representation. The object-centred representation is the product of the final stage of low-level visual analysis and the input into high-level vision. It provides a description of the object based on the object itself, and affords some of the crucial information needed to identify it. By making no reference to any viewer or viewpoint, this representation reveals more about the structure of the object than the 2-D sketch, and allows the person to perceive that an object is the same despite changes in its viewpoint, orientation or distance. In other words, it deals with the problem of object constancy.

To form an object-centred representation, the visual system, according to Marr, has to deduce where the major axes of the figure lie and then work out how the object and its parts are arranged around these axes. Marr claimed that most objects, however complex, can be described in terms of a number of simpler structures which he referred to as generalized cones. A generalized cone is the shape which results from moving a cross-section of constant shape but variable size along a common axis. This may sound rather complicated, but at a glance at figure 3.9 should clarify the idea for the reader.

Figure 3.9 shows a single generalized cone or cylinder meant to represent a human figure. This is then further broken down into more detailed cones. The figure is now shown as six cones standing for head, trunk, two arms and two legs. These can in turn be split into their component parts. For instance, an arm consists of an upper arm and a forearm. A forearm splits into a main part and a hand. A hand into a palm and fingers. Each time a part is divided it is described in terms of even smaller cones or cylinders. Matching or recognition then occurs by linking the 3-D model described in these terms with a set of previously stored descriptions about the object's structure.

The key to forming the object-centred description is to locate the object's major axes. While the full details of how this might be done are not yet clear, the principle that contour outlines can be used to determine the make-up of an object is generally accepted, as children who enjoy finger shadow displays will confirm.

Forming and then using the three-dimensional representation to achieve recognition and identification are not fully independent processes in Marr's theory. The two run together and complement each other. Because prior knowledge of what the object might be and how it is structured is used to guide its visual analysis in this way, the final stage in Marr's theory involves a certain amount of top-down processing. Memory and perception interact at this point in Marr's theory.

Marr's system is one of the best worked out theories of vision we have to date. It accounts for all the important stages of visual analysis from sensory reception to recognition. It makes few assumptions in advance about the visual world and many of its components have now been implemented as working computer programs (see chapter 11). Nevertheless, since its

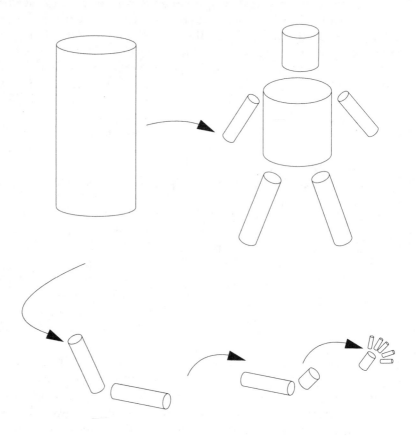

Figure 3.9 The hierarchical representation of a human figure in terms of generalized cones. (Based on Marr and Nishihara, 1978)

inception there have been further suggestions, differing from Marr's, about how various representations are computed (Biederman, 1987; Pentland, 1986; Watt, 1988) and about the adequacy of the scheme as a whole (Morgan, 1984). Despite these qualifications and criticisms, it is fair to say that Marr has offered a solid foundation for subsequent work. We agree with Humphreys and Bruce (1989) that although detailed aspects of Marr's theory are 'not necessarily correct . . . the kind of approach exemplified by Marr's theory almost certainly is the most successful of recent approaches to vision' (p. 21).

Dynamics of Vision

An account of the visual analysis mechanisms alone is necessary but not sufficient. There are other issues which a full account of perception must address, as we indicated at the beginning of this chapter.

First, although Marr acknowledged the importance of moving objects in working out three-dimensional structures, a major focus of his account was the perception of static images by a static observer. Yet, as we saw earlier, both objects and people move and human perception is quite capable of dealing with this.

Second, accounts of visual processing such as Marr's are often concerned with how we perceive and recognize objects and surfaces. But visual perception also involves spatial layouts. Objects and other aspects of the visual world are found in different positions. The visual system can only deal with one small area of the entire visual field in detail at any given time, and the most detailed visual analysis takes place over a very small visual angle in the centre of this field. Before information from other areas can be dealt with, therefore, the centre of visual attention must be shifted either overtly through body, head or eye movements or covertly by changing the focus or range of an internal mechanism. Understanding how attention is shifted from one location and fixed on another and discovering the precise function of visual attention is very important but is not really covered by Marr's theory.

Third, as we also indicated earlier, perception is not merely there to allow us to look at things. Perception probably evolved in the first place to help guide action. Knowing how visual input is coordinated with response output is also essential if we are to understand the skill of perceiving fully. We will briefly review these issues in the following sections.

Motion perception

To perceive moving objects, the visual system must be able to pick up changes in a stimulus over quite brief time intervals and recognize the same stimulus in different positions. It turns out that the visual system is quite adept at doing so and can often use movement to distinguish the shape of the object in question. Experiments have shown that only a few sensory cues are needed for this. Johansson (1973) fixed small lights on the elbows, shoulders, knees and other major anatomical joints of actors and asked participants to view them in the dark. When the actors stood still, participants perceived a random collection of points, but as soon as the actors moved, the structure of a human figure leapt into view. Johansson's findings fit well into Gibson's analysis of variant and invariant aspects of information, since the perceiver is responding to certain variant and invariant aspects of the human form such as the relative proportions of the trunk, the limbs, the positions of joints and the relative movement of body parts.

So powerful is this tendency to respond to real movement that the visual system picks up apparent motion where none is really present. Even simpler studies than Johansson's reveal our ability to do this. If two lights of sufficient brightness are placed at a suitable distance apart and alternately switched on and off at an appropriate rate, a compelling impression of movement from one location to another is created (Wertheimer, 1912). This 'phi phenomenon', or perception of apparent movement, not only occurs when lights are switched on and off but is also apparent when lines, dot patterns and more complex shapes are presented at neighbouring locations. Without it there would be no motion picture industry, since films depend on the rapid presentation of static images. In fact the impression of apparent motion is often stronger when structured shapes rather than simple stimuli are used, suggesting that form and motion perception are intimately related, and also indicating that different neural systems may be used for perceiving the motion of simple and complex stimuli (Braddick, 1980).

Since the impression of apparent movement and real movement are so similar, Bruce and Green (1985) argue that the perception of real movement can be thought of as the integration of a succession of discrete views. The implications of this approach are that motion and shape perception are closely linked, and that movement is perceived by working on perceptual representations of shapes and objects. A rather different approach, taken by Clocksin (1980), and inspired by Gibson's ideas, assumes that motion is perceived directly and that shape can be derived from an analysis of optical flow. Clocksin has shown that the edges of an object can be discovered by examining the way in which the background texture is successively obscured and revealed by an object. As a shape moves across a surface, its leading edge covers the background which its trailing edge uncovers. In other words, Clocksin shows that shape can be revealed by motion, and not the reverse.

Whether shape or motion is perceived first, the two are clearly closely related, yet, despite this, studies of the brain-injured show that problems can separately arise in either the perception of either movement or static form. This indicates that, although mutually supportive, the systems which analyse form and motion are not completely identical and are at least partially dissociable (Humphreys and Bruce, 1989; Bruce and Green, 1985; also see chapter 12 for more information on disorders of motion perception).

Whereas both image analysis and optical flow accounts have been applied to the perception of moving objects, motion of the observer as a whole has been treated mainly from a Gibsonian perspective. As we stated earlier, the changes in the optical flow pattern caused by motion are deemed sufficient for its perception by Gibson, and two such changes, whether the flow is expanding or contracting, indicate forward or back-ward motion. Another important feature of optical flow during motion is the part which remains stationary during motion. This optical centre is the point toward which the observer is moving and movement of the optical centre across the flow field denotes a change in the direction of travel.

With simple ideas like these it is possible to describe the changing patterns of information which surround movement of the observer, but, as yet, there is no detailed algorithm or theory which explains exactly how these flow patterns are processed.

Eye movements and visual attention

Compared with gross movements of the observer, rather more is known about the nature and function of eye movements and the covert deploy-ment of visual attention. Later in this book, in chapter 9, we will consider the role of eye movements in reading. Here we review the nature and role of eye movements in general.

Eye movements The major function of eye movements is to bring information into central or foveal vision and to keep it there. Whenever a scene or picture is inspected or a line of print read, the eyes move in a series of rapid movements from one location to another. These movements or 'saccades' have a ballistic quality which means that, like a shell fired from a gun, once they are started they cannot be modified. The eyes then rest or 'fixate' at the end of each saccade. In contrast to the jerky movements which characterize saccades, smooth tracking or pursuit movements are used to follow fixated objects which move across the field of vision, as when someone watches a bird fly across the sky. A third type of eye movement, convergence, is used to keep clearly and centrally in view objects which approach the observer. Convergence movements point the gaze direction of the eyes towards the nose and, up to a certain minimum distance, allow the perceiver to maintain a single image of the object.

There is yet another type of eye movement, which can only be detected with special equipment. The eyes are held in dynamic equilibrium by three major sets of muscles which are in a continuous state of low amplitude, physiological tremor. This tremor causes the eyes to vibrate rapidly and shifts the image on the retinae back and forth over a small visual angle. One possible reason for these very fast eye movements is revealed by experi-ments which arrange for the retinal image to be stabilized (e.g. Pritchard, 1961). To do this, a small contact lens equipped with a miniature projector is attached to the outer surface of the eye. The effect of any eye movements are immediately cancelled out by this arrangement, since whenever the eye moves the projector moves too, and any image it displays is stabilized on the same region of the retina. The results of this procedure are fascinating. Both form and colour perception are quickly disrupted and when whole words are presented, organized chunks consisting of letter groups and parts of letters disappear then reappear in turn. Neural systems, as we saw earlier, thrive on change and when this is prevented they shut down or at least cease to operate properly. Even when apparently at rest during a fixation, the eyes are never completely still.

The fact that the eyes are constantly in motion raises an important though not fully resolved question as to how information from a series of fixations is combined coherently. There are actually two major issues here. First, the content of successive views must somehow be joined up. So, for example, when looking at a house, successively fixated information about the windows, chimneys, roof, walls and so on must be combined to give a complete representation or 'percept'. The direction and accuracy of eye movements seem to play an important role here, but some means must also exist to create and retain a representation of each view for welding together into the whole. Clearly, some form of temporary visual memory is required for this and various suggestions have been made concerning the nature of this mechanism. Second, as the eyes move around, it is important that the immediately preceding perceptual information does not interfere with that currently being processed. If you are looking at the chimney of a house you do not want your view to be disrupted by the previous glance at the door. The reader may feel that there is something of a paradox here: on the one hand information from successive views must be joined up, but on the other, there must be some means to prevent successive views interfering. The issue is a complex one, but progress has been made in unravelling it. At the risk of oversimplifying, to join up views of the same object, the interpretations or outcomes of a series of fixations must be combined. This suggests that scene analysis depends on three things: the products of high-level visual processes involving pattern recognition, short-term storage of information, and some underlying knowledge about what one is seeing, and not merely on sensory or low-level processing details. On the other hand, to avoid confusion between successive views, the system must prevent the more temporary records of the processing sequence becoming tangled.

Visual attention   Most of the time we attend to that on which we are fixating, but careful experimental work has shown that it is possible to attend to locations other than those currently fixated (Posner, 1978, 1980). People can, in other words, look in one direction but keep a (mental) eye on another. To describe what is going on when we attend to different spatial locations, psychologists often use the spotlight analogy. According to this metaphor, which goes back at least to the time of William James (1890), attention can be likened to a bright light beam which illuminates the darkness, with a brightly lit focus, a reasonably well-lit margin and a dimly lit fringe. The direction of the beam is assumed to be partially under the participant's control, and to enhance the processing of information on which it focuses. The strength of a good analogy in science is that it can be taken reasonably seriously and used to make predictions. Thus, if visual attention is like a spotlight then, presumably, the width of the beam is limited so that only a restricted amount of information is in the centre of attention, but presumably also, its width cannot be reduced beyond some minimum so that any information within the focus is processed. Empirical work supports this idea. Eriksen and Eriksen (1974) showed that partici-pants were unable to reject potentially confusing information when this fell within one solid degree of visual angle from the centre of attention, but were relatively unaffected by information more than one degree distant.

They concluded, therefore, that the attentional spotlight's size is fixed at about one degree. There is also evidence that, again like a spotlight, visual attention can only be pointed in one direction at a time (Eriksen and Yey, 1985), and that the efficiency of attentional processing varies at different retinal locations (Downing and Pinker, 1985).

Despite such support, the spotlight theory is not the only way to conceptualize visual attention. Another currently popular account describes visual attention in terms of a zoom lens. A zoom lens can back off from a single focus and cover the entire scene, or zoom in to look at a single area in detail. Evidence can be marshalled to support the zoom lens account too, and supports the idea that attention can be weakly spread over a large area of space (Eriksen and Murphy, 1987).

Deciding between the two theories of visual attention is difficult. As Humphreys and Bruce (1989) point out, the data, at present, are 'at least as consistent with the zoom lens account as with the spotlight proposal' (1989, p. 154), but whichever is the better, neither the spotlight nor the zoom lens analogy clearly describes the role of visual attention. To state that information in the focus of attention is 'brightly lit', or 'magnified', and therefore processed more efficiently, is all very well as a rough description, but it is important to explain precisely what visual attention does. A theory which tries to do this has been developed by Anne Treisman and her associates (e.g. Treisman and Gelade, 1980; Treisman, 1988). To simplify Treisman's theory somewhat, she argues that we can think of visual perception as comprising two major stages. The first involves the rapid detection of simple perceptual features such as colour, elementary shapes and orientation. No attention is required for this and several features can be processed in parallel at different places in the perceptual field. Evidence for this stage comes from visual search tasks where participants are asked to look for target letters embedded among a set of distractors, such as looking for a letter T among a set of letter Rs. Treisman and Gelade showed that when the target letter can be distinguished from the distractors by the presence of a single perceptual feature, then the search time is unaffected by the number of distractors. So, a participant finds it as easy to find a T embedded among 12 Rs as among four. Quite a different situation arises when the targets and distractors can only be separated by the presence of two or more features, as is the case when looking for green Ts among a set of red Ts and green Ss. The only way to spot the target in this condition is to find the combination of green-and-T; 'greenness' or 'T-ness' alone will not distinguish the target from the distractors. To find this combination, each item has to be checked in turn until the correct one is detected and so, search times increase in line with the number of distractors. The serial checking which is needed to find feature combinations demands attention and characterizes the second stage of visual analysis. As Treisman herself puts it, visual attention provides the glue which sticks features together and allows us to see coherent, integrated objects.

Other supporting evidence for the feature integration view of attention has emerged over the past few years. An important prediction of the theory is that when attention is diverted, the features of different objects can be erroneously combined to form illusory conjunctions (Treisman and Schmidt, 1982). Another idea is that the theory allows one to determine just which perceptual features are basic, since these can be searched for in parallel (Treisman and Souther, 1985). Despite this support, there are some problems for the feature integration account. It is not clear, for example, whether the component letters of words must be processed in a serial fashion. As we shall see in chapter 9, studies of skilled readers suggest that word perception and identification may involve extensive parallel processing. Also, shape or outline perception seems likely to involve more parallel processing than the theory allows. Finally, recent evidence suggests that unattended objects can still be processed quite thoroughly, indicating that attention may not be strictly necessary for the perceptual integration of shape (e.g. Tipper and Driver, 1988). These problems set aside, the issue of how different features such as shape, orientation and colour are combined still remains, and feature integration is probably the best account of this we have at present.

Visual feedback and action

At the beginning of this section we pointed out that vision probably evolved to guide action, and vision and action are certainly closely linked (see also chapter 6).

A number of studies of fully developed and of developing perception illustrate the role of vision in steering action and the role of action in developing visual skills. A dramatic demonstration of the involvement of vision in action was provided many years ago by Stratton (1897). Stratton equipped himself with lenses which both inverted and reversed the visual field. With this arrangement, objects not only appeared upside down but were also transposed from left to right. Not surprisingly, the consequent visual distortion made even simple movements difficult and for the first few days Stratton constantly bumped into things and had problems with straightforward activities such as eating, washing and dressing. As he himself wrote, 'I did not feel as if I were visually ranging over a set of motionless objects but the whole field of things swept and swung before my eyes' (1897, p. 342). Stratton's and other similar experiments show how important it is to coordinate visual input with response output, but equally important, they show how rapidly the system as a whole readjusts to even quite gross distortion. Within a few days, Stratton was able once again to perform everyday tasks and experienced quite severe disruption when he finally removed the lenses and reverted to normal vision.

As well as examining the effects of distorting vision, researchers have also studied what happens when vision is restored, when people blind from birth, usually because of congenital cataracts, are given back their sight following an operation which implants artificial lenses in their eyes. (Other sorts of visual disorders are also considered in chapter 12.) A number of these cases have now been studied (e.g. Senden, 1960; Gregory and Wallace, 1963; Valvo, 1971). Although such patients normally learn to see quite adequately within a comparatively short period of time, they initially experience problems of one sort or another. Typical findings are that these patients not only have difficulty in coordinating movement with seeing, but also experience severe problems in interpreting the very products of the visual system itself. Gregory and Wallace's participant, SB, often found it hard to recognize everyday objects by sight alone which he could do so easily through touch, but could recognize them as soon as he felt the objects in question. Prior knowledge, particularly about an object's critical features, often seemed to be used to deduce an object's identity. Patients studied by Senden, for instance, could determine the difference between a triangle and a square only by counting the number of corners, and SB was able to recognize an elephant instantly because of its long trunk, but expressed surprise at the crescent shape of the quarter moon, having expected it to look like a slice of cake! Despite these problems of interpretation and pattern recognition, other perceptual abilities, such as figure–ground separation, scanning of the outlines of figures and tracking moving objects, seemed to be reasonably intact.

These results are interesting and bear on some old philosophical problems asked originally by John Locke, who questioned whether people born blind and later given their sight would need to learn to see. Locke's claim, borne out at least partly by the more recent data, was that they would, but given the unusual early learning experiences of participants such as these, and the fact that degeneration of aspects of their unused perceptual systems may have occurred during their development, we must be cautious in interpreting such phenomena.

We have just looked at the effects of distorting vision and of restoring sight on visual and visual–motor skills. Another way to examine vision's links with action is to see what happens when action is restricted during perceptual development. Ethical reasons, of course, preclude this type of research with human participants, but some workers argue that it is legitimate to inflict such procedures on animals. Held and Hein (1963) reported a classic study in which pairs of kittens, after being reared in the dark for about ten weeks, were placed in a carousel arrangement which allowed them to walk around in circles (see figure 3.10).

One member of each pair, known as the active kitten, was free to walk around within the constraints of the apparatus; the other, known as the passive kitten, was transported around the vertically striped, cylindrical container as a result of the actions of its fellow. Thus, both kittens should have had an identical visual development with the crucial difference that one could actively sample the environment, while the other was a passive spectator. The results were clear. After ten days, the depth perception of the active kitten was found to be far superior to that of the passive kitten. Movement alone appears to be insufficient to guarantee adequate perceptual development. Rather, it seems to be important for animals to perceive the consequences of their own actions.

Given that vision and action are closely yoked and that their links can be disrupted by various means, what is the precise nature of the linkage? A comprehensive answer to this question is well beyond the scope of this book, but we can discuss one very important aspect of visual–motor coordination here, the computation of the 'time to contact' (Lee, 1980). Consider the following situations. A gannet dives into the sea to catch a fish. Just before the bird enters the water it shifts its wings back into a streamlined position to create less resistance under water. If the wings are moved back too far and too early the bird enters the water too fast and loses control. If the wings are moved back too late, the bird is likely to injure itself as it enters the water with outstretched wings. Driving on a poorly lit road in the dark, a person brakes as she approaches the car in front. Or think of pedestrians on a busy city street who manage to avoid bumping into one another. What all these situations have in common is the approach of or movement towards an object and the crucial timing of an appropriate action. Studies of humans, gannets, flies and other creatures show that a simple but important variable, the 'time to contact', t, computable from an analysis of optical flow, can be used to synchronize visual input and action.

An examination of the problems of braking in the dark should illustrate this informally. The minimal information available to a driver coming up behind another vehicle in the dark is provided by the tail lights of the vehicle in front. As the driver moves closer, the tail lights seem to move further apart from the optical centre, as their image on the retina covers a wider angle. Moreover, if the driver rapidly approaches the vehicle in front, the speed with which the lights diverge is greater than if the approach is slow. Conversely, if the driver starts to fall back, the visual angle subtended by the tail lights

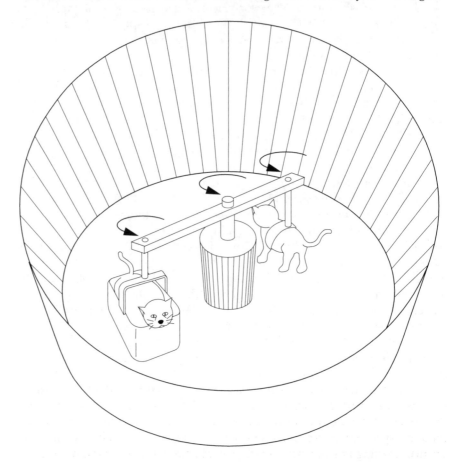

Figure 3.10 Held and Hein's experiment showing the active and passive kittens. (Based on Held, 1965)

on the retina diminishes. By reasonably straightforward application of differential calculus, Lee (1980) has shown that in these and similar situations the ratio of the distance of a point (such as a brake light) from the optical centre and the speed with which the point is moving away from the centre give an accurate index of the time to contact the surface; that is, the time, t, to make contact with a surface is given by the following formula:

$$t = \frac{\text{displacement of the projection on the retina of a point on the surface from the optical centre of the flow field}}{\text{speed with which point is moving away from the optical centre}}$$

This means that the visual system could use just two simple pieces of information, both readily available from the retina, to estimate the time left to make any behavioural adjustments such as braking, catching or stepping to one side before collision or contact occurs. It seems that this simple metric is used in a variety of situations, from the braking of a car when approaching an obstacle to precise timing of a long-jumper's run-up (Lee, 1976; Lee et al., 1982).

Finally, an important part of action is knowing how to stand still! Babies have to learn to stand before they can walk, and sailors have to get their 'sea legs' during the early part of a long voyage. For many years it used to be thought that balance and stance were largely controlled by (proprioceptive) feedback from internal senses such as the stretch receptors in the ankles and calf muscles and the organs of balance in the semicircular canals of the ear. According to this view, the role of vision is minimal in maintaining accurate stance. It is, instead, concerned with outside objects and events or exteroceptive information. Another series of experiments by Lee and colleagues (Lishman and Lee, 1973; Lee and Aronson, 1974; Lee and Lishman, 1975) have disproved this. Lee's team made use of an apparatus known as the moving room. This consists of a large bottomless box, suspended from the ceiling, inside which participants stand; see figure 3.11.

The walls of the room are covered in wallpaper to provide visual cues and the room can be silently moved backwards and forwards. When the room is moved towards the participant an illusion of forward movement or falling is produced; conversely, when the room is moved away from the participant an illusion of falling backwards is experienced. These illusory feelings of movement are so strong that participants try to counteract them by swaying in the opposite direction.

Lee and colleagues investigated the role of such visual feedback in a variety of conditions which manipulated the quality of feedback from the muscles and balance organs. In some experiments, for example, participants were asked to stand on spongy surfaces or to adopt a variety of unusual stances (Lee and Lishman, 1975, see box 3.2 for more details). In all cases, the visual feedback was powerful enough to elicit compensatory action, though especially so when muscle-based feedback was poor. Infants who are just learning to stand are particularly affected by this apparatus, and fall over easily when the room is moved. As Lee and Aronson (1974) indicate: when there is a conflict between mechanical (muscle-based) and visual information, infants tend to rely more heavily on the visual. From these experiments, it seems that correct interpretation of mechanical feedback during development may depend heavily on vision, which helps explain why congenitally blind children often take longer to learn how to stand and to walk than sighted children.

The vital role of vision in human actions is well illustrated by Lee's work. Vision is not merely an exteroceptive sense, it provides proprioceptive feedback too, but not all actions, of course, are as highly dependent on concurrent visual feedback as the ones we have discussed here. Some, such as dart throwing or playing an arpeggio on a piano, take place so rapidly that they run-off

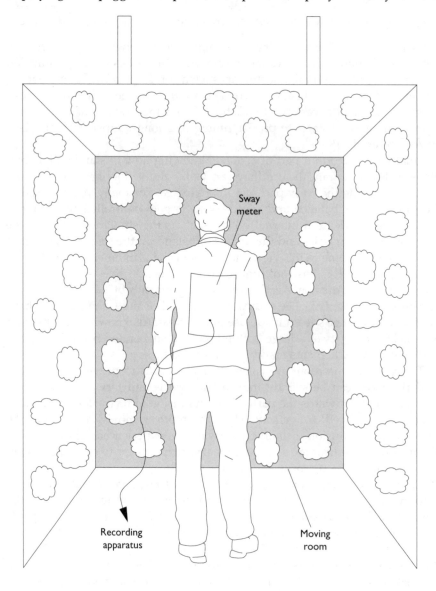

Figure 3.11 The moving room. The room is suspended from the ceiling and can be silently moved backwards and forwards. Participants' body sway is picked up by the sway meter.

without modification in a pre-programmed fashion. We will discuss the way in which these and other actions are controlled in more detail in chapter 6.

Conclusions

The reader may be forgiven for thinking that the range of issues covered in the psychology of vision is vast and unmanageable. In some ways, psychologists' own views of the problems of vision have expanded over the past decade or so. It is no longer possible to assume that visual perception is the intake of information from static objects for the intellectual delight of the viewer via a powerful pattern recognition system. Information, its visual analysis through perception and memory, and human action are intimately linked and our knowledge of any of these affects our understanding of the others. Nevertheless, we hope that we have shown that the problems of vision are tractable and that good progress is being made in unravelling at least some of the details of the perceptual cycle.

Further reading

A good background to the approach taken in this chapter and to other aspects of human cognition can be found in U. Neisser 1976: *Cognition and Reality*. San Francisco: Freeman and Co. A recent, excellent text on vision which covers both visual perception and cognition is G. Humphreys and V. Bruce 1989: *Visual Cognition*. London: Lawrence Erlbaum Associates. For more information on visual analysis, pattern recognition, Gibson's and Marr's approaches and other aspects of visual perception see V. Bruce and P. Green 1990: *Visual Perception*, 2nd edn. London, Lawrence Erlbaum Associates. Also, P.N. Johnson-Laird 1993: *The Computer and the Mind*. London: Fontana, provides a good cognitive science perspective on vision. Details of Marr's work and general research philosophy are fully described in a book which is already a classic: D. Marr 1982: *Vision*. San Francisco: Freeman and Co. Likewise, Gibson himself has provided full details of his ecological approach in J.J. Gibson 1966: *The Senses Considered as Optical Systems*, Boston: Houghton Mifflin, and more radically in J.J. Gibson 1979: *The Ecological Approach to Visual Perception*. Boston: Houghton Mifflin.

Discussion points

1   Why did vision evolve?
2   Discuss the implications of Neisser's view of perception for vision in particular and for cognition in general.
3   What is the point, for psychology, in trying to create artificial visual systems?
4   What sorts of perceptual illusions are there and what do they tell us about perception?
5   How do we perceive depth?

Practical exercises

(a)

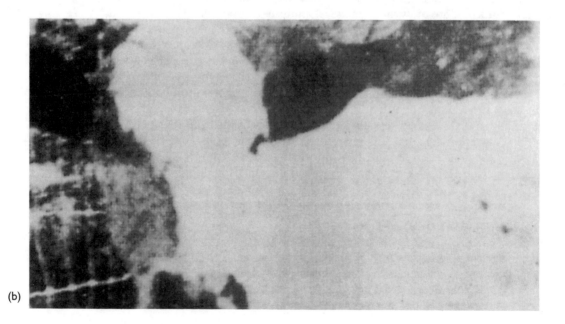

(b)

Figure 3.12   Two difficult to identify pictures

1 Treisman's feature integration theory suggests that single perceptual features can be detected in parallel while a serial search is needed for feature combinations (see text). Make up cards with targets and distractors on them. Try out different combinations of targets and distractors and note people's detection times. Make sure that you include conditions where targets and distractors can be distinguished by a single feature (e.g. a red L among green Ls) and others where a combination of features must be detected (a red L among green Ls and red Cs). Vary the number of distractors and note the effect on searches for single and multiple feature targets.

2 Have a look at figure 3.12(a) and (b). Can you identify these pictures? Try to do so before reading on. Did you succeed? It might help to know that 3.12(a) is an energy map of the world collated from about 40 satellite photographs while 3.12(b) often provides us with milk. Select three groups of people, show them these pictures and ask them to identify them. To be sure that they have done so, in the case of figure 3.12(a) you could ask them to identify the pattern of light coming from the continent of America, and in 3.12(b) to identify the cow's nose. Give the first group of participants no prior information about the stimuli, provide the second group with some general information such as 'a view from space' and 'an animal', and provide the third group with more detailed information such as 'a map of the world at night' and 'the head of a large, grass-eating, farm animal'. Note how many people in each group correctly identify the stimuli and how long it

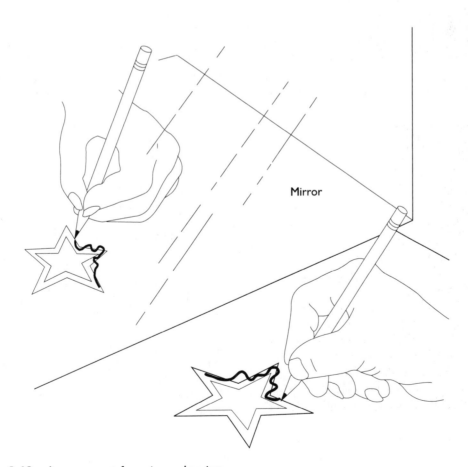

Figure 3.13 Arrangement for mirror drawing

takes them to do so. What does this simple experiment indicate about the relation between perception and cognition?

3   As we explained in the text, one way to appreciate the links between perception and action is to disrupt them and observe the effect. You can do this by trying some mirror drawing. Draw a series of irregular shapes on a piece of paper. Next face a mirror, placing the page of shapes on a table in front of you, so that it is reflected back to you (see figure 3.13). Now, attempt to copy the shapes onto another piece of paper using the reflection in the mirror. Make sure that you cannot see your hands or your drawing directly by interposing a sheet of cardboard or other screening material between you and your work. Practise this task every day for five days using different shapes. Time yourself and note the accuracy of your performance. Do you get faster? Do you become more accurate? What is happening to your use of visual feedback?

Box 3.1
Face detection in the macaque monkey

Perrett et al. (1988), using a methodology similar to that of Hubel and Weisel (1962) and others, measured the electro-physiological response of single cells in the temporal cortex of macaque monkeys to various aspects of faces. A major reason for their interest in this brain area was that damage to parts of the temporal cortex in humans, particularly those parts bordering on the occipital region, has been found to produce severe difficulties with various aspects of face recognition, a disorder known as prosopagnosia. Patients with prosopagnosia are often unable to recognize even the familiar faces of friends or family members, and careful testing shows that the problem is specific to faces and does not include other classes of stimuli. The researchers suspected that careful investigation of the intact brain of a member of a related species could shed light not only on the nature of prosopagnosia but also on the mechanisms of normal face perception.

The general technique used by the team entailed the surgical implantation of micro-electrodes in the brain areas of interest. Once implanted, these devices allow the electrical discharges of individual neurones to be recorded and, because brain tissue contains no pain receptors, do not harm the animal unduly. When a neurone fires it gives off bursts consisting of rapid pulses of electrical activity or 'spikes'. The number of neuronal spikes per second in response to different sorts of stimuli was thus the major dependent variable of interest in this work. Another variable was the length of time which elapsed between stimulus presentation and the start of a cell's response, the response latency.

Perrett et al. first established that the areas in the superior temporal sulcus of the macaque monkey did indeed seem to be involved in face perception. Strong responses were found to pictures of different sorts of faces, but not to those of other stimuli, when recordings were taken from single cells in this area. Stimuli which failed to evoke a response included simple geometric shapes, and complex three-dimensional objects which might resemble faces. The cells in question were activated by faces irrespective of their position in the visual field, and produced strong responses to faces in a receptive field extending 20 degrees on each side from the fovea, or area of maximal retinal sensitivity. Response strength was similarly unaffected by the orientation of the face; equally vigorous responses were recorded to upright, horizontal and inverted faces, though response latency was longer to faces which were not upright. Nor did the distance of the face from the monkey, over a range of 10 cm to 5 m, seem to alter their response. As Perrett et al. themselves put it: 'These findings indicate a role for the cells in a very high level of visual representation of information about faces' (1988, p. 140).

Although manipulations of the faces' gross spatial position had very little effect on the cells' responses, various alterations to the faces themselves did cause them to vary. Pictures and 3-D models of faces whose features where arranged in the wrong places, such as with the mouth above the eyes, produced far weaker responses than normal, unjumbled faces. Also, by covering up particular facial features such as the mouth or the eyes, the researchers discovered that some cells responded most strongly to features in the region of the eyes while others responded to the mouth or the hair.

The sensitivity of some cells to the eyes was then shown to interact with another important variable, head view. Perrett et al. first discovered that cells were highly tuned to respond to faces with the head pointing in a particular direction. In all, they identified six types of cell which responded to either frontal, left profile, right profile, rear, head-up or head-down views of a face. Next, they made the fascinating discovery that these responses often depended on gaze direction as well. So, in about half of the cells which responded most strongly to a full frontal view of

a face, the strongest response of all was found when the eyes were also directed at the monkey. Furthermore, the response of these cells, which diminished as the face was moved away from the frontal position, could be strengthened by arranging the eyes to look sidelong at the monkey (see box figure 3.1.1).

Cells which responded best to profile views were rather different. They were most active when the gaze was averted from the monkey. As Perrett et al. point out, the reason for such neural sensitivity to direction of looking is presumably because gaze direction is of vital importance 'to communication in social interactions in both human and monkey species' (1988, p. 142).

A final set of findings related to the identity of specific faces and to facial expression. About ten per cent of the cells studied showed a strong response to familiar rather

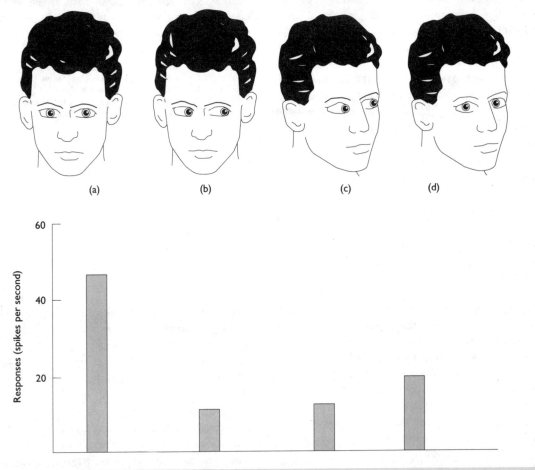

Box figure 3.1.1 Neuronal responses to head view and gaze direction. The strongest response was obtained with (a) full face and eye contact. Low responses were obtained with (b) gaze averted and (c) half-profile face with no eye contact, but an increase in responses was recorded with (d) half-profile face with eye contact. (Based on figure 8.1, Perrett et al., 1988)

than unfamiliar faces, and were totally unaffected by other manipulations. These cells, which clearly play a big part in detecting individuals familiar to the monkey, still fired even when, for example, the surrounding illumination, context or orientation of the face was changed, and certain cells responded most strongly to only one but not to other equally familiar faces. Another important discovery was that these individual-specific cells were unaffected by facial expression, whereas other cells, sensitive to facial expression, appeared to be insensitive to an individual's identity.

The picture which emerges from this work is on the one hand of the complexity of the overall process of face recognition, but on the other of the elegant simplicity, and logic, of what populations of particular cells are specialized to do. But, like all neurophysiological work of a similar nature, it is not possible to be sure that the activity of a cell as recorded under these artificial conditions is as it would be normally. Although unlikely, the very act of using a recording electrode could perturb a cell's response. However, no scientific work can proceed without observation and measurement of some sort, and to demand a totally unbiased observation might be to chase a spurious and unattainable objectivity. Another limitation of the work, though not really a criticism, is that while the authors

identify some of the major components of face perception in the monkey, they do not indicate how these different facial characteristics are integrated into a perceptual whole. Two ripostes to this are that it is presumably of vital importance to identify the individual components first before trying to tackle their integration, and that impressive progress has been made in showing how at least two of the variables, gaze direction and head position, are yoked.

A final problem with this and other work with animals is that we cannot be sure that work on animal populations can be generalized directly to humans. A common complaint is that animal models are useless in helping us understand the more complicated and probably quite different human being. We think this is too extreme a position. Because of evolution, humans and higher mammals are often more alike than different, simple systems are often very helpful in helping us understand more complicated ones, and animal models are often a source of testable hypotheses when studying people.

Based on D.I. Perrett, A.J. Mistlin, A.J. Chitty, M.H. Harries, F. Newcombe and DeHaan, E. 1988: Neuronal mechanisms of face perception and their pathology. In C. Kennard and F. Clifford Rose (eds), *Physiological Aspects of Clinical Neuro-Ophthalmology*. London: Chapman and Hall.

Box 3.2
Vision, stance and balance

Lee and Lishman argued that vision is a vital part of the control system for maintaining stance, in contrast to the classical view which held that vision is an exteroceptive sense, one solely concerned with external events and objects. Their experiments were designed to investigate the relative contribution of vision in controlling stance compared with 'mechanical' proprioceptive information, particularly from the strain on the ankle and calf muscles and pressure on the feet. They reported two experiments in their paper, the first of which we consider here, referring only briefly to the second.

Apparatus
Lee and Lishman's apparatus consisted of the swinging room and a sway meter. The room was constructed from

expanded polystyrene foam sheets. It was open at the bottom and at one end, and was 3.6 m long, 1.8 m wide and 2 m high. Lengths of wallpaper with a floral pattern were hung in the middle of each wall and the ceiling, to provide visual cues. The room could be moved in a straight line silently backwards and forwards by means of four ropes, 5.2 m long, by means of which it was suspended .022 m above the floor.

Participants stood in the same spot on the floor and the room moved relative to them. Their body sway was measured electronically, using the sway meter. As the participant swayed, the varying distance between his back and a 30 × 40 cm plate caused the electrical energy, or capacitance, between the plate and the participant's back to vary. This capacitance was then converted into a voltage and the rate of change of voltage over time was used to indicate sway velocity. As well as the continuously changing sway velocity, average velocities were also computed for each 10 sec period.

Procedure

In experiment 1 the effect of room movement on four stances, one normal and three less well practised, were investigated. Lee and Lishman reasoned that muscular control in less common stances would be imprecise because of the poorer information from muscles and that balance would be more sensitive to vision as a result. Participants were tested barefoot, in the stances listed below.

1 Standing normally on a good surface.
2 Standing on a ramp. Participants were required to stand, with their feet pointing downhill, on a ramp with a slope of 25 degrees. In this stance the feedback from the ankles is different from usual.
3 Standing on a spongy surface. Participants stood on a stack of ten, 2.5 cm thick foam pads. On such a surface, the ankle no longer provides reliable information about the relation of the body to the vertical.
4 Standing on toes. Participants stood comfortably on their toes on a stable, horizontal surface. In this stance, the feedback from the ankles is, once again, different from usual, but, in addition, the angle between the foot and the toes must be precisely controlled to maintain the stance.

Four male and four female participants, paid for participating in the experiment, were tested on the normal stance and on one of the other stances. During each test, the room was either stationary, moving sinusoidally (in a regular backward and forward motion) or moving irregularly backwards and forwards. Five tests, lasting 80 sec each, were given in each stance. They were:

Test 1. Eyes open, room stationary
Test 2. Eyes shut, room stationary
Test 3. Eyes open, room moving sinusoidally
Test 4. Eyes closed, room moving sinusoidally
Test 5. Eyes open, room moving irregularly

Tests 1 and 2 allowed Lee and Lishman to assess the general effect of vision on balance. Test 3 was particularly important. If visual cues are vital in maintaining stance, then the participants would be expected to sway backwards and forwards with the room. Test 4 acted as a control condition against which to assess the effects of test 3. Finally, before test 5, participants were told that the experimenter would attempt to make them sway by moving the room and that they were to try to ignore this and to try to stand still while looking straight ahead.

Participants' body sway and any losses of balance were noted. A loss of balance was defined as a change of stance by either lifting or sliding a foot or dropping down from the toes. If a participant lost balance three times, the test in question was ended.

Results

Measures of body sway were taken from the middle 60 sec of the 80 sec records. This allowed the participant time to settle into the test. Two main indices of balance were used, 'S' and 'D', as well as other measures not discussed here. S was the average sway speed of the body, and D was the percentage of time the participant was swaying in the same direction as the room. A number of important effects were observed. First of all, participants used visual feedback to control their balance in all stances. This was particularly apparent when the room was moved sinusoidally in test 3, during which participants were effectively 'driven' backwards and forwards by the room's motion. For example, when the participant was standing on a normal surface, in test 3, $D = 27$, indicating that body sway was in line with the room movement for a considerable amount of the time, while in test 4, with eyes closed, $D = -2$. When standing on the padded surface, differences in D values were even more apparent ($D = 42$ for test 3, $D = -3$ for test 4). The authors showed that the D values for tests 3 and 4 were significantly different ($p < 0.001$), whenever the room was moving, using a simple statistical measure known as the related t test. Secondly, there was a beneficial effect of visual feedback on balance in all four stances when the room was stationary. As the top line of figures in box table 3.2.1 shows, the percentage of body sway was reduced by having the eyes open in all stances.

Next, the deleterious effect of inappropriate visual feedback can be seen in a series of important comparisons in the lower part of box table 3.2.1. These figures show the quite marked percentage increase in S values when tests 5 and 3, the moving room conditions, were compared with test 1, the stationary room condition. Increases in body sway were also apparent in some but not all of the conditions where sway in the moving room is compared with sway in the stationary room with eyes closed, test 2, indicating that inappropriate visual feedback is often worse than no feedback at all.

Box table 3.2.1   Effects of visual feedback on balance

	Standing	Ramp	Pads	Toes
Percentage improvement in balance with visual feedback (Reduction in S, test 1 vs. test 2)	31	34	70	56
Percentage impairment of balance by misleading visual feedback (Increase in S, test 5 vs. test 1)	80	108	219	204
(Increase in S, test 3 vs. test 1)	66	48	122	63
(Increase in S, test 5 vs. test 2)	12	17	−7	30
(Increase in S, test 3 vs. test 2)	9	−7	−37	−30

Source: Based on table 2, Lee and Lishman, 1975

Finally, the type of stance or surface on which the participant stood clearly affected balance. The more unusual the surface or the stance, the more important visual feedback became. Presumably this is because the role of mechanical feedback is poorer and visual feedback must make up the shortfall. This can also be seen in box table 3.2.1, which shows that balance was most improved by appropriate visual feedback and most disrupted by inappropriate feedback on the padded surface, next when standing on toes, and least improved (or disimproved) when standing on the ramp or standing normally. (One minor criticism of this part of the results is that the claims regarding stance and surface are based simply on inspection of the percentages of sway induced by these conditions and not on statistically tested differences.)

Experiment 1 demonstrated that visual proprioception was helpful but not essential for maintaining stance. In a further experiment, Lee and Lishman investigated the effect of the moving room on three stances for which they found visual feedback to be essential. These were balancing on a low beam, standing with heels together and feet splayed out perfectly in line (the Charlie Chaplin stance), and a stance in which participants stood on one leg with the other behind the calf, with the opposite arm extended holding a weight!

The authors chose the 'pinstripe stance' as the label for this since it reminded them of a civil servant hailing a taxi with his brief case! In each of the cases, inappropriate visual feedback not only caused participants to sway, but in 52 per cent of cases actually caused them to fall over.

Both experiments indicate the important role of vision, but it could be argued that the small number of participants tested somewhat reduces the generality of the results. However, the basic effects which the authors report are so clear, and have since been shown to occur in other studies with different participants, that their generality seems assured. A second criticism might be that participants noticed that the room was moving, inferred what was supposed to happen and reacted accordingly, perhaps to please the experimenters. While this explanation cannot be completely ruled out, it again seems unlikely on the grounds that participants frequently claimed to be unaware that the room was moving at all. As Lee and Lishman conclude in their own summary of their experiments: 'The participant is like a visual puppet; his balance can be manipulated by simply moving his surroundings, without his being aware of it' (1975, p. 94).

Based on D.N. Lee and J.R. Lishman, J.R. 1975: Visual proprioceptive control of stance. *Journal of Human Movement Studies*, 1, 87–95.

4 Language

All human beings, with the exception of those unfortunate enough to have suffered severe and specific brain damage, develop a skill in communicating in at least the language of their own society which is quite unequalled by any form of communication used by other animals. Once language has been acquired it is used almost continuously. People talk to other people, write to them and, when not talking, writing, listening, or reading, much of the remaining time is spent in thinking in which an inner voice using familiar words is normally experienced. Language is, in other words, central to human activity. As language is studied, more of its complexities become more apparent. This chapter will reveal some of the complexities of the cognitive processes associated with language. The result may be an increase in respect for the cognitive systems that allow such processes and processing to take place, while at the same time the impossibility of briefly summarizing all the cognitive processes underlying language should become obvious.

The chapter is divided into four main sections. The first deals with the general structure of language and the relation between language and thought, the second with specific theories of language structure, the third with the production of utterances in a language, and the fourth with the comprehension of language when spoken or written by others.

The Structure of Language

Semantics

Compare the letter strings *child* and *table* with *dilch* and *batel*. The first two are meaningful words in the English language while the second two, although pronounceable, are non-words in English. If we are told *the child is on the table*, we understand what is meant and will probably go to tell him to get down. If we hear *the table is on the child*, this has quite a different meaning and we will rush to rescue the unfortunate infant.

The study of semantics is the study of the meaning of words both by themselves and when put together to form sentences and longer statements. Language is essentially a means of communication, and it is successful only if meaning is communicated by the person uttering a statement to the person who hears or reads it. The study of meaning and its communication is therefore central to the study of language. A traditional model of verbal communication has been what has been called the code model (Sperber and Wilson, 1986). In this model, thoughts are translated by some linguistic encoding device into words which can be transmitted either vocally or in writing. These messages are then received by the hearer and decoded via a linguistic decoding device into the appropriate thought and intended meanings. As we will describe later in the chapter, such a code model is inadequate to describe fully and properly the nature of language communication. It does, however, form a useful starting point for identifying some of the steps involved in language communication. The essential aim is the communication of meaning and to do this words which are themselves meaningful are used. However, the construction of the words into longer utterances, and the context in which they are spoken, may produce a meaning that is quite unexpected from a knowledge of the individual words available.

Syntax

It is rare for anyone to utter single words at a time. Normally we speak in single sentences, or several sentences. For communication to be possible it is necessary for the words to be put together to satisfy the rules of the particular language being spoken. The study of syntax is the study of the appropriate and inappropriate orderings of words in any particular language. *The child is on the table* has the words in an appropriate order while *child table the the on is* is not acceptable in English. The words are the same but communication of the meaning depends upon their proper ordering. There are rules about word order which are, at least at first sight, independent of the meanings of the word themselves. This is illustrated by the famous example 'colourless green ideas sleep furiously'. While the sentence is meaningless we can tell that the words are all in their proper places for nouns, verbs, etc. in English. Most people will agree that such a sentence is grammatically correct while the sentence 'sleep ideas green furiously colourless' is not grammatical. In 1957 the study of syntax and linguistics in general was revolutionized by the publication of Chomsky's *Syntactic Structures*. In it Chomsky provided a framework for the structure of language. We will turn to Chomsky's approach to syntax shortly.

Pragmatics

The third domain of the study of language to be considered here is pragmatics. The study of pragmatics investigates why, in a given situation, a particular utterance is chosen. Why, for example, do people say 'lovely weather!' on a rainy day and how do other people understand that this is an ironic comment on the weather rather than a crazy and false statement? In recent years the pragmatic aspects of language and the influence of the particular situation the speaker and listener are in have become important issues in the study of linguistics, but because these issues blend into the more social and communicative aspects of language we will examine them only briefly in this chapter.

Before considering some of these basic aspects of language in more detail, however, we wish first to explore the general relation between the language and words we use and how we perceive and think about our world around us, or the link between language and thought.

Language and thought: the linguistic relativity hypothesis

In our introductory paragraph about semantics we described the code model of verbal communication. This model assumes that thought is the currency of the cognitive system and that language is used merely as a code for communication to another person. Thoughts are translated into words so that they can be transmitted to the other individual. When linguists, at the end of the nineteenth and the beginning of the twentieth centuries, began to study the culture and languages of different societies this independent but subservient role of language was questioned. Franz Boas, for example, recorded many of the unwritten languages of the North American Indian and highlighted the many different structures and implicit assumptions of the Indian and the English languages. For example, English and other European languages used past, present and future tenses depending on the time at which the event being spoken of occurred. In contrast, the Hopi Indians in Arizona have no such tenses. The time of occurrence has to be inferred from the context of any statement. On the other hand, Hopi Indians have grammatical devices which indicate whether statements are general, timeless truths, reports of known happenings, or descriptions of uncertain events, including those to take place in the future. Kwakiutl Indians, in their language, also do not have tenses based on time but in their case it is obligatory to indicate whether or not the speaker personally observed the action that is being reported.

Linguists were very impressed by these variations in the form of languages. Some began to speculate whether the available words in a language, and the ways in which they had to be used, would determine the way in which individuals in each culture thought. Sapir (1929), for example, argued that the way in which individuals conceptualize the 'real world' is largely and unconsciously built upon the language habits of the group. The result being, he argued, that 'the worlds in which different societies live are distinct worlds, not merely the same world with different labels attached' (Sapir, 1929, p. 209).

However, the person most commonly associated with the idea that language determines or at least strongly influences the way people think was Benjamin Lee Whorf. Whorf was a chemical engineer who worked for the Hartford Fire Insurance Company, but who studied North American Indian languages as a hobby. Whorf noticed that many fires were the result of careless behaviour by people near 'empty' petrol drums. Whorf pointed out that the term 'empty' ignores the fact that the drums were in fact full of invisible but highly explosive petrol vapour. Whorf suspected that the use of the word 'empty' influenced the careless behaviour of these people, causing the fires. He went on to study Indian languages, including Hopi, pointing out many differences in, for example, words referring to time and arguing that these influenced the Hopi culture.

The proposal that particular languages strongly influence ways of thinking became known as the 'linguistic relativity hypothesis', sometimes known as the 'Sapir–Whorf hypothesis'. Testing the linguistic relativity hypothesis is not easy, although examples that seem, at first sight, to fit with the hypothesis are relatively easy to find. Eskimos have many words they use to describe different states of snow while English speakers have just the single word which, if necessary, they have to qualify by adjectives, and in the Philippines the Hanunoo have 92 names for different varieties of rice. Whorf believed that the rich variety of such terms allowed speakers of the language a richer perception of the world. However, it may be that the lifestyle and life experiences of experts in snow and rice lead to the need for many more words. It may be the perception of the world and lifestyle, not the words of the language, that determine the linguistic richness. Furthermore, the size of the Eskimo vocabulary of words for snow was probably exaggerated by Whorf.

One area of research attempting to test the hypothesis has been in the naming and perception of colours. In English there are eleven basic colour words while, for example, the Dani, a traditional people of New Guinea, use just two basic colour terms: one for dark, cold hues and one for bright, warm hues. If the richness of the English language influences perception then English speakers should perceive colours in a more refined way than do the Dani. For each of the eleven colour terms in English there is one generally agreed colour, termed a focal colour, that is generally thought to best represent that term. Has this dominance of certain colours developed from the vocabulary of colour words? Focal colours are certainly easily identified, and English speakers find it easier to associate nonsense names to focal than to non-focal colours. At first sight this looks like evidence for the linguistic relativity hypothesis. However, Rosch (1973a, 1973b) showed that the Dani have the same tendency to learn focal colours more easily than non-focal colours even though they have no names for these colours (see box 4.1). Other research similarly fails to support the linguistic relativity hypothesis. Nevertheless, it is hard to accept that the existence or non-existence of words in one's common language will not have some influence upon thinking. It may be that the use of concrete, physical stimuli in testing the linguistic relativity hypothesis may have been inappropriate. The nature of the physical world may determine the concepts by which people think and be less influenced by language than would be abstract concepts such as freedom, democracy, religion and tranquillity.

Also, a weaker version of the linguistic relativity hypothesis probably has more to recommend it than the strong version. According to this idea, the language we use can constrain (rather than strongly determine) the way we think about things by affecting the available labels we have to help us remember information. For instance, the 92 names for different varieties of rice used by the Hanunoo presumably provide a sophisticated code which allows them to categorize, remember and later retrieve information about rice more easily than a non-Hanunoo would. Similarly, people who have acquired the technical vocabulary of a new subject can remember facts about the subject in question more efficiently than lay persons.

Despite this, and despite the wide variation in human languages, it still does seem to make good sense to disentangle language from cognition and to study it in its own right, starting with syntax.

Theories on Language Structure

Syntactic structures

A major development in linguistics that had a massive effect on the psychological study of language followed the publication by Noam Chomsky of his small book *Syntactic Structures* in 1957. Before Chomsky's new approach came to dominate thinking, psychologists, under the influence of the behaviourist tradition, tended to think of spoken language as a learned habit that could be understood in terms of the then dominant conditioning theories. Skinner, for example, in the same year that Chomsky published *Syntactic Structures*, published his own account, *Verbal Behavior*, of the use of language in terms of reinforcement, conditioned responses to stimuli and generalization from one situation to another. Chomsky (1959) when reviewing Skinner's book, in addition to savagely attacking the undefined and arbitrary use of the terms stimulus, response and reinforcement in Skinner's *post hoc* explanations of verbal behaviour, emphasized that one of the major features of language is the originality and creativity displayed in much that is spoken. If the conditioning model of Skinner was correct then most spoken remarks would be the same as those uttered previously in similar circumstances. The reverse is the case and a major feature of language is that it is about saying something new to the listener.

Chomsky argued that conditioning models, which deal merely with the frequency with which some behaviour occurs as a result of past reinforcements of that behaviour in similar circumstances, could never give an adequate account of language. What was required, he argued, was a model in which the speaker was able to draw upon a large collection of rules which specified what would and what would not be acceptable utterances in his or her particular language. Chomsky's interest was in the structuring of words in sentences. He was, thus, concerned with the syntactic rules that determine what is and what is not correct spoken language. He proposed that there were separate semantic and syntactic components in language production. The form of an acceptable utterance would be generated by syntactic rules. These start with the sentence to be analysed and produced, and successively rewrite components in the sentence until a final acceptable form is reached.

Suppose we wish to generate the sentence 'the boy kissed the girl'. The syntactic tree structure derived from Chomsky's system is illustrated in figure 4.1.

We start with a sentence (S); by application of one of Chomsky's syntactic rules, this can be rewritten into symbols that stand for a noun phrase (NP) and a verb phrase (VP). This rule says, in effect, that sentences in English consist of a noun phrase followed by a verb phrase. The symbol NP can be rewritten in several ways, but for our present purpose we rewrite the noun phrase as an article plus N where N stands for a noun. By further application of linguistic rules the full syntactic tree in figure 4.1 can be constructed.

Chomsky claimed that a limited number of rules (known as phrase structure rules), similar to those used to generate the sentence in figure 4.1, can be used to generate a very large, potentially infinite number of new but acceptable utterances. However, Chomsky pointed out that phrase structure rules are insufficient to specify all the important features of language.

Chomsky was interested in capturing the underlying similarity between many sentences which seem to share the same meaning but have quite different structures in their wording. One particular example is the relationship between active and passive sentences. The sentences *the boy kissed the girl* and *the girl was kissed by the boy* express the same meaning but

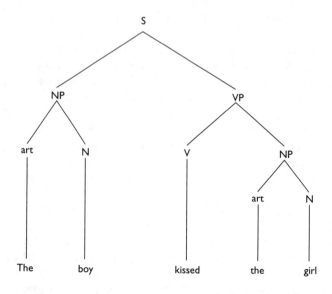

Figure 4.1   A syntactic tree for a simple sentence. S = sentence; NP = noun phrase; VP = verb phrase; art = article; N = noun; V = verb

have different syntactic structures. Chomsky (1957, 1965) thus drew a distinction between surface structure and deep structure. Surface structure refers to the actual order of words in the sentence. Deep structure represents the basic grammatical relationships from which such a sentence is generated. The two sentences (*the boy kissed the girl* and *the girl was kissed by the boy*) have different surface structures but share the same deep structure. Chomsky developed transformational rules that were designed to map deep structures onto surface structure and vice versa. In Chomsky's model, phrase structure rules generate deep structures and from these further, transformational rules produce the final surface structures which are the actual, spoken form of the utterance.

Competence and performance

Chomsky drew an important distinction between people's competence at recognizing acceptable and unacceptable utterances in their language and their actual performance when speaking. Not everything that people say will fit with the idealized rules of syntax. Nevertheless, when asked, people can normally say whether a particular string of words is or is not properly formed in their particular language. For various reasons, perhaps reflecting memory limitations, distractions, absent-mindedness, etc., the actual performances of spoken language may contain errors but, according to Chomsky, mature, adult speakers of a language have a competence in that language which should form the basis for deciding what is and what is not correct. For Chomsky, therefore, the decision about the correctness of the grammatical rules that he posed depended upon the intuitions of the speakers of a language as to whether the strings of words generated by a transformational grammar were or were not correct. Chomsky's grammars were not, therefore, intended as prescriptions telling people how they should speak, but only as descriptions of the way in which people actually do, or at least try to, form sentences.

Psycholinguistics

Chomsky offered his theory of syntactic structure as an abstract, neutral description of the way that language is constructed. He did not claim that people actually go through the procedures of using phrase structure and transformational grammar when they prepare to speak a sentence. His claim was only that this activity could be most neatly described by his grammars. Nevertheless, if phrase structure and transformational grammars so well describe language then it seems a reasonable question to ask whether the actual psychological processes in preparing speech do indeed follow the same steps. In the 1960s and 1970s considerable psychological research attempted to test the relationship between Chomsky's linguistic theory and the actual psychological processes that people use in constructing language. This research came to be known as psycholinguistics.

Miller and McKean (1964) were among the first in this new field when they investigated how long it takes to carry out transformations such as changing from active to passive and positive to negative. They hypothesized that participants start with a kernel string that is positive and active (e.g. *John kissed Mary*). This must then be transformed using Chomsky's grammar if the negative or the passive forms (i.e. *Mary did not kiss John*, *Mary was kissed by John*), or the negative and passive forms (*John was not kissed by Mary*) are to be used. In their experiment they told their participants to turn active sentences into the passive form or vice versa and to find the appropriate transformed sentence (active, passive, negative, positive and so on) in a list of alternative sentences. Participants were told to press a button when they were ready to search this list of sentences, and the time taken before pressing the button was assumed to be a measure of the time required for the transformation. Using this technique, they found that passive transformations took approximately 0.9 sec, negative transformations about 0.4 sec, and the combined negative and passive transformation required 1.5 sec. Miller and McKean claimed that this demonstrates that transformations are single operations which are carried out one after the other, since the time for the combined passive and negative operation was about the same as the two operations carried out separately.

However, Miller and McKean had explicitly asked their participants to carry out the transformations. Their results do not prove that such transformations are conducted naturally on the way to obtaining negative or passive statements.

Further qualification of Miller and McKean's findings is also provided by later research which showed the importance of the context in which statements are used, and their meaning, and demonstrated how some seemingly difficult linguistic forms can often be quite easy to understand. So, for example, Wason (1965) claimed that the ease of use of active, passive or negative forms depended on particular conditions of their natural use. He argued that one major function of the negative form is in what he called the 'context of plausible denial'. In his experiment, Wason presented participants with eight numbered circles, seven coloured red and one coloured blue. With red as the norm in this experiment, the blue circle stands out as an unexpected colour, and participants will be more likely to think of it as 'not red' rather than thinking of the red circles as 'not blue'. He therefore predicted that it would be more natural to use a negative form when referring to the blue circle than when referring to the red ones. In line with this prediction, if circle 3 was the blue circle, Wason found that participants took less time to complete the sentence 'circle 3 is not . . .' where the answer is 'red' than they did to complete a sentence such as 'circle 7 is not . . .' where the answer is 'blue'. Negative statements can, therefore, in an appropriate context, be made more quickly than positive statements.

Slobin (1966) also tested participants on a sentence verification task. The participants were shown both a sentence and a picture and had to indicate whether the sentence was true or false. As in the Miller and McKean experiments, the sentences were in active, passive, negative, or passive negative forms. In terms of Chomsky's (1957) theory, the active sentences should require no transformations while the passive and the negative sentences require a single transformation and the passive negative sentences need two transformations. In which case, these transformations should be reflected in the time to take the decision on the truth of the sentence. Slobin did indeed find that active sentences are judged more quickly than passive and negative ones which in turn are quicker than the combined passive negatives. However, this support for Chomsky's theory was undermined by a second finding. Slobin included sentences that were 'irreversible' because switching the subject and the object of the sentence led to nonsense. For example, the sentence *the girl is watering the flowers* would be nonsense if the subject and object were reversed to form *the flowers are watering the girl*. Slobin found that irreversible passive sentences (e.g. *the flowers are being watered by the girl*) took no longer to be judged than irreversible active sentences (*the girl is watering the flowers*). Slobin concluded that the implausibility of flowers watering girls offsets the syntactic complexity of the transformation. If so, Chomsky's assumption that syntactic analysis must always be completed before semantic processing begins must be untrue, and it may be that people can bypass a full syntactic analysis when the meaning of a sentence allows this to be possible.

On balance, solid evidence for the precise application of Chomskyan rules when speaking and listening was not discovered. What the psycholinguistic research in the 1960s and 1970s did was to establish that people are sensitive to gross syntactic features of language, particularly units such as phrases, but while affected by other aspects such as negatives, passives and other transformations, people's response to these often depends strongly on the context and plausibility of the utterance.

From syntax to semantics

Gradually, problems in demonstrating that people perform syntactic operations in the ways described by Chomsky's theories led psycholinguists to re-evaluate the processes they believed to be taking place. Whatever the attraction of Chomsky's theory as a description of the structure of language, it was always implausible as a model of the psychological generation of a sentence. When a generative grammar begins to assemble a sentence it starts with a single abstract symbol 'S' which it unpacks into a sentence frame, and only at the last stage inserts actual words corresponding to particular meanings. As a model of the way people plan their utterances this seems nonsensical, and always confused the first author when he was an undergraduate! People do not first frame a sentence and then decide what to say; they begin with a message they wish to communicate, which has its own structure, and this will determine the structure of the final sentence.

Because of these problems, psycholinguists started to consider the importance of the meaning of the message itself. They also became more interested in what people can actually do when using language, considering their performance, rather than abstract models of competence. While, for example, a linguist may be happy that a generative grammar can produce an infinitely long, infinitely complex sentence with one clause after another embedded within it (e.g. the man, the dog, the hat, the door, . . . hit, sat on, ran, shut). Real speakers neither produce such sentences nor can they understand them when they encounter them. In real life, as we indicated at the beginning of the chapter, we speak for a purpose and in a particular context and both the object of the communication and the information that is shared by the two communicators are essential to understanding what people actually say. It is towards these factors that modern psycholinguistics has turned.

Semantics

To some extent, the success of Chomsky's theories of syntactic structures distracted psycholinguists from the main reason for the existence of language, which is to convey the meaning of one person's thoughts to another individual. Words must contain meaning or the process would be pointless. What, however, is meant by saying that a word has meaning and a non-word does not? Why should seeing the letters 'cat' produce a different effect from the letters 'cta'? The meanings of 'meaning' have challenged philosophers for many years and it is not possible in this chapter to do more than indicate one or two of the approaches taken by psycholinguists to understand a meaning, and some of the problems that philosophical analysis has demonstrated with such theories (see also the discussion of semantic memory in chapter 2).

Feature theories   Feature theories assume that the meanings of words are stored in a mental dictionary in terms of lists of features that are possessed by the objects named by the words. So, for example, the word cat might be defined by a list of features including 'has fur', 'purrs', 'has claws', 'is domesticated' and so on. Such feature theories have been explored by Schaeffer and Wallice (1969) and Smith et al. (1974). The attraction of feature theories is that they allow an explanation of the time that people take to make certain decisions. People are quicker at saying that *a sparrow is a bird* than that *an ostrich is a bird*. Feature theories explain this as the result of more features being shared by sparrows with the defining characteristics of birds than are shared by ostriches with the concept of bird. Such feature theories can cope with the fact that people are slower to say that *a bat is not a bird* than they are to say that *a table is not a bird*. Here, the overlap in features between bats (e.g. having wings, flying, being small, warm-blooded animals) means that a decision process judging between sets of features will take longer where more features are shared in common.

Feature theories have their attractions but run into serious problems as soon as they move away from the most concrete of nouns. For example, what features define the meanings of abstract words, of adjectives, verbs, prepositions, and so on? What is more, as Wittgenstein (1953) pointed out, there are many concepts which cannot be defined by a single set of features. To illustrate this, Wittgenstein analysed the concept of game, pointing out that the way the word 'game' is used means that no single property of games is common to all the things we call games. Rather, games share a 'family resemblance'. By family resemblance Wittgenstein was drawing an analogy with the appearance of members of the same family. There may be no specific set of features (e.g. turned-up noses or green eyes) that are shared by all members of the family. Nevertheless, children normally share sufficient features with their parents, although a different set of features from one child to another, to make the resemblance of parents and children easily recognizable. In a similar way, Wittgenstein suggested that words may be used in different ways depending upon the particular situation and the social activity and social rules that apply in the given situation. Each of these uses of the word will have similarities to other uses as children have similarities, in different ways, to their parents.

Wittgenstein emphasized that words have their meaning defined within the particular activity that the speaker and listener were engaged in at the given time. He called these different activities 'language games' to emphasize that speaking a language is part of an activity or a form of life. As examples of language games he gives the following: giving orders and obeying them; describing the appearance of an object, or giving its measurements; constructing an object from a description (a drawing); reporting an event; speculating about an event; forming and testing a hypothesis. Within these, and many other types of language game, Wittgenstein argued that the meaning of the words depends upon the use to which they are put, and that it is useful to think of words as tools. In a famous passage, he comments on the variety of tools as follows:

> Think of the tools in a tool-box: there is a hammer, pliers, a saw, a screw-driver, a rule, a gluepot, glue, nails and screws – the functions of words are as diverse as the functions of these objects. (1953, para. 11, p. 6)

Wittgenstein's argument was that words do not merely stand for objects but rather play an integral part in all the many aspects of our lives, and like tools have many different jobs to do. He comments that 'commanding, questioning, recounting, chatting, are as much a part of our natural history as walking, eating, drinking, playing'. A further implication of his approach is that the same word or sets of words can take on quite different meanings depending on the situations or contexts in which it is used, so that to speak of the meaning of a word as if it were fixed for ever is mistaken.

Psycholinguistic theories of meaning have yet to reach sufficient sophistication to cope with the way words are used in different language games. The models of psycholinguistics have often been restricted to attempts to capture the meanings of common concrete nouns. Such concrete nouns form a special set of words, that is, those for which objects in the world exist, for which they might be used as tokens and in terms of whose physical properties the word might be defined. A very large proportion of the words that we use are outside this concrete noun category, and for these a more sophisticated account of word meaning will be required.

Procedural semantics Procedural semantics (e.g. Miller and Johnson-Laird, 1976) begins with the assumption that the meaning of words can be represented in a form similar to computer programs. Such programs could include lists of features and so incorporate feature theories of meaning. However, it is possible to build into procedures other logical operations that are not catered for within the feature theories. So, for example, it would be difficult, in a feature theory, to define the concept 'sister-in-law'. However, this presents no difficulty for procedural definitions where a sister-in-law can be defined as either 'one's brother's wife' or 'one's spouse's sister'. Procedural semantics also offers possible means of analysing the meanings of verbs and, in so doing, begins to capture the dynamics of language within a theory of the meaning of words. Research in this area has if anything emphasized the interdependence of language on other cognitive functions such as perception and action, by showing how closely related are the activities of perceiving, doing and understanding.

Constructing Speech: The Production of Language

Spoken, or for that matter written, language is produced as a serial list of words. A fluent speaker talking on a familiar topic will produce this string of words rapidly and smoothly. Nevertheless, an examination of what is said and how it is produced indicates that the activity of composing speech takes place within a hierarchical set of units rather than one word at a time. These units are constructed and modified prior to being spoken. At the higher levels of this hierarchy are the ideas that the speaker has decided to convey. These ideas must be communicated in a form that takes into account the current situation. The knowledge and expectations of the listener must be catered for, the speech must be syntactically well formed, appropriate words must be recalled from memory and the correct sequence of speech sounds composed.

Higher levels of speech planning

A research technique that has been very useful in identifying the processes of higher-order planning in speech production is the study of the pauses that occur in normal speech. Goldman-Eisler (1961, 1968), for example, had participants either describe a cartoon or interpret its meaning. The latter task is more intellectually demanding and produced more hesitations in the flow of speech as the speakers constructed their ideas. However, when asked to undertake the description of a cartoon for a second or third time the speech was far more fluent, even though the individual words used were often different. The more fluent speech reflected the existence of the high-level ideas that the speaker wished to convey, indicating that the pauses had largely reflected these high-level planning activities.

Deese (1978, 1980) recorded people talking in committees, business meetings and academic seminars. He found that his speakers spoke in grammatically correct sentences, most of which were fairly short, lasting less than ten seconds. Butterworth (1975) studied the speech of participants who were asked to make the best case that they could in support of given social or political positions. Independently, another group of participants divided transcripts of these speeches into idea units. Butterworth found that the hesitations of his participants tended to coincide with the boundaries of these idea units. The speaker became hesitant while developing an idea, then fluently expressed it and became hesitant again while constructing the next idea.

Clauses and speech errors

The notion that there are idea units is closely, though not perfectly reflected in the structure of language. Language is often clearly divisible into clauses, that is, verbs with their subject and predicate, nouns and their associated adjectives and adverbs. For example, *Mary stroked the cat, then put it on the floor* is a sentence with two clauses, one involving Mary's stroking of the cat, the other her putting it on the floor.

Clauses seem to be an important unit in speech production. In spontaneous speech, pauses occur at or near the beginning of clauses (e.g. Boomer, 1965; Butterworth, 1980). Sometimes, speakers pause a word or so into a clause since this indicates to the listener that more is to come while the speaker properly composes his utterance.

Speech errors, or slips of the tongue, have proved a very valuable means of highlighting the construction of spoken language. By collecting such errors when they occur spontaneously in conversation, and by careful analysis of their nature and comparison with the intended utterance, psychologists have been able to illustrate some of the units that must be used in speech construction. The following example is given by Ellis and Beattie (1986), where I is the intended utterance and E gives what the speaker actually said (i.e. the error).

1 I: SPOON of SUGAR   E: SUGAR of SPOON
2 I: I put the BOOK on the BED   E: I put the BED on the BOOK

The displacement of the words *spoon* and *sugar* and *book* and *bed* show that at the point when, for example, book was to be spoken, the rest of the clause up to and including bed had already been planned, otherwise the substitution of the words could not have occurred. Garrett (1975, 1976) found that around 80 per cent of the exchanges of words in slips of the tongue involved two words within the same clause. The evidence from pauses and slips of the tongue, therefore, suggests that speeches are composed in clauses before they are spoken.

We shall now examine other sorts of errors and their role in speech production.

Speech output lexicon

Language production involves more than clause selection. The actual words that we use in speech must be selected from memory. The particular part of memory that retains the store of words in their spoken word forms has been termed the speech output lexicon (Ellis and Beattie, 1986). So just as errors can give useful information about the syntactic processes of language production used to generate clauses, speech errors and pauses also provide a useful source of information about the speech output lexicon.

An obvious source of error occurs when the speaker simply cannot retrieve a word he or she wants to say. When we have problems in retrieving words from this lexicon, we may experience the 'tip of the tongue' phenomenon. We know the word that we want to say but are unable to retrieve its exact spoken form. Brown and McNeill (1966) studied the tip of the tongue phenomenon by reading dictionary definitions of rare words and requiring their participants to supply the word defined. If the participant felt that the subject was on the tip of the tongue they were asked to guess the initial letter, the number of syllables, and other details of the word. It became clear that several of the features of the word were available to the participants. For example, 57 per cent of the time they were correct at guessing the word's first letter.

At other times, retrieval may not fail completely, but it can take longer than usual. During speech, when a person pauses within a clause, it is usually prior to saying a word that he or she uses relatively infrequently, or which is unpredictable in the particular context (Beattie and Butterworth, 1979). Some speech errors involve the retrieval of words from the lexicon that are similar in meaning to the intended word. Ellis and Beattie (1986) give the example I: Can you wriggle your ANKLES? E: Can you wriggle your ELBOWS? Other errors occur when similar-sounding words are retrieved. Ellis and Beattie (1986) give the example of a person describing otters as 'fantastic APRICOTS' when they intended to say 'ACROBATS'. Finally, some speech errors occur when two words of similar meaning appear to have been simultaneously activated and have been combined to form a 'blend'. Ellis and Beattie (1986) give the example I: Have we PERSUADED/CONVINCED you? E: Have we CONSUADED you?

The picture that emerges from errors such as these is of a sophisticated, rapid, though not trouble-free retrieval process in which various candidates for production are activated, often similar in meaning to each other.

Speech errors involving morphemes and phonemes   By looking at yet another sort of speech error, we can see that speech production is even more complex than this, and that words may be retrieved and assembled from smaller constituent parts. Examples were given earlier of speech errors where whole words change their place within a clause. Other forms of speech error involving exchanges of morphemes and phonemes frequently occur, which can also shed light on the speech output lexicon. The best known of these are Spoonerisms, named after the English clergyman, William Spooner. Examples attributed to him include 'You have hissed all my mystery lectures' and 'I assure you the insanitary spectre has seen all the bathrooms'. Spooner's 'errors' may or may not have been deliberate but such errors do occur accidentally in everyday speech. Examples given by Ellis and Beattie (1986) include:

1 I: The HILLs are SNOWy   E: The SNOWs are HILLy
2 I: The Sun is SHining   E: The SHun is Sining

An error such as 1 is interesting as it shows that the morpheme stem of the words 'hills' and 'snowy' can become separated from their suffixes so that the morpheme stems of the words can be transposed while the suffixes remain in their correct places. This suggests that not only are the morphemes and their suffixes separately selected at some stage in the process of speech production, but also that the words of the clause, with its constituent morphemes and suffixes, must be held together prior to the actual articulation of the clause otherwise the transposition would not occur. The second example above shows that the individual speech sounds must be held in some separable form prior to articulation to allow for the possibility of the phonemes 's' and 'sh' to be transposed in the speech.

Conversational maxims

Selecting clauses and words is not sufficient for accurate and appropriate language production. The process of putting an idea into words involves an evaluation of the knowledge shared by the speaker and the listener. Suppose Mary says to Tom 'George was vulnerable'. Such a statement might be interpreted by Tom as a description of George's psychological sensitivity. With no available context Tom would be puzzled why Mary should make such a statement. On the other hand, if we imagine Mary and Tom watching George play bridge and assume that Tom has asked Mary, who is a more experienced player, why George was more cautious than previously in his bidding, then Mary's statement has sufficient information to convey a specific and wholly different interpretation to Tom. In doing so, however, Mary has to be confident that Tom's knowledge of bridge is sufficient for him to appreciate the implications of winning and losing at the particular stage George has reached in the game. Mary needs to construct her utterance so that it is informative to Tom, assuming the knowledge that he does possess but not presuming knowledge of which he is ignorant.

Most speech is carefully constructed so that it activates the existing knowledge of the listener and specifies succinctly the person or thing to whom the speaker is referring. The rest of the utterance conveys new information about that person or thing. What is said is said in a social context (a language game in Wittgenstein's terms) and is normally constructed to maximize the communication of appropriate, new information with the minimum of elaboration upon information already possessed by the listener. This cooperation between speaker and listener has been called the *cooperative principle* by Grice (1975). He suggests that speakers follow at least four conversational maxims in constructing what they say. The most powerful of these is the *maxim of quantity*. This requires the speaker to be as informative but not more informative than is required. In our example above, Mary did not need to describe what vulnerability was to Tom. If Tom had been completely naive about the rules of bridge, then she would have had to explain her usage of the word 'vulnerability' before she could tell him that George was vulnerable. Grice's second maxim, the *maxim of quality*, requires the speaker to be truthful. There are accepted situations when this maxim is violated, for example when the speaker makes a sarcastic remark (e.g. 'Conservative politicians have always loved social scientists'). There are, however, verbal and non-verbal cues used by the speaker to indicate when the maxim is being broken. Grice's *maxim of relation* requires what is said to be relevant to the conversation. Frequent, gross changes in the subject would be interpreted by a listener as evidence of thought disturbance on the part of the speaker. Finally, Grice's *maxim of manner* requires the speaker to attempt to be clear. The speaker, by the very nature of the process of communication, is expected to try to convey her or his message in a way the listener can understand.

As well as ensuring an appropriate linguistic content, there are various other skills involved in participating in a conversation. In particular, participants work together to ensure smooth and efficient 'turn-taking'. Many of the cues involved here are cognitive, but are deployed without either of the conversationalists necessarily being aware of what they are doing. For instance, speakers who wish to signal that they have reached the end of their current utterance allow their voice to drop in pitch, and may look directly at their listener. At times, these skills may go wrong, resulting in less than perfect conversational switches. A study of the former Prime Minister, Margaret Thatcher, revealed that she tended to give her interviewers the impression that she had finished an utterance when she was still, in fact, in mid-speech. The result of this was that she was interrupted more often than any other politician (Beattie et al., 1982; see also box 4.2).

Learning to produce language: children's acquisition of language

Within their first few months of life children begin to understand a great deal that is said to them. However, they are usually around a year old before they start using single words to communicate. A further six months or so passes before they move on to two-word utterances. When they do so they usually position the words in the correct order for their linguistic community. As they move on to more complex sentences, they produce statements which have been described as telegraphic since they miss out the less important words, such as function words like 'a' and 'the'. So, the child might say *Put truck table* rather than *Put the truck on the table*. The speech of two and three year olds demonstrates how they are acquiring general rules for constructing speech, at the expense of falling foul of the irregularities in the language. They will speak of 'mouses', 'foots' and 'sheeps', apparently overgeneralizing the rules they have acquired (though see chapter 13 for an alternative suggestion of how well-formed linguistic utterances might be learned).

Later, as Chomsky (1970) showed, children whose speech is well formed may still be learning the complexities of unusual words. He found that given the sentence 'John promised Bill to leave' they think it is Bill who leaves because the sentence resembles the more common structure 'John (asked, told, requested) Bill to leave'.

By age six children have mastered most of their language, though they still go on learning. The knowledge they have acquired to date is procedural knowledge, knowing how to say what is correct and to identify what is not, but not being able to describe how the decisions are taken. They are linguistically skilled, but they are most assuredly not professional linguists nor psychologists. Children of this age, in the authors' experience, frequently (and proudly) state that they now know *how* to talk, unlike babies who, they claim, do not, but we have yet to come across a child who discusses in any meaningful and detailed sense the processes of word retrieval and language production! Their learning has been by listening to older children and adults, not by learning that language has various qualities. Formal instruction is rarely given and even more rarely seems to have any influence.

There seems to be something special about this learning of the first language. Chomsky (1965) has argued that there are language universals that limit the possible variations in grammars and that children have an inborn preparedness to set the parameters of their language community. For example, languages are normally left or right branching when analysed for their tree structures (see figure 4.1) and children may be born ready to identify which was the case in their linguistic community and to set their expectations accordingly. Children may also have innate expectations about other regularities of languages, such as that adjectives will be near the nouns they modify. Without some limiting of all the possible ways in which languages may be structured, it would be impossible for children to begin to cope with the complexity and variety of the language that they hear.

Disorders of language production (aphasias)

Following brain damage in the left cerebral hemisphere, language problems frequently arise. Studies of these *aphasias* (see Ellis and Young, 1988 for a review) reveal a wide range of specific problems among individual patients. Some, for example, have *syntactic deficits*. The patients know what they want to say but have difficulty constructing grammatical sentences. Saffran et al. (1980) give the example of a patient trying to describe a picture of a woman kissing a man: 'The kiss ... the lady kissed ... the lady is ... the lady and the man and the lady ... kissing.' The content words are available to such patients but are difficult to order properly and integrate with function words. Another form of aphasia is *anomia* where patients have problems with semantic descriptions. An example from Allport and Funnell (1981) of a patient trying to describe a kitchen scene includes: 'Well, it's a ... , it's a place, and it's a girl and a boy, and they've got obviously something which is made ... some ... some ... made ...' Cases of *neologistic jargonaphasia* involve patients having problems with lower-frequency words, often pronouncing them incorrectly. Ellis et al. (1983) give the example of the following mispronunciations for a patient they studied: 'skut' for *scout*, 'tet' for *tent*, 'cherching' for *chasing*. As we discuss in chapter 12 on neuropsychology, these deficits in language can provide one route to studying the intact language system. The very existence of these separate deficits supports the independent existence of the processes involving the syntax, semantics and phonological representation of language within the cognitive system.

Language Comprehension

The comprehension of spoken language can be thought of as involving various stages. The first stage is the perception of the changes in air pressure on the ears produced when a particular word is spoken. (Words must be identified out of the continuous changing pattern of air pressures that we call sound.) The next stage, known as parsing, attaches a particular meaning to the words heard so that a mental representation of the message conveyed by the words can be formed. Finally, we can think of the uses of these meanings in building up a representation of what is happening, and the utilization of the meanings derived. We will consider these stages in turn, though it is worth remarking that this is at least partly for convenience rather than because the three stages are entirely discrete. Rather, they tend to interact to improve the efficiency of the comprehension process.

A record of the patterns of air vibrations during speech, made by a speech spectrogram, shows a continuously varying pattern of stimulation at several frequencies and with varying intensity (see figure 4.2).

The first noticeable feature is the absence of any simple match between pauses in the sound input and the division into words. Studies using synthetic speech have shown that vowel sounds are heard when there are bursts of sound at two frequencies together, the particular combination of frequencies determining the vowel heard (see figure 4.2). The perception of consonants is more complicated and seems to depend upon the clues in the stimuli to the way in which the speaker's vocalizing was produced. For example, a rising or falling burst of energy revealed on a spectrogram may point to a particular frequency, although no sound actually was emitted at that frequency. However, that frequency (e.g. 1,800 cps for the sound /d/)

THIS IS A RECORDING

Figure 4.2   A speech spectrogram. Type B/68 sonagram © Kay Elemetrics Co., Pine Brook, NJ

is the key starting point for the vocal system when the consonant is spoken, and the listener is able to abstract this starting point.

The processes by which sound energy is processed as words are too complex and still too poorly understood to be discussed in detail here. A full discussion can be found in Garman (1990). However, it is worth pointing out that, like most perceptual processes, speech perception is not a step-by-step analysis of the input but the construction of a representation using all available evidence such as context, what has been said already etc. One demonstration of the importance of the surrounding context is that if single words are taken from a tape recording of people carrying out a normal conversation, about half of them will be unintelligible. Within the context, however, the listener has no problem and hears the words clearly. Thus, Lieberman (1963) found that when the words 'borrower' and 'lender' were taken separately from speakers saying 'Neither a borrower nor a lender be', 'borrower' was recognized only 45 per cent of the time, and 'lender' only 10 per cent!

That the processing system uses every source of evidence it can is illustrated by the McGurk illusion. McGurk and MacDonald (1976) made a video of someone saying 'ba–ba–ba . . .' repeatedly, but replaced the sound track with a voice saying 'ga–ga–ga'. Anyone watching the film then hears neither 'ba–ba . . .' nor 'ga–ga . . .', but 'da–da . . .'. The perceptual system compromises the acoustic signal and the visual one and the conscious perception of the sound is the intermediate one (in terms of how the articulation is produced) of 'da–da'.

A further source of information for the language processing system is the various linguistic regularities which have already been briefly mentioned. Within any language, there are regularities in the way in which words are uttered that determine the relationship between the concepts named by the words. For example, English speakers know that when they encounter a sentence in the form *noun1 verb noun2* it is whatever is named by noun1 that has the relationship defined by the verb to noun2. So, the sentence 'Mary kissed John' is interpreted as Mary being the person who kissed John, and not vice versa. On the other hand, a sentence in the form *noun1 was verbed by noun2* is understood as meaning that the action conveyed by the verb is relating noun2 to noun1. So, the sentence 'Mary was kissed by John' is interpreted as John who did the kissing. In the first case the agent of the action is Mary, in the second it is John. Most language utterances consist of stating relationships between agents and objects, and of building these up with further assertions of relationships. Each of these assertions forms a clause within the sentences, and each clause requires comprehending for the meaning of its words and the relationships between them that are being asserted. This need to comprehend the meaning of the clauses is reflected in several ways in sentence processing. If, for example, passages are shown to participants a few words at a time, they are comprehended better if the breaks match the clause boundaries rather than dividing up clauses (Graf and Torrey, 1966). Another example comes from Aaronson and Scarborough (1977) who required participants to read sentences that were shown one word at a time, the participants pressing a button to move on to the next word. They found that the longest pauses over the words came at the end of each phrase, when presumably, its meaning was being fully processed. Once the meaning has been deduced there is no further need for the retention of the exact words that had been heard. Jarvella (1971) had participants recall passages that had been read to them. Verbatim recall of the last sentence was good, with 80 per cent or better recall, but there was a very sharp drop in the recall of the words in the immediately preceding sentence, with recall poorer than 30 per cent. Clearly something happened in the processing of the preceding sentence that, once it was complete, led to a verbatim record no longer being retained.

While it is clear that the phrases and clauses of a sentence are an important division, it would be misleading to imply that understanding has to wait until the whole of a sentence has been heard or read. Full analysis has to wait, admittedly, but people seem to extract as much meaning as possible from the words as they go along, sometimes selecting a wrong interpretation and being led 'up the garden path' by the apparent meaning of what they read. For example, when most people read 'The face that he had loved was now gone for ever, he would never be able to climb its challenging gullies again', they have to reinterpret the meaning of face from that of a beloved human to that of a mountain. We do analyse the words we hear as we go along, selecting the most likely meanings in the context. Further support for this garden path theory comes from studies of eye movements during reading. Just and Carpenter (1980) showed that when a sentence is read we fixate longest on unfamiliar or surprising words. Not all words in a sentence are fixated, but words with most meaning – nouns and verbs – get fixations often for over 500 msec, while function words such as 'of' or 'the' may receive fixations of less than 100 msec. It is not that function words are not processed, clearly they must be for proper interpretation, but that they require less processing to extract their meaning.

There are always degrees of ambiguity in any statement that has to be parsed, but some are more ambiguous than others, with a permanent ambiguity once the statement is complete. For example, 'They are hunting lions' could mean that the lions are hunting or that someone is hunting lions (see box 5.1, chapter 5 for an investigation of the role of attention in decoding ambiguity). The correct interpretation is only possible in a fuller context. It seems likely that where a word has more than one meaning, these meanings are all briefly activated when the word is encountered, but only one is selected for retention in building the mental representation. The other meanings are probably inhibited by spreading activation from the concepts already activated. One method for looking at such activations is the lexical decision task. For example, Swinney (1979) required participants to indicate by a button press whether letter strings were words or non-words. If the participant had just listened to a passage about insects and the word 'bugs' was followed by 'ant' or 'spy' within 400 msec, then both *ant* and *spy* were judged as words quicker than control words, suggesting that both the insect and surveillance device meaning of 'bug' were momentarily activated. However, if the decision task was delayed for a mere 700 msec only the word 'ant' was judged more quickly, suggesting that the alternative meaning of 'bug' had been suppressed.

Conclusions

This chapter has covered many research areas of interest to psychologists, linguists and other cognitive scientists. Language is central to so much of human life that it is inevitably intertwined with almost all that we do. But at the same time, it is so familiar to us that we can overlook its complexity, and the challenge faced by those who try to unravel the parts that it plays in our lives. We hope that we have at least indicated some of the challenges facing researchers in this area. As we stated at the beginning of the chapter, language is a multi-levelled activity. It is also a cognitive function, which draws on a variety of other cognitive functions, such as memory and perception, and it is used for communicative purposes. These wider social and communicative aspects of language, however, lead beyond the boundaries of cognitive research, and beyond the scope of this book, into the province of social psychology. Readers interested in such aspects are referred to the Further Reading section below.

Further reading

A good survey of issues covered in this chapter, and the wider, communicative aspects of language, can be found in A.W. Ellis and G. Beattie 1986: *The Psychology of Language and Communication*. London: Weidenfeld and Nicolson. A thorough review of psycholinguistics can be found in A. Garnham 1985: *Psycholinguistics: Central Topics*. London: Methuen, and M. Halle 1990: Phonology. In D.N. Osherson and H. Laznik (eds), *An Invitation to Cognitive Science*, Vol. 1: *Language*. Cambridge, Mass: MIT Press, covers phonology very well. See also part V of P.N. Johnson-Laird 1993: *The Computer and the Mind*. London: Fontana, for a survey of speech, hearing, grammar and meaning, and a reasonably accessible introduction to Chomsky's work can be found in N. Chomsky 1972: *Language and Mind*. New York: Harcourt Brace Jovanovitch.

Accounts of children's language acquisition can be found in H.H. Clark and E.V. Clark 1977: *Psychology and Language*. New York: Harcourt Brace Jovanovitch, P. De Villiers and J. De Villiers 1979: *Early Language*. London: Fontana, F. Kessel (ed.) 1988: *The Development of Language and Language Researchers*. Hillsdale, NJ: Lawrence Erlbaum Associates and M. Harris 1992: *Language Experience and Early Language Development*. Hove: Lawrence Erlbaum Associates. Both adult and child language are also covered in M. Harris and M. Coltheart 1987: *Language Processing in Children and Adults*, London: Routledge and Kegan Paul.

Discussion points

1 How are language and thought related?
2 To what extent can models created by linguists serve as psychological theories of language?
3 How do we plan utterances?

4   Are children explicitly taught to speak? If not, how do they learn to do so? Do children acquire rules of language, are these rules innate, or do they speak without using rules?

5   What can the study of speech errors reveal about the structure of language?

Practical exercises

1   two or three participants to keep a diary of speech errors for a period of about ten days. How well do these fit into the categories discussed in the text? Do errors occur more when individuals are stressed or under pressure? How might you test this?

2   Either record, after obtaining permission, samples of speech in different social contexts, for example at the family dinner table, or in a more formal setting such as a meeting. Examine the speech samples you collect for pauses and hesitations. How do these differ in different situations? Or, examine pauses in speech samples obtained from participants who are asked to describe a picture or something from memory, such as the appearance of their house. Which task elicits more pausing: describing a percept, or describing a memory?

3   Make two tape recordings against background noise, one of complete sentences, the other of words from the same sentences in random order. Ask different participants to identify the word they hear. Is there a difference in participants' ability to perceive words on the two tapes? What does this tell us about speech perception?

Box 4.1
The primacy of perceptual categories

Labelling of the colour continuum affords a good test of the linguistic relativity hypothesis. Colour perception is a psychological response to a continuously changing physical dimension. If language strictly determines perception and then thought, it ought to be possible to divide up the visible spectrum, using language, in various ways. By contrast, if humans are predisposed to see certain colours as more central or prototypical than others, irrespective of the language they use, then these colours should be easier to label and remember. Rosch investigated this with the participation of members of the Dani tribe of New Guinea. The Dani are a traditional people who lack all of the basic colour terms, save 'mili' (roughly 'dark') and 'mola' (roughly 'light'). She attempted to teach members of the Dani to use colour categories to refer to either focal colours (colours which in the West would be considered to be good examples of reds, greens, blues and so on), or to use the same labels to refer to non-focal colours (indeterminate shades such as greeny-blue, or reddish-yellow). She hypothesized (i) that sets of colours in which focal colours were central to the category would be learned faster than other sets, (ii) that focal colours would be learned faster than non-focal, and (iii) that participants would define the colour category by means of a focal colour, even where focal colours were peripheral.

Sixty-eight Dani males screened for colour blindness participated in the experiment. Dani do not record or measure age, but participants were judged to be 12–15 years old. Colour category sets of three colours each were constructed using Munsell colour chips with a glossy finish. In some sets, focal colours were central, in other sets in between or 'internominal' colours were central, and in yet other sets focal colours were peripheral. This set structure was repeated eight times, so that the sets in

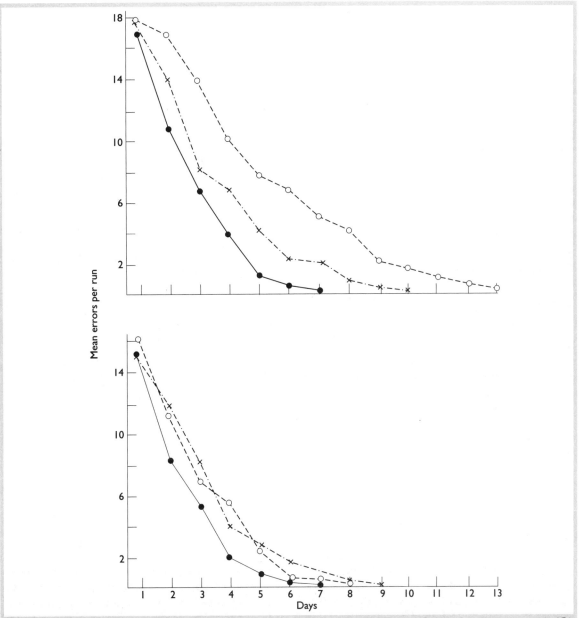

Box figure 4.1.1 The learning of focal and non-focal colours by the Dani: (●) focal colours central; (○) internominal colours central; (×) focal colours peripheral. (Based on figure 1, Rosch, 1973b)

which the focal colour was central were consistent with the eight basic colour terms: pink; red; yellow; orange; brown; green; blue; purple.

However, the crucial comparison in this experiment, and for simplicity the one reported here, is between set 1 in which focal colours were central and set 2 in which internominal colours were central. Rosch taught the Dani to associate arbitrary sib names (rather like clan names)

with the colours. She introduced the task as learning a new language for which the participant would be paid when the task was complete. At the beginning of each test session, colours were placed in random order in front of the participant, and he was told the 'name' of each which he repeated back. Then, the colour cards were shuffled, and shown one at a time to the participant who was required to name each colour. Correct responses were praised and incorrect responses were corrected. Five runs a day were presented on successive days until one perfect run through was achieved. After learning, the extent to which the colour concepts transferred was tested by asking participants to name colours which they had not been trained on, but which were close to the central colour of each category. Finally, participants were again shown all three colours from each category and asked to point to the most typical (best) colour in each set.

Sixty-three of the Dani managed to complete the task, and the learning transferred well. Turning first to the ease with which the two colour sets were learned, there were on average only 8.54 errors made by each participant during the learning of set 1, and 18.96 for set 2. On a t test this was significantly different ($p < 0.05$). Thus, sets in which focal colours were central were learned more easily (and more quickly) than sets in which internominal colours were central (see box figure 4.1.1).

Rosch then tested the second hypothesis, that individual focal colours would be learned faster than non-focal colours, even when focal colours were peripheral in the category. She performed an analysis of variance on the number of errors per stimulus. The focal vs. non-focal dimension was significant ($p < 0.01$), while the centrality or peripherality of the stimulus was non-significant. So focal colours were learned with fewer errors than non-focal, irrespective of the centrality of the colours in their sets.

Rosch was not able to support her third hypothesis, that focal colours would be seen as the best examples of each category. Her participants were unwilling to choose one colour chip as the most typical of a three-member category.

Generalizing from these data alone to conclude that perception always precedes language would be dangerous. The colour continuum could well be a special case of perception in which the neurophysiology of vision constrains the way in which certain colours are more easily perceived than others. However, we can have more confidence in the primacy of perceptual categories since, in a further experiment with the Dani, Rosch showed that good (Gestalt) shapes were more easily learned than poor shapes. In this further study her Dani participants showed none of the reluctance that they did with colour to pick the good forms as the 'best' members of their categories.

Based on material in E.H. Rosch 1973b: On the internal structure of perceptual and semantic categories. In T.E. Moore (ed.), *Cognitive Development and the Acquisition of Language*. London and New York: Academic Press.

Box 4.2
Conversational interruptions and turn-taking cues

For conversation to run smoothly, the interlocutors have to take turns to speak, and agree on the points when turns are to be taken. Some turn-taking signals are part of the message itself, such as the end of a sentence or phrase, some are non-verbal involving gestures, posture etc., but most are transmitted by the pitch, intensity and timing of the speech. For example, both pitch and loudness of the voice drop at the end of a speaker's turn. Beattie et al. argued that interruptions can occur when mistakes are made in the transmission and reception of these subtle signals, though also noted that interruptions can also occur because one participant is trying to dominate the conversation.

In their experiment, they studied turn-taking in an interview with a well-known figure, the former British Prime Minister, Margaret Thatcher. In previous work, Beattie and co-workers had noted that Mrs Thatcher was interrupted in her interviews more than any other politician; a pattern which was consistent across different interviewers. They hypothesized that this was because 'she displays turn-yielding cues at points where she has not completed her turn' (p. 745).

To test this idea Beattie et al. selected 40 extracts from an interview of Mrs Thatcher for *TV Eye* (ITV, April 1979) by Denis Tuohy and compared ten 'turn-final' utterances (utterances where a smooth speaker-switch took place), 20 turn-medial utterances (utterances from well within a turn) and ten turn-disputed utterances (utterances immediately before an interruption by Tuohy). The extracts were presented to participants as follows: video versions were shown to 79 participants, an audio version only was heard by 29 participants, vision only was presented to 14 participants and typescripts of the extracts were shown to 20 participants. For each extract, participants had to judge whether or not Mrs Thatcher's turn was complete or not.

Results

These can be seen in box table 4.2.1. An overall analysis of variance showed that there were significant effects on participants' judgements of both type of utterance (p < 0.0001) and mode of presentation (p < 0.0001), and the mode of presentation and type of utterance also interacted significantly. In the case of the video, vision-only and audio-only analysed separately, there were significant effects of type of utterance (p < 0.0001 for video and vision and p < 0.02 for audio-only) but in the case of the typescript presentation there was no effect (p = non-significant).

Using the Tukey HSD procedure, it was found that for all conditions except the typescript, turn-disputed utterance judged complete scores were significantly higher than turn-medial scores. Finally, completion scores for the video, vision-only and audio-only conditions correlated well (p < 0.0001 or better), but none of these conditions correlated well with the typescript version.

Having thus established that independent observers judged the turn-disputed utterances as significantly more likely to be a completion than the turn-medial utterances, Beattie et al. then proceeded to investigate the character of turn-disputed utterances in more detail. By analysing characteristics of the speech spectrogram, they were able to show that turn-disputed utterances were like turn-final utterances in some respects, but like turn-medial utterances in others. So, like turn-final utterances, turn-disputed utterances showed the same fast fall in pitch of speech at the end, and both were significantly faster than the turn-medial utterances (p < 0.02). On the other hand, the

depth of the fall in pitch was significantly greater in turn-final utterances than either of the other two (p < 0.01). On this dimension, turn-disputed and turn-medial utterances did not differ significantly.

The interesting situation arises, therefore, that there are conflicting cues in the speech of Mrs Thatcher's turn-disputed utterances. As Beattie et al. put it:

> This suggests that while the speaker is actually giving a number of cues to the end of her turn, the cue which she considers paramount may be different from the cue which her interlocutor considers paramount. If she considered that her most decisive cue to the end of her turn was letting her voice drop to around 140 Hz instead of keeping it no lower than 160 Hz, whereas her interlocutor considered that her most decisive cue was a rapidly executed final fall [in pitch] rather than a slow fall, their respective decisions as to whether or not she had finished her turn would differ in precisely those cases which were disputed in the present sample of utterances. (p. 747)

To provide further substantiating evidence for this conclusion, Beattie et al. then had one of the authors, who was trained in phonetic transcription, transcribe the phonetic quality of the 40 utterances without knowing their position in the sequence of turn-taking. When this was done, the turn-final and turn-disputed utterances resembled each other more closely than they did the turn-medial utterances.

It is worth remembering that the participants in the vision-only channel also rated turn-disputed utterances as more likely to be completions than turn-medial utterances. In this case it seems that gaze direction was the major cue. In 100 per cent of turn-final utterances Mrs Thatcher was looking directly at the interviewer at the end, compared with 80 per cent of turn-disputed utterances but only 55 per cent of turn-medial utterances.

Box table 4.2.1   Percentage of utterances judged complete

	Percentage of utterances judged complete			
	Video	Vision only	Audio only	Typescript
Turn-final	83.350	76.430	62.230	63.500
Turn-disputed	40.120	38.570	55.860	50.500
Turn-medial	23.045	18.570	32.405	58.250

Source: Based on figure 1, Beattie et al., 1982

This experiment was very carefully done and the results are very compelling. However, it should be noted that conversational interruptions may occur for social as well as cognitive reasons. As we indicated earlier, one or other party may wish to establish dominance and some control in the situation. Interviewers of Mrs Thatcher may have been particularly affected by this need, especially as other data by Beattie had already indicated that she invariably spoke longer when interviewed, compared with other leading contemporary politicians. This resulted in her interviews typically having fewer conversational switches overall!

Reference

Beattie, G.W. 1982: Turn-taking and interruption in political interviews: Margaret Thatcher and Jim Callaghan compared and contrasted. *Semiotica*, 39, 93–114.

Based on G.W. Beattie, A. Cutler and M. Pearson 1982: Why is Mrs Thatcher interrupted so often? *Nature*, 300, 744–7.

5 Attention

'Everyone', wrote William James back in 1890, 'knows what attention is. It is the taking possession by the mind, in clear and vivid form, of one out of what seem several simultaneously possible objects or trains of thought. Focalization, concentration, of consciousness are of its essence.' James was, of course, right in the sense that we all know what it is like to attend to one thing and to miss another. He was also right in his description of what is happening. At any time there are many different possible aspects of the world upon which we could be concentrating, from which one is selected. This then becomes the clear centre of our current conscious experience. However, James is misleading in one way. The very familiarity of attending to one thing rather than another is so common, so much a part of what it is like to be human, that it is quite hard to see the key psychological question of why we should function like this. Why is it that if two people start speaking to us at the same time, it is hard to understand what either of them say, and just about impossible to understand them both? Why is it so difficult to carry out two tasks at the same time unless one of them is very well practised to the point that it becomes automatic? Why cannot you hold a pen in either hand and write two essays at once? A silly question? But you can do some tasks simultaneously. You can walk and talk simultaneously. If you are an experienced car driver you can even drive and talk. Why can you do some things at the same time and not others? What has happened when a task like driving or walking has become automated?

It was misleading of William James to say that we all know what attention is; in fact, as we will show below, no one yet has a complete account of why we need to select between things to attend to, or how we distribute our attention between several tasks. It would be safer to say that no one knows what attention is. However, as with many areas of psychology, even if the full answers are still awaited, we can at least eliminate many common explanations of attention; we do have some idea of what it is not!

Selective Attention: Some Early Experiments

It is often useful when trying to understand the way psychological research has progressed to follow historically the questioning and the resulting experiments of researchers. Modern research on attention developed from a concentration upon a specific question. Cherry (1953) began it with what he called 'the cocktail party problem'. At a cocktail party, how do people follow the conversation that they are listening to and ignore the rest? How do we manage to stay listening to that voice and not be continuously distracted by all the other talk that is going on around? Variations on the cocktail party problem frequently occur in everyday life. In some, the resemblance to Cherry's situation is obvious. On a bus we converse with a fellow passenger and avoid being confused by other similar conversations. In the international money markets, dealers shout to each other amid a hubbub of noise. In other situations, however, the resemblance to the original cocktail party is less obvious. When we try hard to concentrate on a book despite a distracting TV programme, or try to focus our attention on an examination despite intruding worrying thoughts of failure, we are attempting to perform one task in the presence of competition.

Concentrating on one's thoughts or reading in a distracting environment are equally valid problems for attention researchers to study, but, to some extent, the cocktail party problem was used as a simpler starting point, and triggered a research theme that ran for many years. However, before considering what was found, it is worthwhile examining the basic assumptions of the cocktail party question. The question assumes that you cannot listen to many conversations at once, but does not ask why not. Rather, it takes the limitation for granted and then directs our attention to the problem of, given such a limitation, how we stick to following just one conversation. As such, the cocktail party question is about what is sometimes called *focused attention*, that is, how we manage to attend to one thing at the expense of other competing messages. Another approach is to study *divided attention*, that is, how we manage to do two or more things at once on some occasions with some tasks. How do skilled drivers talk and drive at the same time? How do we listen to and watch a film simultaneously? How do airline pilots monitor a vast amount of information from a variety of sources? Why are some task combinations possible, and some difficult, why are some combinations possible in some situations but not in others? These are all issues in the study of divided attention.

The distinction between focused and divided attention tends, in practice, to become blurred. One reason is that focused and divided attention are studied in the same way, by giving people two tasks to do and seeing how they get on. Also, as Hampson (1989) pointed out, it turns out that many, though not all, of the factors that improve selective attention also improve attention division or sharing. In the past 20 years or so, most interest has been in divided attention, in that, as will become apparent, people quickly gave up Cherry's original question about how people keep monitoring one conversation, and began asking why so little seemed to be remembered about the other conversations. The research focus also turned to consider the sorts of tasks that can be easily combined.

However, this is to anticipate what came later. In the early days of attention research, Cherry (1953) devised a clever experimental set-up to study the cocktail party problem. He had his participants sit with earphones on and presented a different tape recording to each ear. The participant's task was to repeat aloud what they heard in a specified ear. The task became known as dichotic listening, and the participant's activity as shadowing (see Neisser, 1976 for a discussion of a visual version of shadowing). In a variation of this task, known as the split-span technique, material was presented simultaneously in a synchronized way to each ear and the participant asked to report all that he or she heard (Broadbent, 1954).

The dichotic listening task is difficult, and involves great concentration. (You are invited to try an informal version of it in the practical exercises at the end of this chapter.) The spoken shadowed message lacks all the usual emotional emphasis as the speaker concentrates upon hearing the appropriate message, and struggles to keep up. It is also worth noting that, as Cherry discovered, the speaker may afterwards have a very poor idea of what the message that he has repeated was all about. However, Cherry's interest was in the extent to which his participants could report on the message that they had not been shadowing, the message to the 'rejected' ear.

Cherry found that when subjects were tested after shadowing, virtually no words from the rejected ear could be remembered. What was more, a change in the language spoken was not picked up. Speech played backwards was noticed as having 'something queer about it' by a few listeners, but was thought normal by most. What was identified was a change of voice from male to female and a steady tone replacing speech.

Cherry had introduced an attractive technique and, as often happens, the technique itself began to define the problems studied. What could and what could not be remembered from the rejected ear became as much of a research question as the original cocktail party problem and interest became more directed towards divided attention than towards the means by which focused attention was possible. This was understandable, since some surprising results soon emerged from shadowing experiments. For example, Moray (1959) showed that even when the same words were repeated 35 times to the rejected ear there was no retention of them. Many hundreds of experiments later the jury is still out on what precisely is picked up from unattended messages, as we shall see.

Models of Selective Attention

If we return to the cocktail party problem, the question it raised was: given that there is a limitation in how much can be processed by the cognitive system at any one time, how do we select the appropriate message and concentrate upon it, excluding all the other stimulation that is presented to our sense organs? Cherry's experiments suggested that people use physical differences between messages to do this. For example, they can easily distinguish a female from a male voice, or speech from music, or messages from the left from messages from the right, or high notes from low notes and so on. Using these data, and those from other experiments, psychologists began to try to work out how the cognitive system could possibly do all this. Their aim was to model the mechanisms of selective attention.

This was and remains an ambitious aim. Any model will need to account not only for the selection of some messages and the rejection of most of the information in the other messages, as Cherry's (1953) findings indicated, but also for the fact that we are able to switch to other messages if necessary. In the situations under which our perceptual systems evolved it would have been extremely maladaptive if we had no way of breaking our attention to one message when, for example, we heard the roar of a lion, or, less dramatically, our own name.

The first comprehensive model of selective attention was proposed by Broadbent (1958). In this model, information from the senses was first retained in a short-term store, from which it could be forwarded to a selective filter which let through only one message to the part of the system that was limited in its capacity (see figure 5.1). The limited capacity system was both the guts and the restriction in the system. It was the guts because it was this component which Broadbent saw as responsible for conducting a thorough analysis of the incoming information. It was a restriction because it was only capable of dealing with a certain amount of information at any one time. The selective filter was assumed to operate upon the

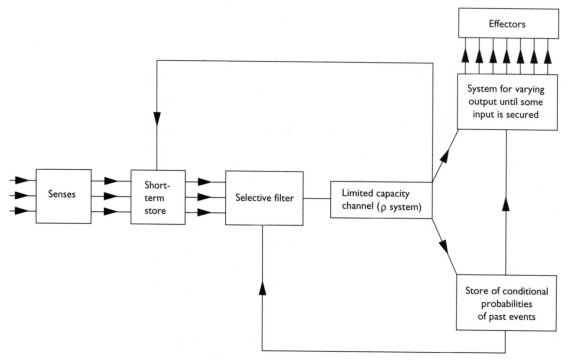

Figure 5.1   Broadbent's model of attention

physical feature of the input, following its superficial analysis, and to use such aspects as the intensity, pitch and spatial location of the input messages to enable one to be selected and another rejected.

Broadbent's model fitted well with the results of Cherry's experiments and, like all good models, it suggested suitable tests of its accuracy. It is a central aspect of the model that the filtering of the messages is based upon the physical aspect of the input. Not only does this follow from Cherry's data, but it makes sense if the reasons for the limitations in the processing capacity of the system lie in the higher cognitive processes, in the limited capacity system, needed to make sense of the messages. The earlier that the filter can operate upon the simpler sources of information, the more it can protect the higher, later stages of processing from overload. From Broadbent's model, Gray and Wedderburn (1960) predicted that if one syllable of a two-syllable word was presented to one ear, and the second to the other, then the shadower should say aloud garbled nonsense, since he or she would not know that the rest of the word was available in the other ear, for that message would have been filtered out on the basis of its physical features before the meaning of the words presented could be analysed.

This prediction, from Broadbent's model, was not supported by experimental data. Using a version of the split-span experiment in which words were decomposed into their component syllables and the syllables presented to alternate ears, Gray and Wedderburn discovered that the two syllables were combined, so that the second channel could not be being rejected purely on physical features of the input. Treisman (1960) also showed that, on some occasions, if the message being presented to the attended ear was switched in mid-sentence to the other ear, participants would follow the sentence using the words from the 'rejected' ear for a word or two to complete the meaning of the phrase that they were shadowing, before switching back to the new message in the correct ear. Again, this shows that the meaning of the input to the rejected ear must be processed on at least some occasions. The Broadbent model therefore clearly suggested tests of its adequacy, which in turn showed its weakness and led to its subsequent modification.

Gray and Wedderburn's and Treisman's findings showed that some processing of the meaning of the second channel must take place. Moray (1959) also demonstrated that on about 30 per cent of occasions people did hear their own names in the second channel. To cope with these data, Treisman (1964a) modified Broadbent's model. She assumed that, in addition to the analysis of the competing messages upon the basis of their physical properties, there are further tests of the sounds, syllable patterns and finally grammatical structure and meaning of the messages. There are, she suggested, really a hierarchy of tests, or a series of filters if you like, that messages pass through. If messages can be distinguished at an earlier stage, on the basis of clear physical differences, then they will be. If messages are physically indistinguishable, perhaps because they are both spoken by similar male voices, then other selective cues will be used. The tests may be pre-biased if particular words are expected because of the context, so that analysis is much simpler for those words that are expected. Where a message is rejected, on, say, the basis of its physical input, it is attenuated rather than rejected completely to prevent it interfering with the selected channel. The point of the attenuation is that, unlike the filtering of Broadbent's model, the possibility remains that the attenuated message can still be selected if the other tests are sufficiently biased in its favour, for example if the word is predicted by the context, or if the system is preset to pick up important cue words such as one's own name which is often used by others to attract our attention.

While Treisman merely modified Broadbent's model, the incompatible data that led her to the modification led Deutsch and Deutsch (1963) to reject the main point of Broadbent's analysis, that one message must be filtered out early to avoid overwhelming the perceptual processing system. The Deutsch and Deutsch model was itself modified by Norman (1968) and it is the resulting Deutsch–Norman model that we will discuss here.

The Deutsch–Norman model implies that the problem in focusing our attention is not to be found in the early stages of processing. In their model no signal is filtered out but all are processed to the point of activating their stored representations in memory, that is, whatever it is in the system that allows us to recognize a word and recall its meaning (cf. logogens in chapter 9). Previous processing will have been performed upon the rest of the message that has been presented before. From this, some events will have been established as pertinent, that is, likely to occur, and these will have also activated the memory representations. The point at which attention becomes selective is when one of these memory representations is selected for further processing. At any one time, only one can be selected, hence the attentional 'bottleneck'.

It may be worth emphasizing just how radical a model the Deutsch–Norman model is. It implies that all information which bombards us is processed, even if only some of it is noticed. The links between attention and conscious awareness are also strong in this model. It implies that we perceive everything we encounter, but are consciously aware only of some of it.

Despite their differences, however, there are clearly similarities between the Treisman and the Deutsch–Norman models. Both assume further processing beyond an initial physical analysis of the input as was the case in Broadbent's theory. The main difference between them is in the attenuation of the rejected channels proposed by the Treisman model, and the extensive processing of unattended material in the Deutsch–Norman. How can one decide between the two models? As before, it comes back to what can and cannot be shown to have been processed from the rejected channel. Treisman and Riley (1969) had participants shadow one of two lists of digits presented simultaneously to the two ears. Occasionally, letters took the place of numbers, and whenever they arose in either of the two ears, the participant was told to stop shadowing. On the Deutsch–Norman model, the prediction was that the performance for the two ears should not differ, since letters are equally pertinent, and for whichever channel they come in, the response is the same. On the Treisman model, however, the accuracy for the shadowed channel should be far greater, since the other channel will be being attenuated. The result was a detection rate of 76 per cent for the attended channel and 33 per cent for the unattended channel. Clearly, this favours the Treisman model. However, it is worth noting the relatively good performance for the unattended ear.

Results favouring the Deutsch–Norman model come from experiments such as that by MacKay (1973). While participants shadowed sentences such as 'They threw stones at the bank yesterday', either the word 'river' or 'money' was presented to the unattended ear. MacKay argued that this word might disambiguate the word 'bank'. Later, in a recognition test, the participants had to choose between the sentences:

(a) They threw stones toward the side of the river yesterday.

and

(b) They threw stones toward the savings and loan association yesterday.

In support of MacKay's hypothesis, participants tended to pick the meaning that went with the disambiguating word that they had received, despite their being unable to remember having heard the word. In this case the results suggest that the unattended message was processed, at least to the point of abstracting its meaning, and this would be predicted by the Deutsch–Norman model but fits less well with the Treisman model (see also box 5.1). However, later studies which have used a different methodology to test the extent of non-attended processing have found that the incidence of such processing often coincides with a momentary disruption or error in shadowing (e.g. Dawson and Schell, 1983), indicating that a momentary shift of attention might have occurred.

So is unattended material fully processed? As is often the case, what starts out as a simple question in psychology ends with a cautious series of more complicated answers. Certainly, people seem to be capable of picking up more information than Cherry's original experiments suggested. It may be that some limited processing of the meaning of unattended material is possible, though whether even this requires rapid attention switching remains to be seen. On present evidence, full analysis of unattended material seems unlikely. Perhaps this should not surprise us. After all, think what it would entail: we could listen to several messages at once with full comprehension though we would only be aware of dealing with one of them. It is difficult to see why the ability to focus our attention and be aware of one among several messages should ever have emerged in the first place, unless, as the Deutsch–Norman model would suggest, it is there to allow us to respond to one input rather than simply to perceive one.

Whatever the outcome of this debate, the fact that people may perceive material in the unattended channel (with or without momentary attention switching) does not, of course, imply that such material is remembered for any length of time. It is logically possible for participants in dichotic listening studies to process unattended material and, after the experiment, to be able to remember little or nothing of it, as Cherry's early experiments suggested, or to retain only a short-term memory for the material. Cherry always tested participants' memories for unattended material after they had finished shadowing, and so his experiments did not shed much light on this issue. MacKay's (1973) work, on the other hand, suggested that a superficial processing of unattended material did take place in short-term memory, but provided no evidence of long-term retention of unattended material. Later studies have examined this issue in more detail. Eich (1984) had participants shadow material at the same time that homophones (words with the same sound but different meaning, and in this case different spellings also, e.g. FARE vs. FAIR) were presented in the unattended ear. The homophones were presented with words designed to bias their interpretation (e.g. *taxi* – FARE). Tested after the experiment, participants were more likely to spell the homophones in line with the bias created in the experiment (F–A–R–E in this case) rather than to offer the more frequent spelling (F–A–I–R), despite being unable to recall explicitly any material from the unattended channel. Thus, despite poor or non-existent explicit memory for unattended material, implicit remembering cannot be ruled out (see chapter 2 for a further discussion of implicit memory).

Capacity Models of Attention ▶ ▶

So far, the models that we have discussed imply a series of stages of processing, starting with superficial, physical analysis and working 'upwards' towards the 'higher' cognitive analysis for meaning. However, these processes may be better thought of as an integrated mechanism with the high and low levels interacting and combining in the recognition of stimuli. In that case, the stage models may not be appropriate and we should look at the overall processing by the system. Kahneman (1973) argued that the problems in attending come about because we possess a limited amount of processing capacity that can be allocated to only so many tasks.

Kahneman's model is summarized in figure 5.2. For our purposes here, the key components in the figure are the available capacity and the allocation policy. Kahneman assumed that, like a computer, any cognitive activity requires a certain amount of available processing capacity. Some activities require far more capacity than others. Some, like walking or humming a well-known tune to yourself, require very little, and there is plenty of capacity left free for a concurrent task. On the other hand, if you were having to walk between landmines laid irregularly before you, or if you were trying to recall a song that you had heard only infrequently, far more capacity would be devoted to such tasks. In Kahneman's view, therefore, any task demands a particular amount of capacity, depending on its inherent difficulty and your degree of experience and practice in dealing with similar tasks. In the model, limited processing capacity is allocated between possible tasks. The allocation policy is determined by enduring dispositions, momentary intentions and your evaluation of the attentional demands. Enduring dispositions refer to rules for the allocation of capacity that are outside voluntary control. They will include allocating capacity to any novel stimulus, to a conversation in which your name is mentioned and so on. Momentary intentions are voluntary shifts in allocation, such as listening to the right-hand earphone in a dichotic listening experiment, or looking for a friend that you hope to meet. In evaluating demands there are usually rules to cope with overloads, such as, for example, if two activities demand more capacity than is available, one is selected and completed rather than both failing. Notice that in Kahneman's model the limitations on attention are non-specific. It is not an overload on the input that necessarily causes limitations on attention, but an inability to supply the necessary capacity for the task or tasks in question.

Kahneman's model can cope with the results of research on dichotic listening by assuming that shadowing one of two inputs is a task that requires almost all of the available resources. What is left is not sufficient to process the remaining channel more than superficially. It is, however, sufficient to identify some target letters in the Treisman and Riley (1969) experiment, though not as many as are found on the channel to which the main resources are allocated. Similarly, some processing of words in the

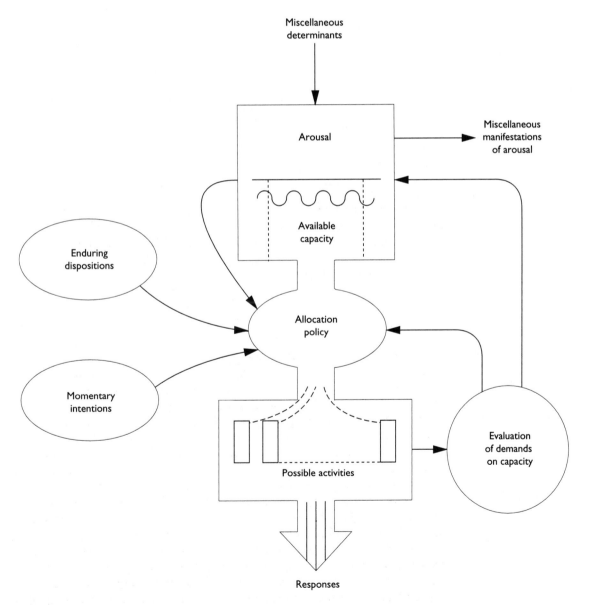

Figure 5.2 Kahneman's model of attention. (Based on figure 1–2, Kahneman, 1973)

rejected channel can take place, and account for the results of MacKay (1973).

One prediction of Kahneman's model is that as a skill develops and becomes more automated, it should be possible to devote less capacity to it and more should be free for other tasks (see chapter 6 for a more detailed discussion of skill and automaticity). It is interesting that Moray, who had tested his dichotic listening abilities for many years, became able to attend to the 'rejected' ear while shadowing well, suggesting that tasks which appear difficult if not impossible at first may well benefit from extensive practice. We will return later to consider the effect of practice in more detail.

Norman and Bobrow (1975) extended Kahneman's discussion of capacity limitations. They introduced the distinction between resource-limited and data-limited processes. A resource-limited process is one which is affected by a reduction in processing capacity or resources, for example the processing of the 'rejected' message in dichotic listening by most people except Moray! Data-limited processing, by contrast, is where the limitation comes from the information supplied from the external world, such as when a sound is masked by a great deal of noise, or is itself very quiet. In this situation, increasing the amount of resources will not of itself improve the situation; only clearer or louder stimuli will do that.

The distinction between the two sorts of process restrictions can help explain performance on attentional tasks. The detection of, say, a tone may require less resources than the identification of the meaning of a word. It may, therefore, be possible to have enough resources left over in a two-task situation such as dichotic listening to identify the occurrence of a tone but not of a word. The word identification is resource limited and perhaps data limited too if the word is not clearly recorded or is in a background of noise. The tone is only data limited and will be picked up unless the background noise is too strong. The problem with such an explanation, however, is that it is only after knowing how the experiment turned out that we can claim that one process is data limited and the other is resource limited. We distinguish between the processes on the basis of the results and then 'explain' the results using our distinction between the two sorts of processes, and a classic circular argument results. Perhaps because of this problem of circularity, Norman and Bobrow's distinction has not been widely applied, but the distinction is interesting nevertheless.

Let us consider further the predictions of a general capacity theory such as Kahneman's. One prediction will be that two tasks may interfere whether or not they are similar, doing so simply because they compete for the same general resource. A second prediction will be that normally the capacity required by a task will depend on that task and not upon the other tasks with which it competes, except where extra capacity is needed to somehow keep that task separate.

There is certainly evidence for the first prediction. For example, Welch (1898) found that the task of reading or of calculating was interfered with by requiring people to grip with their hands as hard as they could. The tasks could hardly be called similar. However, the second assumption fares less well. It is common for tasks which seem to share similar processes to cause more interference to one another than when the same tasks are paired with others. A good example is quoted by Eysenck and Keane (1990). They pointed out that Segal and Fusella (1970) looked at the ability of participants to detect a faint visual or auditory stimulus while forming visual or auditory images. Visual imaging reduced the accuracy of detecting visual stimuli, but had a much less severe effect on auditory ones, and auditory images impaired the detection of auditory stimuli, but had a lesser effect on visual ones. Here, clearly, the competing tasks cause problems not only because they are both sharing the same resources common to all cognitive activities, but also presumably because imaging and perceiving in one modality compete for the same cognitive processors.

Multichannel processing

Capacity models introduced a much needed element of flexibility that was lacking in the earlier structural models. Based essentially on an economic metaphor of supply and demand, they try to do justice to the idea that we can pay attention, often to more than one task at a time. Capacity models, therefore, account naturally for data from many dual-task experiments. However, capacity models of attention have been criticized for their vagueness by several psychologists, most notably by Allport (1980). The concept of a limited capacity is sufficiently vague to make it easy after many experiments to offer a capacity explanation for the results, but the notion has been noticeably ineffective in generating research to extend our understanding of cognitive processing. It is difficult to see how the neurology of the brain could produce a system of processing capacity that was completely open to use in any of the tasks that might be presented. In the early days of computers, when machines were limited in power, it was easy to see the problems that a limited capacity for processing could raise. But the development of computing has revealed problems that may be even more important limitations. For example, whatever the power of your computer, if you have not developed appropriate programs, or if you cannot retrieve the programs that you possess, then you can still not use the machine. It may be that many of the limitations upon divided attention are a mixture of competition for the means of processing or of inadequately learned skills to cope with the task. Let us consider this possibility.

The position adopted by Allport (1980) is that much of the limitation upon divided attention occurs because the tasks compete for the same processing mechanisms (see also Navon, 1985 for another non-capacity account of divided attention). For example, there may be one working memory that is capable of holding meanings of words as they are heard when someone speaks to us, up until the point at which enough of the sentence has been spoken for its meaning to be selected and synthesized from the many possibilities that the ambiguities of language and the multiple meanings of words provide. This may or may not be so, but let us use it as an example. If it is so, then any task which is added to another task for which the working memory is committed already cannot be properly carried out. We will, for example, have a job understanding what two people say to us at the same time. In a similar way, there may be other mechanisms at many points in the cognitive system that, if already committed for one task, will not be available for another. If this is the case, then problems over divided attention will occur when the tasks that someone tackles share such cognitive mechanisms. Equally difficult tasks that do not compete for the same mechanism may be possible to perform simultaneously.

Support for this view comes from experiments that have looked at performance on competing tasks in the same and in different modalities. So, for example, Allport et al. (1972) showed that while people cannot learn lists of words that are spoken to them during a simultaneous shadowing task, they can do reasonably well if the words are shown to them visually, so avoiding some of the competing verbal–auditory mechanisms. Single capacity models would have to predict similar performance here.

What is more, Allport et al. (1972) showed that if the material to be learned while shadowing was pictures, then 90 per cent of them were correctly remembered. It does appear here that it is not so much the fact that there were two competing tasks, but the exact natures of those tasks that decides whether or not both can be done at once. Treisman and Davies (1973) have similarly shown that when two tasks involve monitoring inputs using different sense modalities, performance is far higher than if the same modality is used.

Revised capacity models

Experiments such as these, and the critiques of Allport and others, led to a revision of the original capacity formulation. The 1980s witnessed a progressive splitting (and refining) of the concept of attentional capacity or resources. So, Friedman and Polson (1981) suggested that there were two, not one, resource pools (see also Dawson and Schell, 1983; Mathieson et al., 1990). The idea that there are two resource pools helps explain the otherwise puzzling results of experiments such as those of Segal and Fusella (1970). Suppose an experimenter has four tasks A, B, C and D and finds that tasks A and B interfere with each other, as do C and D, but that tasks A and C, and tasks B and D, are reasonably easy to perform together. One simple suggestion is that tasks A and B draw on a separate resource pool from C and D. So, in Segal and Fusella's experiment visual imagery creates more problems for visual than for auditory perception because visual imagery and visual perception draw on the same resource pool, whereas auditory imagery interferes more with auditory perception since they both depend on the second, non-visual resource pool. However, a shared resource pool is still needed to explain these results fully, since some small amount of conflict does arise between tasks from different modalities (visual and verbal). Very quickly the simplicity of the two resource pools has to be supplemented with a third!

Later it became apparent that this in turn was too simple. Different combinations of tasks produce different patterns of interference that are not easily explained with only two or three major resource pools. After an extensive review of the literature, Wickens (1984) showed that attentional conflict was apparent when tasks shared similar input modalities (vision, audition, tactile etc.), similar internal codes (visual, verbal etc.) and the same stages of processing (input, central, output), at which point, having constructed a system in which there are at least 12 pools of attentional resources, his model begins to look very like the suggestion made by Allport that there are simply many separate processing mechanisms for which tasks compete!

Doing Two Things Well ▶ ▶

So far, most of the examples of doing two things at once that we have discussed have involved very poor performance on the second task. In the last section we suggested that two things can be done at once if they do not compete for the same cognitive processors. One way that this can come about may be through sufficient practice at carrying out both of the tasks, especially both of them together. We will discuss the effects of practice on performance in chapter 6; here it is sufficient to point out that one of the effects of practice is to diminish the need for repeated conscious inter-vention in the carrying out of the task. When we first come to learn a skill like cycling we have to concentrate upon our balance and steering. After many hours of practice we can cycle without thinking about what we have to do and can think about other things, sing to ourselves and so on.

Several studies have shown that people who are highly skilled at one task can often combine it with another task, so long as the two tasks do not compete in their demands for the cognitive processors. For example, Allport et al. (1972) showed that expert pianists could play music that was shown to them while shadowing spoken speech. Shaffer (1975) studied an expert typist who could similarly type from sight and shadow speech. In these two cases it would appear that the skills of playing the piano and typing were so highly learned and free from competition over cognitive mechanisms that they could be carried out together. Novice typists or pianists find the tasks impossible.

Finally, Spelke et al. (1976) demonstrated the development of the skills of doing two tasks at once. They persuaded two students to spend five hours a week training at doing two tasks at once. To begin with they had to read short stories while writing down words that were dictated to them. At first this was very difficult and reading and writing suffered. However, after six weeks their students could read as rapidly, and with the same level of comprehension, as when reading without dictation. At this stage the students could remember virtually none of the words that they wrote to dictation. Spelke et al. now changed the task to require writing down the category to which the words belonged, so demanding far more processing of the meaning of the words. At first this proved very difficult, but eventually the students were able to do it without loss in their reading skill. Clearly, with considerable practice it is often possible to do together two things that at first seem impossible (see also box 5.2).

Conclusions

It should now be clear that William James was misleading when he said that we all know what attention is. Obviously, from our discussion above, attention is far from fully understood by psychologists. We know that it is not based upon a simple, early blocking of most of the information from the outside world, as Broadbent once proposed. It is obvious also that we often cannot do two things at once, and that there is a limitation somewhere. Perhaps the biggest mistake may be to assume that there is just one reason for the limitations to the number of tasks we can do at once. Within our cognitive system, there will be all sorts of restrictions on the amount of processing that can be carried out at the same time: there will be limits to the number of objects that we can classify, to the items that we can concurrently retrieve from memory, to the meanings that we can construct from the sentences we are hearing, to the schema that can be guiding our interpretations of what we are receiving and so on. Any or all of these and other limitations on processing capacity will prevent us doing more than a certain number of things at one time. The study of attention has been very useful in directing psychologists to think more carefully about just what is happening when we do tasks like shadowing and dichotic listening. The nature of attention has turned out to be more complicated than it appeared to William James, but the very recognition of the complexity is a step forward for psychology.

Further reading

The starting point for all modern theories of attention is D.E. Broadbent 1958: *Perception and Communication*. Oxford: Pergamon. The interest in capacity models dates from D. Kahneman 1973: *Attention and Effort*. Englewood Cliffs, NJ: Prentice-Hall. R. Parasuraman and D.R. Davies (eds) 1984: *Varieties of Attention*. Hillsdale, NJ: Lawrence Erlbaum Associates, contains several penetrating theoretical and empirical papers as does M.I. Posner and O.S.M. Marin (eds) 1985: *Attention and Performance XI*. Hillsdale, NJ: Lawrence Erlbaum Associates. The relation between attentional and motivational factors is discussed in M.W. Eysenck 1982: *Attention and Arousal: Cognition and Performance*. Berlin: Springer Verlag, and there is a useful general chapter on attention in M.W. Eysenck and M. Keane 1990: *Cognitive Psychology*. Hove: Lawrence Erlbaum Associates.

Discussion points

1   What is wrong with the filter theory of attention?
2   What happens to unattended messages? Are they ignored totally, processed then forgotten, or processed and remembered?
3   Discuss the strengths and weaknesses of capacity models of attention.
4   What types of tasks are easy to do together and what types are difficult to combine?

5   Is attention ever really divided or are processing systems and mechanisms shared?

Practical exercises

1   Unless you have quite sophisticated tape recording facilities, it is difficult to create materials which are precise and suitable for a full laboratory investigation of shadowing. However, you can investigate shadowing in a basic fashion with two ordinary tape recorders as follows. Record different messages on each tape and play them simultaneously to your participants, asking them to repeat aloud one message as it comes in, and to try to ignore the other. You can investigate various issues with this simple set-up. For example, what factors make shadowing difficult? Try comparing conditions in which both messages are presented in the same or different voices. Vary the spatial separation of the messages. Manipulate the content of the messages.

2   Using the above set-up you can also investigate what, if anything, is remembered from the unattended message. Try various forms of memory tests to investigate this. Perhaps merely asking participants what they remember is too insensitive. Do participants have any implicit memory for unattended material (see chapter 2 for a discussion of implicit memory)? Eich (1984) found that participants exposed to homophones (words with the same sound but two meanings) paired with a word to bias their meaning in

the unattended ear (e.g. taxi – FARE) were subsequently more likely to spell the word in line with the bias (in this case F–A–R–E rather than F–A–I–R). Can you replicate this effect? If you decide to attempt this experiment you will need to determine how likely each spelling of your homophones is with other participants who do not do the full experiment. Does the effect depend on the speed of shadowing? Eich used quite a slow rate.

If you find it difficult to replicate Eich's effect, can you think of any other implicit memory procedures which you could use to study the retention of unattended material?

3   Create various combinations of pairs of tasks to test participants' abilities to do two or more things at once. For instance, you can ask them to attempt to perform two verbal tasks at once (such as saying nursery rhymes while they attempt to read), a visual and a verbal task (saying nursery rhymes while they match shapes one after another) or two visual tasks (imagining a rotating wheel at a fun fair while matching shapes). Which combinations are easy and which are difficult? How do the task combinations improve as a result of practice? (See box 5.2 for some ideas of how to set up an experiment to test the effects of practice.)

Box 5.1
The extent of processing of unattended verbal material

MacKay tested whether material from the unattended channel in a dichotic listening experiment could still be processed. His general methodology was to have participants shadow (repeat out loud) a message played on the attended ear, or, in some conditions, to write out the message as it was being presented. Messages on the attended channel contained ambiguous sentences which could be potentially disambiguated by material presented

on the unattended channel. The extent to which attended material was affected by the unattended material was used as a measure of the processing of unattended material. Here we look at two of MacKay's experiments which investigate these phenomena.

In study 1, 26 sentences containing ambiguous words were presented in which the ambiguous word appeared towards the middle of the sentence. A typical ambiguous sentence was: 'They threw stones at the bank yesterday', in which the word 'bank' could be interpreted as referring to part of a river or a savings and loan institution. At the precise moment when the ambiguous word was presented to the attended ear, half the participants were presented with the word 'money' and the remainder were presented with the word 'river'. After hearing all 26 sentences, participants were then given a recognition test and asked to decide between two sentences and choose the one closest in meaning to the one they had heard. So, in this case, they would be asked to choose between 'They threw stones toward the side of the river yesterday' and 'They threw stones toward the savings and loan association yesterday'. In this way, MacKay was able to determine which meaning the participant had remembered without the participant knowing that the experiment had anything to do with ambiguity.

Two statistical techniques were used in the studies. First a measure known as 'Bias Shift' (BS) was computed by subtracting the initial bias in meaning (BI) from bias produced by the experiment (BE):

$$BS = BE - BI$$

To understand this consider the above sentence containing the ambiguous word 'bank'. Suppose that 45 per cent of people presented with this word spontaneously adopt the river interpretation for this sentence. The BI for this word before the experiment is thus 45 per cent. Now suppose that 75 per cent of participants adopt the river interpretation after being presented with the word RIVER in the unattended channel. The experimental bias, BE, is now 75 per cent and the overall bias shift is given by the formula: $BS = 75 - 45 = 30$ per cent.

MacKay's second measure employed a statistical technique known as the Chi-square test to see whether the number of participants adopting the predicted meaning was greater than that predicted by chance. Chi-square is used to check whether observed frequency data (in this case numbers of participants) are statistically greater than chance.

In study 1, a mean bias shift of 4.2 per cent was recorded in the direction of the predicted meaning, a shift which, though small, was statistically significant ($p < 0.03$ using a sign test). A reliable Chi-square statistic was also recorded, indicating that a greater number of participants had adopted the biased interpretation than could be predicted by chance alone. MacKay concluded from these data that unattended single words could be analysed at the meaning level.

In study 4, MacKay investigated whether more sophisticated forms of ambiguity could be resolved by unattended material consisting of phrases rather than words. This time ten sentences were used in the attended channel, such as 'They knew that flying planes could be dangerous' in which there is deeper ambiguity (planes which are flying vs. the flying of planes). These were accompanied by phrases in the unattended channel such as 'growling lions', intended to bias towards the planes which are flying interpretation. This time, no statistically reliable biases were discovered, nor were such biases found in further replications of this study.

Considering these and other studies together, MacKay argued that whereas the meaning of single words can be determined without attention in a temporary (short-term) memory, the more complex analysis of grammatical and meaningful groupings of words requires attention and the full resources of secondary (long-term) memory.

Intriguing though they are, there are some difficulties with MacKay's experiments. For a start, all the sentences were ambiguous, and this may have alerted participants to the purpose of the experiment. Somewhat more seriously, the unattended material was the only material presented in the unattended ear. It could thus have had an alerting effect. Thus, although checks were made by MacKay to see whether participants were aware of any of the unattended material, it is still possible that they may have switched attention briefly during the experiment to the disambiguating material. Later experimental work by Newstead and Denis (1979) indicates that this may have been the case, though there is evidence, from other sources, that unattended material can be processed.

Based on material in D.G. MacKay 1973: Aspects of the theory of comprehension, memory and attention. *Quarterly Journal of Experimental Psychology*, 25, 22–40.

Box 5.2
Sharing attention without alternation: the power of practice and attention as a skill

In their original study, Spelke et al. trained two participants to copy words from dictation at the same time as they read and understood stories. The authors interpreted their results as evidence in favour of attention as a skill which can be learned, rather than as capacity limitation. Their later study (reported here) was designed to test two alternative accounts of the earlier work: that participants were rapidly alternating between writing and listening, or that the writing task had become so well practised that it used up no attentional capacity at all.

Experiment I was designed to test the switching or time-sharing hypothesis. Participants were trained, while copying words from dictation, to read either easy, highly redundant prose from short stories or more difficult selections from an encyclopaedia. After training, participants were then tested on the non-trained material, from the encyclopaedia for the group trained on easy material, and on the easy material for the group trained on the encyclopaedia. The attention-switching hypothesis predicts that participants trained on the short stories should find the overall combined task of reading and writing easier to acquire in the first place, but that transferring to the encyclopaedia material should be more difficult.

The experiment lasted 14 weeks. Sessions lasted one hour per day, five days per week. After an initial three days of pre-testing of dictation and reading with comprehension skills, the training proper began. Four participants were trained on the short stories, from a variety of American and European writers, and four on material from the *Encyclopaedia Britannica*, though one of the latter group dropped out for personal reasons. There were three reading trials on each day. The first was a control trial when participants read without dictation. The other two were experimental trials which involved reading with dictation. Participants were tested together, and timed their own reading speeds with a stop watch. After each reading trial, they were given a comprehension test consisting of ten short questions based on significant points in the story. The training stage was terminated for each participant when he or she could read as well, and with roughly equal comprehension, on experimental and control trials, tested over a period of five days. To ensure that the effects of training were stable, for the following five days participants were tested with one experimental and one control trial on

the type of reading matter on which they had been trained. Finally, on each of the last five days, participants were tested with one experimental and one control trial on the non-trained reading matter. Participants from the short story group were tested on the encylopaedia material and vice versa.

All participants began by performing poorly on the dual task of reading and writing, but mastered it after practice. Participants trained on the short stories took, on average, around 38 days to acquire the skill, while those trained on the encyclopaedia took around 43, though, given the variation between participants, this difference was not statistically significant. This indicated that the short story material was only marginally easier to deal with than the encyclopaedia, and suggested that attention switching was not taking place.

This interpretation was further supported by the crucial data from the final test phase. As can be seen from box table 5.2.1, experimental reading speeds and comprehension scores are not obviously worse in the group who were trained on short stories and switched to the encyclopaedia (the S–E group), compared with those who first trained on encylopaedia material and were tested on short stories (the E–S group). In all, six of the seven participants showed successful transfer to untaught material. Interestingly, only one participant, Mary, was statistically worse ($p < 0.05$) on her final experimental (with dictation) tests of reading speed on encyclopaedic material (245 words per minute), compared with her control speed. The authors conclude that Mary, the fastest reader in the group, may well have used a switching strategy when learning on the short stories, and then found it difficult to transfer to the harder material.

Thus, although attention switching appeared not to occur in general in this experiment, it cannot be ruled out absolutely since at least one participant may have been using this strategy. As with the earlier experiment, the small number of participants used makes any definitive interpretation difficult, and from the authors' discussion, a wide variety of learning methods were apparent. Also, it could be that participants with the determination to participate in an experiment for 14 weeks have various non-cognitive, motivational traits which aid their concentration on this task.

Box table 5.2.1   Performance (reading speeds and comprehension scores) following transfer to untrained material

	Reading speed		Comprehension	
	Experiment	Control	Experiment	Control
S–E Group				
Don	334	311	67	68
Conrad	243	228	51	41
Mary	245	305	59	62
Jeff	237	227	57	45
E–S Group				
Debbie	280	293	83	82
Paul	327	293	54	48
Tom	305	287	58	51

Source: Adapted from table 2, Hirst et al., 1980

Experiment 2 was designed to check whether the writing task had become so automatic (was simple and routine) that it put little or no strain on the attentional system. In this experiment, two participants were trained to copy sentences as well as single words while reading. On subsequent testing, it appeared that they understood the meaning of the sentences they had copied. They made fewer copying errors with sentences than with unrelated words, they recalled sentences better than words, and they were able to join together information from a set of sentences. The authors conclude that such high levels of semantic processing of the dictation task would be difficult to perform in an automatic fashion.

The results from experiment 2 are impressive, but the reservations concerning participants apply even more acutely than with experiment 1. One of the participants was Mary, the fast reader from experiment 1, while the other, Arlene, had previously worked as a secretary and reported being able to type from copy while talking on the telephone. The extent to which such skills are shared by the population at large is unknown. A third participant, Tom, made little or no progress at the task, and resigned from the experiment!

Based on W. Hirst, E.S. Spelke, C.C. Reaves, G. Caharack and U. Neisser 1980: Dividing attention without alternation or automaticity. *Journal of Experimental Psychology: General*, 109, 98–117.

6   **Skills**

You are a highly skilled person. You normally take these skills for granted but they are worth stopping and valuing occasionally because they represent the end result of years of practice. You can fluently speak at least one language, and read and write it too. Perhaps you are good at solving crosswords. You can probably ride a bicycle, perhaps drive a car and almost certainly kick or catch a ball. You can walk and run over bumpy ground, dodging protruding branches and puddles, yet it takes a child a year to reach the stage of stumbling around, and few three year old children can catch a ball. Learning to speak English fluently took you many years, and anyone who has helped to teach children to read and write will confirm how long it takes.

The difficulty of such skills, the amount of learning that underlies them, is emphasized to us when we tackle the learning of new skills – when first we learn to drive, to type, to speak a foreign language or play a musical instrument or learn a new sport. When we begin it often seems almost impossible to believe that with practice we will eventually be able to carry out skills fluently and effortlessly.

In this chapter we will discuss the acquisition of skills and say a little about how people skilled in certain ways perform some tasks differently from novices. Variation in skill is one of the main differences between individuals – between adults and children and between adults themselves. It influences how each perceives their world and how they behave.

Sensory–motor and Cognitive Skills

In the introduction to the chapter we included as example of skills the driving of a car and the solving of crosswords. Both are skills that improve with learning. However, the former is mainly concerned with the control of movement; specifically your movements that control the car itself. Solving crosswords, on the other hand, is not about movement but about finding the correct word from your semantic memory when the cues to its retrieval are complex and based upon special convention. Car driving is an example of a sensory–motor skill in that what is involved is the use of sensory information in the selection and modification of the movements that you make. Crossword solution is a cognitive skill that is not dependent upon learning how to use sensory input to continuously modify movement. Instead, it is dependent on how to carry out a cognitive task. The distinction is important since not all conclusions that may be reached about one type of skill will necessarily apply to the other. Nevertheless, there do seem to be many similarities in the processes that underlie both types of skill acquisition. For most of the chapter we will be able to ignore the distinction, at least as far as we are able to discuss skilled performance in the present book. At a more detailed level, a careful particular analysis of any skill that is being acquired will be necessary to fully understand its complexities and its control.

Declarative and Procedural Knowledge ▶ ▶ ▶

For many skills, it is easy to explain what must be done at a gross level; the problem is in the doing. To ride a bicycle, all that you have to do is to sit on the saddle, push around the pedals with your feet and turn the front wheel with the handlebars to steer. Simple. Well, perhaps not when you tried it for the first time. Riding a bicycle actually depends on knowing how to do many things that are easy to take for granted: knowing how to balance, knowing how to compensate for turns in the wheel when steering or when looking behind for traffic, knowing how much effort to put into each foot while turning the pedals. The example of riding a bicycle illustrates the differences between declarative (or propositional) and procedural knowledge (e.g. Anderson, 1985). 'Declarative knowledge' is knowing facts, knowing *that* something is the case; 'procedural knowledge' is knowing *how* to do something – perhaps with no conscious ability to describe how it is done. Describing to someone what riding a bicycle entails, in declarative terms, is not sufficient for them to acquire the procedural knowledge needed to ride one. On the other hand, possessing procedural knowledge of how to ride a bicycle does not equip you with declarative knowledge. Most of us who can ride bicyles well do not possess the declarative knowledge that we are actually turning the handlebars so that the curvature of the bicycle's path is proportional to the angle of its imbalance divided by the square of its speed (Polanyi, 1964).

The skill acquisition with which we will be particularly concerned in this chapter is the study of the acquiring of procedural knowledge. One of the problems daily facing driving instructors and sports coaches is (as with riding bicycles) the difficulty of translating what is often a simple amount of declarative knowledge into procedures that you can actually carry out. Their main tool is practice, but practice with as much guidance as possible.

Practice

Practice does not make perfect but it certainly goes on making improvements for a long time. Crossman (1959) studied the speed of industrial cigar making using a hand-operated machine. He found that the speed of the operators continued to improve with their years of experience for up to four years, when the speed of operation of the machine itself was setting a limit to further improvement. Even after making several million cigars the machine operators were probably still gradually improving. However, the amount of improvement was very small. In general, improvement with practice is most rapid at first, and decreases with further experience.

The amount of improvement with practice is normally found to fit a simple relationship: the logarithm of the time taken to carry out the skill decreases with the logarithm of the amount of practice. This relationship, known as the power law or log–log linear law of practice, has been found for many different types of tasks, including perceptual tasks like visual search, perceptual motor skills and verbal and problem-solving tasks (Newell and Rosenbloom, 1981). For example, Seibel (1963) trained three participants to type on a ten-finger keyboard in which any of 1,023 combinations of the keys could be required to be pressed. As figure 6.1 shows, the learning curve was a simple log–log straight line for the first 30,000 trials and then the slope changed, though again it seems to be a straight line function.

Why does the power law occur? What is happening with practice? In fact, there are various stages in acquiring a cognitive skill described by Fitts

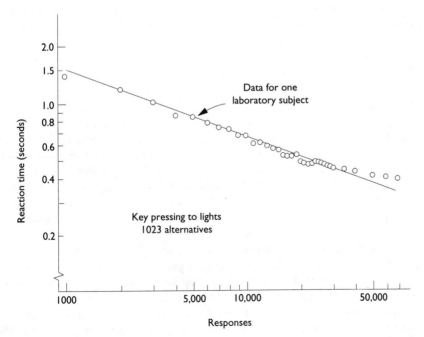

Figure 6.1 The effects of practice. Improvement in typing skill shows the log–log law. (Based on Seibel, 1963)

(1964) and by Anderson (1985), the first of which precedes the practice phase, and we will discuss these stages in the next section. However, other psychologists have emphasized the changes that underlie practice itself. Crossman (1959), for example, assumed that people become more efficient in selecting methods of performing. One of the features of skilled performance of a motor skill is its economy of effort. Also, Kamon and Gormley (1968) found that trained gymnasts have shorter bursts of muscle activity than novices; their movements are more organized sequentially and are better coordinated. The expert gymnast requires less expenditure of muscle effort than do novices. This all suggests that at least part of the improvement with practice is the result of selecting the best ways of performing.

While the power law of practice is a widespread finding, certain other conditions are necessary for improvement to occur. Improvement with practice requires maintaining the participant's motivation, and providing knowledge of the results that he or she has obtained (Fitts and Posner, 1967).

A further improvement in performance, even when the best ways of acting have been discovered, comes from the 'tuning' of the system. Repeated practice of the same action (which as Gallistel (1980) has pointed out is the way babies spend a great amount of their time) allows the neural circuitry to be adjusted so that the parameters that need to be set for controlling movement can be tuned for the best performance. We will return to how actions are modified by feedback later in the chapter.

Another reason for improvement with practice may be, as Newell and Rosenbloom (1981) suggest, that people form and store chunks, or organized collections, of the elements involved in the task. The idea of chunks of information was suggested by Miller (1956). He was particularly interested in short-term memory, and noted that the memory span (the amount that can be recalled without error after one presentation) seemed to be roughly constant at seven items, but that this consistency was often obscured because the size of the items could vary. So, we may have a memory span for only seven letters if those letters do not form a word. However, we may remember up to seven words, and consequently far more letters. The words form a meaningful chunk that can stand on its own in the memory and be 'unpacked' later if necessary into its component letters. The learning of many skills may involve the acquisition of the appropriate, higher-level chunks that can simplify not only memory but other parts of the control of the skill. Thus, as skills at chess develop, combinations of pieces are perceived as dynamic wholes, defending, threatening and so on. One of the earliest of such combinations, the arrangement of the pawns, king and rook after castling, is just a simple example.

The development of higher-level chunks, and the consequent changes in the whole experience of the developing expert, was one of the findings of a classic study of Morse code operators by Bryan and Harter (1899). They studied two employees in a railroad telegraphic office. As the operators became more proficient, Bryan and Harter noted major changes in their perceptual organization. At the start operators had to interpret the incoming Morse code as forming single letters. However, after considerable practice they could 'hear' the Morse in terms of words or even phrases. The same seemed to be true when the operators transmitted Morse. They began by spelling out each word, translating each letter into its Morse equivalent. Much later they were transmitting by constructing the key presses for whole words at one time.

Learning Morse code may seem to be a rarefied skill, but all of us have been through a similar training when learning to write. To begin with we had to spell out every word, and the process was slow and laborious. After plenty of practice, as adults we can scribble away with very little thought about what letter comes next, except when we encounter a word that we have not properly learned how to spell. If you have learned to type proficiently, you will have been through the same experience again. One of the main results of practice seems to be the development of the organization of the elements of the skill into chunks or similar organized wholes that can be dealt with as separate units in their own right. We will return to this when we consider the planning and control of actions.

Management of practice

Given that practice is so important to the development of a skill, the question arises as to whether all practice is equally effective, and how to organize practice to maximize learning.

One major concern in this area has been to compare massed and spaced practice – that is, practice with all trials immediately following one another, or with intervals in between. As a general rule, spaced practice is better, though this must obviously be qualified by limitations on the length of the intervals. One example of the relative efficiency of spaced practice is a study by Keller during the Second World War (reported by Woodworth and Schlosberg, 1954) who found that the learning of Morse code was just as good by participants who had four hours' practice a day for five weeks as for those having seven hours each day. The extra three hours every day were ineffective and, no doubt, very tedious. After a further three weeks the participants with the four hours a day practice were actually considerably better than those who had had seven hours a day.

Somewhat more recently, Baddeley and Longman (1978) describe a study of training schedules for teaching postmen to touch-type, following the introduction of letter-sorting machines. The postmen received either one- or two-hour training sessions either once or twice a day. In terms of hours spent in training, the distributed practice of a one-hour session once a day was easily the most effective. The group having two hours' practice in two sessions a day took 80 hours to reach the proficiency which the one hour a day participants had reached after 52 hours! Spaced practice also shows up well in other situations where the spacing is a matter of seconds or minutes rather than days. For example, people take fewer trials to learn to keep a pointer on the small rotating target of a pursuit rotor (a rotating disc) if the trials are spaced rather than following in quick succession (Woodworth, 1938). Similarly, the learning of lists of words is better with a pause of a couple of minutes between tests of the list than just a few seconds' rest.

All the evidence for spaced practice must be balanced against the practicalities of the learning situation. On some occasions it is easy to use the intervening time for other useful study, but at other times it is not. Baddeley and Longman (1978) note that the postmen from the group receiving only one hour's training each day became dissatisfied at having to spend 12 weeks acquiring a skill that others were learning in four weeks. An optimal training schedule obviously must balance the best learning conditions with what suits the learners and their trainers.

Another aspect of practice is whether to train on the entire skilled sequence as a whole, or to break it up into components to be practised separately. This question of whole versus part learning will obviously not have one simple answer, since the relative advantages and problems of whole and part learning will vary from task to task. Part learning reduces the load on memory and can prevent the swamping of the learner by too much to be controlled. On the other hand, whole learning allows skills appropriate to the integration of the final skill to develop, while there is a danger that part learning may encourage strategies that are not the best when the whole task is tackled.

Much of education involves decomposing the complex skills that are an eventual aim of education into their component skills and teaching these prerequisites first. Gagne (1973) has argued that successful education depends upon identifying the correct hierarchy of subskills in such a part learning approach.

Overlearning

Overlearning is the term for continuing practice beyond the point where the skill appears to be adequately acquired. It should already be clear from our discussion of the power law of practice that improvement can continue for a long time. The value of such extra practice is not so obvious to the learner when the criterion for success is simply success or failure. Someone trying to memorize a poem or a set of facts could feel that they had completed the task once they had successfully recalled the material without making an error. However, as the power law would suggest, further practice can still improve performance, in particular in making it less likely that the information will be subsequently forgotten. An example of an early experiment on the overlearning of word lists is that by Krueger (1929). He had his participant learn lists of twelve nouns, presented at a rate of two seconds per word. In some cases, learning stopped when the participants could correctly anticipate every word that was to come next in the list. In other cases, learning continued for 50 or 100 per cent as long again as the time to reach the correct recall of the list. When tested over periods of up to 28 days, the amount of overlearning was strongly related to recall, so that, for example, after a gap of two days, the group who experienced 100 per cent overlearning were able to recall about two and a half times as much as the group who did not overlearn. After 28 days the recall of all the groups was virtually zero, but when they relearned the lists, the groups who had overlearned the lists showed a 20 per cent or more saving in time to relearn, compared with virtually no savings for the participants with no overlearning.

Bahrick (1984a) has examined the retention of highly overlearned information such as the basics of a foreign language studied throughout school or the faces and names of school classmates. He found that such knowledge was particularly resistant to forgetting and could often be recalled 25 or 50 years later. While normally acquired information is steadily lost over time, that which has been highly overlearned may be virtually permanently retained.

Stages of Skill Acquisition

We stated earlier that the practice phase is only part of the entire process of skill acquisition. In fact, three major stages of skill development have been identified (Fitts, 1964). In the first, or 'cognitive phase', success depends upon understanding what is involved. The learner needs to attend consciously to the cues from the environment and the movements to be made. Instructions and demonstrations are at their most effective at this stage. For example, a driving instructor will first explain the rudiments of controlling the car to the learner and, during the first few lessons, will continue to talk the learner through the drive. At this point, the learner will be concentrating very hard, and the experience of the task from his or her point of view is one of considerable effort and memory load. The learner finds it hard to do several new actions simultaneously and has no spare capacity for other things, such as conversation. In this initial phase, the individual is learning the declarative knowledge that is necessary for the skill; he or she is memorizing *what* to do as a necessary precursor for developing the procedural skills for actually implementing the knowledge smoothly. Coping with this stage dominates consciousness, and people can give detailed verbal reports of their decision processes and strategies for carrying out the tasks. However, the learner may have little memory of other events that happened at the same time. This is a time when considerable demands seem to be placed upon whatever part of the cognitive system it may be which has limits to its processing capacity (cf. chapter 5), and learners frequently express surprise at the demands of the task and whether it is possible at all!

In the next stage, which Fitts called the 'associative phase', component parts of the skill are tried out and a set of appropriate actions for the skill assembled. In the cognitive stage, there was a selection from the available pool of already learned skills of those that seemed appropriate to the new activity. So, changing gear in a car or controlling the foot-pedals draws upon the already well-developed skills for moving our hands and feet. What must be learned next is the exact movements of the hands or feet at the appropriate time and in the right sequence. This begins to develop in the associative phase. Fitts and Posner (1967) described behaviour at the cognitive phase as 'truly a patchwork of old habits ready to be put together into new patterns and supplemented by a few new habits' (p. 12). This putting together into new patterns takes place in the associative stage. Old habits are tried out and new patterns begin to emerge. Errors are gradually eliminated. Obviously, the time that this takes depends upon the task and the student. For difficult skills, like learning Morse code, ten hours of practice are required to eliminate most errors (Woodworth and Schlosberg, 1954). Similarly, fatal errors are sufficiently rare for instructors often to allow trainee pilots to make their first solo flight after only about ten hours' training (Fitts and Posner, 1967).

It is at this associative phase that much of the benefits of practice, discussed earlier, will be taking place: chunking of information, the integration of the components of the skill and their appropriate tuning to the specific task.

In the third stage, which Fitts calls the 'autonomous phase', the component parts of the skill become increasingly automatic. People are no longer able to say how or why they do what they do, and too much thought about the way to carry out the skill may even be detrimental. For example, you will be unable to say how you control your hand while writing. A skilled typist has often forgotten the layout of the typewriter keys and is no better than a complete novice in looking for a single letter, yet he or she could type a sentence using all the alphabet with only 60 msec between striking each letter's key. Skills that are so highly practised seem to demand very much less conscious intervention. They seem to be carried on without conscious awareness at all, in that afterwards the person may have no recollection of them. Drivers may remember very little of an uneventful drive to work, even though they controlled the car skilfully, and far better than they did in the early days of learning to drive, when just driving safely occupied all their attention. Skills that have become automated can often be carried out at the same time as other activities, so long as none of them is competing for the same input or output mechanisms (see chapter 5).

At times the smooth performance of a seemingly well-automated skill can break down, especially if the performer is under pressure. One reason for this is that the skilled person may revert to an inappropriate, earlier phase of skill learning and begin to use his or her explicit, declarative knowledge rather than performing automatically. Masters (1992) provides a good example of this in an experiment in which individuals given practice in golf putting are either encouraged in, or actively discouraged from, building up a rich declarative knowledge base about the skill (see box 6.1). When mildly stressed by the suggestion that level of performance will determine monetary rewards for participation, those with more explicit knowledge about the skill performed worse than those with less knowledge!

It is important to recognize that to describe a skill as automated is not to explain how it is carried out. That remains to be investigated, and the very opaqueness to consciousness of a skill often makes the unravelling of its processes more difficult. Nor does the disappearance of the subjective experience of mental effort from an automated task mean that the task itself does not involve complex control and considerable processing. Consciousness may have been freed for other purposes, but an automated skill is a complex psychological process which remains to be understood.

Controlled and Automatic Processing

The emergence of automatic processing in one particular type of task has been studied by Schneider and Shiffrin (1977). Their interest was in the conditions that allow automatic processing to develop. They distinguished between 'controlled processes', which are those in command of skilled activity in the cognitive phase of Fitt's three stages, and 'automatic processes', which are those used in the third, automatic stage. Control processes are limited in capacity so that only a limited amount of such processes can take place at one time. They also require conscious attention. However, they have the strength of flexibility, being usable in changed circumstances. Conversely, automatic processes are freer from capacity limitations and the need for attention, but once learned they are very difficult to modify.

The experimental procedure used by Schneider and Shiffrin was to have the participants memorize a set of items (e.g. one or more letters) and then to show displays of one to four letters to which the participants had to respond as rapidly as possible, indicating whether any of the shown items were in the set that the participant had memorized. Sometimes distractor items (e.g. digits instead of letters) would be included in the displays.

The most interesting manipulation by Schneider and Shiffrin during their experiments was of the target items that the participants had to memorize. These could be chosen consistently from one class of items or could vary between classes. In the 'consistent condition' the target items might be always consonants while the distractor items would be always digits. In the 'varied condition' the targets would be a mixture of consonants and digits, and so would the distractors.

Schneider and Shiffrin gave their participants several hours of practice at these tasks. At the end of this practice, the consistent and varied conditions were producing marked differences in the time taken to analyse the displays for the target items. In the consistent condition, participants were able to report equally quickly on the presence or absence of one or four memorized targets in displays of one, two or four items. The number of memorized items, and the number of items to be examined, had no effect on the processing time. All targets could be searched for and all items displayed could be examined 'in parallel', that is, at the same time. On the other hand, the varying of the type of target and its sharing the same class as distractor items meant that in the varied condition the more targets to be searched, and the more items in the array to be analysed, the longer the participants took. More errors were also made in this varied condition. According to Schneider and Shiffrin, the difference between the conditions occurs because in the consistent condition the participants can learn which are the pool of items that can be the memory set items, so that any of them can trigger an automatic response. However, in the varied condition there is no consistent connection between any items or type of item and the response, so no learning of an automatic response is possible.

In another experiment, Shiffrin and Schneider (1977) consistently used the consonants from B to L as one set (e.g. always targets) and the consonants from Q to Z as the other set (e.g. always distractors). After 2,100 trials the participants appeared to identify the targets automatically. Shiffrin and Schneider then went on to show a problem with automatic processing – its resistance to change. They now reversed the conditions so those letters that had been targets in the first part of the experiment now became distractors and vice versa. They found that this markedly impaired performance. It now took their participants nearly 1,000 trials to reach the level that they had been at right at the very start of the experiment.

Feature integration theory

Although Shiffrin and Schneider provide good evidence of the development of automaticity, it is still not exactly clear what counts as an automatic process, or, more precisely, at what point automatic responding sets in. Thus, while their participants in the consistent mapping conditions tend, following practice, to be less and less affected by the number of distractors, it is difficult to determine the point at which the shift occurs to processing completely free from capacity limits. A theory proposed by Treisman and her associates deals more directly with this problem of pinning down automatic processes (e.g. Treisman and Gelade, 1980; Treisman, 1988). Treisman and Gelade (1980) argued that perception involves two major stages. First, incoming stimuli are analysed into a number of distinct perceptual features. So, when you look around, your perceptual system breaks down the visual world into different features or dimensions of shape, size, colour and so on. In the second stage, these features are then combined or integrated to provide you with coherent percepts of your surroundings. What you actually finally consciously see, the products of the second stage of perception, are objects of a certain size, shape, colour and orientation at particular locations. The initial feature detection stage occurs rapidly and without attention, since the perceptual system, Treisman claims, is capable of simultaneously analysing stimuli along a whole series of dimensions at once. Feature analysis, in other words, is fully automatic. Integrating features, on the other hand, is rather different. Here, the system must combine sets of features, in one location at a time, so that a series of separate conjoinings of features are needed to perceive a scene made up of several separate objects. This second, feature integration stage does consume attention; attention which, as Treisman suggests, is needed to 'glue' the separate features together.

There is now good evidence to support the feature integration theory, and a typical experiment involves visually searching for targets among a set of distractors, as when looking for a red letter among a set of green letters. So, Treisman and Gelade (1980) have shown that when people are searching for targets which differ from distractors by only a single perceptual feature, such as looking for a red letter 'T' among green 'T's, then they can search just as fast when there are several as when there are only a few distractors. On the other hand, whenever people are searching for targets that involve particular combinations of features, such as a green 'T' among a set of green 'S's and red 'T's, then the search is affected by the number of distractors since each stimulus must be inspected in turn until the target is found. In recent formulations of the theory (Treisman, 1988), the location of stimuli acts as a key feature or master map which can be used to direct attention appropriately. Another prediction of feature integration theory is that when attention is not directly focused on a set of stimuli, their component features will be processed but will not necessarily be properly combined. This suggests that chance or 'illusory' conjunctions of features may arise where features of one object or stimulus become attached to those of another. This prediction has been confirmed by Treisman and Schmidt (1982).

The experiments of Shiffrin and Schneider and Treisman and co-workers have followed the development of automaticity, illustrated its strengths, and highlighted its weaknesses and limitations. However, exactly what takes place when a skill becomes automatic still remains poorly understood. Treisman's work, in particular, suggests that there are limits on what aspects of perceptual processes can be fully automated, though she does agree that, with practice, 'unitization' of feature compounds can occur. Since automated skills make up so much of everyday behaviour, further understanding of the processes that underlie them must be one of the aims of psychologists in the coming years.

Feedback

Knowledge of how a skilled action is progressing and of how successful it has been are crucial for most activities. Without knowledge of the results of an action it is, obviously, difficult if not impossible for the skill to be modified and improved. Feedback on the state of the action and its success is an important aspect of the control and development of most skills. But as well as providing information that can be used to modify performance, feedback also contributes to the rewards and punishments for an action and so is involved in motivating future actions. Nevertheless, in this chapter we will concentrate upon the information conveyed by the feedback. There are several aspects of feedback of information that we need to consider in detail. The first of these is whether feedback is available during the task itself or after it has been performed.

Open and closed loops

Some information can be used either during the actual performance of some task or afterwards when preparing for the next time. Skills such as driving require modification while in progress, but others cannot be modified at the time, though they can be improved when they are next run. If, for example, when throwing a dart it hits the board lower than the target point, you modify your next throw to go higher. Skills that can be modified by feedback while they are actually in progress are known as 'closed loop' since a simple circuit like that shown in figure 6.2 is in operation, with the action being modified by feedback on its accuracy. By contrast, some actions, especially fast ones or some of those that have become highly automated, do not appear to be modifiable while they are being carried out. Since there is no opportunity for feedback to change the action while it

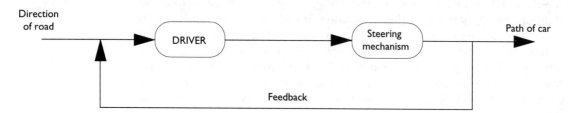

Figure 6.2   'Closed loop' skills depend on feedback

takes place, the feedback element of figure 6.2 is missing and the action is known as 'open loop'. Notice that open loop skills can be modified by a knowledge of their success, but only so that the next attempt can be more successful.

How can we find out whether an action can be modified by feedback while it is being carried out? One indirect way is to time the action, and then to compare its speed to the speed with which feedback information is known to be processed and used in other situations. Various estimates of the time needed to use visual feedback have been obtained, and, although these differ, they do allow an estimate to be made of the minimum movement time during which feedback cannot be used. Thus, Christina (1970) suggested that a minimum of about 200 msec was required to make use of visual feedback. More recent estimates have been lower, perhaps down to 100 msec (Smith and Bowen, 1980). If a movement takes less than this time then it is most unlikely that it will be modified while it is actually taking place to take into account the sight of its going wrong.

A more direct test of the use of feedback during a skilled movement can be made by making the feedback impossible and examining how performance is affected. For example, visual feedback can be easily removed by switching off the lights during a skilled action. Henderson (1975) used such a technique when studying dart throwing. Another example of the use of feedback in a skill that at first sight might not seem to require it has been provided by Sewall et al. (1988) (see box 6.2). Sewall et al. demonstrated greater improvement in the power clean movement in weightlifting when weightlifters practised with a mirror compared with those who practised without a mirror, provided that the mirror was also available on the final critical test of the skill. Removal of the mirror on test resulted in a less impressive increase in performance as a result of practice, suggesting that performers not only profit from the presence of feedback during skill acquisition, but come to rely on it subsequently.

Adams (1971) argued that motor learning was based upon the refinement of perceptual–motor feedback loops. Adams' closed loop theory involved the correction of errors in the skill through feedback on the success of the action. The role of feedback in skill performance is, however, not so clear-cut as this would imply. Many skilled actions such as reaching and walking, at least once acquired, do not require feedback during the action itself for it to be carried out successfully (Rosenbaum, 1991). Also, Winstein and Schmidt (1990) showed that explicit feedback given on 50 per cent of trials led to more permanent retention of the movement being learned than did feedback after every trial. This is a difficult finding for Adams' closed loop theory since 100 per cent opportunity to use feedback might be expected to be the more successful in the development of the skill.

Types of feedback

We have already mentioned the study by Henderson (1975) in which the lights were put out during a dart throw. Henderson found that expert dart players had a good idea of the accuracy of their throw, even when they had no chance to see where it went. To do so they must have had feedback not from the outside world but from their own body. Such 'kinaesthetic feedback' from the muscles and joints of the hand, arms, etc., is just one type of 'intrinsic feedback'. Intrinsic feedback is any information that comes as a natural consequence of the action itself. Henderson's experiment shows that there is intrinsic feedback from the body without vision. However, an enormous amount of feedback does come visually. As such, it is an important source of intrinsic feedback so long as it is a natural consequence of the movement. On some occasions, however, people are supplied with extra information over and above that which they naturally experience or see. They may be told their score when shooting at a target, or perhaps told when a move is closer to the one that their coach wishes them to produce. Such feedback is known as 'extrinsic' or 'augmented'.

Feedback in action

We normally take our skill of being able to balance for granted, but even this requires constant monitoring of several systems. Feedback from them leads to adjustments so that we can stand or walk without swaying noticeably, or falling over. There is kinaesthetic feedback from the joints and muscles, and other feedback from the vestibular system in the ear. Perhaps more important still is the visual feedback from the world around us. If we sway forwards the visual world will seem to move backwards and this can be used to correct our posture. Lee and Aronson (1974) showed how important such movement was for balancing by building a room which could itself be moved! They were able to swing the room forwards or backwards a few inches and observe how adults and children responded. Adults swayed away from the movement of the room, showing that they were correcting for this misleading feedback. Young children who were just learning to walk were often knocked right over by the movement of the room, indicating their heavy dependence on visual feedback for their newly learned skill of balancing. There is a further discussion of these experiments in chapter 3.

It is very difficult to remove all sources of feedback, so most studies of the use of feedback have involved modifying the usual sources rather than eliminating them completely. Visual feedback can be relatively easily changed. Try for yourself the effect of changing visual feedback by looking at your hand in a mirror while you draw around some shape. You will need to screen your direct vision of your hand. Everyone finds such drawing difficult at first; some people find it almost impossible. If you persevere you will soon discover that you are getting better. You are quickly learning to use the novel visual feedback that is often contradictory to your normal use of vision. Improvement normally follows the power law of practice that we discussed earlier.

Simple hand movement

One of our simplest but vital skills is our ability to move our hands from one point to another to pick up a pen, press a button or do whatever we wish. Yet even such a simple skill can reveal a lot about the complexity of skilled movement. To begin with, there is a well-established relationship between the speed with which the movement can be carried out and both the distance to be moved and the size of the target to which the hand is moved (Fitts, 1954). (For readers interested in the mathematics: movement time is proportional to the logarithm of twice the distance to be moved divided by the width of the target.) This relationship, known as Fitts Law, has been demonstrated to apply to a wide range of movements (Keele, 1981). While it is not surprising that the time to make a movement depends upon the distance to be moved, it is interesting that the size of the target plays an important part in such simple movements. The smaller the target the slower the movement itself, and also the more time which elapses before any movement begins (Klapp, 1975). When movements towards targets are carefully analysed they are found to consist of two components (Welford, 1968). The first one is a fast movement that covers most of the distance from the starting point to the target. This seems to be a ballistic movement and takes a relatively short time in comparison with the second component, which involves the slowing down of the first movement and the controlled homing onto the target. This second component markedly increases as the target is made smaller. Thus, even a very simple movement can be analysed into separate components which may be influenced differently by the conditions at the time. It is in the latter stage that visual feedback is very important in directing the action.

Transfer of Training ▶ ▶ ▶

Some skills are composed of subcomponents that have been learned already. In such a case, these component skills can be capitalized upon and, as a result, the new skill can be acquired far more quickly than if one was starting completely afresh. The influence of prior learning upon new learning is called transfer, and the example just given is of positive transfer, that is, where prior learning speeds new learning. In some situations, however, the earlier learning makes it harder to acquire the new skill. This is 'negative transfer'. We have introduced one example of negative transfer already when we described how the participants in the Schneider and Shiffrin (1977) experiment, who had always used one set of consonants as targets and another as distractors, had to take far longer to become automated in the task when the target and distractor groups were switched than they had taken originally to learn the skill.

Another example of negative transfer comes from an experiment by Summers (1975) who taught participants to carry out a sequence of nine key presses with a set rhythm so that the intervals between the key presses might be, for example, 500–500–100 msec, or 500–100–100 msec. Once they had learned the sequence the participants were told that they should forget the timing and now press the keys in the given sequence as quickly as possible. Nevertheless, their original learning of a rate of pressing transferred to the new task and caused a slowing down that was not observed in participants not taught a given rhythm.

Most people probably have some memory of negative transfer. Changing from playing squash or badminton to tennis or vice versa requires quite different stroke making, the first two using a wrist flick while the latter requires a locked wrist, and can lead to tennis balls flying over the fencing of the court while still rising! Car drivers who change the model they are driving may find that they have switched on the windscreen wipers when they intended to flash their lights, or whatever, if the controls have changed in their positions. Nevertheless, while negative transfer does occur, positive transfer is the more common occurrence. Normally, one skill will help us tackle another related skill.

One explanation for negative transfer suggested by Newell (1981) is that it occurs when similar groups of muscles are activated in the two tasks, but the ratio of activity between the muscle groups is different. While this probably accounts for many examples of negative transfer, it does not account for the type of error where a wholly inappropriate action is transferred from one skill to another. Schema theories may help in this case.

Schema Theories of Skill Acquisition ▶ ▶ ▶

When an expert tennis player or a cricketer hits a ball the action is an interesting mixture of old and new. The stroke will be smooth and well practised and each backhand lob or cover drive may resemble all the others that the player has executed. However, it is also true that the action has to be adjusted for the particular circumstances of the ball's velocity and bounce and the placing intended by the hitter. In this sense, then, the stroke is a novel one, though it bears a strong family resemblance to other strokes. The point is that the mechanism for making the stroke must be one that can be modified for the given circumstances. It will not be a simple reflex that fires off independently of the situation. Thus, the mechanism for making such actions must be one that is sufficiently open to be adjusted to the prevailing parameters.

The idea of schemata for movement was proposed by Bartlett (1932) and developed by Schmidt (1975) to capture the various aspects of skilled movement. Bartlett (1932), when discussing how he made a tennis stroke, commented, 'When I make the stroke I do not, as a matter of fact, produce something absolutely new, and I never merely repeat something old. The stroke is literally manufactured out of the living visual and postural "schemata" of the movement and their interrelations' (p. 202). The idea is that the general nature of the response is remembered and the particular response that is appropriate is generated, or constructed, at the time.

A major problem with using the concept of schemata in this and other areas, such as comprehension (see chapter 9), is the vagueness over specifying exactly what they are and how they function. No one would deny that past experience helps when making a similar response or when understanding what is happening; the question is whether introducing the term 'schema' aids our understanding of the role of past experience in guiding new actions. This limitation of the idea of schemata is discussed further in chapter 7.

One important part of the schema concept, emphasized especially by Neisser (1976), is that schemata set expectations of what will happen next and what is important to attend to and abstract from the flood of sensory information that we face continually. So, in skilled movement, a schema will help determine what aspects of the situation need to be evaluated and will prepare the action for the appropriate input when the environment provides the necessary information.

Schmidt (1975) suggested that through experience we develop 'recall schemata' that can generate an appropriate motor program when it is needed, and 'recognition schemata' that help in guiding the movement by generating the expected consequences of feedback from the movement which can be compared with the actual feedback obtained. Support for the idea of a recognition schema generating feedback comes from experiments like those of Henderson (1975), mentioned earlier, where expert dart players can give a good report of the result of their dart throw even though the light is switched off before the dart left their hand. Presumably, the recognition schema generated a pattern of feedback which was compared to the proprioceptive feedback from the body when the dart was thrown, and the accuracy interpreted from the match or mismatch between them.

A prediction from the idea that schemata guide action is that variability of the conditions of practice should improve learning. Several studies have supported this prediction (see Rosenbaum, 1991 for a review). For example, Carson and Wiegard (1979) looked at the accuracy with which children could throw a bean bag at a target. The accuracy of throwing a bag of a different weight to that on which they had practised was better for children who had trained with a range of weights of bean bag, rather than just one weight. Interestingly, this better learning generalized so that they were also more accurate in throwing a ball of wool.

It may be that schema theory will eventually help in the understanding of skill development, and of the situations under which positive or negative transfer will occur. For example, positive transfer should follow those changes which help to develop a schema, as in the Carson and Wiegard experiment, but negative transfer will occur where similar schemata compete or where an inappropriate schema is activated, perhaps as a sub-routine in a bigger skill.

The concept of the schema has been used in the understanding of the control of actions at a higher level than that considered by Schmidt. Reason (1984) has spent several years studying slips of action where people switch from doing one thing to another absentmindedly. He has collected samples such as those of people going to change clothes for an evening out finding themselves in bed in nightclothes because they switched to the normal routine for going to bed. Reason has tried to analyse such 'strong but wrong' actions as the activation of inappropriate schema taking over. It is often possible to understand human errors as being the activation, inappropriately, of a schema that is either easily activated because it is commonly used or because it has been primed by the current conditions. For example, Reason and Mycielska (1982) describe an aircraft crash in which the pilot, during take-off, knowing that his co-pilot was feeling depressed, said 'cheer up' to him, at which the co-pilot retracted the undercarriage before the plane had left the ground, because he had been expecting shortly the command 'gear-up'. The schema for raising the undercarriage would have been primed and ready for activation, and the similar-sounding comment from the pilot would have activated the schema, with most unfortunate consequences (see also chapter 8).

Conclusions

As this chapter illustrates, to achieve skilled performance requires considerable practice and appropriate feedback. It also involves the development of processes which draw heavily on past learning and fit well with the unique demands of the immediate moment. The acquisition of skills is also clearly related to changes in the attentional requirements of a task, and, not surprisingly, the psychological literature on skills blends (though not always neatly!) with that on attention. Work on automaticity by Shiffrin and Schneider and Treisman and Gelade, which we discussed in this chapter, has implications for our view of how we construe the role of attention in skill, while, conversely, the reading and dictation studies of Hirst et al. (1980) discussed in chapter 5 treat attention itself as a skill to be mastered. Unfortunately, there has been a tendency for separate groups of workers to be involved in both areas, though, from work conducted in the past ten years, there are signs that this separation may be coming to an end.

However, what is clear is that skilled action underlies almost everything that we do, and that it is an essential prerequisite for higher cognitive activity since without it we cannot act effectively on the world. For this reason, other references to skill occur in other places in this book, particularly chapters 4, 7, 9 and 13 on Language, Remembering, Reading and Connectionism respectively.

Further reading

General reviews of motor control and skill learning will be found in D.A. Rosenbaum 1991: *Human Motor Control*. San Diego: Academic Press, and D. Holding 1981: *Human Skills*. New York: Wiley. Useful information, especially on aspects of feedback and control, can also be found in M.M. Smyth and A.M. Wing (eds) 1984: *The Psychology of Human Movement*. London: Academic Press. A text which reviews skill and relates it to training is J. Patrick 1992: *Training Research and Practice*. London: Academic Press.

The first chapter by D. Kahneman and A. Treisman 1984: Changing views of attention and automaticity. In R. Parasuraman and R. Davies (eds) *Varieties of Attention*, New York: Academic Press, is a good general review of automaticity. The specific relation between automaticity and skill is well discussed in G.D. Logan 1985: Skill and automaticity: relations implications and future directions. *Canadian Journal of Psychology*, 39, 367–86; see also G.D. Logan 1988: Toward an instance theory of automatization. *Psychological Review*, 94, 192–211, for an interesting account of automaticity.

Cognitive skills are considered in J.R. Anderson (ed.) 1982: *Cognitive Skills and their Acquisition*. Hillsdale, NJ: Lawrence Erlbaum Associates, and J.R. Anderson 1987: Skill acquisition: a compilation of weak-method problems, *Psychological Review*, 95, 492–527.

Discussion points ▷ ▷ ▷

1   Why is a distinction drawn between declarative and procedural knowledge?
2   What is the best way to organize practice to maximize learning?
3   Can you apply Fitts' analysis of the acquisition of a skill into three stages to a skill that you have acquired?
4   What part does feedback play in the control of skilled actions?
5   Why might a person's age affect their ability to learn a new skill?

Practical exercises

1   A good way to increase one's understanding of what is involved in learning a skill is to tackle the learning of a new one. A skill that requires relatively little equipment to practise is that of mirror drawing. The basic set-up involves a table, a mirror standing vertically up from the table and some form of screen to prevent you looking directly at your own hand. Watching your hand in the mirror, you should attempt to draw around particular shapes and to measure the time taken and the number of errors made. You might, for example, try to join up a series of dots on a page. Most people find mirror drawing very difficult to begin with and some people find it nearly impossible to get started. Normally, however, there is a rapid improvement in performance. If, therefore, you record the time taken to draw accurately around the same set of dots, you should find a steady improvement in speed that resembles the power function of improvement of a new skill with practice. Vertical and horizontal movements tend to be easier than those diagonal to the mirror and to yourself. You could, for example, compare how long it takes you to draw around

patterns of dots that are shaped in a square pattern or a star or diamond.

2   Reason and Mycielska (1982) asked people to keep a record of even the most trivial errors when an action they had intended was carried out differently to the way that it was planned. Keeping a similar diary, or perhaps persuading as many friends as possible to do the same, will often reveal a surprising number of errors that one normally ignores or takes for granted. It is worth keeping a detailed record of the circumstances whenever an error occurs. For example, you should record the time, the intended action, the action that actually occurred, and any thoughts about why the error took place.

3   Normally, someone who has been driving for many years can carry out conversations with passengers without having to pause in the discussion except at difficult decision points such as turning at roundabouts. New drivers, however, often find that they need all their attention to be directed to the skill of driving. A reasonably rigorous test of this difference in skill can be carried out by asking new and long-

experienced drivers the same set of questions and timing how long it takes to complete the correct answering of them. It is, of course, very important to point out to the drivers that safely driving the car is the paramount task. After all, you are with them too and want to get home safely.

There are, clearly, several different manipulations that you could make in this experiment. For example, you can arrange for there to be different degrees of complexity in the driving task, from straight empty roads to busy rush-hour city traffic. It is possible also to vary the difficulty of questions being asked. Does switching from easy to difficult questions cause more of a problem to a novice than to an expert driver? You would need a long enough set of questions so that some of the variability in individuals' knowledge and performance can be evened out. You could consider asking a similar set of questions to the same people while *not* driving so that you can see how their performance changes with the driving task.

Box 6.1
Putting players off their stroke: the role of explicit knowledge in the breakdown of complex skills

Masters was interested in the idea that expert skill can fail where performers are highly motivated to succeed. Typical examples of this are found in many sports, where the phenomenon is known as 'choking'. For example, tournament tennis players often score a double fault when facing a match point, and golf players frequently miss extremely easy putts when on the verge of winning a competition. As Masters points out: 'The classic example of choking is the situation where the athlete performs outstandingly in practice but poorly in competition' (p. 344).

Why does choking occur? After all, the lay person would simply put these failures down to stress and nervousness. It is of course obvious that competition athletes are under pressure, but why should stress cause a well-learned skill to break down? Masters' hypothesis was that skill involves the reinvestment of explicit (declarative) processing in what should be an automatic, implicit procedure. 'That is, under pressure, the individual begins thinking about how he or she is executing the skill, and endeavours to operate it with his or her explicit knowledge of its mechanics' (p. 345). It follows from this, that persons who have less explicit knowledge about a skill should be less troubled by the intrusion of unwanted declarative knowledge when under pressure than those with more explicit knowledge about it.

Masters' experiment had two phases. In the first, participants learned the complex motor skill of golf putting

either with the opportunity to think about the skill actively encouraged (explicit learning), with the opportunity to think about the skill permitted but not specifically encouraged (control), or with the opportunity to think about the skill actively discouraged (implicit learning). Explicit learning required participants to read detailed instructions on how to putt before practising. Participants in the control group simply practised without any special instructions. Implicit learning participants were given no instructions about putting, and were also asked to generate letters aloud in a random fashion when practising to try to stop them thinking verbally about the skill.

Following practice under these conditions, half of the participants in the implicit learning and control groups were put under mild pressure by telling them that financial rewards for participating in the experiment could be increased or diminished depending on their performance. Checks during the experiment using a paper and pencil measure of anxiety showed that these 'stressed' groups had indeed been made a little more apprehensive.

In all, 40 participants were used and placed in one of five conditions: explicit learning (EL); implicit learning followed by stress (IL); implicit learning followed by no stress (ILC); control group followed by stress (SC); control group followed by no stress (N-SC).

Four practice sessions consisting of 100 putts each and a final test session of 100 putts were held. In order to keep the final test as equivalent for all the groups as possible, the EL group were not required to re-read their putting instructions prior to the final test, and the implicit learning groups were not required to generate letters on the final test.

Among the various measures taken by Masters were the number of putts entering the hole (out of 100) achieved by the five groups on the test session, and written reports taken after the test session on what participants thought were the factors influencing a successful putt. These written protocols were then scored in terms of the number of different rules for putting which each participant produced.

As can be seen in box figure 6.1.1, there were some clear differences between groups. An overall analysis of variance of the data showed, not surprisingly, that all groups' performance improved during the experiment and that there were differences at each session between groups. In particular, the implicit learning groups were less successful initially in learning the task.

However, the crucial comparisons in the experiment involved the groups' performance on the final test session. In fact, because there was so much variability in performance between the groups at session 4, Masters concentrated on the *change* in performance of each group from session 4 to session 5. Among the various predictions which he made, of interest here is that the explicit learning and stressed control groups should get worse under the pressure of the final test because they would tend to have more intrusive thoughts about the skill, whereas the implicit learning and unstressed control groups should not show a decline in performance. As predicted, the EL performance decrement was not different from the SC group ($t = 0.11$, $p > 0.05$) but the decline in performance of both of these groups was highly significantly different from the performance increase of the IL, ILC and N-SC groups ($t = 3.63$, $p < 0.001$).

So it seems that while the implicit learning groups were slower to acquire the skill of putting, they suffered less from being put under pressure than the explicit learning

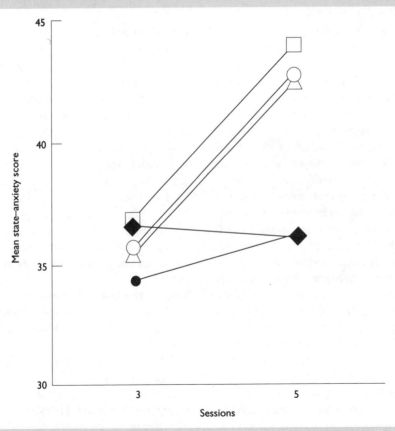

Box figure 6.1.1   The effect of knowledge on the skill of putting: (△) implicit; (□) explicit; (◆) implicit control; (○) stressed control; (●) non-stressed control. (Based on figure 3, Masters, 1993)

and stressed control groups. The assumption that this is because the explicit learning group had readier access to verbal descriptions of the task was borne out by the analysis of the written protocols. The EL group produced many more putting rules than any of the other four groups (t = 5.6, p < 0.001), while the IL and ILC groups had the least knowledge of all, and even significantly less than the control groups, SC and N-SC (t = 3.08, p = 0.004).

A difficulty with this study is that it was impossible to match participants in terms of skill on the task in question before they commenced practice as this would have exposed the implicit learning groups to contaminating experience on the task. Aware of this problem, Masters did check for pre-experimental skill differences as well as he could by examining whether there were any differences in putting skill on the first five trials of session 1. None were found, indicating that the groups started out reasonably matched.

Based on R.S.W. Masters 1992: Knowledge, knerves and know-how: the role of explicit versus implicit knowledge in the breakdown of a complex skill under pressure. British Journal of Psychology, 83, 343–58.

Box 6.2
Visual feedback in weightlifting

The importance of visual feedback in the development of skills is well known, but its wide applicability is only just being discovered. In this experiment, Sewall et al. investigated the role of videotaped feedback and concurrent feedback using a mirror on the acquisition of the power clean movement in weightlifting. The aim of the power clean is to lift the dumb-bell from the floor to the shoulders in one clean movement.

Eighteen men from beginning weight training volunteered to take part. All had had a minimum of eight weeks' training at weightlifting, but no experience with the power clean. Participants were randomly allocated to two groups of nine participants each. One group was asked to observe their movements during the power clean in a mirror positioned at 45 degrees from the sagittal plane of the participant. The other group had no mirror. The experimenter encouraged and reminded participants in the first group to use the mirror.

After a brief description of the experiment, given by the experimenter, all participants were shown the first video-taped demonstration of the lift. Next, each participant was required to perform three repetitions of the movement, using a 40 kg weight, while being videotaped from a 45 degree angle to provide the same view as that seen in the mirror. Data from these lifts provided a score of pre-training ability. Then, participants saw the next section of the instructional videotape. Every 1.5 minutes the video-tape was stopped and participants performed two sets of three lifts as practice, with a two-minute rest between sets. The process was repeated four times, yielding eight sets of three lifts or 24 practice lifts in all per participant. After the last section of instructional videotape, participants were then videotaped while they completed three lifts without the mirror, followed by a two-minute rest, then three lifts with the mirror.

Scoring of the videotapes before and after practice was performed by a competitive weightlifter, experienced in coaching, using the US Weightlifting Federation scoring system. In this system, points are deducted from a maximum of ten for each technical fault. Thus over three lifts a participant could score a total of 30 points.

Results

Results can be seen in box table 6.2.1.

The experimenters first compared the scores for both groups on the post-test without the mirror with those from the pre-test. There was, not surprisingly, a highly significant effect of practice, with post-training scores higher than pre-test (on an analysis of variance, p < 0.01), but no difference in improvement between the group trained on the mirror and without the mirror when tested without the mirror (p > 0.2). However, the mirror-trained group was found to be significantly better than the non-mirror-trained group when tested with the mirror (p < 0.05), though the average group scores, 20 points as opposed to 16.2 points, were not highly significantly different.

The results of this experiment are intriguing, but we hope the reader can see that the conclusions which can be drawn from it are somewhat limited. To begin with, both groups in the study used video, so there is no baseline to see whether the videotaped instruction was effective.

Box table 6.2.1   Means of scores on the weightlifting technique

Practice group	Pre-test (no mirror)	Post-tests	
		Without mirror	With mirror
Mirror	11.8	18.7	20.0
No mirror	12.2	17.0	16.2

Source: Based on table 1, Sewall et al., 1988

Turning to the effects of the mirror, a strong expectation could have been created by the experimenters that the mirror would be helpful. This alone might have contributed to the improvement in the mirror-trained group. The results do indeed show a difference between training groups on the post-test with the mirror, but as the experimenters themselves point out there are various explanations of this. A simple explanation is that participants do best when tested under the same condition as they practice in. Participants trained without the mirror perform poorly with the mirror, perhaps because they find it distracting. A second related possibility is that the mirror-trained group came to rely on external feedback, and so performed better when the feedback was available, while the group trained without the mirror came to rely on intrinsic feedback from joints, muscles and tendons, and had not learned to coordinate this with visual information.

Nevertheless, the study does indicate that motor skills can benefit from the provision of appropriate visual feedback, but the safest conclusion is the one the authors themselves draw: '... concurrent visual feedback during practice aided subsequent performance only when that feedback was also available' (p. 718).

Based on L.P. Sewall, T.G. Reeve and R.A. Day 1988: Effects of concurrent feedback on the acquisition of a weightlifting skill. *Perceptual and Motor Skills*, 67, 715–18.

Part II

Using Cognition

7 Remembering

Having examined the basic elements of cognition, it is now time to consider its functions and examine cognition in action. In chapter 2, we introduced the basic principles that determine what is remembered and what forgotten. However, while the laboratory research that formed the basis of that chapter can guide our understanding of many of the fundamental processes that underlie memory, it is very useful to examine the role that memory plays in a range of real-world situations. One reason for this is that it was easy for the early researchers on memory to believe that they were capturing in their studies most of what was basic to remembering. However, these laboratory studies minimized many of the features that may be central to memory in our everyday life. For example, we are rarely in a situation where we do not have considerable knowledge accumulated from the past that will be relevant to what is happening to us now. When we visit a friend, go to the doctor's, watch the news on television or play a game we have a rich store of knowledge that makes sense of what is happening, what others are saying and doing, and what is likely and unlikely to happen next. This expertise that we all possess is continually put to use. In contrast, the participant in the early memory experiments was likely to be given a list of nonsense syllables (e.g. XUW, VAQ), or at best unrelated words, to be learned under intense time pressure (e.g. two seconds or less per item). Inevitably, such research ignored the benefits of all the past knowledge that the participants possessed. Studies of tasks taken from the real world provide opportunities for this knowledge to manifest itself in the participants' performance. Equally importantly, examining the use of memory in realistic situations introduces the researcher to memory tasks that do not naturally spring from laboratory research (which concentrates on controlling both the encoding and the retrieval conditions), but which are nevertheless very important in our everyday life. Examples are prospective memory (remembering to do things), cognitive maps (memory of the spatial relationship between places), eyewitness testimony and memories associated with particularly important, emotional or unexpected events. In this chapter we will expand the general principles discussed in chapter 2 by examining research on these and other situations in which we use our memories in our everyday life. Morris (1988) gives a fuller discussion of the early history of research on memory and the omissions to which it led.

Combining Knowledge: Scripts, Schemata and Cognitive Maps

For many years, psychologists interested in semantic memory studied small-scale aspects of knowledge such as the nature of, and links between, simple concepts or the representation of single words or mental images (see chapter 2). However, in the past 20 years or so, there has been an increased interest in what can be called larger-scale knowledge structures. This has coincided with an interest in the functioning of cognition in the real world. In this section, two areas of this large field are briefly considered: scripts, which derive from earlier work on schemata, and cognitive maps.

Scripts and schemata

It was Bartlett (1932) who borrowed the concept of a schema (pl. schemata) from the neurologist Head and extended the idea. Schemata are knowledge frameworks built up through experience that guide the interpretation of new information and control our actions (see chapter 5 for a further discussion of the role of schemata in action). For remembering, the important point is that, as described above, in any situation there is usually organized past experience that is likely to help make sense of our new experiences. Bartlett argued that we make a constant 'effort after meaning', trying to make sense of all that is happening. Our past experience is not unstructured, but supplies us with expectations about the way events will occur, on the basis of their regularities in the past. Bartlett showed how stories told by one person to another were stripped of their unusual contents in the transmission, so that the result was a summary in words and events that were familiar to the participants. Using an Indian folk tale, Bartlett demonstrated how the unfamiliar elements tended to be forgotten or 'normalized' in the recall of individuals.

The War of the ghost

Bartlett's work was regarded as vague and difficult to develop by the researchers of the 1940s and 1950s who were heavily influenced by the demands of behaviourism. Behaviourism, as we explained in chapter 1, required that psychological explanations only refer to observable entities such as stimuli or environmental settings on the one hand and responses on the other. By appealing to internal entities, Bartlett stepped outside of this tradition. However, the development of the computer, and the need to incorporate world knowledge within the new computing machines as part of the development of artificial intelligence, led computer scientists to refine Bartlett's ideas. Minsky (1975) introduced the term 'frame' to refer to structured chunks of knowledge. In the same year, Rumelhart (1975) suggested that the structure of stories could be understood using the idea of a story grammar. This resembled the transformational grammar popularized for the analysis of the syntax of sentences by Chomsky (1965). However, the story grammar dealt with the larger units of a story. Rewrite rules provided ways of expanding a high-level analysis of a story in terms of SETTING, GOAL etc., into EVENTS, ACTIONS, CAUSES and so on. The essential feature of the story grammar was that at least some classes of story, such as fable and fairy stories, had a structure upon which the story was built and which was known to the listener who would use it to help understand what was happening. Subsequent research by Thorndyke (1977) did show that people remember the higher-level themes of stories better than the lower-level details, and that disrupting the structure of the story led to poorer recall, with the benefits for the higher-order themes disappearing.

Taking this idea further, Schank and Abelson (1977) suggested that we have acquired schemata, or scripts as they called them, for the commonly experienced structured events in our lives. Their most famous example is the script for going to a restaurant. This involves expectations about what will happen when one enters a restaurant (e.g. looking for a table), what happens during ordering (e.g. reading a menu, selecting from the menu), eating (e.g. that the waitress will bring the food) and leaving (e.g. that there will be a bill, giving a tip). Someone possessing such a script can make sense of what to do next when in the restaurant. Furthermore, they can comprehend statements about restaurants that contain, in themselves, little information. So, for example, the remark that 'I caught her eye and finally got the bill' would be wrongly interpreted by or meaningless to someone who did not know about paying for a meal.

restaurant script

Alba and Hasher (1983) reviewed the ways in which schemata might influence memory. They suggested that there are four such ways. Schemata could guide the selection of what is to be encoded, so that only some of the multitude of different stimuli being encountered by the individual will be encoded while those not identified as relevant within the given schemata would be ignored. Secondly, schemata could allow the abstraction of information, allowing the storage of the meaning of the message without reference to the specific details of the original words or actions. Thirdly, schemata could aid interpretation, providing relevant prior knowledge to aid the comprehension of current experience. Finally, schemata provide integration, with a single, holistic memory being formed as the product of the three previous operations. At retrieval, schemata would provide the framework for the reconstruction of memories.

S. influence on memory

Research on schemata

Schank and Abelson (1977) produced a computer program that was able to answer questions about restaurants and interpret stories about restaurants. The memory implications were followed up by Bower et al. (1979). They first drew from participants descriptions of what was involved in several routine activities. They confirmed that their participants gave similar accounts of the stages that normally were followed in going to a restaurant or a doctor or a dentist. When participants recalled short stories derived from the scripts, they tended to reorder the randomized statements in the stories so that they fitted the original script. Errors in recall were likely to be statements that might have been from the scripts but had not been included in the stories, showing how the participants were using their knowledge of the scripts to generate possible statements. Bower et al. found that when they included interruptions in the flow of a script, such as the waiter spilling the food he was bringing to the table, this was better remembered than either statements from the script or irrelevant statements inserted in the story. This highlighted that the object of a story will rarely be to communicate a script already well known to the listener. Rather, the point of recounting any story is to communicate an interesting way in which normal expectations were modified or unfulfilled. In fact, Brewer and Lichtenstein (1981) found that stories that were constructed from scripts without any deviations were rated as not being like stories by their participants.

Brewer and Treyens (1981) explored the influence of schemata on visual perception and memory by asking participants to wait in a room for 35 seconds. The room looked like an office, with 61 different objects. Some were relevant to an office schema, such as a table, a typewriter and a coffee pot. Others were unusual in offices, including a skull, a toy top and a piece of bark. Other participants had rated the objects on two scales, one for how likely they were to appear in such an office, the other for how noticeable they were. Both the schema ratings and the saliency rating predicted recall. Best remembered were what Brewer and Treyens called frame objects which formed a part of the room itself. The more bizarre items like the top and the skull were also quite often recalled. Errors reflected attempts to use an office schema to generate ideas. So, for example, nine of the 30 participants reported books, though none were in the room. When places were described, objects tended to be 'returned' to their usual places, so, for example, a note pad was reported as being on the desk when it was really on the seat of a chair. This experiment illustrates how the expectations given by schemata can allow rapid encoding, the identification of unusual items, which are therefore the ones to which attention needs to be paid, and the influence of the schema in trying to reconstruct the recall.

Schank (1982) extended his concept of scripts to take into account features of reminding that he had observed. He had noticed that he would be reminded of memories that were apparently related to other scripts when he was in the middle of a familiar script. For example, Schank reports a friend as having been reminded of people who go to petrol stations just to buy a small amount of petrol, when the friend was waiting in a long queue at a Post Office and someone bought a single stamp. On the face of it, the Post Office and the petrol station should require different scripts to guide behaviour. However, they obviously shared enough in some way for the unusual event related to one to remind the observer of the other. Bower et al. had also observed that there were considerable confusions between scripts for going to a doctor and a dentist. Schank proposed that the structures supporting memories were richer than the script model had allowed. He suggested that there are further levels into which the scripts are organized, on the basis of the sharing of similar features. So, for example, visiting doctors and dentists shares general properties of visiting health professionals. Schank's new formulation included 'plans', 'scenes', 'memory organization packets' (MOPs) and 'thematic organization points' (TOPs). Plans cover specific motivations and goals and are a low level in the structure. Scenes involve a setting, a goal and actions to try to reach that goal. Each scene may be a part of many memory organization packets. Thus, the scene of waiting in a waiting room could form part of packets for dentists or doctors, while the MOPs themselves will incorporate several scenes. In this way, Schank was able to account for the apparent relatedness of many of his scripts. However, he was left with some instances of reminding that seemed even more general and dealt with more abstract relationships. Schank postulated thematic organization points as higher-level analogies. The reminding of the petrol buying by the stamp queue is an example of the link being made via a TOP. Other TOPs might be 'getting what you want' or 'failures in service'.

The research discussed so far seems to support schema theories. On the other hand, such theories have been criticized on several counts. For example, Alba and Hasher (1983) point out the lack of specificity of many explanations based on schemata. In their review of the four contributions to encoding that schemata may make that we described earlier, Alba and Hasher conclude that memory for complex events is far more complex than such processes would suggest. Some schematically unimportant details are often remembered, some details are stored no matter what the degree of prior knowledge the individual possesses. They concluded that the stored record of any event is far more detailed than prototypical schema theories would suggest.

critique

Cognitive maps

Another form of mental representation in which information is combined is the 'mental map' or cognitive map of our environment that we develop through experience (see, for example, Smyth et al., 1994 for a review). Such maps seem to start off from a developing knowledge of routes until a more map-like representation is acquired through fuller experience (Appleyard, 1976). However, such representations often include simplifications. So, for example, Byrne (1979) found that when asked to draw how familiar roads meet at roundabouts there was a strong tendency to err towards 90 degree angles, despite the distortions that this often involved. Tversky (1981) argued that we use heuristics or strategies to simplify our representations. Thus we tend to think of geographical relationships as simple north–south, east–west orientations, with the areas (such as countries or states) being simplified as shapes. For example, Stevens and Coupe (1978) found that participants believed that Los Angeles was west of Reno, Nevada, presumably because their cognitive maps were of north–south oriented states and they missed the east–west slope of the State of California. British people similarly say, wrongly, that Bristol is west of Edinburgh, because they forget the western slant of Scotland in comparison to England. There is still a long way to go before psychologists fully understand these 'macro-chunks' of cognition: scripts and cognitive maps. One obvious question, which may have occurred to the reader but which cannot yet be answered, is how are large-scale knowledge systems like these combined and managed? For instance, suppose you are *en route* for an important interview, navigating through a town you barely know. Unexpectedly, you are diverted from your usual route and find yourself in a slow-moving queue of traffic and risk being seriously late for your meeting or missing it altogether. Remembering that the railway station is nearby, you decide to park your car and go by train instead. You will still be late, but not as late as if you had gone by car. Notice here that your knowledge of the likely consequences of slavishly using a particular cognitive map must interact with your interview script (or MOP) to allow you to resolve your difficulty. Laboratory-based research is only just beginning to cope with simple conceptual combinations and relational structures (e.g. Costello and Keane, 1992); it is likely to be some time yet before a truly general account of high-level knowledge is produced sufficient to deal with problems like this.

Memory and Expertise

The possession of schemata is one way that an expert in a particular topic differs from a novice. Most of us are experts at eating in restaurants or buying stamps. The results of the schema research described in the last section can be thought of as illustrating how expertise will modify what is and what is not recalled. The studies of schemata showed how the possession of the schema gave a framework for rapidly classifying what is seen or heard as familiar and in its normal place or as unusual and needing attention, while the schema also gave a framework for recall. One would expect experts to show a similar superiority to novices in those areas where most of us are novices.

In general, experts are found to recall more than novices if both are allowed a similar time to study the material. De Groot (1965) and Chase and Simon (1973) have studied the recall of positions from a chess game when seen briefly by chess masters and novices. Chase and Simon found that after a five-second exposure to a position in middle game, a chess master could, on average, place 16 pieces in their correct position, while novices could manage only four. However, not only did the difference disappear with randomized positions to be recalled, but the experts found this unpleasant.

The studies with chess experts have been extended to children by Chi (1978) who showed that young chess experts recall more from the boards than adult novices. Baddeley (1990) reports a study by Bradley, Hudson, Robbins and Baddeley which combined the Chase and Simon task with concurrent tasks designed to interfere with components of the working memory. The tasks were articulatory suppression (to interfere with the articulatory loop), tapping a pattern on a keyboard hidden from view (to interfere with the visuo-spatial sketch pad) and generating random numbers (to occupy the central executive). Both for weak and strong players, the tapping and the random number generation tasks led to poorer performance in comparison with a control condition, indicating the involvement of both the sketch pad and the central executive in memorizing the board positions.

The basis of the better recall by chess players reflects their richer store of schematic relationships. Chase and Simon (1973) found that the chess master memorized larger groupings of pieces at one glance, with these chunks involving meaningful clusters of related pieces involved in attack, defence, support and so on.

Similar results to those for chess have been found with other skills. Reitman (1976), for example, replicated them using expert and novice Go players. McKeithen et al. (1981) tested expert, intermediate and novice computer programmers on their ability to recall a 31-line program either in its proper form or when scrambled. Recall was highest for experts, next best for those with intermediate skills and poorest for novices with the normal program, but the groups did not differ with the random order. Spilich et al. (1979) showed that participants who had a high knowledge of baseball not only recalled more of a match commentary but tended to remember the significant aspects from the game. Morris et al. (1985) showed that the recall of real soccer scores correlated 0.82 with a soccer knowledge questionnaire that had been previously administered (see box 7.1). However, for simulated scores the correlation was only 0.36. Recall of real and simulated scores was the same for the quarter of the participants who knew least about soccer, but as knowledge increased, so the performance diverged. The recall of the simulated scores was predicted not by the soccer knowledge questionnaire, but by ability at free recall of a word list. Morris et al. argued that the high knowledge participants would process the implications of the real score, and would be emotionally involved with the outcomes for teams that they supported or disliked. This was partly supported by a second experiment which found strong predictions of the matches where scores were correctly recalled from the strength of liking and disliking of the teams involved as well as the amount that the participants knew about the teams.

One prediction that might be drawn from interference theories of forgetting (see chapter 2) is that experts who know more about any given topic in their area of expertise will have more interference from this knowledge and will forget more quickly than novices. Morris (1988) tested this by telling groups of high and low soccer knowledge participants that the scores they were to be shown were real results from ten years earlier. It was hoped that this would trigger the involvement of the high knowledge group, and this seems to have been so, since they recalled far more than the low knowledge group. To control for rehearsal, the participants were then told that the results were actually invented. It was hoped that this would stop the experts discussing the scores more than the novices. Their recall was tested either immediately or after a three-day delay. Recall declined over the three-day period for both high and low knowledge; however, the slope of the decline did not differ, indicating that the soccer 'experts' had not forgotten at a faster rate than the 'novices'.

Eyewitness Testimony

In the case of experts, and even everyday tasks such as going to a restaurant, the flexibility and power of human knowledge is evident. This flexibility of human memory, however, is also combined with a certain fallibility. Memory, as we discussed in chapter 1, does not provide us with a perfect record of events, as is apparent from the study of eyewitness testimony.

In many legal cases the testimony of witnesses is a major source of evidence. Witnesses may be required to identify the person who carried out the crime or to give an account of what happened. Lawyers for the defence will try to undermine the testimony by identifying inconsistencies and by discrediting the witness. The accuracy of testimony and ways to improve it are, therefore, of considerable importance.

One major area of such testimony is the recognition of the criminal, perhaps from police mug shots or from identity parades. In one study Buckhout (1974) illustrated one of the dangers of identity parades. He arranged a purse snatching by a confederate on campus and had 52 witnesses try to select the culprit from one of two successive line-ups of five individuals. The 'criminal' was in the first line-up and someone of similar appearance in the second. Of the witnesses, ten were unable to pick out anyone, seven selected the culprit on the first line-up, but changed their mind to the look-alike on the second line-up. A further 28 selected another innocent person from one or the other of the line-ups. Only seven of the 52 witnesses picked out the right person on the first line-up and stuck to their decision. The poor performance shown by Buckhout and replicated in other studies indicates that recognition can be unreliable. In part, this is a result of the stress and surprise of the crime but also of the changes in context and in the appearance of the accused. For brief glances at unfamiliar faces it is the external features such as hair that most influence recognition, and these are easily altered in different contexts, either deliberately or just through normal growth and changes in style.

A further difficulty facing the police when interviewing witnesses is that it is very hard to describe a face with any accuracy. We are not bad at recognizing faces, assuming that we have reasonable time and the features are not changed, but we do not have the skill or the vocabulary to convey the appearance in words. Deffenbacher (1988) summarizes five studies that found no, or only a very small correlation between the accuracy of a verbal description and the accuracy of visual identification. Various methods have been tried to overcome this. One was the development of the photofit technique where a composite face was constructed from a large collection of different eyes, noses, mouths and other facial features. Unfortunately, the photofit technique led to poor recognition, even under good conditions for memorizing the face. Ellis et al. (1975) found only 12.5 per cent accuracy in selecting the target face from a group of other reconstructions, and Christie and Ellis (1981) found that targets were recognized better by using verbal descriptions than from photofits. Among other factors affecting face recognition are that it is harder to recognize an individual from another race than from one's own race (e.g. Barkowitz and Brigham, 1982; Buckout and Regan, 1988).

Eyewitness testimony is further complicated by the fact that we are best at knowing that we have seen a face before, and not so good at knowing where we have seen the face before. Experimental evidence of this comes from studies such as that by Brown et al. (1977). In this the participants identified whether or not they had seen a set of photos of faces before, and in which of two rooms it had been shown. Recognition of old faces was very good but the participants were much poorer at identifying which room they had seen them in. This can have implications for the wrongful identification of people who are familiar from other contexts. If the face looks familiar the witness may draw the conclusion that the person must be the criminal. One example of this is given by Baddeley (1990). A psychologist in Australia who had appeared in a TV discussion on eyewitness testimony was arrested some time later, picked out in an identity parade by a clearly very distraught woman and told he was being charged with rape. It became clear that the rape had been committed at the same time as he was taking part in the TV discussion. When the psychologist told the police that he had a large number of witnesses including an Assistant Commissioner of Police, the policeman taking the statement replied 'Yes, and I suppose you've also got Jesus Christ and the Queen of England too!'. It turned out that the woman had been watching the TV programme when the rape had occurred and she had correctly recognized that she had seen the face at the time, but not the circumstances.

When witnesses give verbal testimony, the accuracy of the recall of an incident depends upon the way in which the recall is elicited. Much research has been directed to comparing the freely given narrative of what happened in comparison with a questioning (e.g. Loftus, 1979). It is well established that the account given by the witness without probing with questions is usually relatively accurate, but tends to leave out many details, often the very details that the police need for their investigations. When questions are introduced much more information can be elicited. However, along with more correct information comes an increase in errors. This is made worse by the ease with which the wording of the questions can lead to the incorrect answers. For example, Loftus and Palmer (1974) asked participants who had seen a video film of a car crash, 'About how fast were the cars going when they (contacted/hit/collided/smashed into) each other?'. The mean speed estimates were highest for 'smashed' (40.8 m.p.h.), next highest for 'collided' (39.3 m.p.h.), lower for 'hit' (34 m.p.h.) and lowest for 'contacted' (31.8 m.p.h.). Furthermore, twice as many participants responded (incorrectly) that they had seen broken glass following the question using 'smashed' rather than 'contacted'. This research led to the studies summarized by Loftus and Loftus (1980) and described in chapter 2 which demonstrated the ease with which the recall of witnesses can be distorted by the implications embedded in earlier questions. While this research may not show that memories are permanently modified, the consistency of these findings shows how easily the evidence of a witness may be modified by unconscious hints given in earlier questioning.

Given that witnesses will sometimes be inaccurate in their testimony, there is a need for judges and juries to decide which of two witnesses is giving the correct account. The commonsense assumption is that the person who is most confident of their evidence is most likely to be correct. Unfortunately, many studies of the confidence and accuracy of recall have shown that the relationship between the two is very small. Bothwell et al. (1987) carried out a meta-analysis of 35 staged-event studies and found the correlation of accuracy and confidence to be only 0.25. Another widely held view is that hypnosis will aid eyewitness memory. However, many studies have found no advantage from using hypnosis (see, e.g. Smith, 1983 for a review) while others have shown that hypnosis can distort recall (e.g. Orne et al., 1984). The Cognitive Interview, as mentioned in chapter 2, has proved to be a much better tool, eliciting 25–35 per cent more correct information than the standard police interview with no more errors (Fisher and Geiselman, 1988) (see also box 7.2). The technique uses four general strategies designed to maximize recall. These are (a) mentally reinstating the environmental and personal context that existed at the time of the crime, (b) reporting everything regardless of its perceived importance, (c) recounting events in a variety of temporal orders and (d) reporting the events from a variety of perspectives such as that of a prominent character as well as from the witness's own standpoint. These techniques exploit known factors that improve recall. For example, Morris and Morris (1985) showed that the starting point that witnesses took for recall influenced the amount that they could correctly remember.

Autobiographical Memory

The memories that eyewitnesses have of their involvement in a crime are specific examples of autobiographical memories. Autobiographical memories are of episodes from the person's own life. As such, they may be of a number of forms. Cohen (1989) distinguishes between declarative and experiential autobiographical memories. A declarative memory would be my knowledge of the fact that my telephone number is such and such, while an experiential memory would resemble reliving an experience with mental imagery and recollection of how I felt at the time. Cohen also distinguishes between specific and generic autobiographical memories. For example, I may have a specific memory of an event in a particular lecture and I have a generic memory of what lectures in that lecture theatre are like, developed over many years.

Conway (1990) has reviewed the history of research on autobiographical memory. The earliest experimental study of such memories was by Galton (1883). He selected a list of 75 words and then timed how long it took him to bring to mind two separate ideas for each word. He repeated this four times at monthly intervals in different places. He found that his recall was much less rich than he had originally expected. While just over half his thoughts were novel, for almost a quarter of the words the same association was generated on each occasion. Galton, then aged 57, was able to date many of his images from his past, and found that 39 per cent were from before the age of 22, 46 per cent from 'manhood' and 15 per cent were from recent events. In another early study, Colegrove (1899) questioned 1,658 people, mostly college students, about their earliest memories, recall from different periods in their lives and the ease of remembering pleasant and unpleasant events. Several of his findings resemble the results of tighter empirical research in recent years. He found that there were few memories for the first years of life, that the memories for different generations reflected the interests of that age group, and that pleasant memories were easier to retrieve than unpleasant ones.

After this early work, little more was done until Crovitz and Schiffman (1974) initiated the modern interest in autobiographical memory. They read 20 highly imageable familiar nouns to their undergraduate participants and required them to write down a few words describing a memory recalled by the word. After completing the list, the participants went back through their responses dating the memories. Crovitz and Schiffman found that the frequency of memories declined with the age of the memories, unlike Galton's finding. In a more direct test of early memory, Crovitz and Quina-Holland (1976) cued students to recall memories from their childhoods. In two studies they found virtually no memories for the first two years and few for the third year. This childhood amnesia had been explored earlier with similar results by Waldfogel (1948) who had required students to recall all their memories from before the age of eight.

Rubin (1982) suggested that the forgetting of autobiographical memories would be a function of time. He carried out a series of studies using variations of the Crovitz technique. One study used diary keepers who were able to establish the accuracy of their dating for a quarter of their memories from their diaries. For these the accuracy of dating was high. Rubin concluded that the forgetting of autobiographical memories was a function of their age. However, the studies by Crovitz and by Rubin used students as their samples. When people over the age of 70 were tested by McCormack in three studies and their lives divided into four quarters, the highest recall was found for autobiographical memories from the first quarter and the lowest from the third quarter. Rubin et al. (1986) plotted the data accumulated from a number of similar studies. The results are shown in figure 7.1. Rubin et al. suggest that there are three separate components to the autobiographical retention. For the most recent 20–30 years of life, the longer ago the fewer the memories that will be recalled. The second component is what has come to be known as the reminiscence peak. Older individuals appear to sample preferentially memories from their early adulthood. The third component is the childhood amnesia of early childhood.

There are several problems with the Galton–Crovitz methodology. One is that the dating of the memories itself depends upon the memory of the participant. Furthermore, the cueing of recall is very open, depending only upon some relationship with the cue word. This can allow the participants to develop idiosyncratic retrieval strategies such as searching for memories related to one time of life. Other researchers have tried to overcome these problems by carefully recording the details of their own or others' experiences and then testing for their recall using cues recorded when the event occurred. Linton (1982) and Wagenaar (1986, 1988) recorded events from their lives over six-year periods. Linton found a forgetting rate of only

5–6 per cent per year. Wagenaar had recorded as cues at the time 'who', 'what', 'when' and 'where'. These he used as retrieval cues in their various combinations. 'What' cues were most effective, followed by 'where' and 'who'. 'When' cued very little recall by itself, but was a highly effective second cue. In general, combinations of the cues were more effective than the cues alone, and the rate of forgetting resembled that found by Linton.

The Linton and Wagenaar studies both involved events of sufficient importance to the experimenter to be chosen to be recorded. When the selection is more random the rate of forgetting is much higher. Brewer (1988), for example, had ten participants carry random alarms and record what they were doing when the alarm went off. These records were used for testing the participants' memories after up to 46 days. He found a much higher rate of forgetting than was implied by the Linton and Wagenaar studies.

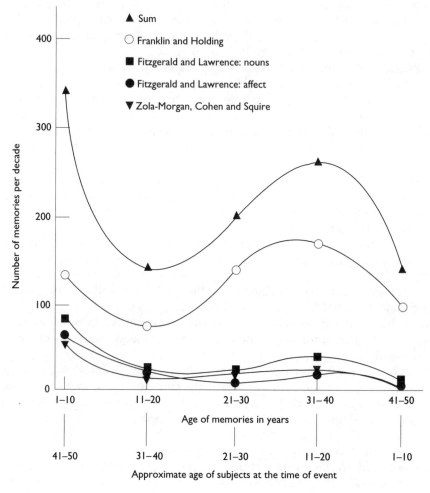

Figure 7.1 Variation in autobiographical memory throughout the lifespan. (Based on Rubin et al., 1986)

Flashbulb memories

One aspect of autobiographical memories that has attracted particular attention is flashbulb memories. These are detailed memories for the circumstances in which one heard outstanding and often surprising news. In such circumstances it is common to be able to remember who you were with, where, how you heard the news and so on. The earliest study of these memories was by Colegrove (1899) who found that 33 years after the assassination of Lincoln, 127 of 179 people questioned could provide these details. Brown and Kulik (1977) questioned 80 participants on their memories of several actual or attempted assassinations. Almost all the participants had detailed memories for John Kennedy's murder, and many had similar memories for the other events. Brown and Kulik argued that there was a special mechanism to record all the details surrounding sudden and important events so that they could be remembered in the future to help cope with similar potentially dangerous events.

There has been much dispute over the correct interpretation of flashbulb memories. Do they represent a special memory process with exceptional recall, or are they just the extreme of essentially normal remembering, with the very good recall occurring for the same reasons that determine the retrieval of other memories? Neisser (1982), for example, argues that flashbulb memories can be inaccurate, that they are well remembered because they are frequently rehearsed, and that they are special only in providing the link between our lives and the course of history. McCloskey et al. (1988) studied the change in flashbulb memories of the Challenger space shuttle disaster. The participants were tested in the first few days after the event and again nine months later. By then, there had been a decline from 100 per cent to between 89 per cent and 100 per cent in recall to questions such as 'What were you doing when you first heard of the explosion?'. McCloskey et al. argue that because some forgetting took place there cannot be a special encoding mechanism that is immune to forgetting. Conway (1990) points out that the level of recall was still exceptionally high and that any special mechanism need not have been activated for all the participants. A few participants might have not shared the interest in the launch and the shock following the disaster. If these did not have a flashbulb memory process triggered at the time of the disaster, then their forgetting would have been normal, and would have accounted for the small loss over the nine months. Nevertheless, whether or not there is a special mechanism for flashbulb memories, and whether or not they are quite resistant to forgetting, there is sufficient evidence that there is a type of memory, perhaps best called a vivid memory, possessed by all of us for events that were surprising and important to us whose memory we retain for decades while others are forgotten (see e.g. Rubin and Kozin, 1984, and Conway and Bekerian, 1988).

When did it happen? Dating autobiographical memories

Many studies of autobiographical memory have asked the participants to date their memories. Wagenaar (1988), however, found that his 'when' cues were poor if not combined with other information. Dating of our memories declines in accuracy with passing time. Thompson (1982) illustrated this in a study in which he had the roommates of his participants record details in diaries that could subsequently be tested. For the first few weeks, memories of when the event occurred and what had happened were related. However, after that time they seemed to be independent. Furthermore, Thompson found that the accuracy of the dating of the events declined by about a day a week.

One way in which memories can be fixed more accurately in memory is when they can be placed in comparison to some highly memorable, landmark event. Thompson (1982) found that his more accurate participants were using such features from their lives, such as breaking up with a boyfriend. Baddeley et al. (1978) found that the accuracy of dating when participants had attended their laboratory showed an average error of 19 days for every 100 days that had passed. However, more accurate recall was given by participants who could relate the visit to an important personal event.

Loftus and Marburger (1983) were concerned about what is known as the 'forward telescoping' of memories of traumatic or unpleasant events, such as being a victim of crime or suffering major health problems. They suspected that such important personal events would be recalled as being more recent than they actually were. This would then introduce a serious flaw into studies that ask how often an event has occurred in the past year or six months. Loftus and Marburger used the landmark event of the eruption of the nearby Mount St. Helen six months earlier to test this. Asking their participants whether they had been a victim of crime since the eruption greatly reduced the incidence of false reports in comparison with a group merely asked about the past six months.

For better or worse, we do not have volcanoes exploding with suitable regularity to help us date our memories! However, Loftus and Marburger also found that other distinctive days, such as New Year's Day, were effective in reducing the forward telescoping of the memories.

Mental Imagery and Memory ▶ ▶

One feature of autobiographical memory is its involvement with mental imagery. Conway (1988) gives the following example of a person recalling her wedding day: 'I can clearly see (closes her eyes) Paul, who was wearing a green velvet suit, my parents . . .'. This imaging is to many people the essence of remembering. It conveys a confidence that the event actually occurred that may be out of proportion to the actual reliability of the images. Brewer (1988) noted the high confidence that went with such images. Morris (1986) found that, when answering questions about a video film, participants were more often correct when they had an image at the time of answering the questions. However, this image could confer an excessive confidence. Morris also reported that the confidence that the answer was correct was so high when an image was available to support an answer that participants were more confident of incorrect answers that were accompanied by an image than they were of correct answers without an image.

Images are affected by the normal factors that determine ease of recall. Morris (1992) asked participants to form images of various people, including friends and relatives and famous persons. The participants recorded the ease of imaging and its vividness. Both these properties of the images were highly predicted by the frequency with which the people had been seen and the recency of the last encounter. For each participant, multiple regressions predicting ease of imaging using the two variables frequency and recency were computed, and the mean multiple correlation was 0.85.

It should not be assumed, however, that the images that are formed during recall are in any sense accurate copies of the original perception. For example, some memory images include the imager himself or herself in the scene. These 'observer' memories were investigated by Nigro and Neisser (1983). They cued memories to common experiences and required the participants to judge the type of memory. Some situations, such as having a conversation, cued many more 'field memories', that is, memories from the original field of view, than observer memories. However, this was reversed for some other situations such as giving a public presentation or running. Nigro and Neisser found that observer memories were associated with high degrees of emotionality and self-awareness having been associated with the original event. Field memories were more common for more recent events. Older memories may involve a higher degree of reconstruction, so allowing the observer viewpoint to be taken.

Memory Improvement

We conclude this chapter with a brief consideration of how memory can be improved. At various times in our lives most of us wish that we could improve our memories, and students are particularly concerned to memorize the material they study. In these chapters on memory and remembering we have demonstrated that the best encoding occurs when the learner is already an expert in the area and is able to bring that expertise to bear in understanding the meaning and implications of the material to be memorized. If the learner is able to consider in elaborate detail the meaning and implications of the new facts, and to integrate them into his or her existing knowledge, then recall is likely to be relatively easy. If what is encoded into memory is itself distinctive and easily discriminated from other stored information, then there is less likelihood of problems from interference by other items that have been or will be stored. If the material has an inherent structure that is known to the learner, then this will guide the encoding and the subsequent reconstruction. If it is possible to incorporate in what is encoded cues that will be available at the time that retrieval will be required, then these will aid the location of the stored information.

Perhaps because a certain amount of effort is required to satisfy all these 'ifs', the temptation for the student is to take a passive role during learning and revising. It is easy to just read one's notes or the set readings, understand them at the time and expect to recall them later. Where difficult material has to be tackled it is easy to simply resort to saying it over and over (rehearsing) but thinking little about what is being said. None of this makes the most of the processes that lead to best recall. A much more active, questioning approach, bringing into play what is already known and guaranteeing a fuller consideration of the meaning of the material, is more effective and is recommended as the basis of most formal study methods (see, e.g. Higbee, 1988). Simple rehearsal is likely to use only the articulatory loop, and be no more than a temporary case of maintenance rehearsal. Rehearsal does little to improve recall if new aspects of the information are not drawn out during the rehearsal and integrated with other existing knowledge. Indeed, it seems that the benefits of pure maintenance rehearsal, in terms of the quantity and quality of the retrieved information, probably accrue from the first few rehearsals in which the rehearsal programme is set up (Naveh-Benjamin and Jonides, 1984a,b; Macken and Hampson, 1993). However, this is not to suggest that reading material just once will suffice. This may be sufficient for immediate recall, but it does not do all that can be done to improve recall at a later time. Overlearning, actively considering in detail material already apparently acquired, will further increase its future ease of retrieval. Information that has been dealt with very frequently may become particularly resistant to forgetting, as Bahrick (1984a,b) found for the recall of old school classmates and foreign languages acquired at school. Spaced practice is also a better use of time than trying to study the same topic too intensely for too long (e.g. Baddeley and Longman, 1978; see also chapter 6). Testing yourself by telling another person, or even yourself, is very beneficial as practice at retrieval and is a salutary reminder of how much has not been acquired.

All of the above can influence recall, but there are some types of material that are particularly difficult to learn because they do not possess the inherent meaning and connections with existing knowledge that normally makes for easier learning. So, for example, learning a new language or attaching names to faces is particularly difficult at least in part because there are no existing links that can be found and developed. It is for these sorts of situations that a solution is provided by the mnemonic methods of memory improvement used by stage memory experts (e.g. Lorayne, 1958; 1990) which also form the basis of commercially offered memory improvement techniques.

Memory improvement techniques normally rely heavily upon imagery mnemonics. These use mental images to link together the items to be remembered. In their simplest form, such mnemonics would recommend that for the learning of a list of unrelated items, such as table, mouse, nail, tree and so on, the list should be memorized by forming a series of mental images that involve the objects named interacting in some way. So, for the first image, a mouse might be imagined on a table, for the second, a mouse perhaps nailed down by its tail, for the third, a nail in a tree, and so on. At recall, the word table recalls the image of the mouse on the table, which in turn recalls the image of the mouse nailed by its tail, and so on. Research on such imaging strategies has shown them to be surprisingly effective (see, e.g. Morris, 1979 for a review), although the most convincing proof is to try it for oneself with a list of concrete words provided by someone else. The fundamental part of the mnemonic is the provision of a meaningful link between the items through their spatial relationship in the image. The imaging of single words does not, in itself, help their recall, though it does improve recognition of the words (e.g. Morris and Stevens, 1974; Morris and Reid, 1973).

The use of imagery is one key component in many mnemonic techniques. Another component is the provision of specific cues to help the retrieval of the appropriate images. Many memory improvement techniques involve the initial learning of 'peg' words, for example to stand for the numbers 1–100. These can then be used to memorize up to a hundred items at a time that can be recalled in any order. The peg words are concrete words, usually constructed using a system of translating the individual digits into consonant sounds and inserting vowel sounds to make familiar words (Morris and Greer, 1984). For example, a hard 'c' sound is usually used to represent 7, and a 't' sound for 1, so that the peg word for 71 might be cat. When the translation rules are known, the peg words are relatively easily memorized, so that the memorizer has a specific object to image along with the relevant item. Thus, if the 71st item to be memorized was 'tie' then a mental image of a tie around the neck of a cat might be formed. At recall, reaching number 71 recalls that the peg word for 71 is 'cat' and that cues the image of the cat with a tie. Peg-word mnemonics have proved to be very effective (e.g. Morris and Reid, 1970; Morris, 1979).

The basic imagery mnemonic can be extended to help in other situations where memorizing is particularly difficult. One such technique is the link word system, commercially available to help the learning of foreign language vocabularies (Gruneberg, 1992). The system involves translating each foreign word into an easily imaged, similar-sounding English word and then linking this with a concrete representation of the meaning of the foreign word. For example, to remember that the French for 'menu' is 'carte' Gruneberg (1987) recommends forming an image of a cart full of menus. Those who try the system find that it provides a very rapid way of acquiring vocabulary. A further, related, imagery mnemonic helps the learning of putting names to faces by linking meaningful translations of the person's name to a distinctive feature of their face via a mental image. This, too, has been found to be highly effective (e.g. Morris et al., 1978).

Conclusions

Although the material in this chapter is, of course, related to that discussed in chapter 2, the work we have covered here has two things in common which make it worth examining in its own right. First, it is more concerned with the activities and examples of remembering, rather than the cognitive structures and processes used to remember. Second, and related to this, it emphasizes that remembering occurs in the real world, with real stimuli, which have real meaning. The focus therefore is more on what memory is for and how it manifests itself, rather than on the abstract mechanics of the memory system.

Remembering underlies most of what we do. Without a record of the past to draw on we would be helpless in our interactions with the world, and probably extremely disoriented about our own lives. But memory is not just about retrieving past information. As we stated in the introduction, pattern recognition and skill run through most of human cognition, and remembering is no exception. In the study of schemata, scripts and chess it is clear that powerful pattern recognition procedures are at work. In interrogating witnesses, actively learning the skills of managing (and mismanaging) the system becomes apparent. There is, of course, still much to discover about the processes of memory themselves and the skills that people have in using them, but the studies reviewed here are now beginning to show how they are used to tackle the world that we encounter. Memory, used with skill, allows us to bring to bear patterns from the past to interpret the present and, as we shall see in the next chapter, to anticipate the future.

Further reading

Good sources for further information on the material in this chapter are: G. Cohen 1988: *Memory in the Real World*. Hove: Lawrence Erlbaum Associates, M. Conway 1990: *Autobiographical Memory*. Milton Keynes: Open University Press, P. Harris and P.E. Morris (eds) 1984: *Everyday Memory, Actions and Absentmindedness*. London: Academic Press, and M.M. Gruneberg, P.E. Morris and R.N. Sykes (eds) 1988: *Practical Aspects of Memory: Current Research and Issues*. Chichester: Wiley (2 vols). Original papers on a variety of topics in everyday memory can also be found in U. Neisser and E. Winograd (eds) 1988: *Remembering Reconsidered: Ecological and Traditional Approaches to the Study of Memory*. Cambridge: Cambridge University Press, U. Neisser (ed.) 1982: *Memory Observed*, San Francisco: Freeman, and D.C. Rubin (ed.) 1986: *Autobiographical Memory*. Cambridge: Cambridge University Press.

Discussion points

1   The use of scripts, MOPs and TOPs suggests that we bring to bear representations (patterns) of the abstract structure of events to interpret present situations. To what extent does remembering rely on efficient pattern recognition?
2   Why exactly do experts remember information from their area of interest better than novices?
3   Review the problems associated with eyewitness testimony.
4   Why do we remember certain events and not others? Why do we forget things from our early childhood?
5   Can memory be improved?

Practical exercises

1   Elicit scripts from people for a number of everyday situations such as attending a wedding, going to see a film or visiting a hospital patient. Make up short stories in which major script elements are missing. Ask other participants to recall your stories as exactly as possible, after a delay of, say, ten minutes. What do you notice about their recall?

2   Investigate people's memories of recent, public events. Do any of these memories constitute 'flashbulb' memories? For instance, how vivid are people's memories of what they were doing when they heard of Margaret Thatcher's resignation? Do flashbulb memories have vivid imagery associated with them? How can you predict when an event will result in a flashbulb memory?

3   Teach people to use the following rhyme as a mnemonic:

One is a bun,
Two is a shoe,
Three is a tree,
Four is a door,
Five is a hive,
Six is sticks,
Seven is heaven,
Eight is a gate,
Nine is a line,
Ten is a hen.

Make a list of ten objects and ask your participants to form an image of each object in turn with the object associated with its number in the rhyme. For instance, if object number three is a sheep, your participant might form an image of a (suitably bemused) sheep in a tree. To retrieve the ten objects your participants should first remember the appropriate line of the rhyme then remember the composite image. So, object number three ... tree ... sheep, would be the sequence in this case. How powerful a memory technique is this? How well do your participants remember the list compared with others who merely repeat the names of the ten objects? Investigate the ease with which objects can be recalled in any order, or the number of the objects remembered by both groups of participants. Why does this mnemonic work?

Box 7.1
Expertise and memory

A number of studies have demonstrated that experts have better memories of new information in their area of expertise than do novices. This has been shown, for example, for chess players (Chase and Simon, 1973) and for accounts of baseball matches (Spilich et al., 1979). A common feature of these studies was that the experts had better ways of chunking and organizing the material, or were more familiar with the meaning of the terms used. Morris et al. (1985) chose a situation in which expertise might play a part without the advantage of either chunking or familiarity. They looked at the recall of soccer scores by soccer enthusiasts and those with less knowledge of soccer.

Two types of results were presented to the participants. The experiment took place on a Saturday afternoon so that the participants were unable to hear the real soccer scores during the afternoon but were presented, for the first time, with the genuine scores in the news broadcast of the results. The participants also heard a set of simulated results. While these results were constructed to be as realistic as possible, using for example the same frequencies of scores as in previous weeks' results, and new but realistic pairings of teams for the matches, the participants were aware that the scores had been simulated.

Expertise in soccer score recall might be merely a reflection of a general better memory ability by the soccer experts. To test for this more general possibility the participants were also tested on their free recall of 30 common words.

Box table 7.1.1   Intercorrelations for experiment 1

	Real scores	Simulated scores	Free recall
Questionnaire	0.82**	0.36*	0.26
Real scores		0.54**	0.32
Simulated scores			0.67**

* p < 0.05 **p < 0.01 two tailed test
Source: Based on table 1, Morris et al., 1985

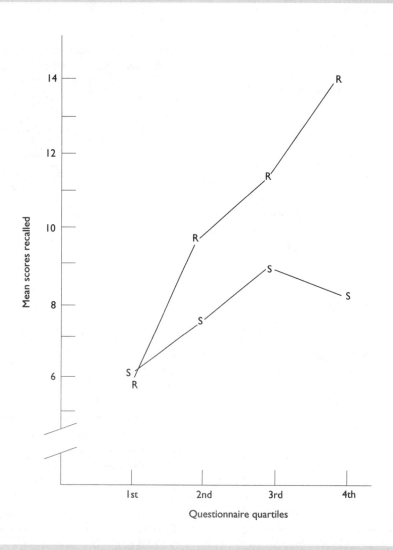

Box figure 7.1.1   Recall of real (R) and simulated (S) scores as a function of knowledge questionnaire. (Based on figure 1, Morris et al., 1985)

Method

Nineteen male and nine female undergraduates were tested as a group. They first completed a soccer knowledge questionnaire consisting of 30 questions testing knowledge of information about soccer, such as 'Where is Chelsea's home ground?' 'What team won the FA cup seven times?'

The football results were tape recorded for the first and second divisions and broadcast on BBC Radio 2. The simulated scores were read at a similar rate and in a similar way. The simulated list appeared indistinguishable from the real results. Half the participants heard the real results first, half the simulated results first. Participants were also given a free recall test of 30 common words.

The participants were given response sheets upon which they had to write the correct scores, following the names of the teams in each fixture. The participants were required to guess where they could not recall, giving a score for every team in every game.

Results

Recall of the real and simulated results was scored as correct only if the number of goals for both teams in a fixture was given correctly. The intercorrelations of the participants' performance on the tests is given in box table 7.1.1. There was a very strong relationship between the recall of real scores and performance on the soccer knowledge questionnaire ($r = 0.82$). However, performance on the simulated scores was far more weakly related to the soccer knowledge questionnaire. Performance on the free recall task did not correlate significantly with the soccer knowledge questionnaire, nor with the recall of real scores, but did correlate highly with recall of simulated scores. Box figure 7.1.1 illustrates the recall of real and simulated scores as a function of knowledge of soccer, measured by the soccer questionnaires. Those participants who knew least about soccer (the first quartile on the questionnaire) had similar recall for the real and simulated results. However, the greater the knowledge of soccer beyond this, the bigger the difference in recall between real and simulated results and the better the recall of the real scores.

Discussion

The greater the knowledge of soccer, the better the recall of the real scores. However, the simulated scores, despite appearing similar in every way except for the reality of the results, led to a different pattern of recall. Real results apparently stimulated encoding or retrieval processes in those who were knowledgeable about soccer which were hardly activated by the simulated scores. There appeared to be two processes or skills being measured. The real scores activated processes in which there were individual differences measured by the soccer knowledge questionnaire. The simulated scores and the free recall scores measured a different individual difference ability.

Morris et al. pointed out that the failure of the simulated results highlighted the difficulty of simulation in memory experiments and the importance of realistic stimuli.

In their second experiment, they showed a strong relationship in the recall of results between the liking or disliking of teams and the recall of their latest results. This relationship is perhaps not surprising but, as with many other findings in psychology which accord with 'common sense', it is still useful to have hard evidence to support it.

Based on P.E. Morris, M. Tweedy and M.M. Gruneberg 1985: Interest knowledge and the memorising of soccer scores. *British Journal of Psychology*, 76, 415–25.

Box 7.2
Eyewitness testimony and the Cognitive Interview

A critical component of effective law enforcement is the ability of police investigators to obtain accurate and detailed information from witnesses. However, eyewitness accounts are known to be frequently fallible and incomplete. Geiselman and his colleagues developed a memory retrieval procedure that they called the Cognitive Interview to maximize the eyewitness recall during an investigation. The Cognitive Interview technique involved four procedures.

1   Reinstate the context. The interviewer and interviewee try to reinstate the context surrounding the

incident before recalling the event. The interviewee is asked to try to recall the surrounding environment, the room, the weather, the lighting, any smells, any people nearby etc.

2   Report everything. The interviewee is asked to report any information even if they consider it may not be important.

3   Recall the event in a different order. The interviewee is encouraged to try to recall in a variety of orders. For example, going through the event in reverse order or starting with the thing that most impressed them about the incident and going backwards or forwards in time from it.

4   Change perspectives. The interviewees try to recall the incident from different perspectives from their own. For example, placing themselves in the role of a prominent character in the incident and thinking about what he or she must have seen.

In experiment 1, Geiselman and his colleagues compared the Cognitive Interview with the standard police interview.

Method

The participants were 89 undergraduate students. The interviewers were 17 law enforcement professionals, police detectives, CIA investigators and private investigators. The participants were shown four-minute films borrowed from the Los Angeles police department and used in their training programme. The films depicted bank robberies, hold-ups, a family dispute and a search through a warehouse. In each film, at least one individual was shot and killed.

Approximately 48 hours after viewing their film the participants were interviewed by the law enforcement personnel. Before each interview the interviewer was told only the title of the crime scenario. All interviews were audio recorded. Three weeks prior to the interviews each interviewer received instructions for one of the interview procedures, that is, the Standard Interview or the Cogni-

Box table 7.2.1   Facts recalled with Standard and Cognitive Interviews

	Cognitive	Standard
Correct items	41.15	29.40
Incorrect items	7.30	6.10
Confabulations	0.70	0.40

Source: Based on table 11.1, Geiselman, 1988

tive Interview.

Results

Each tape recorded interview was analysed for the recall of persons, objects and events. Information elicited was matched against the information contained in the four films for accuracy. Each participant's report was scored for:

1   The number of correct bits of information recalled;

2   The number of incorrect bits of information generated (e.g. wrong hair colour of a suspect);

3   The number of confabulated bits of information generated (e.g. a description of a participant's face when a face was not shown in the film).

The results are shown in box table 7.2.1. The Cognitive Interview elicited approximately 35 per cent more correct items of information than the Standard Interview, but the two types of interviews did not differ in the number of incorrect items generated, nor in the number of confabulations.

Geiselman went on to report several more experiments investigating the Cognitive Interview. He found that the interview was effective with participants other than students and that the negative effect of asking misleading questions was reduced when the Cognitive Interview was used.

Based on R.E. Geiselman 1988: Improving eye witness memory through mental reinstatement of context. In G.M. Davies and D.M. Thomson (eds), *Memory in Context: Context in Memory*. Chichester: Wiley.

8 Planning and Actions: Successes and Failures

You have arranged to meet a friend at 7 p.m. At 6.30 p.m. you lay down the book you have been reading, put on your coat, pick up a letter to post on the way, and start out. On the way you meet another old friend. You chat for a while, start looking at your watch and become anxious about meeting your first friend. Eventually you say that you must go, and you run to meet your first friend. The next day you discover that you still have the letter you intended to post in your coat pocket.

There is nothing unusual in this sequence of events. We do not normally forget to post letters, but it can be a common error if posting letters is something that we do relatively rarely and at different times and places. What we want to emphasize initially is that all of this behaviour is best understood in terms of the plans that you were following. Your main goal was to meet your friend. To do this you had to organize yourself to leave at an appropriate time, walk an appropriate route, perhaps involving several streets and crossing a number of busy roads. When you unexpectedly met your other friend you were capable of suspending your initial plan, or rather, of modifying it to allow you to achieve your new, temporary goal of talking with your friend. However, much of that conversation will have been influenced by your need to keep the meeting short. You will not have launched into any long anecdotes; you will have kept the topics of conversation at a fairly superficial and brief level; you will have shown signs of fidgeting, by the position in which you stood so you were ready to hurry on, by looking at your watch and so on. Your friend would probably guess that you have an appointment elsewhere.

The example given above illustrates both how the plans and goals that we have shape our behaviour, and also the flexibility of those plans. Plans can also go wrong – we forget to post letters, to keep appointments or to watch TV programmes. This chapter discusses how our behaviour is organized to fulfil our plans, and the ways in which we sometimes fail to carry out what we plan. We will look at actions, errors and absentmindedness. We also examine the link between cognition and emotion and its relation with action and the relatively new field of prospective memory: remembering what we are going to do.

The Planning and Control of Action

In this section the basic principles in the control and planning of actions are considered, and models designed to account for these are discussed. Some of these date from the early days of cognitive psychology, others are somewhat more recent.

Plans, TOTEs and schemas

Perhaps the classic book on the planning and control of actions was Miller et al. (1960) *Plans and the Structure of Behavior*. At the end of the 1950s, the dominant view in psychology was still behaviourist. However, there were several alternative approaches from which Miller et al. were able to draw ideas. One was the British tradition exemplified by Craik and Bartlett, who were encouraged, by the pressures of wartime, to study complex skills such as those of aircraft pilots (chapter 6). Another was the progress being made by Chomsky and others in developing grammars in linguistics which were not compatible with current behaviourist views of language (chapter 4). Most important, however, was the developing field of computer simulation and artificial intelligence. When Craik had been writing in the 1940s there had been few complex machines for him to use as analogies to human cognition. By the late 1950s the groundwork of cognitive science had been laid and more powerful computers were making the simulation of human cognition by computers seem plausible, as well as revealing the types of complexities that a computer simulation of human behaviour would have to face.

Miller et al. (1960) emphasized, as we have done, that our lives have structure, that as we think about our coming day we construct plans to meet what we intend and foresee. They agreed with the behaviourists that what an organism does depends upon what happens around it. However, they identified two ways in which this dependency should be described. The dominant view at the time, that of the behaviourists, they called the optimists' view. For them the relation between the environment and the organism's actions was simple and straightforward. However, the alternative view was provided by the pessimists 'who think that living organisms are complicated, devious, poorly designed for research purposes, and so on. They maintain that the effect an event will have upon behaviour depends on how the event is represented in the organisms's picture of itself and its universe' (p. 7).

Miller et al. are among the pessimists, and they proposed a new set of concepts for tackling the analysis of actions. They found it 'quite obvious' that behaviour is organized simultaneously at several levels of complexity. To represent how the organism does this they proposed two general concepts: the 'Plan' and the 'Image'.

A Plan was defined by them as 'any hierarchical process in the organism that can control the order in which a sequence of operations is to be performed' (p. 16). An Image is 'all the accumulated, organized knowledge that the organism has about itself and its world' (p. 17).

Miller et al. assumed that normal adult humans have access to a very large number of Plans which they might execute if they chose to do so. They assumed that the parts of a Plan that are being executed have special access to consciousness and that we have a quick-access 'working memory' that is used to store the information on the current state of an uncompleted Plan. For Miller et al., intentions are the uncompleted parts of Plans stored in working memory.

For the more detailed analysis of Plans, Miller et al. introduced the Test–Operate–Test–Exit (TOTE) unit (see figure 8.1). The TOTE unit is a simple flow chart indicating the transfer of control of processing through a series of tests for incongruity with the Plan, the employment of an operation that may alleviate the problem, and the constant circuiting of test and operation until the necessary conditions have been fulfilled so that the test shows no incongruity and the next stage in the programme can be implemented.

The example of a TOTE unit given by Miller et al. is for hammering a nail flush with the surface. If the head sticks up then the test shows incongruity and Hammering is initiated. The loop continues until the nail head is flat. Miller et al. illustrate how hierarchies of TOTE units can be built up,

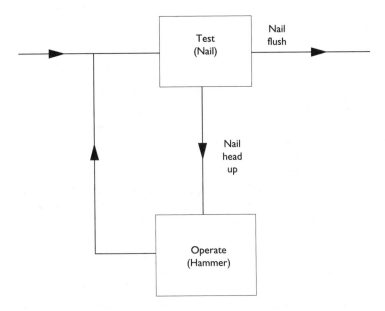

Figure 8.1   A Test–Operate–Test–Exit (TOTE) unit. (Based on figure 3, Miller et al., 1960)

embedding lower-level instructions within the higher-level parts of the Plan. An example of a hierarchical Plan for hammering nails is given in figure 8.2, where the Hammer operation has been elaborated into two necessary TOTE units for Lifting and Striking.

The idea of hierarchical Plans bears considerable resemblance to that of the schemata that were discussed in chapter 6. When Bartlett (1932) adopted the concept of a schema that had been first used by Head, he used it to discuss the role of organized past experience in the interpretation and control not only of stories but also of actions. For Bartlett, ' "Schema" refers to an active organization of past reactions or of past experiences, which must always be supposed to be operating in any well-adapted organic response' (p. 201). Schemata have been used to explain the way past experience can be used to make sense of similar situations when they recur. As we discussed in chapter 6, schemata for actions, based upon past experience, have been a popular if rather vague concept when considering actions from Bartlett onwards.

Some modellers of the human action system have preferred the vaguer concept of schemata to that of Plans and TOTEs. While the TOTE concept has many attractions, one of its weaknesses may be in the emphasis upon feedback. Of course, feedback on the success of our activities is very important in many circumstances, but it may not always be the case that feedback is evaluated and utilized, especially at so many stages in an action sequence. Also, the emphasis on feedback and testing can obscure the even more important question of what is involved in the Operate stage of the

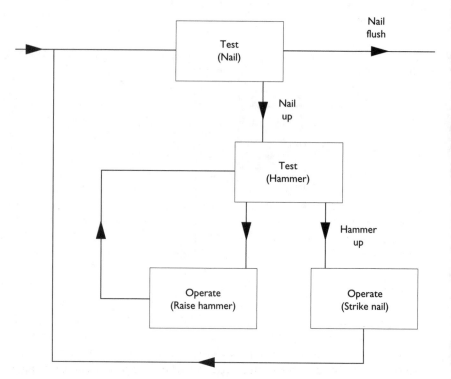

Figure 8.2   A Plan for hammering nails. (Based on figure 5, Miller et al., 1960)

TOTE, which is where the real activity takes place. Finally, a simple TOTE structure would be a very dangerous one if it was not supplemented with some system to prevent continuous looping if the Test could never be satisfactorily accomplished. The vaguer concept of schema has the advantage of emphasizing the structured use of experience without specifying prematurely the form in which it is used.

Norman's activation–trigger–schema system

An example of a schema theory of action has been proposed by Norman (1981) which he calls an activation–trigger–schema (ATS) model for the control of action sequences.

In Norman's model it is assumed that we all possess a very large number of schemata, which are organized bodies of knowledge, including procedural knowledge that can control motor activity. Each schema has only a limited range and any given action must be specified by many schemata, organized together and controlled by higher-level schemata. This idea of hierarchical control will be familiar from earlier sections in the chapter. Norman called the highest-level schema the 'parent' schema while those initiated by that schema he called 'child' schemata. There can be several levels of control since child schemata may themselves be parent schemata to other schemata which they control. Intentions are related to the highest-order parent schemata. Because most action sequences require considerable time to be completed, several intentions may be active at any one time. So, in our example, there were intentions to walk to your friend's house, to post the letter and to talk with your friend that you met on the way, all active, or potentially active. Since you forgot to post the letter, that intention and its related schema may have ceased to be active, but we will consider this further later.

Many schemata can, in Norman's model, be active at one time. For well-practised skills only the highest-level schema need be specified. Once activated, the lower-level components of the action sequence complete the action without further need for intervention from higher-level schemata except at critical choice points.

Each activated schema has a set of specific conditions that are required for it to be triggered. There are, thus, two stages prior to the use of a schema. It must be activated, often by higher-level schemata, but sometimes by cues from the environment. Once activated, it will not actually be implemented in initiating some behaviour unless the appropriate triggering conditions exist. To continue our example of visiting a friend, the intention to do so activates a host of schemata necessary for walking safely through the town and for following a well-known route. At appropriate points, for example at the kerb when crossing a road, the activated schemata for road crossing will be triggered, and you will carefully survey the traffic and choose when to cross. Because such skills are very well practised it is not necessary to think about them except where critical decisions must be taken.

Levels of control of actions

As we have just suggested when discussing Norman's model, and the earlier TOTE model, a common idea in discussions of action planning is that there should be different levels of control. This is especially well illustrated by a quotation from Kenneth Craik, a British psychologist writing in the 1940s and using a wartime analogy:

> the C-in-C Fighter Command presumably says: 'we want a sweep carried out over such and such an area'; he does not have to add: 'this means that Spitfire number so and so on such at such a station must have so many gallons of petrol in its tanks and care must be taken that its plugs are clean and guns loaded.' These latter details are delegated to subordinates. In just the same way, for rapidity and certainty in action, it is essential that certain units of activity, such as looking at an object, walking, grasping, using words, or balancing one's body, should be delegated to lower levels. (Craik, 1966, p. 38)

In other words, Craik is suggesting that an efficient system for controlling behaviour will be organized so that all of the details of common actions are handled by specially developed subsystems, so that the planning of the strategy for our actions will be freed from the need to deal with such mundane details.

Broadbent (1977), who quotes this passage from Craik, comments that this idea of multiple levels of human processing was generally accepted by Bartlett and his associates (including Craik) at Cambridge during the 1940s. Indeed, Broadbent traces the view back to Hughlings Jackson writing in the nineteenth century.

The idea of Craik and Bartlett is that the efficient control of any complex system is best accomplished by organizing the separate components into modules and in having further systems in overall control of these modules (see also chapter 12). Under normal circumstances, these higher-level systems do not have to be concerned about the detailed functioning of the lower-level systems. This frees the higher systems to plan and control events at a level appropriate to the complexities of the world with which they have to cope. For human behaviour there are many necessary skills such as walking, breathing, shaking hands, opening doors and saying goodbye, which in themselves are quite complex and flexible skills, but which need to be controlled and regulated appropriately for us to live safely and sanely. It is the norm in biological and human systems for such hierarchies to exist (Koestler, 1975; Simon, 1981). They are not special to the control of human actions.

In the case of our own actions, it is at the higher levels that we are most aware of what we are doing and of our own plans and intentions. Unless we are learning a new skill, we normally think about what we do and describe what we are doing, or will do, at the general level of walking, waving, making tea, posting letters, rather than talking about individual movements. It is at this high level that we are conscious of our actions. We are not conscious of what is involved in undertaking many of the complex skills that we can perform. We know how to write a sentence that we have thought of, but not how this is accomplished in terms of programming our muscles to move the pen in the appropriate sequence. As we discussed in chapter 6, a skilled typist often cannot describe the position of the letters on the keyboard, but can type using them at a very fast rate. It is sometimes remarked that he or she has the memory 'in their fingertips'. Nevertheless, even the most skilled typist is aware of the nature of the action he or she is carrying out, to whom the letter is to be sent, its general content and so on. Hence, while well-practised skills are carried out non-consciously, the fact that their associated actions are being carried out together with their goals, is generally present in consciousness. We know what and why we are doing many things even if we do not know exactly how we are doing them. So, the control of action, at its highest level, is associated with consciousness and awareness. A model to account for this has been proposed by Morris and Hampson (1983).

The BOSS–Consciousness model

When discussing the control of actions and the place of consciousness in the cognitive system, Morris and Hampson (1983) followed the example of Craik, Bartlett and Broadbent, and argued for a hierarchy of systems controlling behaviour. The components of the system that are in overall control of actions we called BOSS and the subsystems to which BOSS delegates and which BOSS supervises we called EMPLOYEE systems. Information about the state of the world and the state of the person were supplied to BOSS by Perceptual EMPLOYEE systems, and movement controlled by Motor EMPLOYEE systems. For some well-practised skills, BOSS was not involved and Perceptual and Motor systems communicated directly. However, when new skills are being acquired and when the main plans and schemes of the individual are involved, then the behaviour is supervised by BOSS.

Morris and Hampson (1983) claimed that conscious experience is associated with the information that is made available to the BOSS system by the Perceptual EMPLOYEES to enable it to monitor what processes it needs to initiate. The proposal is not that we are conscious of the actual activities of BOSS, but of the processed information made available to BOSS, including the feedback from BOSS's own activity. Thus, we are conscious of perceptual information that has been highly processed, so that it is at the level appropriate for BOSS to interpret what needs undertaking. We are conscious of the end products of perceptual processing; of tables, chairs, people – the categorized objects that the system has identified – but not of the steps that lead up to that point. We are also conscious of deciding to do things (such as to visit a friend in this chapter's example), but we are not aware of the full details of how this decision is taken.

In Hampson and Morris (1989) and Morris (1992) we reviewed further arguments and evidence that support and extend the model. However, whether or not we were correct in our discussions of consciousness in the cognitive system as a whole, there is wide agreement that consciousness is associated with these higher-order control processes (see, e.g. Mandler, 1975; Reason and Mycielska, 1982; Harré et al., 1985).

Cognition and Emotion

So far, in our discussions of action we have presented a rather rational and controlled view of human activity, but of course people act for various reasons, and then evaluate the outcome of activities. Activities mean something to people and have emotional significance. Cognition in general and action in particular are not arbitrary operations, they are significant activities carried out by a person with real needs and real emotions. We are not able, in this book, to review all the work in this area, but we can indicate some of its relevance for theories of action.

The relationship between cognition and emotion has become of more interest to psychologists in recent years. Emotion has, of course, always interested psychologists (see, for example, Strongman, 1987, for a review of psychological theories of emotions). However, cognitive psychologists have tended, until recently, to see emotions as outside the realm of cognition. Cognitive theories drew heavily on metaphors derived from computing, or earlier models of information processing, and these had no place for emotion. Furthermore, in that emotions did seem to interact with cognition, they seemed, as Plato had argued, to be enemies of reason, distorting rational thinking.

At some point, however, our theories of cognition must dovetail with our accounts of emotion, since emotions involve all aspects of psychology. They have clear physiological concomitants, and often seem to depend upon social situations for their interpretation, but there is, also, a growing consensus that cognition and emotion are directly related. Several accounts of this relationship have appeared in recent years (Oatley and Johnson-Laird, 1987; Ortony et al., 1988; Scherer, 1984). They have in common the view that emotions reflect assessments of current cognitive processing, and its implications for the goals of the individual. Understood thus, emotions can be defined, in part, as evaluations of the implications of the cognitive processing that is taking place.

As an example of this approach, consider a theory proposed by Scherer (1984). He argues that when any new event occurs, it is processed by a series of Stimulus Evaluation Checks (SECs). Scherer's first check is for novelty; only new patterns of stimulation are processed further. Next, there is an intrinsic pleasantness check, to determine whether the response should be approach or avoidance. Scherer's third check is for the goal or need significance of the event. Is it relevant to the organism's goals or needs (the relevance sub-check)? Is the outcome consistent with the state expected on current plans (the expectation sub-check), and is it conducive to reaching goals or satisfying needs (the conduciveness sub-check)? The fourth check is for the coping potential. What is the cause of the event (the causation sub-check)? What degree of control does the organism have over the event and its consequences (the control sub-check)? Can the organism change or avoid the outcome (the power sub-check)? Can the outcome be adjusted by internal restructuring (the adjustment sub-check)? Finally, there is the norm/self compatibility check. Does the event conform to the expectations of significant others (the external standards sub-check)? Is it consistent with

Table 8.1   Stimulus Evaluation Checks, and the outcomes for two emotions

Stimulus Evaluation Checks	Facets	Fear	Sadness
Novelty	Expectation	unexpected	open
Intrinsic pleasantness	Pleasantness	open	unpleasant
Goal/need conduciveness	Relevance	high	relevant
	Conduciveness	obstructive	obstructive
	Justice	open	irrelevant
Coping potential	Agent	other	open
	Motive	malevolent/chance	open
	Control	low	low
	Power	low	low
Norm/self compatibility	Norm compatibility	open	irrelevant
	Self compatibility	open	irrelevant

Source: From Scherer, 1984

the individual's own norms and standards (the internal standards sub-check)?

We will not, here, go into the justification for all of Scherer's checks and sub-checks. You will recognize many of the evaluations that seem to be made consistently by individuals; others, perhaps less well known, have been identified by social psychologists, while yet other checks fit with the importance of goals and plans in the direction of behaviour. Scherer sees particular patterns of the outcomes of these checks as leading to different emotions. These summarize the state of the situation. Some examples of the predicted SECs for fear and sadness are shown in table 8.1. Because of their cognitive evaluation component, strong emotional states should leave a clear trace in memory with records of the sorts of checks and evaluations which have taken place. In support of this, Morris (1992) reported studies of autobiographical memories of emotional events where the properties of the remembered events fitted well with the evaluations that Scherer predicted should have taken place.

In our BOSS–Consciousness model (Morris and Hampson, 1983; Hampson and Morris, 1989; Morris, 1992), emotions reflect the reporting to the BOSS system on the current processing activities, as they affect the overall well-being of the system, and its success or otherwise in reaching its goals. Oatley and Johnson-Laird (1987) argue that emotions are related to junctures in our plans. If sub-goals are achieved, we experience happiness, but when the unexpected occurs, or when progress towards a goal changes unexpectedly, emotions make the system ready, prompting towards the next phase of actions, and communicating non-verbally to others how we are functioning. For Oatley and Johnson-Laird, the function of emotions is to communicate changes in our planning to ourselves and others.

There has, therefore, been a recognition by many theorists that cognition and emotion are not unrelated, and that emotions are not a malign threat to accurate cognition. Rather, cognition and emotion are seen as related aspects of the key processes of planning and controlling our actions, and in evaluating our success and failures so that further actions can be planned.

Human Errors ▶▶▶

The greater willingness of cognitive psychologists to consider the role of emotion in cognition is, we believe, indicative of a more fundamental change in the discipline. As cognitive psychology has matured it has increasingly acknowledged that cognition is not simply a rational or sterile activity which takes place in controlled, laboratory conditions, but an impressive, flexible, if at times messy activity which takes place in the real world for real reasons. Cognition generally goes right, but it sometimes goes spectacularly wrong, and it does so in the real world! In chapter 12 we shall look at some reasons why cognition goes wrong because of brain injury; here we examine some of the more mundane types of human errors which occur, particularly those involving slips of action.

In our initial example, we imagined that you set off for your friend's house intending to post a letter on the way, only to discover the letter in your coat pocket the next day. Such an example of absentmindedness will be familiar to everyone, but why do such errors occur, and what about other examples of absentmindedness? If the cognitive system is organized hierarchically, this will be one potential source of errors in acting. On some occasions, the running of the systems within the hierarchy will get out of line – if, for example, an EMPLOYEE subsystem carries out its habitual processing without being properly modified for the special occasion. This is what happened in our example when your normal walk was not interrupted by remembering to post the letter.

Slips and lapses

Reason has collected many examples of failures to carry out intentions (e.g. Reason, 1977, 1979). Reason and Mycielska (1982) describe two studies in which volunteers kept diaries in which were recorded deviations from intended actions. In the first study, 35 people kept diaries for two weeks and a total of 433 incidents were recorded. In the second study, 63 university students similarly recorded their slips of action during seven days, but in this case they answered a standard set of questions each time they noted an error. The questions asked about the nature of the intended action, the nature of the erroneous action, wrong actions that could be recognized as related to another activity, the person's mental and physical state and the prevailing environmental conditions. A total of 192 slips were recorded in this way.

The total pool of 625 slips of action from both studies was initially analysed into four categories. In one, some intended action was repeated unnecessarily (e.g. sugaring coffee twice). In another, the intended actions were made but in relation to the wrong object (e.g. throwing a dirty shirt into the toilet rather than the laundry basket). In the third, unintended actions became incorporated into the sequence (e.g. taking out one's own front door key when approaching a friend's house). In the final group, actions were left out of the sequence (e.g. getting into bed still fully clothed).

Both Norman (1981) and Reason and Mycielska (1982) have tried to interpret these and other errors through models of action planning and control. They recognized that a mistake in the way we carry out our actions can only be understood in terms of the system for controlling our actions. A breakdown in this system, when it fails for some reason, can give an insight into the normal functioning of the system.

Returning to our example from the beginning of the chapter, in Norman's account the reason why you forgot to post the letter was probably because you needed to modify the normal set of schemata for walking to your friend's house by setting up a new schema for posting the letter that must be activated and triggered at the correct point. If the activation was not sufficient, or the trigger conditions not well enough specified, or the trigger conditions not adequately processed, then the schema will not be invoked and the letter not posted. So, for example, seeing the letterbox might be enough to trigger the schema, but the trigger conditions may not be sufficiently specified for you to post the letter if you happen to be looking the other way when you pass the box.

In their analysis of their pool of errors, Reason and Mycielska (1982) note that absentminded errors occur in tasks that have some degree of automaticity. They arise in familiar and mostly constant environments, and are associated with distractions and preoccupation. In such situations, the error is often what Norman (1981) calls a capture error where a more familiar habit substitutes itself for the intended action sequence. Reason and Mycielska give as an example the error of one of their participants who took off all her clothes as if for bed when intending merely to change from jeans to a dress. In another example, the person sprinkled sugar over his cornflakes, even though he had wanted to cut down on sugar and eat them without it.

Another major set of errors are those defined as 'data-driven' in Norman's classification, where external events activate schemata independently of the plans and intentions of the individual. Other examples of such faulty triggering can be found in Young et al. (1985; see also box 8.1) who investigated the sorts of slips that occur in face recognition. In one of their largest categories of error, participants misidentified the person, either by identifying an unfamiliar person as a familiar person, or by mistaking one familiar person for another. In both cases, a more frequently used face recognition unit was presumably activated by resemblances between the mistaken person and the familiar person. Reason and Mycielska also provide several examples of this, such as people forgetting what they intended doing when they go into another room, and starting to perform another activity instead, after being cued by an object or event in the room. Another person reported to them 'On leaving the room to go to the kitchen I turned the light off, although there were several people there.' In this case, the light switch triggered the familiar, if inappropriate schema.

There are many other possible opportunities for errors to change actions as planned into those that are not planned, or to fit with planning, but to lead to undesired or undesirable consequences. Errors can occur at any stage in the models proposed by Norman (1981). In Norman's account, the errors reflect faults in either the activation or the triggering of a schema. The wrong schema may be activated, or activation may be lost; schemata may be triggered at the wrong time, or fail to be triggered appropriately.

However, there are yet other ways in which human errors can occur. Reason (1990) has reviewed the complex background that underlies the making of errors. We will first look at his framework for understanding the levels at which cognition takes place, and the ways that weaknesses inherent in the nature of the cognitive system lead to errors.

The Generic Error Modelling System (GEMS)

Reason (1990) describes the Generic Error Modelling System (GEMS), developed by Rasmussen (1986), which is illustrated in figure 8.3.

There are three levels at which actions are controlled. First of all, the skill-based level of control of behaviour involves the control of behaviour in routine environments. The skills are well developed and conscious attention (i.e. the BOSS system in our model) can be occupied elsewhere. The system does carry out attentional checks on the progress of the action, but if these match expectations then attention can be directed elsewhere. However, if the skilled action is not proceeding as expected, then attention (the BOSS system) must be directed to solving the problem. The system then moves to the rule-based level.

In the rule-based level, the situation is examined and the current circumstances matched with existing schemata and stored past experience of similar problems. These stored condition–action rules ('if the situation is X then do Y') will often allow the problem to be solved, and routine, skilled behaviour to recommence. However, if the rules that are retrieved and are applied fail to solve the problem, the person is forced to analyse the problem at a higher and more demanding level. In this third level, that of knowledge-based responding, knowledge about the processes and the system that is failing has to be evoked to try to understand what is going wrong. (See chapters 6 and 10 for more details on the development of automatic, skill-based actions, and on the knowledge and skill requirements of problem solving and decision making.)

We can illustrate these three levels with the rather simple example of opening the door into a room. Normally, you do not have to think about the well-learned skill of turning the door handle and pushing the door open with the required amount of force. If, however, the door fails to open as expected, you may, operating now at the rule-based level, think of one or two reasons why the door has failed to open before. Perhaps it is locked, perhaps something is blocking it from opening from the inside. You try various actions that have worked in similar situations before – perhaps turning a key in the lock, or looking through a window in the door to see what, if anything, is blocking it on the other side. If these learned rules fail, you are forced to consider what it might be about the nature of the door that could be causing the problem. By thinking of what you know about wooden objects, hinges, the weather and so on, you may be able to form

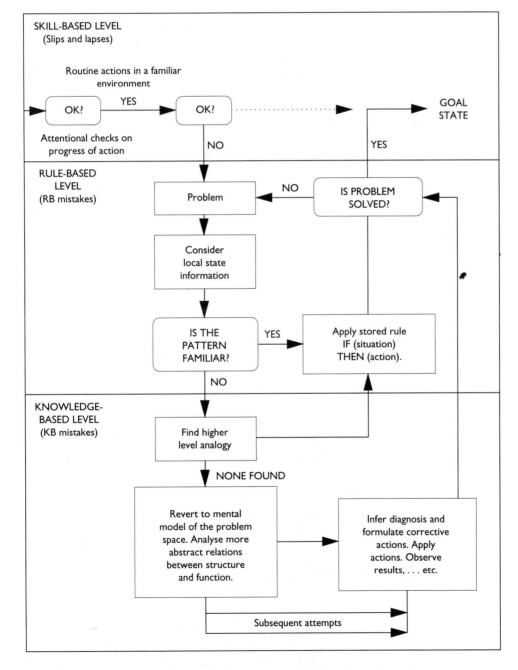

Figure 8.3 The Generic Error Modelling System (GEMS). (Based on figure 3.1, Reason, 1990)

various hypotheses about what may have happened – maybe the damp weather has swollen the wood, maybe the hinges are breaking. In these latter cases you are having to use your knowledge to infer diagnoses and develop new solutions.

The types of errors reported by Reason and Mycielska (1982) were often ones where faults occurred at the skills level. The errors were ones of slips or lapses where the normal functioning of the skill broke down, often through a 'strong but wrong' error where an action or schema that was more frequently carried out than the intended one took control. Reason (1990) goes on to examine errors that arise at other stages in the GEMS system. The types of errors are classified in table 8.2.

We have already discussed two of Reason's error types, slips and lapses; we will briefly consider the other two types, mistakes and violations.

Table 8.2   A catalogue of errors

Skill-based performance	
Inattention	*Overattention*
Double-capture slips	Omissions
Omissions following interruptions	Repetitions
Reduced intentionality	Reversals
Perceptual confusions	
Interference errors	

Rule-based performance	
Misapplication of good rules	*Application of bad rules*
First exceptions	Encoding deficiencies
Countersigns and nonsigns	Action deficiencies
Informational overload	Wrong rules
Rule strength	Inelegant rules
General rules	Inadvisable rules
Redundancy	
Rigidity	

Knowledge-based performance

Selectivity
Workspace limitations
Out of sight out of mind
Confirmation bias
Overconfidence
Biased reviewing
Illusory correlation
Halo effects
Problems with causality
Problems with complexity
    Problems with delayed feedback
    Insufficient consideration of processes in time
    Difficulties with exponential developments
    Thinking in causal series not causal nets
    Thematic vagabonding
    Encysting

Source: Based on Reason, 1990

Mistakes

Mistakes take place at the knowledge- or rule-based levels of GEMS. Many very serious accidents (for example at the Three Mile Island and the Chernobyl nuclear power stations, and the sinking of the Herald of Free Enterprise ferry) involved mistakes where decisions taken by individuals in immediate control of the situations led to the disaster because they were not aware of the possible consequences of their actions, or of more appropriate interpretations of the situations. So, for example, the crew carrying out the testing of emergency procedures at Chernobyl were not aware of the characteristics of the nuclear reactor which made their actions so dangerous. At Three Mile Island, a failure to diagnose properly the main problem of a valve jammed open reflects a typical error of problem solving. One common mistake is that people tend to seek and evaluate evidence in support of whatever hypothesis about the world they currently hold, rather than seek to test hypotheses in the most effective way (see chapter 10 for a further discussion). The result is that people rarely properly test the rules they use. In general, from a review of many examples of mistakes, Reason concludes that mistakes often come from the misapplication of good rules, or the application of inappropriate rules at the rule-based level, with a tendency to go for 'strong but wrong' rules, combined with a tendency to overlook or explain away evidence that the rule is inappropriate. Errors at the higher, knowledge-based level are also similar to those uncovered by laboratory research on problem solving (see chapter 10). For example, confirmation bias, overconfidence, difficulties with the estimated frequency of events or of dealing with information that is not immediately present have all been noted as sources of error in the laboratory and in real life.

Reason (1990) also discusses how the nature of complex organizations and projects can lead to human errors. Pressure for optimizing production, combined with optimism that all is well, and an ignorance of the ways in which the complex components of the operation may interact to cause a major error, often underlie major tragedies. For example, operating procedures that led to the sailing of the Herald of Free Enterprise with open bow doors came from inadequate procedures for checking the closure of doors. There was no positive check built into the system, and arrangements for the location of the crew meant that the possible error could go unmonitored. However, the actual disaster came about when the ship had been trimmed nose down so that it could dock at a berth that required this. Otherwise all might have been well. Reason documents many examples of failure to develop systems to monitor for the possible combinations of circumstances that are usually the final determinants of a major tragedy that is ascribed to 'human error'.

Violations

Reason also considers in detail violations, that is, the deliberate breaking of rules. While the reasons for such violations are important if accidents are to be avoided, they are not really relevant to this chapter, and the interested reader is referred to Reason (1990) for more information.

Experimental Studies of Prospective Memory

Planning cannot occur in a vacuum; to plan we need to use some key elements of cognition. In recent years a number of studies have been carried out upon our memory for future actions – 'prospective memory', as Meacham and Leiman (1975) have called it, in contrast with 'retrospective memory' for things that have already happened.

Most of the research on prospective memory has been carried out in the past 15 years (see Morris, 1992 for a review). However, perhaps the earliest study was made during the Second World War by Drew, using the Cambridge Cockpit built by Kenneth Craik. In this first flight simulator, 140 experienced pilots were required to keep checks upon temperature, pressure gauges and fuel indicators. As the experiment progressed, more and more of the pilots forgot to check their petrol and radiator gauges, and more than 80 of them 'landed' with the undercarriage up.

This early study illustrates both the strength and the weakness of laboratory studies of actions. The control and monitoring of the simulator allowed clear recording of what the pilots did or did not do. However, it is always open for anyone to explain the high failure rate by claiming that the pilots, knowing that it was a simulation, did not try as hard as they would do if their lives depended upon a real landing! Nevertheless, Reason (1977) and Reason and Mycielska (1982) provide several examples of aircraft crashes or near disasters that have resulted from human errors. Failure to reset the altimeter to local barometric pressure has been blamed on several occasions. For example, in 1966 a Britannia aircraft crashed short of the runway at Ljubljana for this reason. The cockpit study may, therefore, have some resemblance to errors that do really occur.

More recent research on prospective memory has been less ambitious in scale. One common design has been to give participants postcards to be returned on specific days (e.g. Levy et al., 1979; Meacham and Leiman, 1975). Meacham and Leiman (1975), for example, found better rates of return of postcards by participants supplied with a coloured tag for their key ring to act as a mnemonic aid.

Another area of prospective memory, reviewed by Levy and Loftus (1984), involves research upon compliance with instructions, usually connected either with attending medical clinics or for taking medication. Obviously, remembering a medical appointment or to take medicine is important, and failure to remember could be potentially harmful. Nevertheless, rates of responding in these situations can often be quite low. Nazarian et al. (1976), for example, found in their study in the USA that only 48 per cent of appointments to see a doctor or nurse in 12 days' to eight weeks' time were actually kept. Reminder cards increased the attendance rate to 67 per cent, and were more effective the longer the interval between appointments.

The examples given so far have been of situations in which there was little control over the conditions under which the memory is cued. In real life, there will be a multitude of different ways of coping with remembering to do things. Harris (1980) questioned people on the memory aids that they use, and found that people reported quite frequently using memory aids such as writing notes to themselves, tying knots in handkerchiefs, and so on. In the homes of the patients or the participants with cards to post, there may or may not be special provision made for memory aids. To understand the conditions under which prospective memory works, much more detail on the situation in which remembering and forgetting takes place will be required.

A first step towards such understanding was taken by Wilkins and Baddeley (1978) who designed a small device that would record exactly the time at which a button was pressed. They used this to study a simulation of pill taking by having housewives press the button at 8.30 a.m., 1.00 p.m., 5.30 p.m. and 10.00 p.m. each day for a week. The vast majority of responses were within five minutes of the set time. Late responses increased across the seven days but were unaffected by the day of the week. The 8.30 a.m. button presses were most accurately remembered, perhaps reflecting that it was easier to 'build' such a button press into one's schema for getting the day started. One interesting point was that no one made an extra response; no one, that is, forgot that they had already pushed the button. Another point of interest was that those participants who did best at the task actually had poorer memories for lists of words upon which they were also tested. This suggests that we do not just have good or bad memories, but that some people may have good prospective memories but poorer memories for other things. This is discussed further by Morris (1984, 1992b).

The Wilkins and Baddeley (1978) study provided more accurate timing of responses, but it still lacked control over what the people did during the research. Harris and Wilkins (1982) designed a situation which allowed for control over the participant's actions, and monitoring of the participant's own monitoring of the time, as the need to respond approaches. Harris and Wilkins' task simulated watching television while waiting for the right time to carry out some action, such as taking food from the oven or making a phone call. In their experimental set-up, participants were shown a two-hour film about a hijack, and were given a set of times, spaced at three- and nine-minute intervals. The participant's task was to hold up the card at the correct time. The only clock was behind the participants, so that they had to turn their heads to consult it. Harris and Wilkins filmed the participants and were able to observe when they consulted the clock, how accurately they showed the cards at the correct times, and how the stages of the film influenced performance.

Over 12 per cent of Harris and Wilkins' participants' responses were more than 15 seconds late. The rates of looking at the clock increased dramatically as the time to show the card approached. However, on over a quarter of the occasions when the participants missed showing the card, they had looked at the clock within the last ten seconds. Harris and Wilkins concluded that people can forget to do things very quickly on occasions, which corresponds to many people's personal experience. They found no difference between the three-minute and the nine-minute delay intervals between cards, and also, surprisingly, no clear relationship between the stage of the film, its degree of excitement as rated by observers, and the errors made. Perhaps, like Drew's (1940) study with which we began this section, there is a problem over the reality of the simulation. You are probably far less likely to get deeply involved in a film while being filmed yourself, and having to glance over your shoulder every few minutes, than you are if settled comfortably at home before the TV while the dinner finishes cooking.

Ceci and Bronfenbrenner (1985) extended the Harris and Wilkins research to the monitoring of cooking by children. While waiting for cup-cakes to cook the necessary 30 minutes, the child's checking of the clock was monitored. Ten year olds in their own homes showed a similar pattern of checks of the clock to the participants in the Harris and Wilkins study. That is, they made several checks in the first five minutes, as if calibrating their internal time monitoring system, then made few checks in the next 15 minutes, and checked frequently over the last five minutes.

Ceci et al. (1988) then tested the theory that the children were first calibrating a psychological clock, and applying a Test Wait Exit strategy (a version of Miller et al.'s (1960) TOTE proposed by Harris and Wilkins, 1982), by the ingenious technique of providing the ten year old children with a wall clock that ran faster or slower than it should. They manipulated the rates to be 10 per cent, 33 per cent, or 50 per cent too fast or too slow. Where the rates were 10 per cent or 33 per cent too fast or slow, the children showed a J-shaped response, adjusting to the new rate and looking frequently in the first five minutes as shown by the clock, but little during the next 20 minutes. In the case of the 50 per cent fast or slow clocks, however, the children did not adopt the J-shaped strategy, but looked frequently at the time throughout the experiment. Ceci et al. concluded that the children were able to recalibrate a psychological clock to speeds within a third of normal rates, but that for the 50 per cent fast or slow clocks the discrepancies with the children's expectations were so great that they became suspicious, and/or anxious, and began to check regularly.

So far, therefore, the experimental attempts to study prospective memory have often been ingenious but still raise more questions than they answer. However, the study of prospective memory is developing with growing evidence of its distinct nature. There is evidence, for example, that the processes of prospective and retrospective memory are different. Where researchers have compared the recall of the same participant in prospective and retrospective memory tasks, performance has rarely been significantly correlated. For example, Maylor (1990) compared the accuracy of several hundred late-middle-aged and elderly participants in remembering to make a telephone call with their abilities at digit span, learning lists of words and free recall, and found no evidence of a relationship. Similarly, when Kvavilashvili (1987) asked her participants to remind her to pass on a message that the participant had been asked to convey, subsequent testing showed that participants who remembered to remind the experimenter were not better at remembering the content of the message. There is also evidence that even though older participants may perform worse than younger participants on retrospective memory tasks, differences in prospective memory are less apparent (Einstein and McDaniel, 1990; see also box 8.2).

That remembering to do things is an important aspect of human life, and one requiring far more research, is illustrated by the large number of memory aids people adopt to avoid such problems (such as diaries, notes, etc.; Harris, 1980) and by the frequency with which such errors are believed, by us all, to occur. Reason and Mycielska (1982) report a questionnaire on memory errors where the respondents indicated how often they thought that the particular types of error occurred. Out of the 30 types of error, most frequent of all came 'attending but not taking in', which hardly seems a memory error at all! Then came 'forgetting plan item', 'blocking on name', 'forgetting intention (to do)' and 'forgetting intention (to say)'. Of these, only 'blocking on a name' is an example of retrospective memory, the others being prospective memory failures. Morris (1984) has argued that the frequency of such failures may be overestimated, but the very reason for this overestimation is their importance to the individual involved, and the inconvenience and embarrassment that a forgotten intention can bring.

Conclusions and Prospects

As we warned earlier in the chapter, the study of the planning and control of human actions is in a very early stage and all that can be offered are attempts by cognitive psychologists to come to terms with the theoretical and empirical problems that the area raises. Nevertheless, it is clear that the control of actions can be tackled by cognitive psychologists. It is also worth noting the considerable interest in human actions among social psychologists (see, e.g. von Cranach and Harré, 1982; Harré et al., 1985).

We must emphasize again the importance of the study of the human planning of actions. This is not only because it is at this level that we conceptualize human behaviour outside the psychology laboratory, but also because the other activities of the cognitive system will not, ultimately, be comprehensible outside the framework of plans and goal-directed actions which determines what people do. To understand how we perceive, remember, speak and think, it is necessary to recognize the purposes that such processes are serving at any one time and the way that the higher-order plans of the individual will influence the products of these processes. Thinking and speaking are tools that aid us in achieving our goals. So too are perception and memory. We solve problems to further our plans, we talk to communicate and obtain information that will aid our intentions. Our perceptual systems exist to guide and control our actions. Our memories supply information so that we can interpret our current situation and plan for likely future occurrences. In chapter 2 we emphasized how what we remember is determined by the task that is being undertaken, by the plan that is being run. We pointed out how, for example, we remember few details about common objects like coins because we do not need to process their specific details when we use them. On the other hand, we can remember many apparently irrelevant details about events that happen just once, but because of their personal relevance to us or because they may involve changing our schemata for interpreting future events, leave us with what have been called 'flashbulb memories'.

The point is that the cognitive system exists to make actions possible, to allow us to carry out plans. A full understanding of the cognitive system will not, therefore, be likely to be achieved without an understanding of how its various components are integrated to this end.

Further reading ▶ ▶ ▶

A classic text on planning and human action is, as we mentioned in the chapter, G.A. Miller, E. Calanter and K. Pribram 1960: *Plans and the Structure of Behavior*. New York: Holt.

Good sources of information on errors and what they reveal about action and planning are: J. Reason and K. Mycielska 1982: *Absent Minded? The Psychology of Mental Lapses and Everyday Errors*. Englewood Cliffs, NJ: Prentice-Hall, J. Reason 1992: *Human Error*. Cambridge, Cambridge University Press and J.E. Harris and P.E. Morris (eds) 1984: *Everyday Memory, Actions and Absentmindedness*. London: Academic Press.

Several reviews of the role of emotion in cognition have been published. Among those worth consulting are C.R. Brewin 1988: *Cognitive Foundations of Clinical Psychology*. Hove: Lawrence Erlbaum Associates, and S.M. Aylwin 1985: *Structure in Thought and Feeling*. London: Methuen. The latter offers an unusual, but stimulating perspective on the area.

Discussion points ▶ ▶ ▶

1   What are the general principles governing the planning and control of action?
2   How are awareness and action related?
3   What is emotion for? How is it linked with action?
4   'To err is human'; what sorts of errors do people make? What do these errors tell us about the nature of human action?
5   In what areas of everyday life is prospective memory important?

Practical exercises

1   Take examples of simple everyday actions, such as digging a hole or writing a letter, and see how feasible it is to analyse these in terms of TOTE units. What actions, or parts of actions, submit to such an analysis, and which are problematic?

2   Either keep a diary yourself (or better still encourage two or three participants to do so) of the lapses and slips of action and memory made over the course of a week. To what extent can you categorize the slips using the categories discussed in the chapter? Or, attempt to replicate the study by Young et al. (1985) (see box 8.1).

3   How do people manage their prospective memories? Construct a survey to discover the sorts of memory aids which people commonly use to remember future actions. Think carefully about how to do this. One way is to give written examples of prospective memory tasks and simply ask participants how they would deal with each situation. Alternatively, you could provide them with examples of memory aids and see which your participants used. What are the strengths and weaknesses of each of these methods? Are there any other ways you can think of for studying prospective memory techniques?

Box 8.1
Everyday errors in face recognition

Everyday difficulties and memory slips can be used to refine and test theoretical models of cognitive processing. Young et al. argued that slips and errors in face recognition could be used to test the model of face recognition developed by Hay and Young (1982).

They asked a number of people to keep records of errors and difficulties they experienced in recognizing other people. They noted the factors that can bias such data. These included a volunteer bias, with people offering to keep records because they think they are particularly prone to the errors being investigated, selection bias where not all errors come to the participants' attention, and recording bias, less information being recorded than is available at the time of the incident. However, Young et al. argued that most of the conclusions they wished to draw were based on the fact that certain types of error can exist, not on differences in their rates of production. They tried to minimize recording bias by providing record sheets incorporating a systematic checklist of things to be recorded.

Method
Eleven male and eleven female participants kept records over an eight-week period. These diarists were asked to record all incidents of mistaken face recognition that they were aware of, regardless of how trivial or inexplicable they might seem. Incidents were recorded individually on record sheets as soon as possible after they occurred. The first week of the study was used as a training week and the records were not included in the analysis.

The record sheets asked for the following information:

1   *Type of incident.*
2   *Source*: details of information available at the time when the incident occurred. A checklist included facial features, hair, beard or spectacles, build etc. Diarists were asked to cross through any of these sources of information that were not available to them. They ranked the other sources in the order in which they felt they had contributed to recognition, or misrecognition.
3   *General details*:
    (a)   whether the incident involved a person known only through the mass media;
    (b)   whether viewing or hearing conditions were poor at the time;
    (c)   whether the diarist was hurried, intoxicated, distracted or in distress at the time;

(d)   whether the diarist would expect to meet the person at that time and place;

(e)   how certain the diarist was while the incident occurred that he or she had correctly recognized the person;

(f)   how long the incident lasted.

4   *People involved*: each person involved in the incident was classified by the diarist in terms of how well they were known and how often they were seen.

5   *The way the incident ended.*

6   *Person details available*: used when the diarist found that he or she was unable to recall some details about the person.

Results

Following the practice week, 922 completed records were obtained from the 22 diarists. A further 86 records of 'resemblance only' experiences were collected and analysed separately. These were records of instances where the diarists thought that someone closely resembled someone else but did not produce the experience of thinking that they were actually the person resembled. The incidents were classified into seven principle types; the details are shown in box table 8.1.1. These seven principal types were, in several cases, analysed into several sub-types as follows.

Principal types

1   *Person unrecognized*   This type of incident involved failure to recognize a familiar person. Analysis of the incidence showed that failures can occur for all types of information used to recognize people and that they can even occur in the case of highly familiar people, and people one was expecting to encounter. Poor viewing or hearing conditions were present in only a minority of the records.

2   *Person misidentified*   In this type of incident, the diarist mistook one person for another. Two sub-types were classified:

(a)   Unfamiliar person misidentified as a familiar person. These misidentifications tended to be brief, and were often associated with poor conditions. They usually ended when a better view was obtained.

(b)   One familiar person misidentified as another. Many of the misidentifications were of brief duration (e.g. ten seconds or less). The person that diarists thought they had encountered tended to be more familiar and more often seen than the person that had actually been encountered.

3   *Person seemed familiar only*   Three sub-types were identified:

(a)   Familiar person successfully identified. Incidents of this sub-type tend to involve people who are not well known and are encountered in an unexpected or inappropriate context. They were often ended by quite deliberate mental searching until the correct context was retrieved.

(b)   Incident not ended when record made. These were similar to the first sub-type but the diarist could not remember why the person appeared familiar.

(c)   Person found to be unfamiliar. As in the first two sub-types, the key factor was the sense of familiarity. The misidentifications were brief in duration and resolved when a better view was obtained.

Box table 8.1.1   Number of incidents of each type of misidentification, identified in diarists' records

Person un-recognized	Person mis-identified	Person seemed familiar only	Difficulty retrieving full details of person	Not sure if it was a particular person or not	Thought it wasn't the person it was	Wrong name given to person	Others	Complete main set
114	314	233	190	35	4	9	23	922

Source: Extracted from table 1, Young et al., 1985

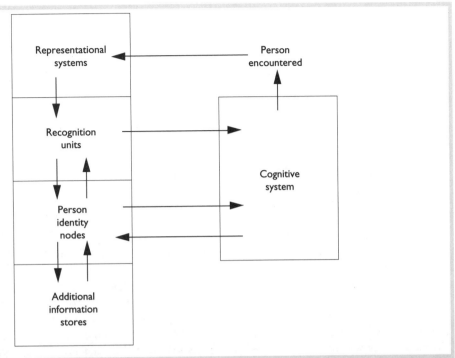

Box figure 8.1.1   A model of person recognition. (Based on figure 1, Young et al., 1985)

4   *Difficulty in retrieving full details of person*   The diarist was able to remember some details but was still searching for others, most usually the person's name. There were two sub-types:

(a)   Difficulty successfully resolved. In the 135 records in this sub-type, there was no instance of a diarist recalling a name without first being able to access some information about the person's occupation and where she or he was actually seen.

(b)   Incident not ended when record made again. No cases were found, in 55 records, in which the name could be retrieved without details of occupation and where the person was usually seen.

5   *Not sure if it was a particular person or not*   The diarist was unable to decide whether or not he or she had correctly identified a person. Only 35 records fell into this type, but they were divided into a first sub-type where the diarist was not sure if they were a particular familiar person or whether they were an unfamiliar one. The second sub-type was unsureness between two familiar people.

6   *Thought it wasn't the person it was*   Only four incidents were reported in this classification.

7   *Wrong name given to a person*   Only nine such errors.

Discussion

Young et al. went on to outline a model of person recognition using the results of the study. The model is illustrated in box figure 8.1.1.

Encountering the person leads to representational processes which create a structural description of the person. This description can activate recognition units whose function is to indicate how closely the face, hair, build etc. resemble that of someone already known. The recognition units can then access information concerning the identity of the resembled person. These are stored in person identity nodes. Both the recognition units and the person identity nodes can activate knowledge about the person from the cognitive system. The person identity nodes can activate additional information stores, including the person's name.

Young et al. argued that the feelings of familiarity indicated blocks in the system between the recognition units and the person identity nodes. Errors arose where information could be recalled about a person, including their occupation but not their name, suggesting blocks between the person identity nodes and the additional information, especially the name, that could be activated by those nodes. Thus, the information collected in the study was used to develop the model of person recognition which could then be investigated under more rigorous experimental conditions.

Based on A.W. Young, D.C. Hay and A.W. Ellis 1985: The faces that launched a thousand slips: everyday difficulties and errors in recognising people. *British Journal of Psychology*, 76, 495–523.

Box 8.2
Ageing and prospective memory

Einstein and McDaniel developed a laboratory paradigm for studying prospective memory, and used it to examine whether or not this type of memory is especially difficult for the elderly. In two experiments, young and old participants were given a prospective memory test where they were asked to perform an action when a target event occurred, as well as three tests of retrospective memory (short-term memory, free recall and recognition). Typical studies of prospective memory have asked participants to perform some action in naturalistic settings, such as telephoning the experimenter or sending in a postcard at a specified time in the future. A problem with such research is that it is so weakly controlled. The participants are free to adopt any strategy that they wish and there is no restriction over what is happening at the time that the prospective memory needs to be recalled.

Einstein and McDaniel developed a technique for bringing prospective memory under tighter, laboratory control. The essential characteristic of their paradigm was to have participants busily working on one task while at the same time requiring them to perform an activity at some future specified time. In their Experiment 1, they embedded the prospective memory portion of the experiment within a short-term memory task. This task involved presenting participants with a set of words on each trial and then having them recall the words. At the start of the experiment, the participants were also given the prospective memory instruction that if they happened to see a particular word (the target event) they were to press a response key on the keyboard in front of them. Three of these target words appeared across the 42 short-term memory trials and the measure of prospective memory was the number of times participants remembered to press the response key when the target event occurred. The latency of responding was also recorded.

In this first experiment they compared the prospective memory of young and elderly participants.

Method

Design and participants
The design was a 2×2 between-participants factorial design with the age of the participants (young, old) and the opportunity to form an external aid (no aid, external aid) as the factors. Twelve participants were assigned to each of the four groups, with the young participants aged between 17 and 24 and the old participants between 65 and 70 years.

Materials and procedure
The words for the short-term memory task were presented at a rate of one every 750 msec on a computer screen. The participants recalled the words orally and in order. After they had been given the instructions for the short-term memory task, participants were told that they had a second task. They were to press a response key on the keyboard whenever the target word *rake* appeared. For all participants, this word appeared three times during the 42 short-term memory test trials. The participants in the external-aid condition were given 30 seconds to formulate some type of memory aid. They were supplied with rubber bands, paper clips, scotch tape, erasers, paper pads, scissors, a stapler and pens in front of them. Before beginning the short term memory task, the participants also completed a free-recall task involving the recall of a 36-word list constructed of six words from each of six categories. They also had a recognition test involving the presentation of 56 nouns at a rate of two seconds each followed by being given a list of those 56 items randomly intermixed with 56 new items and being allowed five minutes to circle the old items.

After these two tasks the short-term memory experiment was run. The 42 test trials were made up of one- and two-syllable familiar words in sets of from four to nine for the young participants, and sets of from three to eight for

Box table 8.2.1 Standardized beta coefficients for regression analyses predicting performance on a range of memory tasks

Predictor variable	Predicted variable			
	Prospective memory	Short-term memory	Free recall	Recognition
Age	−0.03	0.36*	−0.27**	−0.16
Memory aid	0.34*	−0.16	−0.15	0.12
Prospective memory	–	0.14	0.00	0.20
Short-term memory	0.13	–	0.21	−0.11
Free recall	0.00	0.28	–	0.46*
Recognition	0.26	−0.15	0.47*	–

* $p < 0.05$ ** $p < 0.06$
Source: Based on table 2, Einstein and McDaniel, 1990

the elderly participants. Following the short-term memory trials the participants were given a questionnaire asking them to rate the degree they had thought about the prospective memory task during different parts of the experiment.

Results and Discussion

The younger participants recalled more than did the elder participants in the free-recall and the recognition conditions. The older participants recalled a greater proportion of words in the short-term memory task, but this reflected the shorter list length.

The particular interest lay in the recall of the prospective memory task and its relationship to performance in the other conditions. Separate multiple regression analyses were carried out to predict performance on the criteria variables of prospective memory, short-term memory, free-recall memory and recognition memory using age, memory aid, prospective memory, short-term memory, free recall and recognition as predictors. Performance is illustrated in box table 8.2.1.

The prospective memory performance was not related to any of the variables except for the use of a memory aid. In particular, the standardized beta coefficient was very low and a long way from significance for the relationship between age and prospective memory. Age was related to performance on short-term memory and the free-recall task. The recognition and free-recall tasks were themselves significantly related.

There was a strong relationship between the rated frequency of thinking about the prospective memory task during the short-term memory task and performance in prospective remembering ($r = 0.59$, df = 46, $p < 0.01$).

Einstein and McDaniel concluded that the results counter the view that prospective memory should be especially problematic for elderly participants. Young and old did not differ on prospective memory, even in the no external aid conditions.

Based on G.O. Einstein and M.A. McDaniel 1990: Normal aging and prospective memory. *Journal of Experimental Psychology: Learning, Memory and Cognition*, 16, 717–26.

9 Reading

Reading and writing have been common skills for only a short time. In the British isles it is only within the past hundred years that most of the population has been taught to read and the majority of the population of the world still remains illiterate. In a literate society, it is possible to get by without being able to read, but, where reading is taken for granted as a skill everyone possesses, the person with a reading disability is at a severe disadvantage. How do adult readers go about translating black marks on paper into meaningful messages? How do children learn these skills? What goes wrong when someone with brain damage loses part of their ability to read? Why do some children have great difficulty in ever learning to read at all? We will tackle these questions in this chapter and offer some answers, as well as showing that reading is a far more complicated process than it might appear at first sight.

Because of its importance, it is necessary to understand reading in its own right. However, we have another reason for wishing to consider it here. Reading is a task that demonstrates a great deal about the integrated functioning of the cognitive system. As we shall see, it involves language, memory, perception, attention, understanding and other cognitive activities working together to extract meaning from print in a most efficient and remarkable way. But first, we must consider the language and spelling systems on which reading rests.

The Structure and Units of Speech and Writing

We are all familiar with the division of written and spoken language into words, made up of letters, and with phrases, sentences and paragraphs composed from words (see also chapter 4 for a discussion of other important dimensions of language). Two less familiar concepts are useful when studying language; they are the ideas of morphemes and phonemes. A morpheme is the smallest unit of meaning. It can correspond to a word, such as *cat*, but some words have several morphemes, each contributing to the overall meaning of the word. So, *hopeful* has two morphemes (*hope* and *ful*) and *hopefully* has three (*hope-ful-ly*). Morphemes can then be divided into the sounds (phonemes) which compose them. Phonemes sometimes correspond to letters, but often a letter can stand for one of several different phonemes, depending upon the word. For example, the *a* in *fat* and *fate* stands for different phonemes. Sometimes several letters combine to represent one phoneme, as with the *ee* in *feet*. Later in this chapter we will discuss the place of all these units of language in reading.

It is obvious, but worth remembering, that reading depends upon writing. The processes that the person learning to read must develop are determined by the way in which ideas are recorded in writing. Some early forms of 'picture writing' developed from the recording of events in pictures into more formal symbols so that, for example, the symbol of a circle for the sun came to represent heat, light and day (Diringer, 1962). Such idiographic writing clearly provided the reader and writer with many of the tremendous advantages of writing, such as the permanent retention of information and its transmission to people at another time and place. However, idiographic writing is limited in what can be represented. Speech is the main way in which people communicate, and, in speaking, we are able to refer to many abstract concepts and relationships not easily represented by ideograms. There must always have been pressure on the evolution of writing towards the accurate recording of all that can be said in a language, so written symbols came to represent words rather than ideas. Nevertheless, some modern writing systems are still based upon a one-word-one-symbol principle. These include Chinese and one form of writing used in Japan (Kanji). Such ways of writing are called 'logographic'. We use a few logographs in English too, for example, £, +, &.

The system of writing with which we are familiar is more flexible than logographic writing. Around 1000 BC the Greeks developed a way of writing using a small set of symbols (the alphabet) to represent sounds. All modern alphabets descend originally from this Greek version. Writing which will record the sounds of speech is both attractive and powerful. Anything that can be said can be written down for posterity. In an ideal world, perhaps, this direct relationship between spelling and speech sounds would be perfect and the cognitive skills required in reading would be far simpler. There would be no irregular words such as *yacht, debt, island, knight* and *colonel*. Some writing systems, such as Finnish and Italian, are much closer to this ideal than English. Why then are there so many irregular words in English? According to Stubbs (1980), before about AD 1500 English words were written as they were pronounced. The first irregularities were introduced to avoid confusing repetitions of up and down strokes, so, for example, *wimin* became *women*. Then the spread of printing led to gradual standardization. Also, there was a move to alter spelling to reflect the Latin or Greek origins of words, at the expense of their actual pronunciation. So, *dette* became *debt* from the Latin *debitum*, *sutil* became *subtle* from *subtilis*, and so on. By the 1650s, English spelling was virtually standardized. Since then spelling has been fixed, but many pronunciations have changed. In the seventeenth century, for example, the 'k' in *knife* and the 'l' in *would* were pronounced, as well as a 'gh' sound in *light*. At the end of its long history, the result is that many words are still 'regular', that is, they are spelt as they are spoken, using the most common sounds associated with the letters of the alphabet. However, many words are 'irregular' with no direct correspondence between spelling and sound. This has major implications both for the way we read and for ways of teaching reading, as will become clear later.

There are some advantages in irregular spelling beyond those introduced to aid writing or to return to Latin or Greek originals. One advantage is to distinguish between words which sound alike (homophones). The spelling of words like 'two', 'too' and 'to' can help clarify their meaning. In other situations, irregular spelling can help to make clear the relationships between words and concepts that would be lost in accurate phonetic spelling. So, the retention of the silent 'g' in *sign* clarifies the relationship of the word to *signature* where the 'g' is pronounced.

Reading by Ear: Phonic Mediation

The reader of English is faced with a far more difficult task than faces readers in languages with few irregular words. In a language in which all words were regular it would be possible to read by converting each letter into its appropriate sound and by recognizing the sound of the word by using the speech recognition system. Reading could be basically dependent upon our cognitive processes which interpret the words we hear. Such a process, known as 'phonic mediation', is superficially attractive as an explanation of how we read for several reasons. One is that, when reading, many people have the experience of hearing the words as if being spoken by a mental voice, a process sometimes described as inner or silent speech, or subvocalization. A second reason is that while speech has evolved over hundreds of thousands, and possibly millions of years, reading and writing are skills invented by modern man which will have to exploit abilities that have evolved for other reasons. So it would not be surprising if the cognitive skill of reading was based closely upon the processes used in speaking and listening. Thirdly, there is no doubt that people can use a sounding-out technique (i.e. phonic mediation), for reading unfamiliar words. Faced with the sentence 'The kurnel sailed his yott', it does not take much effort to form an internal acoustic code so that the auditory recognition system that we normally use for understanding spoken words will allow us to interpret the sentence as 'The colonel sailed his yacht'. Given the task of deciding whether or not a string of letters is a word, people take longer to reject non-words that sound like words (e.g. *burd*) than other non-words, e.g. *losp* (Rubenstein et al., 1971; Coltheart, 1978); a finding known as the 'pseudohomophone effect'.

However, while people do appear to be able to use phonic mediation, there are several reasons why it cannot be the basis of all reading. At best, the phonic mediation strategy should be applicable only for regular words, leaving the reader unable to understand irregular words, of which there are many in English as we have seen. Yet, regular words which are pronounced according to standard pronunciation rules are judged as words no more quickly than are irregular words (Coltheart et al., 1979). Secondly, when we read *yott* we are aware that it is different from *yacht* and that we are adopting a slow strategy for finding its meaning. Thirdly, there are some pairs of words, technically known as 'heterophonic homographs', which are spelt the same but are pronounced differently. The correct pronunciation of *minute* and *tear*, for example, can only be decided after the meaning has been determined, so that pronunciation is unlikely to be the means of identifying the meaning. The conscious experience of inner, silent speech is not, in itself, hard evidence for phonic mediation, since the sounds of the words could be being accessed after the word has been read rather than as a step in its reading. Finally, there is a type of reading difficulty (dyslexia) that sometimes occurs following brain injury and is known as 'phonological dyslexia' (see also chapter 12). Patients suffering such a problem are quite unable to read aloud any nonsense words (e.g. PIB, ZUG) but can pronounce and understand almost any familiar real word (Patterson, 1982; Funnell, 1983). Since these patients cannot read non-words, they appear to be unable to use the usual letter–sound conversion rules necessary for phonic mediation. Their ability to read familiar words implies that they possess routes to the meaning of words that do not require phonic mediation. It is, therefore, not possible to maintain that phonic mediation is the sole basis of reading. It is, however, one way that the reader may tackle an unfamiliar word, and a very important way, as will be seen at the end of the chapter.

Word Recognition by Eye

It is now generally agreed that skilled readers often recognize words visually as familiar letter strings. Repeated experience of a word will lead to the development of a visual word recognition process specific to that word. Encountering the word will lead to its processing and, normally, its recognition, along with the activation of the stored information about the meaning of the word. Much research on reading has concentrated upon how a familiar word is processed by the visual word recognition system to enable the word to be identified. Some psychologists have concentrated upon the recognition of just one or two words at a time, in an attempt to simplify the reading conditions and to make manipulations of likely factors influencing reading easier (see, for example, Mitchell, 1982, and Taft, 1991). Some studies have involved degrading the appearance of words by, for example, displaying them for only a fraction of a second and following the display with a jumbled collection of parts of letters, known as a pattern mask, which prevents further processing of the word, in order to see what can be extracted from letter strings when the reader does not have the time to check the original, and when viewing conditions are poor.

There are, of course, various sources of information that the reader could be using to help identify a word. One would be by first identifying all of the letters in the word. Another might involve the way the letters are combined, using regularities in spelling (orthographic rules). A third could be the whole appearance of the word, its length, outline shape, parts that are dense, in straight or curved lines and so on. A fourth possibility is the use of the context of the passage being read, which could help to bias likely words.

Studies of word recognition have tried to specify which of these types of information are used in reading. When considering this work, however, we must bear in mind an inevitable problem with such research. This is that even though a particular source of information may or may not be demonstrated as being used in experiments where one word is read at a time (often under difficult conditions for the reader) this information may not be necessary to normal reading. The processes involved in reading a continuous text, clearly printed, at the reader's own pace may differ from those used when one word is flashed briefly to a participant in a tachistoscope or on a computer's video display. With this proviso, we now consider some relevant research.

Does word recognition involve first recognizing the letters?

An experiment by Cosky (1976) suggests that the letters of a word do not need to be identified before the whole word is recognized. Cosky argued that if some letters are more difficult to identify than others, then words made up mainly of the difficult to identify letters should take longer to recognize if the letters have to be recognized prior to the word's identification. Cosky first tested the ease of recognizing letters by timing how long it took participants to name letters when shown them, or to report if a letter was the normal way up or inverted. Having classified letters as easy or difficult to identify, he then tested the time it took to pronounce words varying in the discriminability of their letters, their length and their frequency of usage. While shorter and more frequent words were pronounced faster, there was no evidence that the ease of discriminating the letters affecting the reaction time. Experiments such as Cosky's led some experts on reading (e.g. Mitchell, 1982) to conclude that letter identification is not necessary for word recognition. One objection to this conclusion is that, as we will describe below, while the alternative sources of information such as a word's shape or its context may help recognition, they do not seem to be sufficiently specific in the information they supply to make word recognition possible.

One solution to the problem that word recognition time is not easily linked to the difficulty of discriminating letters is the possibility that our cognitive systems can process several letters at the same time (i.e. in parallel). If so, then the speed of recognizing a word will depend upon the speed of discriminating the least discriminable single letter in the word. This should be sufficiently short a time for no differences to be readily apparent in Cosky's experiment. There is, indeed, evidence that up to 12 letters may be processed simultaneously. The task involves indicating by a button press if a string of letters (e.g. BBBB) are all identical or if one is different (e.g. BBAB). When this is done, the time to indicate that all the letters are the same is independent of the number of letters shown. However, the problem with this research is that the participant may be responding to the regularity of the pattern rather than processing each of the letters. Whether or not it is necessary to identify the letters of a word before the word can be identified, it is worth noting that most models of word recognition do assume letter recognition plays a major part in the process. Secondly, we should not assume that all the letters in a word need be recognized. It is not too difficult to read *gardxn flxwxrs*, with several letters replaced by 'x'. There is, indeed, what Smyth et al. (1994) have dubbed 'the letter restoration effect', first demonstrated by Pillsbury (1897). Pillsbury showed that people will confidently report seeing letters in words they have been shown briefly when those letters were either smudged or replaced by other letters. It is also worth noting that it is necessary to encode not just what letters are present but also their position in a word. Even the miscoding of the position of one letter could make a big difference to the word recognized (e.g. *diary* and *dairy*; *causal* and *casual*).

Do word recognition processes make use of orthographic regularities?

One experimental design that has been used to examine whether the ordering of letters found in words helps word recognition involves showing very briefly strings of letters that either do or do not conform to normal English spelling rules (e.g. *blunth* vs. *trilbhu*). Gibson et al. (1962) found better performance with the orthographically regular strings, that is, those using normal spelling. When Baron (1979) asked participants to compare two strings of letters as to whether or not they were identical, orthographically regular letter strings were judged more quickly. There have, however, also been experiments which do not fit well with the belief that letter strings that fit spelling rules are more quickly processed. Both Manelis (1974) and McClelland and Johnston (1977) compared combinations of letters that are either common or rarely found in English. Common combinations might be expected to be more quickly processed, but neither study found any difference. Doubt therefore remains about the use of such spelling regularities in normal reading.

Does word recognition use the shape of the word?

Reicher (1969) briefly displayed a set of letters to participants, followed by a pattern mask, and finally showed two letters. The participants' task was to say which of the letters had been in the first list. Reicher found that performance was better if a four-letter word was shown rather than four unrelated letters, or even a single letter. This has been called the 'word superiority effect' and has been repeated in many other experiments.

Manelis (1974) showed the word superiority effect to be bigger for real words than for non-word letter strings that followed English spelling. One obvious way in which letter strings and words differ is in the overall shape of the familiar word. McClelland (1976) tested this by varying the shape of the words by printing them in letters alternating in their case (e.g. RaGe). In this condition, identification of the letters in the word was poorer than when the word was printed consistently in one case. This strongly suggests that there is some property of the word shape itself, above and beyond the letters composing it, which helps word perception.

The technique of manipulating upper and lower case letters to study their effect upon reading has been used by other investigators. Baron (1979), for example, had participants read aloud lists of 30 words, either proper names (e.g. *Ann, Dan*) where the first letter is normally in upper case, or words that are only rarely seen beginning with a capital letter (e.g. *ate, ant*). When the reading of these words was compared with less familiar type setting – all lower case for the proper names (e.g. *ann, dan*) and a first letter in upper case for the others (e.g. *Ate, Ant*) – the result was significantly longer reading times for words presented in the unfamiliar form. Again, this suggests that the visual shape of the word is involved in its recognition. However, the contribution of word shape in reading may be quite small. Cohen and Freeman (1978) found that the reading aloud of a short passage in alternating upper and lower case letters was slowed by 11 per cent for slower readers, but only by 2 per cent for faster readers. As with so many studies on reading, this result can be interpreted in several ways. It appears to show that alternating the case and disrupting word shape has little effect on reading. However, Mitchell (1982) argues that, especially for the fast readers, any differences are obscured by the slow task of reading aloud.

When people are asked to cross out a particular letter throughout a piece of text, they tend to make mistakes and miss letters in words more than they do in random lists of letters (e.g. Healy, 1976). This suggests that the perception of the word, as a word, inhibits the identification of the letters that make it up. Further, more errors are made in high frequency words, as would be expected if high frequency words have formed stronger representations of their shapes in the recognition system.

Context and word recognition

Tulving and Gold (1963) showed that the time for which a word such as *avalanche* needed to be displayed was reduced if participants had previously seen a context sentence such as 'The skiers were buried alive by the sudden ...'. Such experiments have often been taken as showing that context improves word recognition. What is more likely is that context improves word recognition under difficult and unusual circumstances. In the Tulving and Gold experiment the participants had to recognize a very difficult to distinguish word, with plenty of time to consider possibilities derived from the context. In normal reading, the words are rarely as highly predictable and are normally clearly printed. Context does not normally clearly specify what the next word is likely to be. Fischler and Bloom (1979) found that the lexical decision that a letter string was or was not a word was speeded by a context sentence only if nine out of ten participants could guess the word. Stanovich (1980) concluded from his review of the use of context that context will help when reading from print is slow, either because the reader is unskilled (e.g. a child) or because the word is poorly presented (e.g. bad handwriting). However, under normal conditions, readers probably make little use of context (see also Mitchell, 1982; Taft, 1991).

Other factors affecting word recognition

There are other properties of the words that we encounter that influence the ease of their reading (see Ellis, 1993 for a review). One such factor is the familiarity of the word. So, letters making up familiar words (e.g. *cat*) are perceived faster than those forming non-words (e.g. *cah*) (Henderson, 1982). Real words are read aloud faster than pseudohomophones (e.g. *seat* faster than *seet*) (McCann and Besner, 1987). Some words are more frequent than others, and high frequency words are easier to recognize than low frequency words (Monsell, 1991). Words that are learned earlier in life are read more easily than those learned later (e.g. Brown and Watson, 1987). Since word frequency and age of acquisition are closely related, it is not easy to reliably determine which is the main contributor to reading ease (cf. Ellis, 1993). These are stable features of word recognition, but in any particular situation the ease with which a word is read may be primed by recent encounters with that word. So, if, for example, you have recently read the word *telephone* you will identify it more quickly than if it had not been met recently (e.g. Carr et al., 1989).

Word recognition experiments: a summary

Despite many ingenious experiments, many of the processes underlying word recognition are still to be determined, and others are in dispute. Probably, at least some letters and their positions must be recognized prior to word recognition. There is evidence suggesting that the shape of words also contributes to the process. Spelling regularities may help too, as will context, but, in the latter case, only if the reader is unskilled or the text to be read is poorly presented.

Models of Word Recognition

So far we have considered some of the empirical evidence on the processes that underlie word recognition. We will turn now to two models that will serve as examples of the types of models which have been developed in an attempt to describe how word recognition takes place. All models of word recognition assume that there is some representation of the words we know stored within our cognitive systems, and that the appropriate representation must be activated by the newly presented word for that word to be recognized. How might this be done? One way might be to search through all the words in the memory store of known words when a new word is encountered, until the correct one is found. It is most unlikely that this is actually the process used. It usually requires less than three-quarters of a second for a participant to indicate whether or not a string of letters is a word. Most readers are familiar with more than 20,000 words, so that if every word in the human memory for words (usually called the 'lexicon') was examined before declaring a non-word is not an English word, the rate of comparison would be faster than one every four milliseconds. Perhaps we could search memory this fast, but it seems unlikely. Admittedly we have painted an extreme picture of search models. For instance, it is possible to think of searches in which some, but not all of the words in memory are considered, thus considerably reducing the search time. There are, however, other reasons for rejecting serial search models. One is that if there was such a search then the time to decide whether a particular word was a word should depend upon its position in the memory and should not vary with the nature of the other words being tested in the experiment. In fact, it is quicker to identify a high frequency word if all the other words are also high frequency than if they are of various frequencies (Glanzer and Ehrenreich, 1979). For these sorts of reasons, most psychologists who have studied word recognition have preferred models which allow direct access to individual words, rather than a search through all the words each time one has to be identified. There have been many models of word recognition, but we will describe just two here. The first, the logogen model, has been popular, especially among English psychologists, and the second, the Rumelhart and McClelland model, represents a development of the logogen model which has been implemented for a limited set of words in a computer program.

The logogen model

This model (illustrated in figure 9.1) was first proposed by Morton (1969). The basic units in the model are called 'logogens' (from the Greek *logos* meaning word, and *genus* meaning birth). For each morpheme that a person knows it is presumed that a logogen has been created. This logogen collects evidence from the perceptual system which is analysing the letter strings encountered for their visual features (e.g. lines, curves, other distinctive shapes) perhaps also using the identification of some of the letters, and also other information based upon the likely meaning of the word derived from the context. The logogen is tuned to receive information appropriate to its own morpheme. As more information accumulates, the unit is activated more intensely, until the activation exceeds a threshold when the unit fires and the word is recognized. If we suppose, for example, that the word *cat* has been presented to the reader, then the perceptual system will analyse the letters and the shape of the word, passing on this information to the logogens. Logogens for words shaped like *cat* will be activated, for example, those for *can* and *eat*. If the reader has been reading a story about cats, then further activation will come from the semantic system (discussed in more detail later) where information about cats has been recently activated. Eventually, the activation for the cat logogen will exceed its firing threshold and the reader will recognize the word and be able to obtain access to the stored information that she or he knows about cats. There are some additional assumptions that are required to make the logogen model compatible with what is known about word recognition. It is well established that high frequency words are more quickly recognized than low frequency words (e.g. Frederiksen and Kroll, 1976; Rubenstein et al., 1970). This can be accommodated in one of two ways: either, as Morton (1969, 1970) originally proposed, by each encounter with a word lowering the logogen's threshold so that high frequency words have a lower threshold than low frequency words, and require less input before they fire, or, as Morton (1979) has later suggested, because it is quicker to check the meaning of a common word, once the logogen has fired.

The interactive-activation model of Rumelhart and McClelland (1981, 1982) develops some of the ideas of the logogen model. It has been implemented as a computer program capable of identifying nearly 1,200 words. The

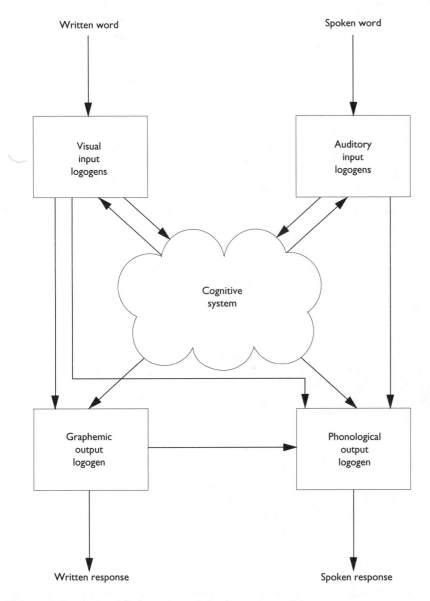

Figure 9.1   A simplified version of the logogen model

difficulty of modelling word recognition is well illustrated by the model, since it can, as yet, cope with only four-letter words, written in one particular typeface with letters made up of straight lines with no curves.

The model consists of a visual analysis system and a visual word recognition system (see figure 9.2). The analysis system is itself composed of a 'feature level' and a 'letter level'. Beyond the letter level is the word level, with a unit for each of the words that the system can recognize. Activation from the letter units feeds to their appropriate words, so that the letter T's letter unit stimulates the word units for all words with the letter T in that particular position. If the word presented was TIME, then that unit will start to be activated, as will those for TAKE, TRIP, TRAP, etc. The rest of the letters from TIME will also stimulate their appropriate units. In addition, as at the feature level, the letter units also inhibit and reduce the likelihood of firing of all those words which do not have a T, an I, an M or an E. So, while T stimulates the TIME unit, as do I, M and E, the other

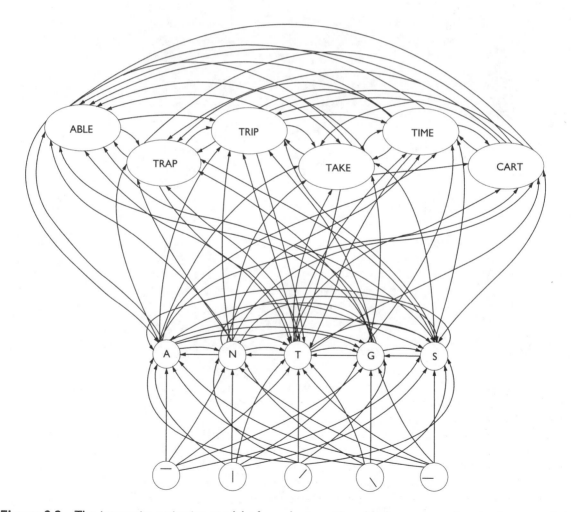

Figure 9.2 The interactive-activation model of word recognition. Nodes representing the features of the letters (/,\,– etc.) connect to nodes for letters with those features, and those nodes to words containing those letters.

words beginning with T are inhibited. As the TIME unit is activated it also inhibits the other word units. In the end one and only one unit wins through and stays active. When activation starts at one level, it is not necessary for one unit at that level to be selected before the units which are being activated can pass on stimulation to the higher-order units. Thus, the activation of the feature detector for the crossbar of the letter T will start to activate the T letter detector, and that will start to stimulate the words containing T, even though the feature detector for the crossbar has not been uniquely selected. This ability to stimulate higher levels before a lower-level decision is made is described as being 'in cascade'. The special features of the Rumelhart and McClelland model are not arbitrary. They are necessary to mimic the way the human recognition system works. The Rumelhart and McClelland model can simulate many of the features of recognition that have been discovered in the empirical studies, for example the word superiority effect (see, for example, Ellis, 1984).

In this section we have considered two major accounts of word recognition, but it should be made clear that these are only representative of a larger class of psychological models of this process. Psychologists have invested an enormous amount of energy, during the past three decades, in trying to fathom out the intricacies of word recognition (Taft, 1991, reviews recent progress). The reason for this interest is that word recognition is a crucial part of the overall reading process, and a comprehensive account of the processes it entails would not only increase our knowledge of human reading but would also speed up progress in the construction of artificial, computer-based reading systems.

Eye Movements during Reading

So far we have been concerned simply with the recognition of single words. While this is an essential first step in the process of reading there are far more processes beyond word recognition that are necessary to the normal reading process. In normal reading we have a page of lines of prose over which we move our eyes as we read. If we are aware of moving our eyes while reading at all, we probably would describe what we do as moving our eyes along the line. While we are capable of moving our eyes smoothly when we are tracking a moving object, that is not the way we move our eyes during reading. When reading our eyes move in a series of rapid stops and jerks. The pauses, known as 'fixations', vary considerably in length, but average about one-fifth to a quarter of a second. Fixations are affected by a variety of factors such as word length, word frequency, word type and so on (see also chapter 4). The movements, known as 'saccades', take on average about a fortieth of a second. When reading, therefore, our eyes are stationary around nine-tenths of the time. Reading takes place during the fixations. Even a strong flash of light will not be perceived if it occurs during a saccade (Latour, 1962). Most eye movements during reading are forward to new words, but, even in the skilled reader, 10–20 per cent of eye movements are back to earlier words. These eye movements are known as 'regressions'. Poor readers make more regressions and have longer fixations than skilled readers (see Mitchell, 1982 and Rayner, 1983 for more information).

When reading a typical line of print we make five or six fixations. In any single fixation only a few words can be seen clearly enough to be identified. You can do a simple experiment yourself by staring at a word in the middle of a line of print that you have yet to read and seeing how many words around it you can make out. You will be able to recognize confidently only one or two words. This effective visual field has been shown to be about 10–12 letters or spaces, perhaps two average words. For readers of English, more information is picked up to the right of the fixation point than to the left (Rayner et al., 1980). Normally, the eye fixates a point about a third of the way along a word. For readers of languages written right to left, the perceptual span is biased the other way, no doubt as an adaptation to the way the text must be scanned (Pollatsek et al., 1981).

Reading and Comprehension

There is far more to reading than recognizing a word and moving the eye on to another word to be recognized. So far we have said very little about the main purpose of reading, that is, the understanding of the message that the writer wished to convey. Reading is about comprehending this message, about constructing for oneself the meaning of the passage. The meaning of individual words must be integrated to construct meaningful sentences. These, in turn, will develop fuller passages. Most written prose has a hierarchical structure. At the highest level, books and stories have plots; articles have introductions, several central passages and conclusions; textbooks have chapters on different topics. Within each textbook chapter there are separate sections. Those sections themselves break down into more specific paragraphs, and those paragraphs are composed of several sentences each making one or more assertions. The reader needs to comprehend and develop an understanding of the message that is being conveyed at all of these levels. The process of skilled reading is essentially the process of retrieving stored knowledge about words, situations, plots and the way of the world, and using it to construct specific representations of the message of the material that is being read, at all appropriate levels of the message. In the next few sections of this chapter we will discuss how the meaning of what is read is constructed and comprehended, beginning with the meaning of individual words and considering, in turn, the higher-order activities involved in inference, comprehension and dealing with extended text.

Accessing meaning and comprehending sentences

Before we can comprehend a written sentence it is necessary to access the meaning of the words we are dealing with, that is, we must *identify* them as well as simply recognize them as words we have seen before. For instance, what do you know about cats? You can probably list a lot of things that you have learned about them, about their appearance, behaviour and so on. One aspect of our memories is a vast store of facts that we have acquired through our experience and which words such as 'cat' can trigger into recall. We must activate the appropriate stored knowledge related to a word, if what we read is to make sense. Models such as the logogen model and the Rumelhart and McClelland model assume that the word recognition units are keys to the accessing of the information stored in semantic memory about the thing named (see also chapter 2).

The activating of the appropriate information in semantic memory is a first step to comprehending a sentence, but much more is involved. Suppose you read the words 'The cat bit the dog'. You must retrieve the meanings of the words and construct the meaning of the sentence. In doing so you must hold the semantic information that you have acquired while reading 'the cat bit' while processing 'the dog'. You need to take into account not just the meaning of the words, but the role they play in a sentence constructed in this way. Just as recognizing letter order is essential to word recognition, so remembering word order is essential to sentence comprehension. You must remember which animal bit which! When comprehending a sentence, therefore, it is necessary to have available the meanings of the individual words and also to know the role that these words were playing in the sentence, whether they were the subject or the object of the action, and suchlike. This information is known as syntactic information (see chapter 4). When understanding a sentence, our cognitive system must have a record of the syntactic and the semantic (meaning) information contained in the sentence. This suggests that such information will be stored in memory, perhaps in special short-term memories developed for the task. There will probably be other short-term memories that retain information temporarily during processing at the other stages. We discuss such memories in chapter 2.

Comprehension and inferences

A person reading a text is continually analysing what they read for its connections with what has been read already. Through these connections it is possible to build up a coherent representation of the message of the passage. A sentence is interpreted and understood in the context of its preceding sentences. Take the example given by Haviland and Clark (1974) of *George thinks vanilla*. Very odd it sounds. We have our doubts about George! But suppose someone had asked the question *What kind of ice cream does Vivien like?* then the statement *George thinks vanilla* would be perfectly sensible.

Haviland and Clark (1974) argue that writers (and speakers) identify what they think the reader (or listener) already knows, and what the audience does not know. The former Haviland and Clark call the 'given information', the latter is the 'new information'. The reader has to identify the given information, which is a cue to information already stored, and then must integrate the new information with the old. Haviland and Clark measured the time people took to report that they comprehended a pair of sentences. Where inferences had to be made the participants took markedly longer. So, when, for example, the pair was

We got some beer out of the truck,

The beer was warm

the participants were quicker to comprehend the second sentence than when the reader had to infer that the beer was in the picnic supplies, as was required in the pair:

We checked the picnic supplies,

The beer was warm.

Many of the links in a story are causal ones, rather than just the mentioning of the same object or event. People can comprehend, and therefore read more quickly, sets of sentences linked by causal relationships. Haberlandt and Bingham (1978) showed this for triplets of sentences that were or were not causally linked. Similarly, if motivational steps have to be inferred, reading takes longer. Smith and Collins (1981) found that it is quicker to read

Rita needed a doctor fast

John got out the telephone book

than

Rita was having stomach pains

John got out the telephone book

where the reading of this second pair is slowed by the need to draw the inference that a doctor is needed.

Reading is, thus, an interplay of identifying links with already acquired information, of integrating the new information with the old and of deriving inferences either in the process of linking the given and the new, or as a result of the integration itself. Readers continually draw inferences from what they have read. Most authors are aware of this and provide only the necessary new statements that are required to carry the story along.

Scripts and schemata

Some inferences in reading can be drawn from simple knowledge about the creatures and objects named. However, many stories assume a knowledge that is used not just at one point, but to aid the comprehension of a whole chunk of the story. Whenever a story describes a car journey, a meal in a restaurant, a visit to the doctor's, attending a lecture, or any one of a large number of events that we have often experienced and which have a known reliable structure to them, then the author will assume that the reader will bring to the story a knowledge of what normally happens on such occasions. No story with a scene in a restaurant requires the author to describe the characters finding a seat, reading the menu, choosing food, etc. To someone from an alien culture such a scene in a novel would be incomprehensible because of the assumptions that the author makes about the knowledge which the reader brings to the passage. Such knowledge has been called scripts by Schank and Abelson (1977) (see chapter 7). They are

Scripts

examples of a rather more general concept, that of schemata (Bartlett, 1932; Thorndyke, 1984), that is, of organized structures of knowledge, derived from past experience which can be retrieved to guide comprehension. For many common activities it is possible to identify events that most people agree are normal features of the activity. Bower et al. (1979), for example, generated accounts of the common events in many activities such as going to a restaurant or the doctor's. They found not only that people agreed upon these common elements but that they played an important part in the recall of short stories based upon them. Statements not explicitly made in the story, but implicit in the script (such as ordering food in the restaurant, or sitting in the waiting room at the doctor's surgery), tended to be imported into the recall or incorrectly claimed to have been in the story in a recognition test. Events that had been deliberately moved in the script tended to return to their normal place.

Perhaps the most interesting finding by Bower et al. was that when they introduced events into the script-based stories that interrupted the normal flow of the script, these events were especially well recalled (see box 9.1). To the reader they seemed to be the whole point of the story. In fact, as Brewer and Lichtenstein (1981) showed, people rate a story that merely recounts a normal, uninterrupted script as hardly being a story at all. Readers read for a purpose, to discover the message that the writer wishes to transmit, and no writer would normally want to describe a completely mundane, common activity.

Readers bring to their reading an enormous wealth of prior knowledge and expectations. People reading a story expect a certain form to be followed, they expect stories to have plots. This influences their reading and their subsequent recall (cf. Thorndyke, 1977). Not just our reading, but all of our life is probably guided by expectations derived from past experience which structure what we expect, perceive, do and remember (Schank, 1982). It is perhaps because reading draws so heavily upon the frameworks that we have developed to deal with life, but then explores their limitations, that reading can be so engrossing and informative.

An Outline Model of the Reading Process

We have completed our review of the stages involved in reading, and they can be put together to give an outline of the basic processes involved in reading. This model will be useful in the next two sections where we will consider learning to read and reading disorders. There are two main types of component in the model that is illustrated in figure 9.3 These represent the PROCESSES being carried out and the RESOURCES used. The model is considerably simplified from that which would be required to fully specify the processes of reading, but it does highlight the main aspects and their relationships.

Our description of the model begins with the input material, that is, the text being read. The first process is to visually analyse each word. We have already discussed two models of the processes that might be involved here (i.e. Morton's 1969 logogen model and Rumelhart and McClelland's 1981 model). The marks on the paper will be analysed using the resources of feature, letter and word recognition units. For familiar words presented in clear type or handwriting, this will be sufficient to identify the word. From the visual analysis system, information (represented by the arrows) will be passed to the systems for identifying the sound and the meaning of the word. Notice that it is possible to get to the process of identifying word meaning either directly or through identifying the sound of the word (phonic mediation). Identification of the meaning of the word is via the stored information on word meaning, that is, semantic memory. Identification of the sound of the word might use the rules for the regular conversion of letters to sound, known as correspondence rules, and also analogies between letter patterns for similar-sounding words. Most readers are probably capable of using both strategies, but the analogy strategy appears to be frequently used by adults (cf. Glushko, 1979). As an illustration, read the non-word *tepherd*. What sound did you give to the *ph* in the middle? Normally *ph* is read as a *f* sound, but many people read it

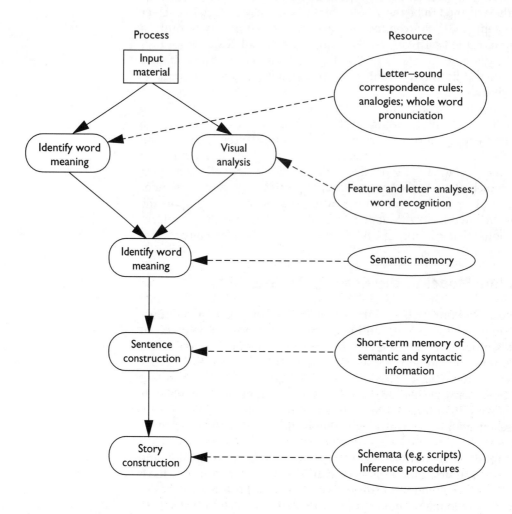

Figure 9.3   The basic processes and resources involved in reading

here as a *p* and *h* because *tepherd* is closely analogous to *shepherd*. In addition to these strategies for deciding how to pronounce new words or non-words, most experienced readers will have learned to link the correct sound of a word with its visual appearance without recourse to correspondence rules or analogies.

Once word meaning has been analysed the process of sentence construction can begin. From these sentences the story being told in the writing can be constructed, drawing upon past experience of stories and of the world. One important feature of the model to be noted is that the arrows showing the direction of flow of information go in both directions. It is assumed that processes higher in the system can influence what happens lower down. So, for example, the context of the story being constructed could influence the selection of word meaning; important when the word is a homonym like *bank* with several possible meanings. Similarly, this influence could spread down to aid the selection of the word's sound or its visual representation. As we discussed earlier, context effects will normally appear only when the visual analysis is hampered by ignorance or poor quality input.

To simplify the model we have not included processes for syntactic analysis, nor for reading aloud. Reading aloud will probably make use of information from most levels, since skilled readers incorporate appropriate inflexions and pauses to show they are using the meaning of the story. However, it is possible to read using just the word-sound process as we do when we read nonsense words.

Learning to Read

The model in figure 9.3 illustrates the skills that an expert reader possesses and which a child must acquire when learning to read. Fortunately, by the age of five, when most children in Britain and Ireland are learning to read, they have already developed adequate skills in several levels of the model. They have learned the meanings of many hundreds of words and can skilfully go from the word sound to the word meaning. They are equally skilled at interpreting sentences and comprehending stories, even though their experience is limited, and they will have problems reading books about topics outside those they have encountered in life, or in stories read to them. Teachers have always recognized that children need appropriate comprehension skills, sufficient command of English, good speaking vocabulary and wide and varied experience when they come to tackle learning to read (Holmes, 1928). It has sometimes been claimed (e.g. Morphett and Washburne, 1931; Bigelow, 1934) that children need to achieve a state of 'reading readiness' before they can be successfully taught to read, and the age of six and a half was often mentioned. Anyone with experience of schools in the UK or Ireland, where children aged four and a half or younger often successfully begin to learn to read, will have their doubts about such a claim. Coltheart (1979) reviews the research upon which the claim that there is a critical stage of reading readiness is based. He shows that the research is quite inadequate to justify this strong assertion. On the other hand, he also reviews studies which show that the age of beginning reading is not very important, since late starters soon catch up once they begin to receive instruction.

The problems for the child learning to read are mainly ones of visual analysis, and of linking the result of that analysis to word meaning and to the appropriate word sounds. They do not possess the resources that support visual analysis and word-sound identification. The skilled adult reader can reach the meaning of most words either directly from the visual analysis, or indirectly through the word's sound. It is useful for the child to learn both of these skills, since the direct visual route is the basis of skilled adult reading but the route via phonic mediation is especially useful to the child who knows the sounds of many words but not their visual appearance.

Methods of teaching reading often strongly emphasize either the visual or the phonic route. For many years what has been called 'The Great Debate' centred upon whether children should be taught to sound out the words they had to read (see Chall, 1967). Some teaching methods advocated 'whole word' or 'look and say' techniques, encouraging the recognition of words by sight, while others emphasized the teaching of skills for sounding out new words. Chall (1967) pointed out that all reading programmes include some training in phonic skills. Since adult reading skill is mainly one of whole-word direct access to the meaning, the challenge from the opponents of training in sounding out words is that this involves training in an immature approach to learning which may inhibit the development of the more mature skill.

Obtaining evidence of the effectiveness of teaching methods is notoriously difficult. Apart from the obvious problems of matching children on their intelligence and home background, teachers themselves are affected by the introduction of the new teaching schemes. Some may respond with more than normal involvement and enthusiasm, producing improvements that are not really the result of the teaching method itself. Others may give only token cooperation and ignore the specified method if they believe that it is harming the learning of some of their pupils. Against this background of difficulty in interpreting the research, it does appear that teaching phonic skills can benefit rather than harm the new reader. The majority of the studies reviewed by Chall (1967) showed an advantage for phonic training. Also, as will be described later, the source of the reading difficulty of many poor readers appears to be in their weakness in using sounding-out skills.

Normal stages during learning to read

So far, we have briefly discussed some issues in the teaching of reading, and have described the components of the adult reading skill. What has not been considered is the way normal children taught in British and American schools usually develop as they learn to read. We will describe the sequence of stages in learning to read that are identified by Marsh et al. (1981). It should be emphasized that these are the stages observed among children taught by the normal methods used in British and American schools. As was pointed out early in this chapter, reading is not a skill for which there can have been any evolutionary selection, and it is not likely that its components are pre-programmed as the learning of speech may be. Different teaching styles could and almost certainly would lead to different stages.

Stage one: 'Glance and guess'   As a first step towards reading, children are often taught to recognize a small number of words by sight. They acquire a small sight vocabulary but have no skills at sounding out words. When they encounter a word that they do not know they will tend to guess, basing their guess upon the context. Faced with the sentence 'The boat is on the sea', a child may read it as 'The boat is on the water'.

Stage two: 'Sophisticated guessing'   At this stage, still within the first year of learning to read, children still guess on the basis of the context, but now draw the word guessed from the growing number of words that they have encountered previously, and normally the word spoken has some visual resemblance to the actual word being attempted. The child appears to be looking for an overlap between the visual characteristics of the new word and the stored information in the visual word recognition units. Perhaps the recognition units have yet to be fully defined. In some cases they may contain only a partial description of the word. At this stage the reading still depends upon the visual perception of the whole word.

Stage three: 'Simple grapheme–phoneme correspondence'   The child now begins to decode new words by sounding them out. In doing so, the translation rules for going from the letters to the sounds may be still inadequately appreciated, so that the more sophisticated rules are missing. This sometimes leads to non-words being produced in the reading attempt. For example, the child will usually not realize that the silent '*e*' at the end of many words (e.g. *tame, line, lane*) has the effect of lengthening the earlier vowel, so he or she will read the words as 'tam', 'lin' and 'lan'. Sounding out the words has been added as a valuable strategy to supplement the increasing set of words that can be recognized visually.

Stage four: 'Skilled reading'   As children become older and more experienced at reading they develop more sophisticated skills. They learn the context-specific rules for letter–sound conversions and begin to pronounce new words by analogy to ones of the same structure. So, for example, they learn that '*c*' is pronounced as an '*s*' sound if the next letter is an '*i*' (e.g. *city, cite*) but as a '*k*' sound if the following letter is an '*o*' (e.g. *cork, cow*). They will sometimes read the non-word *faugh* as 'faff' because it is analogous to words they know like *laugh*. By this stage, when the average child is aged eight to ten, they have acquired the basic adult reading skills. From then onwards they will enrich their vocabulary and their efficiency at reading, but, according to Marsh et al., they will not change qualitatively in their reading technique.

The four stages identified by Marsh et al. (1981) can be seen as reflecting three strategies in learning to read. The earliest strategy, used in Marsh et al.'s first and second stages, involves the direct recognition of the words as wholes. Frith (1985), when re-describing the Marsh et al. stages, calls these 'logographic skills'. In the third stage in Marsh et al.'s model children use a knowledge of the usual correspondence between particular letters and their sounds. The children are using what Frith calls 'alphabetic skills'. Finally, in Marsh et al.'s stage four, the child is able to go beyond simple letter to sound conversions, combining this with an ability to break down words into components. Now the child is able to use regularities in the structures of the words to obtain their pronunciation. At this stage, where spelling regularities and the sounds that go with sets of letters are used in reading, the child is using what Frith calls 'orthographic skills'. Recent evidence has been presented by Goswami (1991) of the ability of children to exploit analogies between words when learning to read. She shows how beginning readers can exploit analogies at the beginning and the end of words in quite subtle ways and argues that this often precedes the ability to break words down into their individual phonological components (see box 9.2).

In the section above we have described commonly observed stages in the development of reading in modern Western countries. However, as Ellis (1993) has argued, these stages are likely to be a reflection of the teaching methods that have been favoured rather than some more fundamental aspect of reading. For example, in America in the 1780s the teaching of reading very heavily emphasized phonics so that the early visual stages may well not have occurred.

As we will discuss in the next sections on developmental dyslexia, the acquisition of these skills may play an important part in determining if children have reading disorders.

◀ Reading Disorders ▶ ▶ ▶

A marked difficulty in the ability to read is often termed 'dyslexia'. There are two general classes of dyslexia. If someone who was normally skilled at reading suffers brain damage, usually in the left hemisphere of the cerebral cortex, as a result of a stroke, a tumour, or a head injury, and afterwards has noticeable reading problems, he or she is described as suffering 'acquired dyslexia'. Several types of acquired dyslexia have been distinguished, and these can often be understood in terms of the model of reading given earlier in figure 9.3. We will discuss some examples of acquired dyslexia shortly. The second class of dyslexia is that of apparently otherwise normal children who have severe difficulty in learning to read. This is often called 'developmental dyslexia'. The term 'developmental dyslexia' is disliked by some psychologists. They point out that it can imply that children with a reading problem have a sort of disease or specific brain damage as is the case with acquired dyslexia. For some children this may be so, but to classify a child with reading problems in a way that suggests brain damage or a medically diagnosable illness can be misleading and harmful to the child, her or his parents, and their associates. Nevertheless, some children of normal or high intelligence do have reading problems, and the term developmental dyslexia is in common use among psychologists who do not misunderstand its implications. The term does not specify a distinct group of children. Within the population there is a spread of reading abilities. Ellis (1984) draws the analogy between the terms 'obesity' and 'developmental dyslexia'. The concept of obesity is important for health, but there is no dividing line between a normal and an obese person; people spread from thin, through average sizes, to very fat. So do reading abilities. There is no dividing line beyond which someone is suddenly obese. The term is used to describe people who need help in losing weight. Developmental dyslexia can be thought of as describing children who need special help with reading.

Acquired dyslexia

We cannot review all the types of dyslexia that have been identified in recent years, but we will select a few examples to show how patients with specific brain damage can show through the reading skills they have lost and those they retain how the cognitive processes of reading are organized. A good brief review of acquired dyslexias will be found in Ellis (1993) and fuller reviews in Coltheart (1981), Patterson (1981) and Ellis and Young (1988).

There are some patients who can pronounce and understand almost any familiar real word. At first sight they appear to have no reading problem. However, when they are asked to read non-words, however simple, such as BIP or GUZ, they are unable to do so. This particular disorder has already been described when we discussed phonic mediation. It is known as 'phonological dyslexia' (Patterson, 1982). If you look at the model of the reading process reproduced in figure 9.3 you will see that the brain damage which the phonological dyslexic has suffered appears to have put out of action the route to reading aloud through translating words to sounds. The route from the visual analysis process direct to word meaning remains intact, and hence these patients have little difficulty with words for which they have already developed visual word recognition units.

If there are patients who appear to have problems with the route through the word sounds, what about that directly from visual analysis to word meaning? The answer is, yes, there are people who have, apparently, suffered damage to this part of the system. They are known as 'surface dyslexics'. The errors which are made by surface dyslexics fit well with the assumption that the direct route from visual recognition unit to meaning has been damaged, and that the patient employs a variety of strategies to try to get around this problem. The surface dyslexic often misreads irregular words, while having few problems with regular words. For example, *phase* may be read as 'face' and *grind* as 'grinned'. The errors suggest that the patient is either using grapheme–phoneme correspondence rules to translate letter by letter (Marshall and Newcombe, 1973) or using inappropriate analogies to the sound (Henderson, 1982). Nevertheless, surface dyslexic patients do manage to read some irregular words. How do they do this? As we mentioned earlier, it is possible to read aloud without identifying the meaning of the words. This could be by sounding out the words read, but it is more likely that the experienced reader learns the direct relationship between the visual appearance of words and their sounds. As well as developing a link from visual appearance to word meaning we also learn to link the visual appearance with its appropriate sound. We do, as we said earlier, usually hear an inner voice while we are reading. Surface dyslexics appear to retain at least some ability to go from the appearance of a word to its correct sound. However, they then must interpret the meaning of that sound. At this point there are problems if the word is a homophone and there are various alternatives with the same pronunciation. Marshall and Newcombe found that a surface dyslexic whom they tested tended to make errors confusing the meaning of the word he had read with a word that sounded the same. For example, he defined *mown* as 'to cry' (cf. moan) and *bury* as 'a hat, headgear' (cf. beret). Surface dyslexic patients, then, seem to have lost the direct link from the visual word recognition units to the meaning of the words stored in semantic memory.

The final type of acquired dyslexia that we will mention is known as 'deep dyslexia'. Like phonological dyslexics, the deep dyslexic patient cannot read non-words, so it is assumed that the route to word meaning via identifying the word sound has been lost. However, the deep dyslexic makes many more errors. They can often read common concrete nouns like *table* or *baby*, but even here semantic errors occur. *Ape* may be misread as 'monkey', *forest* as 'trees', *student* as 'thinking'(!!). Abstract words cause great problems, as do function words like *the* and *has*. Other function words are sometimes substituted. Visual errors are also common, 'brush' for *bush*, 'wedge' for *edge*, for example. Clearly, the deep dyslexic has suffered considerable damage to his or her reading system and there is still debate about the actual components that have broken down. The semantic errors suggest failures in the identification of word meaning in semantic memory. For a fuller discussion of deep dyslexia the reader is referred to Ellis (1993) and Ellis and Young (1988).

Poor readers (developmental dyslexia)

Why do some children who have average or high intelligence have problems learning to read? No doubt there will be many reasons, since there are many components in the reading process and in the cognitive system which makes it possible. Any of these may not have been properly developed and may cause reading problems. All that can be done here is to offer a few possible reasons. The interested reader should consult a fuller review such as that by Mitchell (1982), Downing and Leong (1982) and especially Frith (1985).

Several possible sources of reading difficulties have been proposed by cognitive psychologists. Here we will consider the following: that poor readers have inappropriate patterns of eye movements; that backward readers have difficulty in extracting visual information; and that poor readers do not use 'word-attack' skills to decode unfamiliar words as well as do good readers and do not follow the normal sequence of skill development described by Frith (1985).

Faulty eye movements   It has been shown many times that children with severe reading problems tend to show more regressions, shorter saccades and longer fixations (Rayner, 1978; Pavlidis, 1981). Of course, this would be expected when reading text, since poor readers will have greater problems in interpreting the words before them. However, Pavlidis (1981) found that when poor and normal readers had to follow and fixate a series of five lights as they flashed in sequence across a display, poor readers appeared to be much less efficient in watching the lights. Pavlidis therefore argued that the cause of the poor readers' deficiency was in their ability to control their eye movements. On the other hand, in an experiment by Stanley (1978) good and poor readers differed when reading a text but not when looking for the picture of an object in a scene. Tinker (1946, 1958) has reviewed attempts to train eye movements to improve reading, and concluded that while eye movement patterns could be trained, the participants in such experiments showed no greater improvement in reading than did those trained in quite different techniques. Stanley et al. (1983) failed to replicate Pavlidis' (1981) study, finding no difference between the eye movements of all but one of their dyslexic participants and their group of normal readers. However, Pavlidis (1983) has criticized the Stanley et al. study over technicalities in its design.

Some experts on reading (e.g. Mitchell, 1982) believe that the differences observed by Pavlidis are the result of the dyslexic children's approach to the task. At the moment, while Pavlidis' research certainly calls for further investigation, it seems unlikely that differences in eye movements will prove to be the crucial cause of developmental dyslexia.

Extracting visual information   Mitchell (1982) criticizes most studies which have purported to show that poor readers have problems in extracting visual information from their environment because the superior performance by the normal readers, which is often observed, could be because the normal readers are more likely to use verbal strategies, for example to name the shapes shown and rehearse the names to remember them. The fact that good readers are more likely to name the stimuli in the experiments is interesting and will be taken up in the next section. However, it does not justify the conclusion that poor readers have *visual* difficulties. Studies where it is hard for the symbols shown to be named, such as that by Vellutino et al. (1975) using short strings of Hebrew letters, have found that poor readers are just as good as normal readers at recognizing and remembering what was shown. Done and Miles (1978) showed that good and poor readers did not differ in their ability to remember the order of a set of nonsense shapes. When, however, they had the chance to learn a set of names for the shapes the good readers did better than the poor ones. Again, it seemed to be a case of the poor readers making less use of verbal strategies. To summarize, it does not appear that poor readers have special problems extracting visual information.

Poor word-attack skills   In our description of the stages through which children normally proceed when learning to read, we described the three types of skills distinguished by Frith (1985), namely, logographic, alphabetic and orthographic. Frith believes that many cases of poor reading occur because for some reason the child fails to develop adequate alphabetic strategies. She argues that while it is theoretically possible for a child to fail to learn to read any words by sight, such cases are extremely rare. Classic developmental dyslexia occurs, according to Frith, where children do not progress from the first, logographic skill to the alphabetic skill. Frith points out that where formerly dyslexic children have been taught to read, they have more problems reading non-words than do normal children, suggesting that they have still not mastered the letter-to-sound rules as well as other children. Frith argues that, for developmental dyslexic children, there may be a basic dysfunction involving phonology, that is, these children may have a problem understanding or making speech sounds. She cites studies which show that dyslexic children tend to be late in starting to speak, to be poor at categorizing sounds and in repeating unfamiliar spoken words, slow in naming pictures, and several other sources of evidence. We noted in the previous section that poor readers tend to adopt verbal strategies for remembering visual shapes less readily than normal readers. This, presumably, is another reflection of the same underlying problem.

As we emphasized at the beginning of this part of the chapter, it would be a mistake to expect that there is one cause of reading problems among children. Nevertheless, it does appear likely that a great many of the problems that poor readers face result from their having difficulty in learning and applying the alphabet strategies that normal readers take in their stride.

Conclusions

In this chapter we have looked at why words are spelt as they are, and the implications this has for reading. A strategy of sounding out each word letter by letter is inadequate as the sole basis for reading, although, as we suggest at the end of the chapter, it is a valuable skill and if it is not developed may lead to poor reading.

The different possible sources of information for word recognition were reviewed. There is still dispute about the relative importance of the identification of the individual letters in a word or the overall word-shape in word recognition, but both are probably used by the skilled reader. On the other hand, the context supplied by the rest of the text probably makes little difference in word recognition if the words are clearly printed and being read by a skilled adult. For children learning to read or for adults struggling with indistinct words then context helps word recognition. Two related models of word recognition were described. Both assume that evidence is accumulated from various analysers and that the mental lexicon can be accessed directly by the word; there is no need to search through it looking for a match between the symbols presented and a stored word unit.

Reading involves far more than word recognition. It requires the use of stored information about the meaning of words, and the making of inferences as well as the interpretation of the text through scripts and other schemata that help its structuring and interpretation. Our outline model of the processes involved in reading not only summarizes what goes on but helps to explain the different types of acquired dyslexia that we reviewed.

The development of reading skills commonly goes from whole-word recognition to alphabetic strategies and then to more skilful use of regularities in spelling. It was concluded that many poor readers may have failed to develop the alphabetic strategies. Here, however, as in so many of the other aspects of the reading process, a great deal remains to be discovered.

Taken as a whole, reading illustrates perhaps more clearly than any other task the multi-levelled and integrative nature of much of human cognitive activity.

Further reading

A.W. Ellis 1993: *Reading, Writing and Dyslexia: A Cognitive Analysis*, 2nd edn. Hove: Lawrence Erlbaum Associates, covers most of the issues in this chapter in more detail. Another good survey is to be found in M.A. Just and P.A. Carpenter 1987: *The Psychology of Reading and Language Comprehension*. Newton, Mass: Allyn and Bacon. A thorough though often quite technical discussion of lexical access is covered in M. Taft 1991: *Reading and the Mental Lexicon*. Hove: Lawrence Erlbaum Associates. M. Coltheart (ed.) 1987: *Attention and Performance XII: The Psychology of Reading*. Hove: Lawrence Erlbaum Associates, is a volume of high-level conference proceedings dedicated to reading.

Useful general accounts of reading development are to be found in M.J. Adams 1990: *Beginning to Read*. Cambridge, Mass: MIT Press, and J.S. Chall 1983: *Stages of Reading Development*. New York: McGraw Hill, and U. Goswami and P. Bryant 1990: *Phonological Skills and Learning to Read*. Hillsdale, NJ: Lawrence Erlbaum Associates, offers a more specialized treatment of the role of phonology in reading development. Finally P.B. Gough, L.C. Ehri and R. Treiman (eds) 1992: *Reading Acquisition*. Hillsdale, NJ: Lawrence Erlbaum Associates, is a recent collection of chapters on the topic.

Discussion points

1   What factors are important in the recognition of individual printed words?
2   Discuss the role of attention, skill and memory in reading and comprehending sentences.
3   What do writers assume that readers already know?
4   What stages do children pass through when learning to read?

Practical exercises

1   Prepare samples of text for participants to read which are distorted in various ways. For example you can create text in **wHiCh ThE cAsEs Of LeTtErS aRe AlTeReD, or WHICH ARE ALL IN UPPER or lower case, orxxwherexxspacesxxbetweenxxx-wordsxxarexxx filledxxwithxxxs, or where there are spelxing errors.** Some of these manipulations perturb word shape or word boundaries. Which of the various manipulations you present slow reading time the most? Are there any particularly disruptive combinations of text? Are some types of word (function vs. content, high vs. low frequency) affected more than others?

2   Do people need to sound out words when they are reading? Select short passages from newspapers or magazines for participants to read. Have one group of participants read the passages (silently) while saying quietly to themselves 'one, two three, one, two, three, one, two, three, …' or some other suitable form of articulatory suppression. Compare the performance of this group on indices such as reading speed and comprehension with the other group of participants who read (silently) without any suppression.

3   Read carefully through box 9.2 on analogies in learning to read, then listen to a child of, say, around six years, who is just learning to read. Write down the words which the child has difficulty in reading, but do not correct them at this stage. Divide the list into two sets. For each word in set I, prepare a suitable analogy and sound this out to your reader before he or she tackles these words again. For the remaining words, encourage the child to sound out the letter groups of each word. Which strategy produces the most improvement?

Box 9.1
Memory for the unexpected: remembering script violations

Bower et al. conducted a series of experiments on script memory. For instance, they demonstrated that people show remarkable consistency in generating major script elements, and are likely to confuse in memory actions in a text that were stated with unstated actions implied by the script. Here, we outline the last experiment of the series (Experiment 7). In this experiment, Bower et al. explored how well people remember unexpected deviations from a script.

In their original theory, Schank and Abelson (1977) mentioned several script interruptions which they called obstacles, errors and distractions. Obstacles occur when a condition necessary for an imminent action is missing, as in being unable to read a French menu. Errors occur when an action leads to an inappropriate or unanticipated outcome, as in ordering steak and receiving fish. Finally, distractions occur when an unexpected situation or action takes the actor temporarily or permanently out of the script, as when an urgent telephone call takes the diner away from the meal. Bower et al. pointed out that as well as these interruptions, various irrelevant statements can also occur in a text. They

defined an irrelevancy as 'something that can occur in parallel with essential actions without impeding the flow of events' (p. 210). Their prediction was that 'interruptions will be remembered better than script actions and that irrelevancies will be remembered less than either' (ibid.).

Script-based stories, 22 to 26 sentences long, were made about making coffee, attending a lecture, getting up in the morning, attending a film, visiting a doctor and dining at a restaurant. Each text contained one error, one obstacle, one distraction, three irrelevancies and about 20 relevant script actions. Twenty-four Stanford University undergraduates read the six stories for five minutes in all. After a ten-minute intervening task to remove any transient short-term memory effects, they were required to recall the stories in writing in as exact a way as possible.

Percentages recalled were as follows: interruptions 53 per cent, script actions 38 per cent and irrelevancies 32 per cent. Even if the type of script was treated as another variable in the experiment (as a mixed effect) interruptions were recalled better than script actions ($p < 0.001$), but the difference between script actions and irrelevancies was only just significant when the scripts themselves were treated as constants or fixed effects (p < 0.05).

Of the three types of interruptions, obstacles were recalled best (60 per cent), followed by distractions (56 per cent) and errors (42 per cent). Obstacles and errors did not differ at all from one another, but obstacles were significantly different from errors (p < 0.001) as were

distractions from errors (p < 0.05). These differences were only significant if the scripts were treated as fixed effects, leading the authors to be uncertain as to whether the differences between interruptions were strong enough to generalize across other learning materials.

Based on material in G.H. Bower, J.B. Black and T.J. Turner 1979: Scripts in memory for text. *Cognitive Psychology*, 11, 177–220.

Box 9.2
The use of analogies in learning to read

Goswami's interest was in the relation between the child's phonological awareness and the use of analogies in learning to read. As she pointed out, it is widely known that there is a strong link between a child's phonological skills prior to beginning school and subsequent progress at reading, but the exact nature of this link is not known. One possibility is that phonological skills and awareness might operate at the phonemic level in which words are broken into their smallest constituent sounds, which correspond in turn to single letters or pairs of letters in words. This would allow the child to build up *grapheme-to-phoneme correspondences*, and is the level traditionally emphasized in phonics approaches to reading. Another level at which phonological skills could work is at what Goswami calls the *intra-syllabic* level. Here, single syllable words are broken into their *onset*, corresponding to the initial consonants, and their *rime*, corresponding to the vowel(s) and final consonant(s). For instance the onset of clip is '*cl-*', and its rime is '*-ip*', and the onset and rime of *cart* are '*c-*' and '*-art*' respectively. Goswami noted that tasks involving rhyme, which operate at the intra-syllabic level (rather than phonemes), are the best predictors of later reading ability. This suggests that grapheme-to-phoneme correspondence may be less important than was thought in early reading and may even

emerge after the grosser intra-syllabic skills have emerged. In two experiments, Goswami investigated whether beginning readers can make use of intra-syllabic analogies, and compared the relative importance of information from the onset and the rime of single syllable words.

Experiment 1
Thirteen girls and seven boys from the infant classes of a primary school participated in the study. Their mean age was 6 years 11 months. Their mean reading age on the Schonell Graded Word Reading Test was 6 years 7 months.

A preliminary session was held in which the participants' reading ages were established. The experiment then took place on two subsequent sessions. At each session, the children were first pre-tested on the sets of nine words which they were to read aloud, to establish any prior knowledge of the words in question.

The basic design of the experiment is shown in box table 9.2.1. The experimenter told the children that the clue words should help them work out some of the words they had just tried. The clue words were then pronounced and segmented to emphasize the consonant cluster relevant in the analogy. For instance, if the onset of 'trim' was the source of the analogy then the experimenter said /tr, /i, /m/,

Box table 9.2.1   The basic structure of Goswami's experiment 1

Clue word	Analogy test	Common unit control	Common letter control
Onset analogy trim	trot, trap, tred	blot, snap, sled	tint, tart, torn
Final consonants analogy limp	camp, dump, romp	caps, duct, rods	grip, slop, clap

'trim'. While if the rime of, say, 'desk' was the focus, the experimenter said /d/, /e/, /sk/, 'desk'. Each clue word was presented either with onset or final consonant analogies, with a given child receiving one or the other. Control words were also tested. Common unit controls began or ended with the same pair of letters as the analogy test words. These words were used to check that any improvement on the analogy test was due to the clue word rather than any other correspondences between the test words. Finally, common letter control words shared less direct analogies (common letters) with the clue words, but in principle allowed participants to draw on a similar phonemic structure to the clue words.

Goswami made two major predictions. First, that a greater increase in performance, from pre-test to test, should be found in the analogous than in the common unit or common letter control words. Second, that onset analogies (*trim: trot, trap, tred*) should be more effective than final consonant analogies (*limp: camp, dump, romp*) since the latter disrupt the rime by not including the vowel.

Results

The results can be seen in box table 9.2.2

Box table 9.2.2   Mean number of words read correctly

Clue word	Analogy test	Common unit control	Common letter control
Onset analogy			
Pre-test	1.2	1.75	1.10
Analogy test	2.6	1.80	1.15
Final consonants analogy			
Pre-test	1.55	1.50	1.55
Analogy test	2.05	1.60	1.75

Source: Extracted from table 2, Goswami, 1991

On an overall analysis of variance there was a significant effect of type of test ($p < 0.01$), a significant effect of clue word type ($p < 0.01$), and a significant interaction between word type and test ($p < 0.0001$). Further testing of these effects showed that children read significantly more analogous words at test than pre-test (Newman-Keuls, $p < 0.01$) indicating that analogies were being made. Also there were significantly more analogy words read in the onset

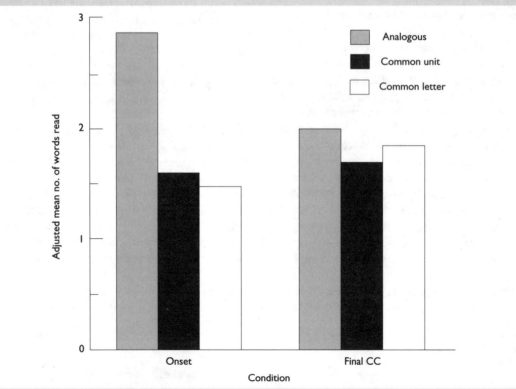

Box figure 9.2.1   The effect of onset analogies on reading performance. CC = Consonant conditions. (Based on figure 1, Goswami, 1991)

than in the final consonant condition (Newman-Keuls $p < 0.01$). Goswami conducted further statistical tests on her data to clarify this effect. In particular she corrected for any previous knowledge of the words which the children might have had using a technique known as the analysis of covariance. This allowed her to partial out the pre-test scores. Having done this, the effects of the onset analogies on performance were clearly apparent (see box figure 9.2.1).

To summarize experiment 1, children can make use of analogies in learning to read and do so most readily when the onset structure is preserved as in *trim, trot, . . .* compared with when the rime is disrupted as in *limp, camp, . . .* Thus words which share consonant blends (two or more consonants) at the beginning act as more effective analogies than words which share consonant blends at the end.

Experiment 2

Experiment 2 used a similar procedure to explore these effects further, except this time Goswami examined the effect of a shared vowel as well as a consonant blend. She contrasted analogies such as *wink–pink*, in which the vowel and the terminal consonants were shared (preserved rime), with analogies such as *trim–trip* in which the vowel extended the common onset. This time, the faithful preservation of the rime provided a more effective analogy than the extension of the onset. In this second experiment, the rime effect was by far the strongest.

Thus, intra-syllabic skills can be used and are often quite subtle. Reflecting on her work, Goswami states: 'Children do not seem to begin by analysing written words into graphemes and spoken words into phonemes, although they can certainly be taught to do so. It is the intra-syllabic phonological units of onset and rime that are the important ones' (p. 1122).

Based on U. Goswami 1991: Learning about spelling sequences: The role of onsets and rimes in analogies in reading. *Child Development*, 62, 1110–23.

10 Problem Solving and Reasoning

The ability to solve problems might be regarded as the pinnacle of human ability. Few animals, except perhaps some of the higher apes, have shown anything like the human ability to solve problems, while the results of the scientific and technical problems which humans have faced and solved in the past are all around us. Nevertheless, it may be that the need to solve problems is relatively rare in our individual lives. The occurrence of a problem may reflect failures in an even more impressive cognitive system which is able to cope with understanding our environment and planning our response to it without the obvious hold-ups that problems, by definition, represent. In the first part of this chapter we will consider the situations in which the need to solve problems arises, the nature of such problems, and common attempts at their solution. Then, we will move to considering whether our thinking represents the use of a mental logic, before moving on to consider an aspect of thinking closely related to problem solving, namely decision making. We frequently need to take decisions that may have considerable effects upon our future lives, and the second part of the chapter will concentrate upon factors which may lead to a distortion in our decision making processes.

When Do We Need to Solve Problems?

Rasmussen (1986) has proposed a model of the control of human cognition. In this model there are three main levels. At the normal level of control our cognition follows well-practised routes with little need for thought about what should be done next. At this 'skill-based' stage, which might be illustrated by our ability to drive if we are experienced drivers, or by our normal routines when getting up in a morning, all goes well so long as the routines that we have learned meet with no novel obstacle. At some stage, however, something will go wrong. This might reflect an error that has occurred, or it may be that our learned habits are inadequate to cope with the present situation. In this case, we move to the second level in the model, which Rasmussen terms 'rule-based'. Having identified that our normal skilled behaviour cannot proceed in its usual way, we examine the current situation and draw from memory rules which we have learned are likely to apply in such a case. So for example, if our usual skill-based routine of climbing into our car and driving to work is interrupted by the car failing to start, we will search our memories for examples of rules which might apply to explain the present situation. We may consider the possibility of the car being too cold and needing more choke, or we may suspect that we have flooded the engine by our initial attempts at starting. We may wonder whether the points need cleaning or even check to see whether there is petrol in the tank. It is only when these rules that we have acquired fail to overcome the obstacle that we have to move to Rasmussen's third level, which he terms 'knowledge-based'. Then, working from our general first principles and a basic knowledge of the situation that we are in, we deduce new information and, for us, novel situations. For psychologists studying problem solving, it is this final stage that has usually been considered. It is, as was remarked earlier, a vital part of human ability, but, as the Rasmussen model implies, we should not overlook the fact that the need to solve a problem is normally a relatively uncommon aspect of the complex and powerful cognitive skills that we possess.

Two example problems

To illustrate what is involved in problem solving, consider the two following example problems.

1   One morning, at sunrise, a monk sets out from a house at the bottom of a mountain to follow the track to the top of the mountain where his monastery stands. For some of the way he walks quickly, sometimes he stops to look at the view or shuffles along as his feet become tired. Sometimes he pauses to look at flowers while at other times he hurries on because the weather looks threatening. Eventually, near sunset, he reaches the monastery. Next morning, at sunrise, he sets out to return to the house at the foot of the mountain. Again he walks at varying speeds, sometimes quickly, sometimes slowly, sometimes sitting to rest and contemplate the view. By evening he reaches his home again. The question is, given that he followed the same path up and down the mountain, was there any time on the two days when he was at the exactly the same point on the mountain on both days. A solution to the problem can be found on page 233.

2   In this second problem, imagine that you are a carpenter cutting up the block of wood shown in figure 10.1. You are going to divide this block into 27 equal cubes. One way to do this would be to hold the pieces together after each cut, and to make the cuts that are illustrated by the dotted lines in the figure. This method involves six cuts. Can you

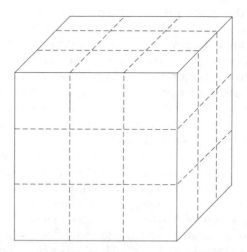

Figure 10.1 Cutting a block of wood into 27 cubes. What is the minimum number of cuts needed to do so?

reduce the number of cuts involved by reorganizing the pieces of wood after each cut? Will it reduce the number of cuts, for example, if you place the two pieces of wood on top of each other after the first cut has been made?

Think about these problems before reading on and note your attempts at solutions.

The components of a problem

What was involved in your attempts to solve the problems given in the preceding section? One vital stage was that you developed a representation of what was involved in the problem as you read it through. Then, a goal was set by the specific question that was asked. In trying to solve the problem you were able to draw upon a vast amount of past experience which brings knowledge of walking up mountains and cutting wood, as well as possible ways of solving similar problems. Finally, you were able to carry out mental operations to mentally manipulate the parts of the problem. You could imagine ways in which the wood might be cut and rearranged. These four elements are the basis of problem solving and the source of the problems themselves. Problems exist where the representation of the problem is inappropriate, where goals may lead to inappropriate general strategies for solving the problem, where past experience helps to obscure possible uses of the available resources and where inappropriate specific processing methods may be chosen, again because of one's past experience.

It is worth pointing out once again that the problems that we encounter represent failures in a generally adequate and powerful system. Normally the representations that we form, the goals that we seek, the past experience and the methods that we employ lead to a smooth and sophisticated control of our behaviour and domination of our environment. For example, when we read the two sentences 'Mary threw the ball to John. John tossed it back' we are able to comprehend what happened and through our past experience understand and draw inferences from what is given. So, for example, we automatically deduce that John must have either caught or picked up the ball to be able to throw it back to Mary. It is only when these sophisticated and normally unconscious processes are foiled in their resolution of the challenges with which they are faced that we become aware of problems to be solved.

Where Problems Occur in Problem Solving ▶ ▶ ▶

Inadequate representation

Many problems are the result of an inadequate representation of the problem being chosen or invented. This is true of the two examples given above. The monk problem will have seemed particularly difficult if your approach to its solution was to think in terms of trying to estimate where he might be because his movements vary in unpredictable and unspecified ways. If, on the other hand, we imagine two monks, one walking up the path and one walking down it, both having set off at the same time of day (see figure 10.2), then it immediately becomes obvious that there must be some point at which they are in the same place on the path at the same time of day, however their progress up and down the mountain varied from minute to minute. Anyone who moved to that representation would not find the problem difficult at all. Similarly, anyone who concentrated upon the middle block of the cube being cut up in the second problem will have little difficulty in realizing that since that cube has six sides it will need six cuts to make it, however the wood is reorganized.

Problems with goals

Since problems have a goal to which the problem solver is working, one common strategy of participants seems to be to attempt to match as nearly as possible the current state to the desired goal state. Such a strategy is known as a heuristic. Heuristics are rules which people choose to follow which may, in many circumstances, lead to a solution but they are not guaranteed to do so. In much of our everyday experience it may be that attempting all the time to match the current state with the desired end state may be a very suitable heuristic. Sometimes, however, it can lead us away from the desired goal. An example of this is given in the three jugs problem studied by Atwood and Polson (1976). The problem, which is illustrated in figure 10.3, is as follows:

> You have three jugs which we will call A, B and C. Jug A can hold exactly eight cups of water, B can hold exactly five cups and C can hold exactly three cups. A is filled to capacity with eight cups of water. B

Figure 10.2 A monk on a mountain (see text for explanation)

A   B   C

Figure 10.3 Water jug problems

and C are empty. We want you to find a way of dividing the contents of A equally between A and B so that both have four cups. You are allowed to pour water from jug to jug.

Atwood and Polson found that as their first move, twice as many participants preferred to pour water into jug B than into jug C. This is a reasonable start and the pouring of water into jug B is more similar to the desired goal than is the pouring of water into C. However, at two points in the two main paths to solution the participants have to pour water out of B, either back into A or into C and in both cases leave B empty. More than half of the mistakes that participants made were at this point where they were deviating from what seemed to be the normally reliable heuristic of seeking similarity between the present and the desired end state.

Inappropriate use of past knowledge

In normal situations one of the most powerful contributions to our ability to understand and control the world that we experience is our memory of the uses and normal properties of the things that we encounter. We remember that chairs are for sitting in, pens are for writing with, candles are for lighting and so on. We could, if necessary, sit down in a chair at a table, light a candle, pick up a pen and start writing with little thought and no problem experienced. However, on occasions, this tendency to classify and perceive objects in terms of their normal uses can lead us into difficulties, as was demonstrated in one of the most famous and early studies of problem solving by Maier (1931). In Maier's two string problem the participants were asked to tie together two strings that were hanging from the ceiling but which were too far apart for the participant to hold on to both at once. In the room there were various objects including a chair and a pair of pliers. The participants tried various solutions, usually involving the chair, but these do not solve the problem. The only solution is to tie the pliers to one string and set the string swinging so that, while holding onto the other string, one can catch the swinging pendulum and then tie the strings together. After ten minutes, less than two-thirds had been able to solve this problem. For the participants, the problem was that they did not perceive the pliers as a weight that could be used as part of a pendulum. A similar demonstration of this difficulty in perceiving the normally less useful properties of objects was devised by Duncker (1945) who termed the phenomenon functional fixedness. As part of what was supposed to be an experiment on vision, Duncker asked his participants to support a candle on a door. He supplied them with a candle, a box of matches, and some drawing pins in another box. The correct solution was to pin the drawing pin box to the door and use it as a platform for the candle. The participants found the task difficult because they did not see the box as a potential candle holder, but only as a drawing pin holder.

Some of the factors influencing the strength of functional fixedness have been explored in various subsequent experiments. In one of these, Birch and Rabinowitz (1951) showed that if an object had been used for its normal purpose in a preceding experiment then the participants were less likely to see it in its novel use. Birch and Rabinowitz repeated Maier's experiment with the two strings, but before testing participants on the problem they required some participants to complete an initial task which involved the completion of an electric circuit by either a switch or a relay. Ten participants used the relay, nine used the switch and six more participants had no prior experience with either relay or switch. When undertaking the two string problem all the participants eventually used either the relay or the switch as the pendulum bob. However, all of the ten participants who had used the relay initially now used the switch as the bob for the pendulum. Of the participants who had used the switch for the electrical circuit, seven used the relay and two the switch for the bob. Of the six participants tested with no electrical circuit prior experience, three used the relay and three used the switch as the pendulum bob. Clearly, therefore, the initial experience with either the switch or the relay made its use as a pendulum bob less likely in the subsequent experiment.

Reductions in functional fixedness have been shown where the normal properties of the objects are minimized and hints given of alternative uses. So, for example, Maier (1931) and Birch and Rabinowitz (1951) both showed that brushing against one of the cords and accidentally setting it in motion increased the likelihood that participants would solve the problem by thinking of a pendulum. Duncker (1945) found that his candle problem was more easily solved if the drawing pins were not in the box so that its use as a drawing pin container was less obvious. Cofer (1951) showed that when participants had learned words like 'rope', 'pendulum', and 'swing' in a memory experiment prior to the two string pendulum problem, they were more likely to solve the problem than control participants who had learned other words. Once the new solution to a problem has been found it becomes part of the individual's past experience and can be used to solve other related problems. So, for example, Maier (1945) had his participants solve the problem of how to hang a string from the ceiling to the floor without defacing the ceiling. They were given several wooden poles, clamps and string. Having found that the solution is to tie the string around a pole and to brace that pole against the ceiling using poles clamped together, Maier's participants were able to make a hat rack using poles clamped together and pressed against the ceiling, and in which the clamp was used as a hook for the hat.

Problems in selecting the right operators

In solving any problem the correct operations have to be performed upon the given state of the world. Operations that have proved appropriate in the past may no longer be the best or even adequate. Nevertheless, there is a tendency to continue with what has been a successful set of operators. The most famous demonstration of this tendency to continue with the same form of actions, what has been described as mechanization of thought, are the experiments by Luchins (1942). The problems for the participants were similar to those used later by Atwood and Polson which we discussed earlier. The participants are asked to imagine that they have three jugs each with a specified capacity, and that they must, using these jugs, measure a given quantity. They are allowed an unlimited supply of water. The set of

Table 10.1   Luchins' water jug problems

Problem	Capacity of jug A	Capacity of jug B	Capacity of jug C	Desired quantity
1	21	127	3	100
2	14	163	25	99
3	18	43	10	5
4	9	42	6	21
5	20	59	4	31
6	23	49	3	20
7	15	39	3	18
8	28	76	3	25
9	18	48	4	22
10	14	36	8	6

capacities and desired quantities for ten problems used by Luchins (1942) is shown in table 10.1. The first five problems can be solved by filling jug B, pouring water from B into C until C has been filled twice, and then pouring water into A. This solution could be used for all but problem 8. However, problems 7 and 9 are much more simply solved by adding C to A. Problem 8 cannot be solved by pouring water from A into C. Luchins found that 83 per cent of his participants continued to use the more complicated solution on problems 6 and 7. In addition, 64 per cent of them failed to solve problem 8. In comparison, participants who began with problem 6 did not see the biasing from the first five problems and only 1 per cent of them adopted the B minus 2C minus A solution and only 5 per cent failed to solve problem 8. Thus, the first five problems had created a very powerful bias in the way in which the participants tackled the problems. This tendency to tackle the problems in a particular way caused considerable difficulty when problems 6 to 10 were encountered.

General Problem-solving Methods

So far we have discussed the general problems in problem solving. Are there appropriate general methods for tackling a problem when it occurs? For some situations it may be possible to discover an algorithm that will guarantee the eventual solution of the problem. Algorithms are procedures which if correctly carried out will always lead to the correct answer. So, for example, most people know the procedure for arithmetic division and, if they carry it out, will reach the right answer in a division sum. Usually, however, the problems that we encounter do not have algorithms that we can easily identify for the solution. We then have to choose heuristics, rules of thumb, that we hope will lead to a solution. One sophisticated heuristic is 'means–ends analysis'. This has been used by Newell and Simon (1972) in a computer simulation program called the General Problem Solver (GPS). Newell and Simon give the following example of means–ends analysis in ordinary life:

I want to take my son to nursery school. What's the difference between what I have and what I want? One of distance. What changes distance? An automobile. My automobile won't work. What is needed to make it work? A new battery. What has new batteries? An auto repair shop. I want the repair shop to put in a new battery; but the shop doesn't know I need one. What is the difficulty? One of communication. What allows communication? A telephone . . . and so on. (p. 416, 1972)

The general feature of the means–ends analysis that their GPS carries out is the breaking down of the main goal into subgoals. GPS identifies differences between the current state and the goal or subgoals and chooses to try to eliminate what it identifies as the most important difference. If this difference cannot be eliminated it is analysed to identify what subgoals must be achieved before this difference can be eliminated, and, eventually, possible solutions will be found. The General Problem Solver proved to be a flexible and powerful means of problem solving. Further introductions to it will be found in Anderson (1985).

Recent Developments in Problem-solving Research ▶ ▶ ▶

Powerful though it is, GPS has mainly been applied to puzzle-like problems, and, as Eysenck and Keane (1990) point out, whether it can be extended to less well-defined, real-life problems is debatable. Complex, real-life problems tend to involve more background knowledge than puzzles. Unlike puzzles, the knowledge needed for their solution is not given in the description of the problems themselves. The goal state, or what counts as a solution to the problem, tends not be known in advance; solutions to real problems are often only recognized when they are reached. Real-world problems, in short, are usually ill-defined and knowledge intensive, unlike the clearer cut, knowledge-lean puzzles. Problems in real life also typically have a strong emotional element, about which cognitive psychological work on problem solving has little to say. In addition, some people are clearly expert at solving certain types of problems. Recognizing all this, psychologists now consider broader aspects of problem solving than those covered by GPS. Two strands in contemporary research are particularly important. The first concerns the differences between expert and novice problem solvers. The second examines the flexible use which can be made of knowledge from other domains when generating solutions.

Problem solving by experts and novices differs in a number of important ways, indicating the importance of the level of skill in problem solving. Many of these are obvious differences such as the speed and ease with which experts solve problems, the few errors they make when doing so, and the complexity of the problems they can tackle. These aspects of 'expert-ease' arise not necessarily because experts are cleverer or faster thinkers than novices, but rather because they know more about the domain in question, and are able to marshall their well-organized knowledge to assess the problem quickly and effectively. Expert chess players, for instance, can rapidly break down or 'chunk' the patterns made by pieces on a chess board into a few well-organized patterns, and are highly skilled at remembering configurations of pieces during a game (De Groot, 1965; Chase and Simon, 1973). Despite this, they are not significantly better at visual memory tasks than non-experts, performing the same when shown and asked to reproduce a random arrangement of pieces on the chess board. Similarly, football fans are better than non-football fans at remembering plausible lists of results, but no better when dealing with randomly generated ones (Morris et al., 1985). The importance of possessing problem-relevant schemata or knowledge structures is well illustrated by this work. Such knowledge not only allows thinkers to generate appropriate solutions, but greatly aids them in structuring the problem in the first place (see also chapter 7). A second issue concerns the open-ended nature of many problems which, as a result, require novel or creative solutions. Thus, if the problem is to write a PhD thesis, or to design a new mode of transport, there are many possible solutions, some more effective and original than others. Creative thinking has often been treated under a separate heading from problem solving, and has sometimes, wrongly we believe, been elevated to the status of something magical or mystical. The ability of a Newton or a Mozart to create new mathematical ideas or new music, seemingly out of thin air, is of course, impressive and awe inspiring, but new ideas, even those which are startlingly fresh and innovative, still rely heavily on old knowledge. Newton acknowledged this when he spoke of standing on the shoulders of giants who had gone before him, and Mozart was a skilled musical performer as well as a composer, and hence had a rich repertoire of musical phrases and expressions at his disposal.

At the heart of creative thinking, then, lies the ability to produce fresh and appropriate ideas, and to create new mental structures from old. For some time, little was known about this associative or linking process save that creative thinking seemed capable of producing many and often quite remote associations. Recently, new light has been shed on innovation in thinking, problem solving and creativity by studies of analogical thinking (Keane, 1988). Many key insights in science and everyday life often involve likening one thing to another and using the analogy to reveal hitherto unnoticed aspects of the problem domain. Analogical thinking is now known to be important in domains as diverse as computer programming and solving problems in electrical circuit design (see box 10.1 for an example experiment on analogical solutions of a problem).

Once again, links between problem solving and memory are apparent here. Information about the problem and the knowledge from which the analogy is generated (the so-called base domain) must be organized in such a fashion that the two can be brought together and compared. One means of doing this is through the process of reminding. Schank (1982) has argued that reminding and the use of analogy are key processes in memory, and, at the highest level of abstraction, structures which he calls Thematic Organization Packages (TOPs) are used to link otherwise quite disparate ideas (see chapter 7 for more details of Schank's work). Keane (1988) has shown that predictions can be made from Schank's theory of the frequency with which participants will use an analogical solution, but has made the important point that the use of analogies is not automatic, as Schank suggests, but rather depends on participants intentionally searching for an analogical solution.

Creative and analogical thinking skills, then, seem to rely on the ability to recognize and exploit common structures (common patterns) in situations which may differ markedly in content. Barnes and Hampson (1993a) have argued that the ability to extract and use such 'domain-invariant information' may be an even more fundamental human skill which underpins several aspects of inference and problem solving. They have shown how predictions from recent approaches to learning theory can be used to explain our general ability to do this. For example, the child who learns that although different families have different family members, nevertheless all families share a similar pattern of interrelationships is, in one sense, using an analogy, albeit a very close one. Learning theory suggests that people need to 'learn how to learn' before they can accomplish these skills. They appear to do this by learning all possible relationships in a limited set of domains before acquiring the ability to transfer or generalize the domain-invariant knowledge to new domains.

If this view is correct, problem solving, especially of a more creative nature, relies heavily not only on specific knowledge about the domain in question, but also on some powerful general purpose pattern recognition abilities and skills.

Logic and Mental Logic

It has long been common to describe *Homo sapiens* as rational creatures and to identify their ability to reason as one of the features that sets them apart from other animals. How then does this reasoning take place? Some, if not most psychologists, according to Johnson-Laird (1983), have postulated a mental logic that operates with rules similar to the formal logic studies by logicians. Some psychologists such as Piaget have asserted this view strongly, but, neverthless, such a view has considerable problems. The major difficulty is that people are not good at reasoning using even the simplest syllogisms such as those studied by Aristotle. For example, many people will accept as valid the following invalid logical syllogism:

Some A's are B's
Some B's are C's
Therefore some A's are C's

There are some invalid syllogisms which people will reject as invalid and others that they will, commonly, accept. For example, people commonly accept the following invalid syllogism.

No A's are B's
No B's are C's
Therefore no A's are C's

To explain this pattern of errors, Woodworth and Sells (1935) proposed what they called the atmosphere hypothesis. They suggested that logical terms such as 'some', 'all', 'not', created an 'atmosphere' that predisposed participants to accept conclusions which included the same terms. So, for example, participants, according to the atmosphere hypothesis, will tend to accept positive conclusions if they are given to positive premises and negative conclusions if they are presented as following from negative premises.

The atmosphere hypothesis does not account for all errors in participants' judgements about syllogisms. (A fuller introduction to the performance of participants with such syllogisms will be found in Anderson, 1985.) Nevertheless, the atmosphere hypothesis does describe many of the errors that do occur and these errors raise a major problem for the theory of mental logic. Some defenders of mental logic such as Mary Henle assert that the mistakes arise because the participants have misunderstood or have forgotten the premises or because they bring to the problem additional and unjustified assumptions that influence their reasoning. Henle declares that she never found errors which could unambiguously be attributed to 'faulty reasoning'.

Johnson-Laird (1983) has attacked this philosophy of mental logic. He points out that logicians have shown that there are an infinite number of distance logics, so that any claim that human beings use mental logic must be qualified by specifying which of them is actually used. It is not possible, in this volume, to do justice to most of Johnson-Laird's arguments against mental logic but we will consider in detail a famous experimental paradigm which supports his view.

Hypothesis testing: the Wason selection task

Wason (1966) devised a simple experimental procedure for investigating participants' ability to judge the circumstances under which a statement is true. In its basic form, the participants are presented with four cards. They know that each card has a letter on one side and a number on the other side. The cards shown might be those illustrated in figure 10.4. The participants are given a rule to test. For example, for the cards shown in figure 10.4 the rule that they might be given could be 'if there is an A on one side of the card, then there is a 4 on the other'. The participants are asked which the minimum set of cards that must be turned over in order to find out whether the rule is true or false. This Wason selection task has been investigated in several experiments. In a review, Johnson-Laird (1977) summarized the results of four experiments. A total of 128 adult participants had been tested. Of them, 59 wanted to turn over the cards with the

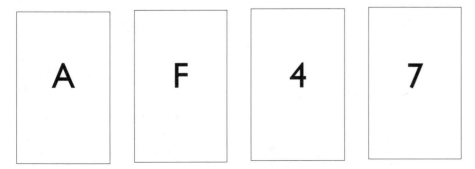

Figure 10.4 The selection task. Which card or cards would need to be chosen to test the rule 'If there is an A on one side of the card, then there is a 4 on the other'?

A and the 4 on them and 42 wished to turn over just the card with the A
showing. Only five participants chose the correct response of turning the
card with the A and the 7. It is clear from these results that most
participants recognize that the card with the A upon it must be turned over.
The problems arise for the cards with the numbers. Many participants
wished to turn over the card with the 4, as if wishing to confirm that an A
is on the reverse side. However, even if that is the case, turning over this
card will not confirm or deny the truth of the rule. If there is an A on the
reverse side then it is merely an instance of the rule while if there is another
letter then the card is irrelevant. On the other hand, turning over the card
with a 7 displayed is essential in testing the rule. If there is an A on the
other side then the rule is invalid. The poor performance of participants on
the Wason task suggests that they do not naturally use a reliable mental
logic in their attempts at a solution.

One interesting subsequent line of research has been to investigate the
performance of participants when the rule is stated in a more realistic form,
especially in a form that the individual will have encountered. In one such
experiment by Griggs and Cox (1982) the abstract letters and numbers of
the original Wason task were replaced by the names of drinks and numbers
representing ages. So, for example, the participants would be given the
cards shown in figure 10.5. The participants were told that they were testing
the rule 'if someone is drinking beer then that person must be over 21'. The
cards represented people of a certain age and the drinks that they were
drinking in the bar. With this rule to test, Griggs and Cox found that the
majority of participants who had been unable to correctly answer the
abstract, traditional, Wason task question were now able to correctly select
the cards labelled 'beer' and '16' and did not wish to turn over the other
cards (see box 10.2).

It is important to notice that in the Griggs and Cox experiment it is the
fact that the participants have encountered a similar law in real life which
makes the difference between their realistic and their abstract (Wason) task.
Participants who are tested on rules involving real objects but ones that
have been arbitrarily created, e.g. 'if I eat haddock, then I drink gin',
perform no better than participants on the original Wason task (Mantelow
and Evans, 1979). It is not necessary for the participants to have direct
personal experience of the use of the rule. For example, Rumelhart and

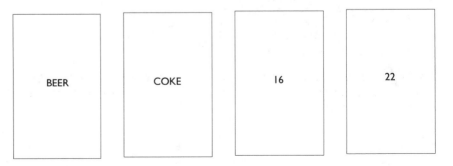

Figure 10.5 A more concrete version of the selection task (see text for
discussion)

Norman (1981) found good performance with the use of the rule 'if a purchase exceeds $30, then the receipt must have the signature of the manager on the back' where participants had to imagine that they managed a store. However, where the participants were given an arbitrary principle they showed no better performance than normally with the Wason task. As Johnson-Laird (1983) comments, 'what is crucial, . . . is that insight into the task reflects an effect of content on the process of deduction. If participants already possess a mental model of the relation expressed in the general rule, or a model that can be readily related to the rule, they are much more likely to have an insight into the task' (p. 33).

If participants made use of a mental logic then the same logic should be used for the abstract and the realistic tasks and no difference in performance should occur. Clearly this is not the case.

Rather than using mental logic, Johnson-Laird suggests that people reason with what he calls mental models. Mental models are rather like cognitive building blocks, and can be combined and recombined as required. Like any models they stand in place of the thing or situation itself, and one of their most important features is that their structure captures the essence of (analogically resembles) the situation they represent. The essential feature of reasoning with models, Johnson-Laird claims, lies not only in the construction of appropriate models to capture various states of affairs, but also in the ability of skilled reasoners to test any conclusions which they reach. Logic, in that it makes any appearance at all, applies when conclusions are tested rather than when they are formed, since testing a model implies that the reasoner appreciates the logical importance of falsifying a conclusion, and does not merely seek positive evidence in its support. Rules for combining models do exist, but these are more like plans for combining physical structures than abstract rules. Another implication of the models theory is that reasoning is better construed as a practical skill than as an esoteric, abstract pursuit. Also, what separates skilled from unskilled reasoners are differences in the working memory space available to construct and manipulate complex models, and persistence in testing previously drawn conclusions (though as we saw earlier, success on everyday reasoning tasks can also depend on a participant's general knowledge and experience).

An example might help make these abstract points clearer. Suppose you are given the following propositions:

The fox is on the left of the dog
The cow is in front of the dog
The hen is in front of the fox

After comprehending these propositions, without any knowledge of formal logic, you can construct a model which captures the spatial arrangement of the terms as follows:

fox   dog
hen   cow

By inspecting the model you can then draw the simple and unambiguous conclusion that: 'The hen is on the left of the cow.'

Clearly, the more involved the original propositions, the harder it will be for you to construct and maintain a well-integrated model. In other cases, the combined statements may admit of more than one interpretation. So, suppose you are told that:

The fox is on the left of the dog
The cow is on the left of the dog

You might quickly form a model like this:

fox   cow   dog

and conclude that: 'The cow is on the right of the fox.'

However, if you are more skilled at reasoning, you will attempt to disprove this conclusion, by looking for another arrangement that still does justice to the original statements, but which falsifies your first conclusion. Such an arrangement might look like:

cow   fox   dog

in which the cow is now on the left of the fox. The existence of two possible models means that in this case there is no single unambiguous conclusion to be drawn about the relation between cow and fox from the original statements.

The power of the mental models theory is that it not only applies to indisputably spatial structures like the one above, but it also accounts for reasoning with more abstract syllogisms which include logical terms such as 'all', 'none' and 'some' (Johnson-Laird, 1983). It has recently been extended to include more complex logical operators such as 'only' (Johnson-Laird and Byrne, 1991). A further attractive feature is that it shows how models and propositions can be used together, and it is sufficiently precise to be successfully implemented as a computer program.

Decision Making and Statistical Reasoning

Should I spend my savings on a new camera or a new jacket? Should I ask Alice Brown out to dinner? Is it safe to overtake this slow lorry in front of me? All the time we are taking decisions and those decisions depend upon our weightings of what we perceive to be the costs and benefits of the alternatives that we can imagine occurring. Fundamental to many of these decisions is our estimate of how likely the various alternatives are to occur. Most of our decisions are concerned with possibilities and probabilities rather than certainties. There is a possibility that Alice Brown will be delighted by my invitation, and also a possibility that she will sneeringly reject me and enjoy telling her friends of my cheeky assumption. There is a possibility that I will overtake the lorry safely and another possibility that I will crash into some obstacle that I have yet to see. All our decisions must be based on our estimates of the size of these risks and the benefits of our success. A major research area for psychologists interested in decision making has been the reliability with which individuals can estimate the probability that different events will occur. Clearly, since most of us manage to stay alive and avoid too many embarrassing experiences while not living the lives of hermits we must, in many cases, be reasonably good at estimating probabilities and taking decisions. Nevertheless, the fact that we get by in our ordinary lives does not mean that our decision making is perfect. Many of the studies of human decision making have suggested that there are several major flaws in the ways that we estimate probabilities and put together the estimate that we have made.

Examples of errors in thinking about probability

Suppose that you have been tossing a coin that you know to be unbiased and have had it land as heads on the last five occasions. What is more likely on your next throw? Is it more likely that the next throw will turn up tails, heads or is there no difference in the likelihood of heads and tails? Following a run of heads most people expect that the probability of tails turning up has been increased. In casinos, a run of red numbers at the roulette table will lead to a rush of money to the black numbers as the gamblers expect the betting to even out. In fact, of course, assuming that your coin and the roulette wheel are unbiased, then the probability at the next throw or spin of the wheel remains the same (i.e. 0.5 for the coin) whatever has gone before. Many people, however, fall into the gambler's fallacy of expecting a run of tails to even out a run of heads or a run of black numbers to counterbalance a run of red numbers because they know that, over an infinite amount of time, equal numbers of heads and tails or blacks and reds are to be expected.

The gambler's fallacy has a powerful effect upon most of us. Consider the following runs of heads and tails thrown with a tossed coin. A: h h h h h h. B: h h h t t t. C: h t t h t h. Assuming h to represent a throw of a head and t to represent the throw of a tail, which of these runs, if any, would you think was more likely when an unbiased coin was thrown six times? The answer is that they are all equally common. On each throw there is a 0.5 probability of getting a head and a 0.5 probability of getting a tail. The probability of getting each of these runs is therefore $0.5 \times 0.5 \times 0.5 \times 0.5 \times 0.5 \times 0.5 = 0.016$. Most of us, however, feel that there is something odd about a run of six heads and even something unusual about three heads being followed by three tails. We expect small samples of events to be representative of their theoretical abstract probabilities. The gambler's fallacy and the belief in the law of averages are examples of erroneous probability estimation.

Another error, which Tversky and Kahneman (1974) call the 'representativeness heuristic', is a little bit like the gambler's fallacy in reverse. They argue that people expect representatives of some class of events or things to be similar to the norm for that class. So, for example, a lawyer, a teacher or a policeman would be expected to match the stereotypes of those professions. In reality, there is considerable diversity amongst individual people even if it is possible to make generalizations about the characteristics of large groups.

The representativeness heuristic can lead people to make quite silly errors, that is, errors which are silly once they have been thought through! Consider this example reported from among several described by Tversky and Kahneman (1982). In December 1980 they asked groups of participants to rate the likelihood of certain events happening in 1981. In one of these they asked the following:

Suppose Bjorn Borg reaches the Wimbledon finals in 1981. Please rank order the following outcomes from most to least likely.

Borg will win the match.
Borg will lose the first set.
Borg will win the first set but lose the match.
Borg will lose the first set but win the match.

The point of interest here is that participants rated Borg as being more likely to lose the first set but win the match, than he was to simply lose the first set. However, if we think about the questions carefully, it should be obvious that for Borg to win the match as well as losing the first set adds the extra condition of having to win the match on top of the one of losing the first set. The combined probability of losing the first set and winning the match, that is, the probability of the two events being true, is less likely than the probability of one of those events being true, namely the losing of the first set. Tversky and Kahneman give many other examples of the same phenomenon. The reason why people fall into the mistake appears to be that they regard the combined statement of Borg losing the first set but winning the match as more representative of what they would expect to happen than they regard Borg losing the first set. The representativeness of the events described is increased by the specificity of the description, although their probability of being true is thereby reduced.

The availability heuristic

Judging probability is difficult, and we should not be surprised that people make mistakes. To make an accurate estimate of the probability with which an event will happen, the participants in experiments would need to have noted each instance of the particular event, and also all the occasions when it did not occur when it could have happened. To do so for all the possible events about which we might need to make a probability judgement in the future would be to place a ridiculous load upon our memories and our cognitive capacities to record what was happening around us. Instead, when a probability judgement has to be made, we will fall back upon ways of estimating the frequency with which events occur. One way to do so is to search our memories for an example. Kahneman and Tversky (1974) suggest that we often estimate the probability of an event occurring by depending upon the availability of examples of the event in our memories. If we can recall many examples easily and quickly then we assume that the event must happen frequently. If, on the other hand, we find it hard to think of many instances then we assume that the event is unlikely. Hence, the availability of the items determines our probability judgements. As such, this may be a reasonable heuristic but, as will all heuristics, it can let us down. Kahneman and Tversky offer several examples where probability judgements have been distorted because of differences in the ease of recalling some things from memory. One of their examples was to ask participants to judge which was more common, words in English beginning with the letter k or words in which the letter k is the third letter of the word. Because of the way information is encoded and retrieved from our memories, it is far easier to think of words beginning with k than to recall words where k is the third letter. Consequently, people judge there to be more words beginning with the letter k than words where k is the third letter. As it happens, there are three times as many words in English with k as the third letter than as the first letter.

The effect of the availability heuristic need not depend upon the use of memory but can also reflect the ability of the individual to imagine instances. One of Kahneman and Tversky's (1974) illustrations of this was to ask participants to estimate how many committees of two and of eight members could be formed by selecting people from a group of ten individuals. It is far easier to imagine groups of two people selected from ten than it is to imagine groups of eight people selected from ten. Nevertheless, the number of each size of committee that can be formed is the same (i.e. 45), since each time a two-person committee is selected a potential eight-person committee remains. The median estimate of the number of committees formed of two members was 70 while the estimate of committees of eight members was 20, clearly supporting Kahneman and Tversky's hypothesis that people would be strongly influenced by the ease of imagining the committees.

It may seem that these imaginary instances of estimating the number of words with particular letters or numbers of committees is far removed from everyday life. However, subsequent studies have shown that people are influenced by availability heuristics in ways that will have far more impact upon their daily lives. People's estimates of the dangers of activities or of possible causes of death may markedly alter the way they carry out their lives. People will avoid travelling in aeroplanes because they suspect there is a high risk of an air crash, while others will be strongly influenced by a recent train or coach crash to consider using an alternative form of transport. Lichtenstein et al. (1978) obtained estimates of the frequency of deaths per year for 41 causes of death. The results are shown in figure 10.6.

In figure 10.6 the diagonal, straight line represents what would be accurate estimation of the frequencies. It can be seen that the relatively rare causes of death are overestimated while the far more common causes of death are underestimated, the former falling above the line and the latter below the line. For many of these examples the frequency of death is being estimated at several hundreds per year when the actual numbers are less than ten per year, while, for the more common causes of death, the estimates are undervalued by a factor of ten.

Why are rare events overestimated and common causes of death underestimated? One likely cause is the frequency with which individuals encounter accounts of such deaths. Newspapers concentrate upon reporting deaths from unusual causes while common causes of dying rarely occur except as explanations for the deaths of famous people. Combs and Slovic (1978) found a close relationship between the number of deaths reported in newspapers and their estimated probability of occurrence. It is likely, therefore, that the estimation of probability of death is being exaggerated through the availability heuristic as people recall instances of such deaths that they have read about in the newspapers or heard on television or radio.

An important aspect of the availability heuristic may be summed up by the adage 'out of sight, out of mind'. An illustration of this was given by Fischhoff et al. (1978). The experiment involved participants estimating the probability of a car not starting. For some participants, six major deficiencies that can cause a car engine to fail to start were provided and the final option of 'all other problems' was added. For other participants only three examples of major deficiencies were provided. The result of giving only half as many major problems was that these participants estimated the probability of the cause being one of those instances as far higher than when the same causes were evaluated as one of six possibilities. For the participants to have been consistent between the two experimental conditions, the 'other' category should have been given a far higher proportion of instances where only three common deficiencies had been suggested. Where six possible deficiencies had been proposed, the 'other' category was assigned 0.08 as its overall proportion. With three suggested deficiencies this rose to 0.14. However, for consistency, it should have increased to 0.47. The results seem to reflect the fact that the participants given only three examples failed to think of alternative examples and to weight them accordingly.

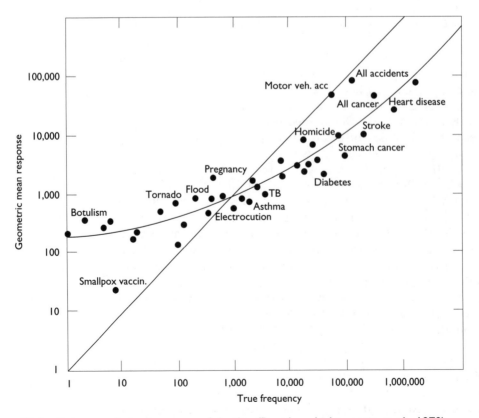

Figure 10.6   Estimates of the frequency of deaths. (Based on Lichtenstein et al., 1978)

Combining information

The examples given so far have been of errors in estimating probabilities when only one judgement must be made. In real life it is often the case that new information arrives that must be used to modify the existing estimates of probabilities. It is possible, using Bayes's theorem, to calculate how the probability estimate should change when new information arrives. Such calculations are beyond the scope of this book, but are introduced in Smyth et al. (1994). It is a common finding that the new information overwhelms the prior knowledge that the individual possesses and so the new probabilities bias the overall judgement. One example of this is given by Kahneman and Tversky (1973), who told their participants that one individual had been chosen at random from a set of one hundred people that consisted of 70 engineers and 30 lawyers. This could be called the engineer-high group. A second set of participants, the engineer-low group, were informed that the individual came from a set of 30 engineers and 70 lawyers. Both groups were able to estimate the probability of the individual being a lawyer or an engineer, that is, the probability of being an engineer was estimated at being 0.7 by the engineer-high group and 0.3 by the engineer-low group. Next, the participants were told that another person had been chosen from the same group and they were given the following description of them:

> Jack is a 45 year old man. He is married and has four children. He is generally conservative, careful and ambitious. He shows no interest in political and social issues and spends most of his free time on his many hobbies, which include home carpentry, sailing and mathematical puzzles.

Participants in both groups estimated the probability of Jack being an engineer as 0.9. There was no difference between the two groups, even though the engineer-high group should have estimated the probability more highly than the engineer-low group. Participants were also given the following description:

> Dick is a 30 year old man. He is married with no children. A man of high ability and high motivation, he promises to be quite successful in his field. He is well liked by his colleagues.

With this description the participants were presented with no information about Dick's profession. In such a situation they should have estimated the probability of Dick being an engineer to be the same as the proportion of engineers in their group. In fact both groups estimated the probability of Dick being an engineer as 0.5, again allowing the uninformative information to change their probability estimates, and ignoring what they already knew about the groups.

Conclusions

In this chapter we have argued that problem solving needs to take place only when our very sophisticated cognitive processes fail to cope with some unusual circumstance. When this happens the problem may result from the initial representation of the problem, from the wrong choice of goals or subgoals, from inadequate or inappropriately perceived past experience or from inappropriately selected operators. The use of heuristics in problem solving were discussed, including the means–ends analysis used in the General Problem Solver. We pointed out, however, that more recent research in problem solving has concentrated on more open-ended problems. The importance of analogical thinking is now seen to be as important as, if not more important than, the mechanistic search algorithms of GPS. The idea that people use a mental logic as the basis of their deductions was then criticized, with particular reference to the Wason selection task which illustrates that people can have problems in making logical deductions with abstract problems but be able to solve problems with the same logical form if they have had experience of analogous situations in real life.

The discussion of decision making concentrated upon the reasons why estimates of probability may often be distorted. In particular, the representativeness and availability heuristics were shown to have their problems. These distortions in probability estimates could make considerable difference to the way in which people plan their lives. Finally, the way in which people may sometimes ignore knowledge that they already possess when new information on probabilities is presented was illustrated.

Further reading

A classic text on general problem-solving methods is A. Newell, J.C. Shaw and H. Simon 1972: *Human Problem Solving*. Englewood Cliffs, NJ: Prentice-Hall. Analogical thinking is well covered in M.T. Keane 1988: *Analogical Thinking*. New York: Wiley. Useful coverage of problem solving, thinking and related issues can be found in K.J. Gilhooly 1988: *Thinking: Directed, Undirected and Creative*. London: Academic Press. Aspects of creativity are covered in an interesting way in M. Boden 1990: *The Creative Mind*. London: Weidenfeld and Nicolson.

P.C. Wason and P.N. Johnson-Laird 1972: *The Psychology of Reasoning: Structure and Content*. Cambridge, Mass: Harvard University Press is a dated but important milestone in the psychology of reasoning. More recent texts are: P.N. Johnson-Laird 1983: *Mental Models*. Cambridge: Cambridge University Press, and P.N. Johnson-Laird and R.M.J. Byrne 1991: *Deduction*. Hove: Lawrence Erlbaum Associates, both of which apply the mental models theory to various aspects of cognition. The notion that human reasoning relies on quite basic matching biases is explored in J. St. B. Evans 1989: *Bias in Human Reasoning*. Hove: Lawrence Erlbaum Associates, and J. Baron 1988: *Thinking and Deciding*. Cambridge: Cambridge University Press, reviews decision making.

Discussion points

1   Discuss the general difficulties which may impede problem solving.
2   To what extent is problem solving a skill? To what extent does it rely on knowledge? To what extent might it rely on pattern recognition?

3   Are problem solving and creativity really different?
4   Do humans reason logically? If not, how do they reason?
5   What are the major biases affecting decision making?

Practical exercises

1   Present the travelling monk problem (see beginning of chapter) to ten people. How many of them successfully solve the problem within two minutes? Now present the same problem to another ten people. This time ask them to visualize the monk walking up and down the mountain, consulting his watch every few minutes as he goes. How many people successfully solve the problem this time? What does this tell us about the nature of problem solving?

2   Test participants on abstract and realistic versions of Wason's selection task (see text and box 10.2 for examples). How effective are instructions in this task? For example, investigate the importance of instructions which bias participants toward rule breaking or falsification. (Griggs and Cox (1982) did this by telling their participants to imagine that they were law enforcement officers.)

3   Explore the nature of biases in an everyday decision-making task such as buying a car, by constructing descriptions of vehicles for sale and manipulating various dimensions of the information you supply. For instance, you could set up a version of the engineer–lawyer task of Kahneman and Tversky (1973) (see text). First, give your participants some statistical information about, say, the likelihood of mechanical failure of second-hand cars within various time frames. Then present descriptions of cars with various aspects manipulated, such as statements about mileage, year of manufacture, number of owners etc., and see how these factors bias participants' estimates of mechanical reliability.

Box 10.1
Analogical problem solving

Gick and Holyoak were among the first to demonstrate empirically that analogies are frequently used to solve problems. Their basic procedure was to provide participants with a story analogy describing a problem and its solution, then to observe how participants used the analogy in solving Duncker's so-called radiation problem. The latter was presented as follows: 'Suppose you are a doctor faced with a patient who has a malignant tumour. It is impossible to operate on the patient, but unless the tumour is destroyed the patient will die. There is a kind of ray that can be used to destroy the tumour. If the rays reach the tumour all at once at sufficiently high intensity, the tumour will be destroyed. Unfortunately, at this intensity the healthy tissues that the rays pass through on the way to the tumour will also be destroyed. At lower intensities the rays are harmless to healthy tissue, but they will not affect the tumour either. What type of procedure might be used to destroy the tumour with rays, and at the same time avoid destroying the healthy tissue?' The solution to the problem is to arrange for weak rays, insufficiently strong to damage healthy tissue, to converge simultaneously from different directions onto the site of the tumour, so that the combined strength of all the weak rays is then sufficiently powerful to destroy the tumour.

Gick and Holyoak report several experiments in their paper in which participants are given stories of problem situations and their solutions which analogically correspond to a greater or lesser degree with the radiation problem. In Experiment 2, which we consider here, roughly equal numbers of participants were given an 'Attack-dispersion' or a 'Parade-dispersion' story to read and summarize in writing prior to receiving the radiation problem. A third, control group of participants was given no prior story at all. The Attack-dispersion story described the activities of a general who wished to attack a fortress in the centre of a small country. Many roads radiated outwards from the fortress likes spokes on a wheel, but all were mined. Small groups of men could pass safely over any of the roads, but larger forces would detonate the mines. Unfortunately, the entire army was needed to capture the fortress. The general's solution was to divide up the army into small groups and have each converge simultaneously on the fortress so as to arrive at the same time. The Parade-dispersion story described a dictator who ruled a small country from a fortress situated in the middle. Many roads radiated out from the fortress like spokes of a wheel. To celebrate his anniversary the dictator wanted a parade more impressive than any seen before. He wanted his army to be seen and heard at the same time in every part of the country. To achieve this, his general divided up the army and sent each group to the head of a different road. When all was ready, he gave a signal and each group marched down a different road. Thus, the general was able to have his parade seen and heard throughout the entire country at once, and so please the dictator.

The resemblance between the Attack-dispersion and the radiation problem are obvious at an intuitive level. Similarities between corresponding aspects of both problems are immediately apparent, such as the tumour to be destroyed and the fortress to be captured, the inaccessibility of tumour and fortress, the impossibility of a 'full strength' assault on either tumour or fortress, the ineffectiveness of a low strength assault and so on. At a more formal level, Gick and Holyoak demonstrated that the correspondence between the number and nature of the propositions (or idea units) in both stories was very close indeed. So, they predicted that participants should find it easy to draw an analogical correspondence between the two stories and use this to generate a solution to the radiation problem. But how close does such an analogical correspondence have to be in order to be useful? The match between the Attack-dispersion and the radiation problem, although not perfect, is very close indeed. Would a story with a weaker correspondence, such as the Parade-dispersion story,

prove less easy to use? More differences are apparent between the radiation problem and the Parade-dispersion story than between the radiation problem and the Attack-dispersion story. For instance, the two problems differ markedly at a fundamental level: to destroy a tumour versus to arrange a parade. In addition, the constraints on the strengths of forces and rays permissible in the Attack and radiation problems are absent in the Parade story. There are also important differences in goals between the stories. Going down the roads is an end in itself in the parade story, whereas it is a means to an end in the Attack story, as is the use of rays in the radiation problem. Not surprisingly, then, Gick and Holyoak found a somewhat lower propositional correspondence between the Parade and radiation stories.

Having read and summarized their stories (or not in the case of the control group), participants then attempted to solve the radiation problem and were allowed to refer back to the analogical stories whenever they wished. They were requested to write down each idea that came to mind while solving the problem, even those ideas which they later rejected. Finally those participants who were given a prior story were given a questionnaire which asked them to rate the helpfulness of the story when solving the radiation problem.

Results

The data from one participant had to be discarded on the grounds that he had solved the problem once before. The major results obtained from the remaining participants are displayed in box table 10.1.1.

There are several things to note about these results. Considering first the total (combined complete and partial) solutions, there was a statistically significant difference ($p < 0.001$) between the experimental and control groups, with 76 per cent and 49 per cent of the former achieving solutions compared with only 8 per cent of the latter, and while the Attack story produced more solutions in total than the Parade ($p < 0.01$), both story groups produced

Box table 10.1.1 Percentages of participants achieving complete and partial solutions to the radiation problem following analogical stories compared with no story (control) group. Numbers of participants in parentheses

Story	Complete solutions	Partial solutions	Total solutions
Attack (47)	57	19	76
Parade (45)	31	18	49
Control (50)	8	0	8

more than the control (p < 0.001) suggesting that even the weaker analogical resemblance between the Parade and radiation problems was sufficient to assist the solution process. Indeed, no differences were apparent in partial solutions between the two analogical stories (19 per cent and 18 per cent), but the greater power of the Attack story was demonstrated by the greater number of complete solutions achieved (57 per cent versus 31 per cent, p < 0.01).

No reliable differences between the groups of participants were revealed by the questionnaire, but whenever participants in a story group discovered a solution they tended to rate the story as most helpful.

It appears, then, that participants can often generate an analogical solution to a problem even when a complete mapping between the prior and the target stories is impossible, but that the closer the mapping the more likely a solution will be found.

However, the nature of the correspondences which participants use to exploit analogies is not clear from this data. Gick and Holyoak used a propositional format to capture the (logical) similarity between the stories, but this need not imply that participants themselves compute analogies in such an abstract way. Acknowledging this limitation of their study, Gick and Holyoak state that: 'numerous subjects ... commented on the importance of

the reference to roads radiating outward like "spokes on a wheel". Intuitively, this phrase seems to elicit a spatial image that represents those essential aspects of the dispersion solution that can be applied to both military and medical problems. Even though these stories were always presented verbally in our experiments, the problems essentially describe spatial relationships. Our use of a propositional representation to describe the correspondences between the stories does not preclude the possibility that some form of analog representation plays an important role in the mapping process' (1980, pp. 346–7). In other words, subjects might be using mental imagery to solve these problems.

Another issue which is not clear from this experiment alone is whether participants need to be explicitly told, as they were in this case, that the stories might be useful. In fact from other experiments which Gick and Holyoak report in their paper it seems that when participants are not told to use previously presented (and remembered) stories, only a minority succeed in solving such problems. Being aware that one has a potential analogy as well as being alert to the analogical relationship itself appears to be a prerequisite for increasing the likelihood of a solution.

Based on M.L. Gick and K.J. Holyoak 1980: Analogical problem-solving. *Cognitive Psychology*, 12, 306–55.

Box 10.2
Reasoning with realistic materials

Griggs and Cox set out to explore further the effect of using everyday or thematic materials in the Wason selection task. They noted that results from previous experiments were inconsistent, with some studies demonstrating that realistic materials improved performance and others showing little or no effect. In the second of three experiments, Griggs and Cox tried to replicate a study originally conducted by Johnson-Laird et al. (1972). Johnson-Laird et al. required participants to solve a version of the selection task using a rule such as 'if a letter is sealed then there will be a 5d stamp on it'; in other conditions in the experiment, stamps of Italian denomination were referred to, as in 'if a letter is unsealed then there will be a 40 lire stamp on it'. Participants were asked to imagine that they were postal workers and to decide whether or not

such rules were violated. They checked the rule by turning over appropriate envelopes to examine the relation between stamp denomination and whether or not the envelope was sealed. Johnson-Laird et al. discovered a facilitating effect of thematic material like this. Their English participants performed equally well with Italian or English stamp versions, and much better than with abstract examples of the problem. Apart from replacing references to English and Italian stamps with American and Mexican ones, Griggs and Cox ran essentially the same experiment with American participants, but found no facilitating effect of thematic materials.

Griggs and Cox noted that in the Johnson-Laird experiment, the English participants in the early 1970s would have had direct experience of the postal regulations concerning the sealing of envelopes, and, although they would have had little experience of 40 and 50 lire stamps, they would probably have been able to use their knowledge of the rules concerning 4d and 5d stamps to solve the Italian stamp version of the task. Their own American participants, by contrast, had little or no experience of such postal regulations and so were unable to profit from the thematic nature of the task.

They hypothesized from this that realistic materials alone are insufficient to ensure correct solution of the selection task, but that the rule itself must be part of the participant's everyday experience, or at least in long-term memory. To test this they ran a realistic version of the selection task using University of Florida participants and the State law governing the drinking of alcohol. In Florida, persons must be 19 years of age to drink alcoholic beverages legally.

Procedure

Forty University of Florida undergraduates took part; 20 received the thematic (drink law) version of the problem first followed by an abstract version (using letters and numbers), the other 20 received the abstract version first followed by the thematic. The thematic problem was presented as follows. Participants were asked to imagine that they were a police officer on duty whose job it was to ensure that people conform to certain rules. They were then told that the cards in front of them had information about four people sitting at a table, and that:

> On one side of a card is a person's age and on the other side is what the person is drinking. Here is a rule: IF A PERSON IS DRINKING BEER, THEN THE PERSON MUST BE OVER 19 YEARS OF AGE. Select the card or cards that you definitely need to turn over to see whether or not people are violating the rule. (p. 415)

Cards labelled DRINKING A COKE, DRINKING A BEER, 16 YEARS OF AGE and 22 YEARS OF AGE were presented to participants.

In the abstract version, participants were told:

> On one side of a card is a letter, and on the other side is a number. Here is a rule about the cards: IF A CARD HAS AN 'A' ON ONE SIDE, THEN IT HAS A '3' ON THE OTHER SIDE. Select the card or cards that you definitely need to turn over to see whether or not people are violating the rule. (ibid.)

Results

Seventy-three per cent of the participants made the correct selection for the drinking-age problem, and no participants selected the correct combination for the abstract version. Also, as can be seen in box table 10.2.1, there was absolutely no benefit in performing the abstract version after the thematic version (as trial 2), which implies that there was no transfer of solution from the thematic to the abstract version.

Box table 10.2.1 Effect of type of problem and when performed on number of participants selecting the correct card combination

Thematic		Abstract	
Trial 1	Trial 2	Trial 1	Trial 2
14	15	0	0

Source: Derived from table 5, Griggs and Cox, 1982

Griggs and Cox then ran a further study with 18 more participants to see if their thematic effect could be replicated. This time, 14 of the 18 participants made the correct selection, indicating that the effect is very robust.

Interpretation

These experiments strongly support Griggs and Cox's suggestion that thematic materials facilitate performance on the selection task when the participant has experience of the rule or relationship in question and can fall back on material in memory to solve the problem. It is not sufficient merely for the material or content of the problem to be concrete, the rule itself must be in long-term memory.

There are, however, other aspects of their thematic version of the problem which may be important. Testing the rule hinges on the ready availability of a counter-example – an instance which breaks the rule – and participants are likely to have experience of this. Also, the 'detective set' induced by the instructions may help get participants to home in on the latter, and the strong imagery evoked by imagining individuals at a table may help concretize the problem. A fuller experiment would be needed to disentangle the relative effects of the familiarity of the rule, the extent to which a visualization strategy is used and the falsification bias introduced by the detective set. From this experiment all that can be deduced is that their combination appears to be very powerful.

But is *reasoning* facilitated? This study suggests probably not. Humans may well try to avoid reasoning as such whenever retrieval from memory, or 'memory cueing' as Griggs and Cox put it, is a viable alternative.

Based on R.A. Griggs and J.R. Cox 1982: The elusive thematic-materials effect in Wason's selection task. *British Journal of Psychology*, 73, 407–20.

Part III

Modelling Cognition

11 Artificial Intelligence

Throughout history, philosophers and thinkers have used the known to try to understand the unknown. The ancient Greeks thought that the heavens were an upturned bowl and the stars were holes through which light shone. Much later, scientists with a better understanding of the solar system likened the behaviour of electrons in the atom to the way in which planets revolve around the sun. The heart is often described as a pump, and the kidney as a filter. In these cases, something seemingly complicated and mysterious is explained in terms of something simpler and better understood.

The workings of the mind have not been exempt from the human tendency to explain using analogies or models. At various times, the mind has been likened to a piece of wax, a bird cage, an hydraulic system and a telephone exchange (Marshall and Fryer, 1978). Many of these early models described the mind in terms of a physical system or piece of technology and were able, after a fashion, to account for some but by no means all aspects of human cognition. Current attempts to model cognition are the subject of this and the next two chapters. In this one, we discuss the use of computers to simulate human cognitive activity and the important research area of artificial intelligence (AI). In chapter 12, the application of models of normal cognition to explain the difficulties of the brain-injured is considered, while in chapter 13 we examine a new approach to cognitive modelling, connectionism.

One of the various definitions of 'model' in *The Shorter Oxford English Dictionary* is 'something that accurately resembles something else'. One problem with earlier attempts to model the mind is that they likened the workings of the mind, something that is essentially abstract and non-physical, to rather simple and concrete physical systems. To say that the mind is like a bird cage and that memories are like birds is all very well, but it is obvious that the analogy is rather limited in its application. According to many psychologists, the emergence of the digital computer has changed all this and has revolutionized the way in which we think about mind. They maintain that the workings of the computer offer an interesting and more accurate model of mental function than any we have had previously. Barely 40 years old, the computer is now widely used in business, industry, research and the home, but it is also affecting the way we view ourselves.

Models, Minds and Thinking Machines ▶ ▶ ▶

Modelling the mind

How can the workings of a computer be used to understand the human mind? To answer this question we must make an important distinction between the computer's hardware and its software. Computer hardware refers to the physical components of a computer and their operation. Modern computers are made up of microchips or miniature electrical circuits which are interconnected in various ways. The user communicates with the computer via a key board or some other device and the results typically appear on a screen or printout. This interaction between person and machine is made possible partly by the electronic signals which pass through the various microchips and other components which constitute the hardware. However, in order to get a computer to do anything useful it must also be equipped with software. Software refers to the various programs, operating systems, and other instructions which tell the machine what to do. Using the same hardware, a computer system can run different pieces of software. This makes computers very flexible and more useful than, say, electronic calculators which can often only perform a limited set of operations.

A computer program is simply a set of instructions or rules which tells the machine how to perform various operations. At its most fundamental level, that of the machine code, the computer program tells the machine which parts to switch on and which parts to switch off. Early computer programs are all written in machine code but nowadays a range of high-level computer languages are available which are much easier to use and which instruct the machine to manipulate and transform various symbols. Equipped with high-level programming languages, the computer is not merely a calculating device, it is a general purpose symbol-processor.

Computer software, not hardware, offers an interesting way of thinking about mind, since the mind can be thought of as a symbol-processing system too. The idea that mind is a set of rules or instructions which operate on symbols or internal representations of reality has been around for some time (Craik, 1943; Miller et al., 1960; see also chapter 1). What we now have is a way of mimicking or modelling mental operations directly using computer programs. Artificial intelligence research takes these ideas seriously and uses computer programs to try to simulate intelligent behaviour and the mental processes associated with it.

How literally is work in AI to be understood? Do programs provide a perfect model of how the mind works, or do they represent just one of many possible ways in which an intelligent system might operate? This is an awkward question. To deal with it, a distinction is sometimes made between AI and computer simulation (CS). The aim of AI is to get computers to perform intelligently in whatever way is most efficient. People interested in AI in this technological fashion do not really care whether AI programs resemble mental processes or not; their goal is simply to get the computer to do the job in question. For instance, most commercial chess programs for microcomputers play a very creditable and seemingly intelligent game of chess, but they do so in ways quite unlike a human player. To make an effective move in chess the player must look ahead to work out its consequences and the possible responses of the opponent. Computer chess programs are able to take advantage of the larger and more reliable memory at their disposal and can look ahead for more moves than a human player. The human, on the other hand, tends to have better pattern recognition skills than the machine and, although restricted in memory, can rapidly assess the consequences of moves in terms of the overall configuration of pieces. Thus, although both the person and the computer obey the rules of chess, and behave appropriately during the game, the way they control their chess playing is quite different.

By contrast, those who adopt the CS approach are concerned to get computers to perform tasks in the same way as humans. So, for example, an ideal computer simulation of language would not only produce meaningful, grammatically correct and appropriate sentences when questioned, but it might also sometimes make some of the slips of the tongue and other errors which frequently characterize human speech. We should add that no such ideal language simulation yet exists!

Although the distinction between AI and CS is important in some situations such as game playing and robotics, in others it is less crucial. For example, some of the best AI models of vision also offer some of the best psychological explanations for how humans see (e.g. Marr, 1982). Psychologists differ in their opinion as to what this means. Perhaps AI programs like these offer the best explanation we have at the moment for how certain aspects of the mind work. Alternatively, perhaps they offer the only coherent explanation of how the mind works. There might, after all, be only one effective solution to the problems faced by minds and intelligent machines.

In the sections which follow many of these points will become clearer as we introduce some of the major achievements in AI. Before that we wish to set AI in its context by briefly examining its history and background.

History of AI Research

Part of the folklore of AI is that it began before the invention of computers! Charles Babbage (1792–1871), a Victorian inventor, was probably the first to try to build a large calculating engine, but it was his friend, Lady Ada Lovelace, who realized that such a machine might also have the ability to manipulate symbols in general, and need not be restricted to numbers. She believed, for instance, that Babbage's device would be capable of musical composition, but was unsure whether it would ever be able to perform novel tasks. By seeing the potential of the computer as a general purpose symbol-processor, Lady Lovelace thus anticipated the development of a program as a set of instructions, and set the scene for later developments. Unfortunately, because of mechanical rather than conceptual difficulties, Babbage's engine never worked properly and the debate about intelligent machines receded for nearly a hundred years.

The Second World War gave the debate a new urgency. Faced with the need to decode enemy messages, the Allies invested time and money in research into computational devices. When the first real computers appeared in the late 1940s, several people already understood that they might be used to simulate human mental processes. One such person was the British mathematician, Alan Turing, who, during the war years, suggested an intriguing test to see whether a computer was really behaving intelligently. Figure 11.1 illustrates a slightly modified version of this test. Imagine that you are seated at a terminal which is connected to a computer and also to another human being at a different terminal. You can communicate either with the computer or with the other person via your terminal, but you do not know which you are dealing with at any given time. Your job is to decide, by posing suitable questions, or setting particular problems, when you are communicating with the computer. Turing argued that if it was not possible to discover which was at the other end, person or machine, then intelligence would have to be attributed to the computer.

The Turing test should not be taken too literally. It is actually quite tricky to use, and first impressions of even quite simple programs can easily convince one that the system is intelligent. ELIZA, a program written by Weizenbaum (1966), simulates the responses of a psychotherapist to a patient, and often fools users into thinking that it is responding in an intelligent and appropriate fashion to their input whereas in fact it responds in a stereotyped way. Here is a brief section of the rather truculent interchange between ELIZA and a human 'patient'; the program used is a smaller version of the original, designed for use with a personal computer:

ELIZA: PLEASE STATE YOUR PROBLEM
Patient: I hate computers
ELIZA: DO COMPUTERS WORRY YOU?
Patient: Yes
ELIZA: YOU SEEM QUITE POSITIVE
Patient: I am
ELIZA: IS IT BECAUSE YOU ARE THAT YOU CAME TO SEE ME?
Patient: No!
ELIZA: ARE YOU SAYING NO JUST TO BE NEGATIVE?
Patient: Why do you ask?
ELIZA: WE WERE DISCUSSING YOU NOT ME
Patient: Sorry!
ELIZA: THERE IS NO NEED TO APOLOGIZE

At first ELIZA seems quite sensible. She appears to understand the input and responds appropriately. In fact, the program works by searching for key words in the input, especially those to do with feelings and emotions, to which it then responds with set phrases. In reality it knows nothing, a lack of understanding which it is not difficult to reveal:

Patient: What was the last thing I said to you?
ELIZA: I AM NOT SURE THAT I UNDERSTAND YOU
Patient: What was the last thing I said to you?
ELIZA: PLEASE DO NOT REPEAT YOURSELF

ELIZA neatly dodges the question but fails to cover up the fact that she never really knew what been discussed, and so she fails the Turing test.

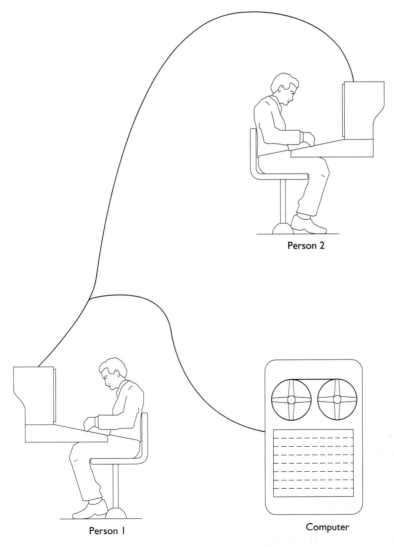

Person 2

Person 1

Computer

Figure 11.1   The Turing test. With whom is person 1 communicating – person 2 or the computer?

A second problem is that the Turing test is too strict. It demands that computers show cleverness in all areas of expertise before their behaviour is judged intelligent. If we stick rigidly to the Turing test when judging AI, programs which many would agree display considerable ingenuity, such as chess programs or vision simulations, would have to be classed as quite unintelligent. A more sensible way to proceed is to assess the computer's behaviour purely with respect to the cognitive skill in question, judging language programs from what we know of language, vision programs from our knowledge of visual perception and so on. This way we do not get sidetracked into rather silly considerations that although the computer may be expert at perceiving objects, or a skilled chess player, it cannot be intelligent because, say, it does not know the price or taste of orange marmalade!

The first AI researchers were quite ambitious and did attempt to produce systems which were intelligent across a wide range of tasks (e.g. Newell and Simon, 1963), but nowadays, there is less agreement that general machine intelligence is a goal worth pursuing. Nevertheless, at least two important AI research groups have recently proposed powerful and successful general frameworks or cognitive architectures which we will describe later (Anderson, 1983; Laird et al., 1987), but, these initiatives excepted, many researchers now believe that AI programs are more likely to be successful if they are restricted to particular tasks. It is also clear, with hindsight, that the types of problem which Newell and Simon examined were ones which did not involve much background knowledge whereas many situations involving human intelligence do.

For these as well as for practical and economic reasons, the emphasis of AI research has now shifted. Current themes in AI research include the study of experts and the creation of expert or knowledge-based systems. Experts are people who are highly skilled in a specific area of knowledge and progress has been made in modelling expert knowledge in a number of different domains. Other current applications of AI are the simulation of human perception, attempts to get computers to understand and use language, and programs which simulate aspects of human memory. We will be examining examples of some of these applications in later sections.

Methods and Tools in Contemporary AI ▶ ▶

How do AI researchers go about the job of producing their programs? What general methods, tools and techniques do they use? What general concepts have emerged from AI?

Forming a theory

Before writing a computer program, it is necessary to have some understanding of the mental processes which are to be mimicked. Sometimes this means constructing a detailed psychological theory which specifies, in precise information-processing terms, the various mental operations involved. Marr (1982) emphasized how important it is to establish what a mental function is for and how it works before bothering with the details of its computer implementation. According to Marr, this prior stage of theory construction should be informed by as much relevant data as possible. It is perhaps for this reason that Marr's theory and its implementations are so impressive and have been so widely acclaimed. Other AI programs are created less carefully than this. At times, AI researchers simply rely on their own intuitions as to how a mental activity works, or merely build on the achievements of previous work in AI. While this may lead to the creation of successful programs, it does not necessarily guarantee plausible simulations. A somewhat less hit-and-miss approach is the technique known as protocol analysis, which requires a person to 'think aloud' or report what they are doing while working on a particular task and their verbal 'protocol' is then taped and transcribed. The protocol is then examined and attempts made to deduce the major steps in the mental process.

Protocol analysis has been widely applied to simulations of game playing, problem solving and, lately, to the elicitation of expert knowledge, but the technique does have its problems. If we ask someone to think aloud while performing a task, we are asking them to introspect or describe the contents and activity of their own mind. Introspection is a notoriously error-prone method of investigation. It can, at best, only give access to mental events which are conscious, whereas other important mental activity undoubtedly takes place at non-conscious levels. It depends on the verbal skills, accuracy and honesty of the introspector. The very fact of introspecting may itself interfere with that which is introspected. Finally, even if the introspectors' reports are accurate and truthful, there is no assurance that what introspectors are consciously experiencing and describing actually reflects what they are doing. Nisbett and Wilson (1977) report several situations in which behaviour can alter without any accompanying change in verbal reports, and also several situations where verbal reports suggest that stimuli are effective in controlling behaviour but which more objective analyses show to be ineffective. In a similar vein, Tulving (1989) has recently warned against the uncritical acceptance of what he calls the 'concordance' hypothesis or the idea that conscious experience, information processing and behaviour necessarily correlate. You can experience some of the problems of protocol analysis for yourself by trying Practical Exercise 1 at the end of this chapter.

After considering the issue, Nisbett and Wilson (1977) urged psychologists to reject data based on introspection and concentrate instead on observable behaviour. Accepting Nisbett and Wilson's conclusions in full would, of course, spell the end of protocol analysis, but, given that it does seem to be of some use, a more fruitful approach is to investigate the relation between conscious reports, information processing and behaviour to see when conscious reports might be accurate indicators of the other two (Ericsson and Simon, 1980; Morris, 1981; Tulving, 1989). Ericsson and Simon, for instance, suggest that introspective self-reports are reliable when they reflect the operation of a central control and Morris (1981) made a useful distinction between self-reports which in certain circumstances may be accurate and reliable and self-hypotheses which may not (see also Morris and Hampson, 1983, and White, 1988).

Despite this limited acknowledgement of their utility, techniques based on self-reports do not always compare well with other methods of finding out what people are thinking of what they know. Burton et al. (1988), for example, compared four methods of knowledge elicitation and found that protocol analysis took longest and produced less information than other techniques. Alternative methods currently used for eliciting expert knowledge include structured interviews, card sorting techniques, questionnaires, examining tough cases or examples and employing various statistical techniques such as multi-dimensional scaling. Current consensus is that no single method, on its own, is completely satisfactory, and so 'knowledge engineers' (people who elicit knowledge from experts and who work on expert systems) generally use a mixture of methods.

AI Languages, Knowledge Representation (KR) and manipulation

Having formed a theory, by whatever method, the researcher then has to program the computer. This task is now made much easier by a range of computer languages that have been developed for AI purposes: these include LISP, LOGO, MICROPROLOG and POP-11. Languages such as these are more convenient to use for the symbol processing of AI than languages such as FORTRAN which are better suited to numerical calculations. As well as suitable languages, contemporary AI workers also have a range of programming environments to choose from. A programming environment includes tools for editing and correcting programs as well as suites of other programs designed to make some of the routine aspects of AI easier (Garnham, 1988).

In addition to all this, today's AI researchers also use a number of general principles or themes to guide their programming. Three themes, in particular, arise time and again and have to be dealt with when writing most AI programs. First, the programmer must make important decisions about how knowledge is to be represented. Second, a way of searching or manipulating the knowledge must be determined. Third, a means must be found to coordinate or control different parts of complex programs.

As we explained at the beginning of this book, the word cognitive means to do with knowledge, and, as we have pointed out in various chapters since then, the issue of knowledge representation is important in many areas of cognitive psychology. AI also has to face the problem of how external reality can be internally represented. In the course of its brief history, AI has developed a number of powerful general notations, and some quite specific frameworks for representing knowledge. Two important general notations or ways of writing knowledge include networks, in which knowledge is represented as a set of linked nodes and production systems, in which condition–action (if . . . then) rules are used to capture complex knowledge relations. More specific and specialized knowledge systems, which have been discussed in various places already, include frames, scripts, MOPs, TOPs, and mental models (see chapters 7 and 10 for more details). By now, many of the important characteristics, strengths and weaknesses of these systems have been worked out, and although a researcher still has to make the important decision about which type of knowledge representation to use, having made the decision he or she can be confident that many of the basic properties of the system he or she chooses have been explored.

Representing knowledge is by no means the end of AI. Knowledge has to be manipulated and examined to be of any use. The closely related concepts of search and control are important here. Search refers to the way in which a body of knowledge is explored. The idea of search originally came from simulations of problem solving and game playing where finding a solution to a problem or choosing what move to make in a game was seen as a search through a set of alternative solutions or moves. Various search procedures are now quite well understood, and search methods are now used widely in memory systems, language programs and some vision simulations as well as in problem solving and game playing. Some involve blind search where, in one way or another, the set of alternatives is slavishly examined while others are more human-like in their use of shortcuts, known as heuristics.

Control is needed where different parts of a complex program have to be coordinated. The control system tells the program, or part of the program, what to do next. Control is really a form of search on a large scale in that the system as a whole is again moving through a set of possible choices. Normally, the control system is conceptually separable from the way in which knowledge is represented, except in the case of production systems where representation and control are rolled into the same set of condition–action rules. Production systems are interconnected representations which control themselves.

There have been some interesting developments in program control in recent years. Agenda-based systems use what is essentially a list to order the computer's tasks. As in a meeting where the topics to be discussed are listed in order of importance and urgency, so an agenda-driven program includes a similar list. An important program which uses an agenda is the 'Automated Mathematician', AM (Lenat, 1977). AM was initially provided with a fairly simple set of rules about how to discover and manipulate concepts and a great deal of information about set theory. With this basic knowledge, and its control system, which ranks tasks in terms of their interestingness, AM proceeded to discover a number of key mathematical concepts, including some which are not yet fully proven by human mathematicians. By far the most interesting thing that AM does is to discover new things to do. While working out new concepts, new tasks to be done are generated, assigned an interestingness rating and added to the agenda. The list, therefore, is modified as the program runs.

Agenda systems are useful whenever a decision has to be made concerning which task to do next. At other times, several different aspects of the same task need to be coordinated. When language is analysed, for example, various aspects of the incoming information, such as its sound, grammar and meaning, have to be interpreted and combined. One way to do this is to use the computer equivalent of a blackboard. Blackboards are, of course, large spaces on which information about many different topics can be written and read at the same time. In AI, a blackboard is the store of information, available in parallel, for all processes or 'knowledge sources' to monitor. A given knowledge source waits for its own particular piece of information, and when it becomes available on the board it 'fires' or 'shouts' and adds its conclusion to the pool of data on the board. Blackboard systems are actually more general versions of production systems, but with two important differences: more complex processes than simple productions can monitor the board and the board can be divided into special sections which only certain knowledge sources are allowed to see (Stillings et al., 1987). HEARSAY, a language-understanding program, uses the blackboard control technique to good effect (Erman and Lesser, 1980).

Once again, previous experience gained with these various systems helps the researcher enormously when writing AI programs.

Program testing

After it is written, an AI program must be tested. This can be done informally, simply by watching the program in operation across a range of tasks, or more formally, by comparing the output or behaviour of the program with objective records from cognitive psychological and other experiments showing how people actually perform in the situation in question. It is important, however, not to assume that the inner workings of the program necessarily constitute a true explanation of the cognitive process in question simply because the behaviour of the program closely resembles human performance. After all, as Garnham (1988) points out, quite accurate estimates of planetary motions can be obtained from elaborate clockwork models based on the now discredited epicyclic theory about the movement of planets. An incorrect theory can sometimes make reasonably accurate predictions.

◀ AI in Action ▶ ▶

With their armoury of languages, programming tools and ideas about knowledge and its manipulation, AI researchers have begun to simulate a wide range of human cognitive activity. We can only focus on a few areas here, but the ones we have chosen, vision, language and memory, do illustrate some of major challenges which AI has had to face. We also briefly consider some applications and problems for AI research in the construction and use of expert systems. Some of these areas will then be further examined in the next two chapters from the neuropsychological and connectionist perspectives. So, having read all three chapters, the reader will be able to compare and contrast three important ways of modelling cognition.

In selecting the simulations and examples for this chapter, we have tried to include examples of classic milestones in the development of AI to help put present work into perspective and to highlight some of the challenges of computer modelling.

Vision

As we explained in chapter 3, one of the first obstacles to be overcome in understanding vision is to realize that there is something to be explained. Perceptual processes are so efficient and take place so rapidly that it is easy to take them for granted.

Notice, for example, how easy it is to work out the contents from the scene in figure 11.2. It consists of two solid objects one in front of the other. How does your visual system perform this task so smoothly? How might a computer be programmed to do the same? One way to appreciate the problems that the visual system must overcome is to try to work out how to build an artificial vision system. This, of course, is the challenge facing those interested in computer vision.

The first computer vision programs were designed to deal with simple scenes, known as BLOCKWORLDs, rather like the one in figure 11.2. Even in such simple scenes, separating out objects from their background and grouping together different parts of the same objects is more difficult than it might appear. SEE, a classic program written by Guzman (1969), analyses scenes like these by identifying key junctions between lines in the scene. Some junctions indicate where the corners and edges of the objects are, while others show that one object is partially obscuring another. The reader may find it helpful to refer to figure 11.2 as we describe the various junction types.

One important junction which SEE locates is the T. A single T junction normally means that three surfaces are in contact but does not indicate which surfaces belong to which object. Where two T's occur close together, one object generally obscures another. When a ruler covers the edge of a page, for instance, two T junctions are formed.

Another junction is formed when three (or more) lines come together at a vertex and form an arrow. These junctions usually show how two regions,

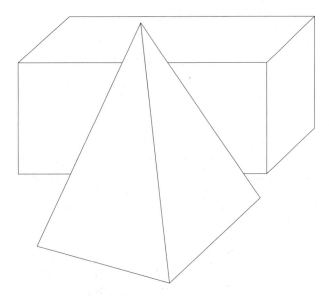

Figure 11.2 A simple world of geometrical objects

separated by the middle line (arrow shaft), are part of the same object. There are several examples of arrow heads in figure 11.2.

Related to the arrow is the fork. Once again, three lines come together but this time there are three regions involved which are generally part of the same object. Have a look for some in figure 11.2.

By programming the computer to identify junctions like these, Guzman allowed it to infer which regions belonged with which 3-D object. Here are some of the rules which SEE uses to do this:

1   Find regions. A region is any area completely bounded by lines. Label each separate region as A, B, C, D etc.
2   Identify junctions.
3   Link regions together at junctions if the junction type specifies that they belong to the same object.
4   Make a diagram showing which regions go together.

It should be clear that what SEE does is to work out how the scene is structured using only a few simple rules and some knowledge about junctions. Guzman's program has no prior knowledge about the nature of the visual world at all apart from this. It 'sees' by working out the structure of objects from first principles.

While Guzman's program fares quite well with simple line drawings it is incapable of dealing with less clear-cut situations. Shadows and areas of brightness cause it a great deal of trouble, because the light–dark boundary associated with a shadow or a light patch may be wrongly interpreted by the program as the edge of a surface. Roberts (1965) dealt with this problem in another pioneering program by writing in knowledge about the structure of objects in advance. To do this, Roberts gave his program information about basic shapes such as cubes, hexagons and wedges. With these 'perceptual building blocks', the program then deduced what objects were present by working out which brightness differences were due to edges and which were due to shadows. When Roberts wrote his program it looked increasingly likely that programs would have to be given more and more knowledge about the structure of the visual world before they could see. Programs like these, which rely on prior knowledge, are referred to as 'knowledge-driven' or 'top-down' accounts; programs like Guzman's, which rely more on the information from objects, are 'data-driven' or 'bottom-up' accounts (see also chapter 3).

Although different in several respects, both Guzman's and Roberts' programs were similar in that they only worked on the BLOCKSWORLD. The reason for using BLOCKSWORLDs was that basic principles about vision could be discovered by simplifying the perceived information. In practice, as with other areas of psychology, it has turned out that oversimplifying the problem has led to a somewhat oversimplified and truly 'artificial' solution. Simple scenes like figure 11.2 do not stretch the visual system in the way that poorly lit, natural objects with vague boundaries do. Nevertheless, some progress was made with BLOCKS-WORLDs in understanding the general problems of object segmentation and some of the techniques discovered can be applied to more complicated objects.

A further feature of the first vision programs is that they were simulations of high-level visual processes. The basic, low-level tasks of finding the edges and other simple features in the image were made comparatively simple, and the main job was to identify objects in the scene. Human perception, however, has to cope with all aspects of vision and an additional set of problems arise when low-level vision is considered.

Low-level vision: Marr's program

Perhaps the most impressive vision program to have been produced in recent years is the one developed by David Marr and colleagues. This forms part of a larger interdisciplinary approach to the problems of vision outlined by Marr (1982) and described more fully in chapter 3. As we pointed out in chapter 3, Marr's theory is not the end of the story as far as our understanding of perception is concerned, there is much still to be discovered, but it happens to be a very good account and it has had a seminal influence on both the psychology and computation of vision.

Marr's program copes with problems that both Roberts' and Guzman's failed to address. It can perceive objects with vague and fuzzy boundaries and copes with everyday objects despite visual noise, texture and subtle shading. Unlike Guzman's program, Marr's relies far more on the patterns of brightness differences in a scene, and, unlike Roberts' program, it uses very little background knowledge about shapes and structures. In Marr's opinion, the early stages of vision are largely a data-driven process, and require far less conceptual support than others have claimed.

Various aspects of Marr's system have been turned into working programs. Here we concentrate mainly on the program which creates the first stage, the primal sketch. The program begins with a picture of the object taken by TV camera. The picture is first 'digitized' or turned into a set of numbers, with each number representing the brightness of the scene at the point in question. This digitized image is then passed through four filters which produce successively blurred versions, each of which is examined in turn. It may strike the reader as odd that the program blurs its initial image; surely it would be better to retain as much detail as possible. The reason for this is that although very blurred images contain no fine detail, they do still show the overall structure and outline of the object, as short-sighted people know. By getting rid of the sharp detail in some images, the major structure can be more easily extracted and the fine detail can be added later from the sharper images.

Each digitized image is processed by a program which searches for brightness changes, the idea being that important information is present wherever the intensity of the image is changing the fastest. An edge, for example, is usually a boundary between a light and a dark area. To find where intensity is changing most quickly, the program uses the mathematical technique of differentiation and applies this over many different areas of the image. Marr and Hildreth (1980) called the crucial points at which intensity is changing fastest 'zero crossings' since they are points at which the change in intensity stops increasing, or becoming more and more positive, and begins to decrease and becomes negative, rather like the top of a hill. (The more technically minded reader might be interested to note that this is determined in practice by the point at which the second derivative of the intensity function crosses zero.)

The result of all these operations is a raw, primal sketch of the object. This is a very messy representation consisting of zero crossings of various sizes known as edges, bars, blobs and terminations. The edges referred to here are not, at this stage, the external edges of the object but are simply boundaries between light and dark areas. Using this rather messy image, the program then begins to group elements into more organized, higher-order structures, such as lines and curves. To do this it employs many of the Gestalt principles of perceptual organization discussed in chapter 3. One simple grouping process, for instance, is based on the proximity of elements. For example, a series of blobs close together get joined up and treated as part of the same line. Another grouping process depends on the Law of Common Fate: bars which point in the same direction are joined together and so on. With these and other simple rules, the program not only separates objects from their background but also teases out their major parts.

Later stages of Marr's system then take the organized primal sketch and work out the different depths or distances from the observer in different parts of the picture. This gives what Marr calls the 2-D sketch of the object. The analysis at this stage is 2-D and not fully three-dimensional because the object is still depicted from one viewpoint.

The third and final stage of visual analysis forms the complete 3-D representation of the object. At this point the visual system not only knows what the object looks like from one angle, but can work out how it is likely to appear from different orientations.

Marr's program and general theory are remarkable achievements. They have specified, in far more detail than any previous account, how the basic problems of visual analysis might be solved. More importantly, some of the mechanisms used to extract information from the image, such as blurring the image and the zero-crossing procedures, may have quite precise neurophysiological parallels (see chapter 3). However, there are a number of bridges still to be crossed before a complete artificial vision system is reached, and, as we keep emphasizing, Marr's account is a psychological theory not a set of established facts. There are alternative accounts for several of the stages which he discusses. Thus, the idea that the 3-D structure of an object can be determined by relating the current view to some ideal or prototypical view is now receiving some attention (Hildreth and Ullman, 1989) as a possible alternative to Marr's account, based on generalized cones. There are, in any case, working programs for only some of the earlier stages of visual analysis in Marr's account; the later stages still need to be fully computerized. Other limitations of Marr's account become apparent when attempts are made to analyse moving objects. There is also more to perception than mere visual analysis. We see where things are as well as what they are and can shift our attention from one location to another. Nor is perception an isolated cognitive function; at some future date vision programs will need to be connected to programs which determine what objects are for, how they can be used, what they are called and so on. There is still a broad gulf between attempts to get knowledge into the computer by means of vision programs and attempts to program computers to represent, organize and use that knowledge. Marr's program has started us on the right road but there remains a long way to go.

Language

The 1960s were very optimistic years. At the beginning of the decade scientists were convinced that computers would soon be able to understand and produce language and to translate from one language to another. By the end of the decade it was clear that these aspirations would take rather longer to be realized. Language has proved quite tricky for AI to deal with. For one thing, it is a many-levelled activity, with phonological, syntactic, semantic and pragmatic characteristics (see chapter 4), and each level or aspect of language has its own range of problems. Another difficulty is that a full computational model of language depends on progress in other areas such as semantic memory, knowledge representation and social perception. Language occurs in linguistic, cognitive and social contexts, and it is in relation to these wider contexts that it must be studied. In this section we briefly review work on speech perception, syntactic analysis and language understanding, concentrating mainly on language reception, though many of the issues we raise apply to language production too.

Speech processing Imagine you are listening to someone speaking. To understand the meaning of the sounds you hear, you must first separate them from background noise, and then identify their major physical characteristics. Phonology refers to the basic processes of speech perception (and production) concerned with the physical characteristics of speech. Several computational methods for phonological analysis have been developed. Some of these are technical methods which bear little resemblance to the way in which people process sounds; others, however, analyse sounds in ways that have some psychological plausibility. Formant tracking, for instance, works by picking out the major energy bands in the speech signal, while linear predictive coding (LPC) is an intriguing method which uses a model of the vocal tract to analyse speech sounds. The model depicts the vocal tract as a tube composed of sections of different diameters, each of which can resonate at a particular frequency. LPC analysis can also be used in reverse to synthesize speech.

After analysing the incoming sounds as human speech the listener must next decide whether or not they are words. Word identification involves important cognitive processes, but it is still only a step on the way to understanding fully the meaning of a word. You may, for example, identify the string of letters 'sesquipedalian' as a word, and realize that you have heard it before, but still be ignorant as to its meaning. You need to do more work to recognize and interpret it fully. Current programs for word recognition and identification are still comparatively primitive and can deal with only around 2,000 words. Some of the more powerful systems identify words (but do not fully understand them) by matching them against templates or copies, a technique which humans seem unlikely to use since template systems are too inflexible to cope with the variations of human speech. Also, people sometimes use syntactic and semantic information to interpret speech. Read the following two sentences aloud: 'It was a hot day so I bought an ice-cream' and 'Whenever I have nightmares, I scream'. Notice how similar the ends of the sentences sound, but how easy it is to distinguish their meanings using syntactic and other cues.

Attempts have been made to incorporate syntactic and semantic factors into word recognition systems. HEARSAY, a program which uses a blackboard control system, concentrates mainly on the infrequent and longer words in sentences because these tend to be acoustically clearer (Erman and Lesser, 1980). After detecting the less common words, it then works outwards from them and examines the commoner words which tend to be spoken less clearly. In fact, HEARSAY probably relies far more on contextual cues than humans since it makes many more semantic and syntactic intrusion errors. It 'recognizes' words which are grammatically or semantically plausible even if these are not the ones actually spoken.

Syntactical analysis   There is more to speech comprehension than recognizing individual words. The way in which words combine must be considered too. For a start, the grammatical structure of an utterance must be analysed or parsed. Computer models of grammatical analysis owe a great deal to the work of Noam Chomsky and other linguists (see chapter 4). Chomsky (1957) demonstrated that a finite set of linguistic rules can be used to construct and analyse a potentially infinite set of sentences and, as we explained in chapter 4, argued against a strictly behaviouristic explanation of language. Although many of the details in Chomsky's original theory are no longer believed to be correct, the basic idea that all well-formed sentences can be broken down or parsed into abstract phrase structures still is.

As with speech recognition systems, not all artificial parsing systems are psychologically plausible. It seems highly likely, for instance, that humans parse spoken sentences in what would be a left-to-right fashion if the words were written down, whereas not all artificial systems follow this rule. Nevertheless, the construction of artificial parsing systems is not completely divorced from the study of people. Among the various issues in the study of human syntactical abilities, two are especially relevant to the construction of computer parsers, namely the construction of the phrase structure tree and the search problem.

Constructing a phrase structure tree from a spoken sentence along the lines illustrated in figure 11.3 is a perceptual as well as a linguistic problem. Like any act of perception, it involves the use of stored knowledge to interpret incoming data, but like other forms of perception the relative contribution of the data (from the words) and the stored knowledge (about sentence structures) must be determined. Do people, when parsing, start from the individual words and try to work from the bottom up to an understanding of the whole sentence, or do they start with a general interpretation of the sentence and work from the top down to predict the word slots? The answer to this question is not yet fully resolved as far as humans are concerned, though some artificial parsers work in both a top-down and a bottom-up direction.

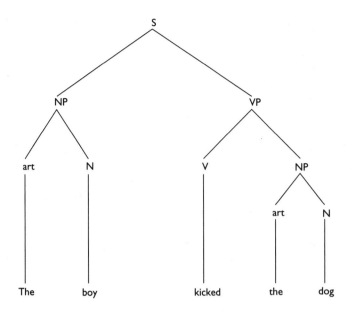

Figure 11.3 A phrase structure tree. S = sentence; NP = noun phrase; VP = verb phrase; art = article; N = noun; V = verb

Another important question for human and artificial parsers is how to cope with sentences which have more than one possible interpretation, such as 'visiting relatives can be a nuisance'. There are essentially two ways of dealing with this problem which depend on whether the set of possible interpretations is searched depth- or breadth-first. With a depth-first search a particular interpretation of a string of words is selected and followed through to completion or until it fails. In a breadth-first search, all possible interpretations of a string are examined in parallel. Humans take comparatively little time in parsing, which suggests that they only consciously adopt one interpretation of a sentence until proved wrong.

Language understanding   Research into language understanding has produced important spin-offs for the study of many other areas of cognition. To understand even the simplest sentence involves a large amount of background knowledge, and so the study of language-understanding systems has led to a general interest in the representation of meaning and the nature of semantic memory.

One way round the large amount of knowledge required by language-understanding systems is to write programs which only converse about limited aspects of the world. This was the approach taken by Winograd (1972) with his classic program, SHRDLU. SHRDLU was one of the most advanced programs of its time, and its performance is still impressive even though it only converses about the simple shapes in the BLOCKSWORLD.

SHRDLU is mainly a language-understanding system. It does engage in simple dialogue but its replies are produced from a small set of ready-made phrases. It consists of three major components: a syntactic analyser, a semantic system and an inference mechanism. The semantic system, in conjunction with the other two, uses a representational framework known as procedural semantics to move blocks around on an imaginary table top and to answer questions about its own performance. Procedural semantics, as the term implies, expresses meanings as procedures or sets of rules. For example, the program represents the meaning of 'block' as a set of rules for checking whether a given object has the properties of blocks, while the meaning of a sentence is a procedure which adds the fact expressed by the sentence to what the program already knows.

SHRDLU's power, however, is revealed by its ability to make inferences: one of the hallmarks of a skilled language user. Its comprehension mechanism can handle pronouns such as 'it', 'one' and 'them'. The meaning of expressions like these depends on the topic of previous sentences, to which a connection has to be made. SHRDLU also detects when it has misunderstood an expression and can ask for more information. Examine the following dialogue between SHRDLU and its user. SHRDLU's responses are in capital letters:

1   Take the green block and put it on the yellow block.
2   OK
3   Now put them both on top of the blue one.
4   OK
5   Which one is at the bottom?
6   THE BLUE ONE
7   Move the red block to the right of the blue block.
8   OK
9   Put the sphere on top of the pyramid.
10   I CAN'T

Note what the program is doing. It interprets the first instruction correctly, but to do so, it must infer that the word 'it' refers to the green block. Similarly, in line 3, the word 'them' is correctly interpreted as referring to the green and yellow blocks, showing that the program has kept track of what has gone before (unlike ELIZA). In line 6, it successfully answers a question and produces some new information: it was never explicitly told that the blue block was at the bottom. In line 10, it uses its knowledge of geometry to decide that a sphere would fall off the sharp top of a pyramid.

Powerful though it is, SHRDLU is, as it stands, limited to discussions about the BLOCKSWORLD, and attempts to extend its procedural semantics to wider knowledge domains have not been entirely successful. A more broadly based system than SHRDLU, outlined by Schank (1975), is known as MARGIE, which stands for Memory, Analysis, Response, Generation and Inference on English. Margie uses scripts (see chapters 7 and 9) to interpret texts which it paraphrases into representations known as conceptual dependency diagrams.

Conceptual dependency makes explicit the meaning or conceptual relationships between idea units in the text. To do this, the main verb in each sentence is given a key organizing role. The idea is that the meaning of a verb can be expressed as a set of simple primitive acts such as the physical or mental transfer of information, the propulsion of one body by another, or the ingestion of food or other substances. With conceptual primitives like these, the system can represent quite complex actions and use them to structure text.

Contrasting SHRDLU and MARGIE, Garnham (1988) observes: 'SHRDLU and MARGIE are two very different responses to the challenge of producing a computer program that can "understand natural language". In SHRDLU Winograd seemed to have provided a complete demonstration of what could be done in a restricted domain ... MARGIE and subsequent Schankian programs, on the other hand, because of their more ambitious nature, continually suggested problems that apparently required new types of knowledge structure' (p. 165).

Our own feelings are that if the work on computerized vision is anything to go by, then only by facing up to the full complexities of language will progress be made. Marr's program could not have emerged from programs which dealt only with the BLOCKSWORLD, and if language programs are similarly confined, all they will discuss, in a suitably banal way, is blocks. Fortunately, current research suggests that the challenge is being met. Key areas for research at the moment involve attempts to deal with dialogue and non-literal languages, both of which introduce wider problems than the BLOCKSWORLD.

Dialogue or conversation depends for its success on both parties having some idea of what the other has in mind. Suppose you were approached at a train station and asked by a man who anxiously looks at his watch, 'When will it arrive?'. Using your knowledge of the context, and the likely intentions of the speaker, you quickly infer that 'it' refers to the next train. Thus, computer simulations of dialogue must have some model of what the other knows and intends as well as a general understanding of language and the setting in which it is used. For this reason, interest in discourse plans is quite intense at present. To date, however, most computer simulations of discourse have been limited to quite restricted conversational domains, in which the plans are relatively unambiguous, and to quite literal forms of conversation, such as Winograd's SHRDLU, though some attempts were made at the end of the 1970s to broaden the range and the flexibility of computer models (e.g. Walker, 1978).

Current research on discourse indicates that there are a number of other important psychological issues to be settled before fully effective simulations can be produced. All human languages, for instance, are full of non-literal usages such as 'it's raining cats and dogs'; 'the stock exchange is going up'; 'the deutschmark is falling'; 'my love is an arbutus'. Language appears to have grown and developed partly through the use of metaphor and simile, so the examination of these forms cannot only be left to the poet or novelist if we wish to grasp fully how language works. The AI community is now beginning to consider these aspects of language, and this research would be helped if, as Carbonell (1982) suggests, a general theory specifying the different types of metaphor could be developed. Other topics for research, reviewed by Grosz et al. (1989), include the use of linguistic gesture, the interpretation of sentence constituents, such as pronouns and noun phrases in different contexts, and recognition of discourse plans.

Memory

To the non-psychologist, using computers to simulate memory might seem a comparatively straightforward task. After all, computers are devices which encode, store and retrieve information and, therefore, already apparently exhibit many key characteristics of human remembering. Presumably all that has to be done is to specify the type of information which people remember, and then put this into the computer in some convenient form. In practice things are more complicated, and the simulation of human memory raises fundamental issues about the representation and use of knowledge and the frameworks which do this which go far beyond merely putting information into a computer. Memory also raises questions concerning the nature and function of subjective experience which current computer models fail to address. Many computer models are primarily models of simplified semantic memories (e.g. Anderson and Bower, 1973), and some psychologists maintain that a full simulation of episodic memory is unlikely to be achieved on the grounds that computers do not have recollective experiences (e.g. Tulving, 1983). Thus, although memory has been reasonably well studied by cognitive psychology, we are still a long way from anything like a complete computer simulation.

Nevertheless, some progress has been made in modelling important aspects of human remembering. Anderson (1983), for example, has used a production system notation to develop ACT* (pronounced 'act star'), a general model of cognition, which simulates not only memory but also the acquisition of various skills such as solving geometry problems, playing chess, programming computers and learning. Further development and extension of ACT* is still continuing (Anderson, 1983; Anderson and Thompson, 1988).

The basic architecture of ACT* is illustrated in figure 11.4. The model incorporates a distinction between procedural and declarative knowledge and has three main parts: a working memory, a declarative memory and a production memory, together with a set of processes (labelled arrows) which operate on and between these memories.

The working memory contains currently accessible information. This includes information retrieved from declarative memory and temporary representations formed by the action of the production system or deposited by the encoding process. Declarative memory is the permanent knowledge repository of the system, and production memory contains the procedures which the system as a whole needs to create new knowledge.

Most of the processes in the model operate on or through working memory. Encoding brings in information into working memory from the outside world. Performance processes convert information in working memory into behaviour. The match process checks the conditions of the various production rules against the current content of working memory. If a match is detected, then the production in question may be allowed to fire, and its results are then deposited in working memory. Finally, the outcome of cognitive activities can be stored more permanently in declarative memory.

Anderson's (1983) approach embodies several assumptions, some of which are merely to do with the technical details of the simulation, but

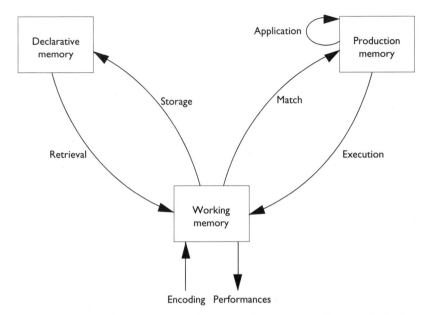

Figure 11.4   The basic architecture of ACT*. (Based on figure 1.2, Anderson, 1983)

others are more important and involve basic decisions about the nature of knowledge. One of these latter assumptions is that declarative knowledge comes in chunks or units which contain no more than five elements. The important units of declarative knowledge, according to Anderson, are images, propositions and strings.

Images and propositions are common features of several cognitive models; strings, a novel feature of ACT*, are used to encode temporally ordered information. So, a string might be used to represent the days of the week, the numbers one to ten, or simply the order of words in a sentence. Anderson suggests that one characteristic of strings is that they are fixed or end-anchored by their first item, and that their subsequent ordering makes it easier to retrieve information in one direction rather than another. As an illustration, it is easier to generate the letter three steps further on in the alphabet after 'M' than it is to provide the letter three steps before.

Another innovative and quite plausible feature of ACT* is that the main elements of declarative knowledge, images, propositions and strings, need not always be used separately but can be used together in what Anderson (1983) calls tangled hierarchies.

Figure 11.5 shows such a hierarchy in which the three types of representations are combined. The strings, in this example, work a little bit like scripts, and order the sequence of information; the propositions capture the important semantic relations and the image economically represents one of the main referents of the hierarchy, a table. Assuming that human knowledge also relies on different internal representations, some similar tangled arrangement of representations is likely to be needed for ideas to be ordered, illustrated and discussed.

Using ACT*, Anderson has managed to simulate a wide range of quite complicated human activities, and ACT*'s performance closely matches the actual behaviour of human participants gathered from controlled experiments. For instance, Anderson has been able to mimic the important skill known as mental rotation, whereby people are able to match two objects at different orientations. Experimental data show that as the angular separation between the to-be-matched objects increases so does the time taken to make the match. It seems likely that people accomplish these matches by mentally turning around images of the objects until the images are in the same position. The further the images have to be turned the longer the rotation takes (Cooper and Shepard, 1973). ACT* behaves in a similar way.

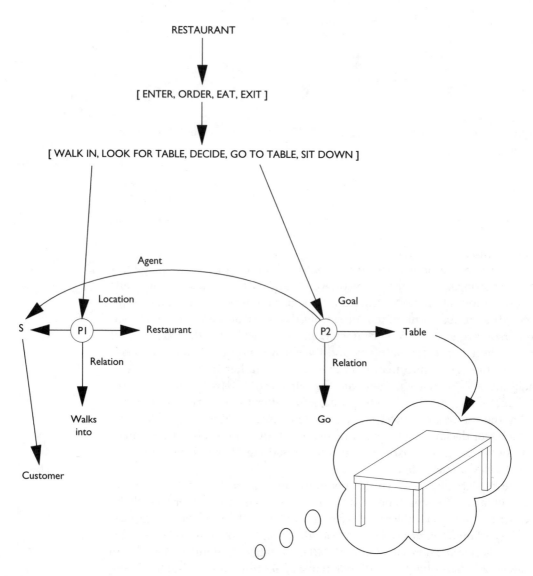

Figure 11.5 Part of a tangled hierarchy comprising strings, shown by [ ], propositions (Ⓟ1 and Ⓟ2) and image. (Based on figure 1.3, Anderson, 1983)

It takes an image of one object and moves it through a number of small angular steps until it matches the image of the other object. Mental rotation in ACT* is also helping to clarify some aspects of mental rotation in humans, such as the effects of complexity of the figures on rotation rates, which are not easily solved with behavioural data alone.

Other ACT* simulations demonstrate how behaviour shifts, as skill develops, from control by declarative representation, through a phase where fairly rough-and-ready procedures govern behaviour, to the final, smooth stage of skilled performance. The shift from declarative to procedural control appears to be a key feature of human skill too. In learning to drive, for example, the beginner initially relies on verbal instructions to know when to depress the clutch and shift the gears, and only later develops smooth control over these actions. Finally, indicating the flexibility of the system, ACT* has been used successfully to model the emergence of grammar in the early stages of language development.

Each of Anderson's (1983) simulations is quite interesting on its own, but the real power of ACT* is that it shows how one common architecture might be used to perform a wide range of cognitive tasks. Even so, ACT* is by no means the last word in general theories of cognition. Another important system, SOAR, capable of dealing with an equally wide variety of tasks, has more recently been described (Laird et al., 1987). SOAR shares some features with ACT*, such as its dependence on a production system, but differs from it in important ways too. Unlike ACT*, SOAR dispenses with the declarative long-term memory and also has better developed links with the external world. It also relies more heavily on problem-solving techniques than ACT*, and is not yet fully expressed as a cognitive theory, but looks well set to develop in this direction in the near future. Further aspects of SOAR are outlined in box 11.1.

The common architecture approach of ACT* and SOAR contrasts markedly with the approach taken by those who maintain that each mental function, such as memory, perception and language, has its own distinctive structure and must, therefore, be studied on its own merits (e.g. Fodor, 1983). The argument between those who believe that a common architecture supports all cognition and those who believe that several specialized architectures are required is likely to continue for some time.

Whatever the final outcome of this debate, there are many other features of human remembering still to be simulated. One such feature is the nature of retrieval. Perhaps because of their emphasis on semantic memory and the representation of knowledge, many current computer models give the misleading impression that retrieval from memory is always a direct and effortless affair. In fact, as experimental cognitive psychology has shown, retrieval is often reconstructive and quite effortful (Bartlett, 1932; Baddeley, 1982). This form of retrieval, akin to reasoning and problem solving, has received comparatively little attention by computer modellers, but work by Kolodner (1983) may mark the beginning of a change. Kolodner has offered a working computer program known as CYRUS that provides the first really explicit account of reconstructive retrieval, and which may well suggest new avenues of research into this phenomenon.

Expert knowledge-based systems and knowledge elicitation

The explosion of and demand for human knowledge, the increase in the power and capacity of computers and the growing sophistication in knowledge representation in the latter half of the twentieth century have been factors responsible for the development of expert systems. Expert systems are programs which give advice on specialized topics, usually within a particular domain such as medicine, law, geology or chemical analysis – advice which is often better than that provided by many human professionals. As knowledge expands, the ability of human experts to keep abreast of new developments in such areas is decreasing, and so the demand for expert systems is increasing as a result. In this section, we briefly outline some of the developments in expert systems with particular reference to medicine, and mention some issues for expert system research with particular emphasis on knowledge elicitation. In box 11.2, PROSPEC-TOR, an expert system which has been successfully used in geological explanation, is outlined.

Expert systems, applied examples of AI, depend heavily on earlier, non-technologically oriented work on semantic memory and problem solving. Their essential components are a knowledge base or store of information about the domain in question, an inference engine or way of generating new knowledge from the database, and an interface for communicating with the user. One of the earliest and most famous expert systems, MYCIN, was designed by Shortliffe (1976). MYCIN, which diagnoses and prescribes treatments for various types of infective meningitis, has been quite extensively used in clinical settings. Its knowledge base of 460 rules allows it to function with some sophistication, but, in contrast to many human physicians, its expertise is confined to one ailment. Accordingly, other expert systems, designed around the MYCIN format and each dedicated to one illness, soon appeared, including CLOT, a small system for diagnosing blood-clotting problems, and ONCOCIN, used for controlling chemotherapy in cancer patients. These purpose-built expert systems can be extremely useful to the specialized consultant, but are of course less helpful to the general hospital practitioner who will routinely encounter and deal with a range of disorders. With this problem in mind, Pople (1982) developed INTERNIST 1, a system which can diagnose up to 600 diseases. INTERNISTS's database includes information about diseases and what are known as their manifestations. The latter include physical symptoms and the results of investigative tests. The program works by linking the likelihood with which certain symptoms define different diseases, and the frequency with which the symptoms occur with a disease. When the physician enters the manifestations for a particular patient, the machine first produces a hypothesis specifying a set of possible diseases. It then compares the evidence for each of the diseases against the manifestations, eventually coming up with one which is best supported by the data. A limitation of INTERNIST 1 is that it only considers one disease at a time rather slavishly before moving on to the next one. This means that it can take up to 20 minutes over a consultation. To get around this problem a further generation of expert systems is being developed, which, like humans, uses heuristics or short cuts to pick the most likely disease, or small set of diseases, to account for a set of manifestations. One of these, CADUCEUS, homes in on likely diseases faster than INTERNIST 1, using a structure which links different sorts of diseases together. Certain key manifestations in the patient's data quickly allow the machine to choose the broad category of disease and then to move into more detailed hypothesis testing within this category.

These examples illustrate the progress that has been made in developing medical expert systems from the first, highly specific systems, through those with more generality, to more recent programs with increased flexibility. This progress looks likely to continue as a result of intensive current research. Three important research issues at present which will benefit future expert system design are: how is knowledge represented by the system, how is new knowledge to be generated from old, and how is the machine to link with its human user? The first two of these issues are related, since the way in which knowledge is represented closely constrains what can be done with it. For instance, knowledge represented in the form of an image can be subjected to inspection, rotation or other spatial transformations, while knowledge in the form of a network can be searched from node to node. At the moment, most contemporary expert systems work with production rules, not unlike those used by ACT* and SOAR, and although these are useful and flexible ways of capturing knowledge, there are suggestions that other representational formats, such as analogical models, would be worth exploring in more detail (Johnson-Laird, 1983).

Work on the interface with the user is also important. Expert systems, by their very nature, are complex and involved, and the more normal or human-like their interaction with their users, the more likely they are to be deployed and accepted. Designing user-friendly interfaces for expert systems is one of the jobs of human factors researchers. These are applied psychologists, often with a background in cognitive psychology, who are interested in human–machine interactions. Recent human factors research suggests that the user interface itself should be intelligent, and should, therefore, be an expert system in its own right, skilled in communication and understanding. As Young (1989) suggests, such 'intelligent front ends' (IFEs) will have to know what the user already knows, and misbelieves, about the topic, what terminology the user understands, what kinds of explanations will be useful and so on. They will, in other words, need a model of the user as well as linking the user with the machine. Just how intelligent and how helpful the IFE must be will depend on the nature of the system and the needs of the user. Young points out that designers of earlier systems such as MYCIN and PROSPECTOR sidestepped the problem of communication and understanding by creating systems which could only be used by people who already knew the technical terms in the area in question. However, he argues that systems designed for a wider usership will have to be more accommodating.

So far we have listed research on characteristics of the expert system itself. A vital prerequisite for getting knowledge into the system is to get it out of the expert! Knowledge elicitation is an important make or break stage in the creation of expert systems. Various knowledge elicitation techniques are now used. Some of these are comparatively informal and resemble interviews between the expert and the knowledge engineer, while others are more tightly structured, and may, for example, involve the expert in ratings or rankings of the importance of various concepts in the domain.

One philosophical difficulty with this area, apart from the methodological problems of particular methods such as protocol analysis which we discussed earlier, is that a singularly inappropriate metaphor is often used to describe the knowledge elicitation process. Knowledge elicitation is often referred to as 'mining' or 'quarrying' knowledge out of the expert, as if knowledge were a substance to be extracted chip by chip. In fact, as Young (1989) again points out, all knowledge elicitation methods require the expert to do something, and the resulting behaviour is then used as evidence to infer what the expert knows. Knowledge is, therefore, to be probed in a sensitive fashion, not mined, and preferably by a variety of different techniques such as examining key problem cases, sorting cards listing issues and concepts in the area, using structured interviews and so on, to reveal different aspects of the knowledge in question.

Another frequent claim made in this field is that the difficulties of knowledge elicitation are the real bottleneck in the creation of expert systems. We agree with Young (1989) here that one of the major difficulties is that the form in which the knowledge will be used or implemented by the computer system is often fixed before the elicitation process ever begins. This means that the expert's knowledge, which may be quite clear when explained to other people, has to be squashed into an often inappropriate format. For instance, an expert might describe a feature of a problem in highly visual and graphic language, perhaps explaining the pumping action of the heart in clear, spatial terms. This implies that imagery is used by at least one expert to think about the issue. However, to get such visual knowledge into the machine, it may then have to be changed into a series of unwieldy procedures. We leave the last word to Young who writes: 'It is hard to believe that this problem will be overcome until a range of varied representation methods is available, so that a representation can be chosen that is suitable for encoding the knowledge, instead of the present Procrustean attempt to force things the other way round' (1989, p. 31).

Conclusions: AI and Cognitive Psychology

Whatever the strengths of its particular simulations, there is no doubt that AI has enriched cognitive psychology. In fact it is unlikely that cognitive psychology would resemble its present-day form but for AI. In this concluding section, we review some of the benefits of AI for cognitive psychology, consider the growth of the new endeavour known as cognitive science and examine some general problems with attempts to model the mind using computers.

Four benefits of AI

The simulation of human cognition on computers and the general approach of AI have several benefits for cognitive psychology. First, together with cognitive psychology, AI offers a common way of understanding all intelligent systems. The assumption behind both AI and cognitive psychology is that minds and artificial intelligence programs are knowledge-based systems which can be understood in functional terms. This has helped liberate psychologists both from the earlier constraints of behaviourism and from the later, though equally rigid, structural accounts of mind.

Second, AI provides a way of modelling or representing the activities of the mind in a formal and well-defined fashion. If human scientists wish to express their theories about the mind in terms of computer programs they are forced to be precise and explicit. Computer simulations act as tests of the coherence or internal consistency of cognitive theories. If the theory contains a contradiction or inconsistency then the program will fail to run properly. Without this safeguard it is too easy and tempting to construct theories which are vague and poorly specified. Broadbent (1987) has developed this argument. He pointed out that experimental techniques in cognitive psychology are now so rigorous that experiments tend to be more replicable than ever before (two experiments performed in the same way are now likely to give identical results), but that the precision with which theoretical concepts are stated has not kept pace with our experimental skills. This means that if an experiment's procedure is altered slightly, our theories are often insufficiently precise to explain the change in behaviour which results. Standard AI modelling techniques are obviously one way of dealing with this problem, but, as Broadbent indicated, large-scale AI models are often too complex to permit clear experimental predictions to be made at the micro level. At the moment, there tends to be a division of labour between the large-scale simulations of language, memory and perception undertaken by AI and the more detailed investigation of component processes examined by cognitive psychology. The answer, he maintained, is to construct small-scale computer models of these more detailed aspects of cognitive processes. By doing this, precision and testability can both be maintained. To illustrate his argument, Broadbent has indicated how small-scale computer models can resolve discrepancies and fill gaps in the experimental literature. For instance, he has shown how just one theoretical model, expressed sufficiently precisely, could be used to explain data from three different experimental situations normally thought to involve distinct types of speeded search, and has also explored, with a small-scale model, the previously uninvestigated issue of the links between the components of working memory.

Third, AI research has offered psychologists a vast range of new concepts and ways of thinking about mind. Here, for example, are just some of the technical terms now used in cognitive psychology which come directly from or have been inspired by work on computer simulation: code; motor program; procedure; symbolic representation; network; database; array; indexing; addressing; storage buffer; flow diagram; control system; search process; modularity; subroutine; contention scheduling; register; parser. The development of such a technical vocabulary has made it far easier for cognitive psychologists, as well as for AI researchers, to think and communicate about mental life. The language of information processing would not be so well developed were it not for computing and AI. Technical vocabularies can however have drawbacks. They can lead the unwary to assume that because there is a handy label for a concept, everything is clear and understood. Also, because researchers, after a time, tend to think about and phrase their theories using these terms, it can become difficult for them to describe their interests in any other way. They can become trapped within a paradigm or way of looking at things partly because of the words they are using. As we shall see in chapter 13, there may be a powerful alternative to the standard information-processing view which may not be immediately obvious to someone steeped in computer jargon.

Fourth, AI provides specific models of mental processes which can then be tested using standard experimental techniques. Several examples of this have been noted in the previous section and in other places in this book. In some cases, the original computer simulation has proved to be a remarkably good predictor of how people behave (Bower et al., 1979). In others, however, human and computer performances diverge. Computer simulations of semantic memory (e.g. Collins and Quillian, 1969) do not always perform in the same way as people. But whether the simulations are eventually borne out by the data or not, clear testable predictions can often be derived from AI models and this is one of the hallmarks of good science.

To sum up, artificial intelligence can be considered as a major branch of theoretical psychology, since it provides a powerful general framework, useful concepts, technical terms and specific models where none existed before. It also affords a rigorous testing ground for theories developed in cognitive psychology, at the micro and macro levels, as well as offering ready-made models which can be checked against behavioural data. It has, on the whole, demystified mind and through the language of information processing has allowed progress to be made on problems that have puzzled humankind for centuries.

Cognitive science

In the past few years the contact between AI and cognitive psychology has become even closer with the growth of a new approach known as cognitive science. Cognitive science is an interdisciplinary enterprise consisting of work in cognitive psychology, AI, linguistics, brain science and the philosophy of mind. It has become clear of late that all these disciplines are concerned with different but overlapping aspects of mental life. Although it is slightly unfair to single out any from this family for special mention, it is probably true that cognitive psychology and AI form the core of cognitive science. This is because AI and cognitive psychology support and complement each other so well. Both are sources of theories about mental function, and whereas, as we pointed out above, AI tests the coherence of psychological theories, cognitive psychology checks their correspondence with reality.

To some extent, cognitive science is as old as cognitive psychology and AI, and could be said to have emerged in the 1950s, but it is only recently that the term cognitive science has become fashionable. Does this new term matter or is this a case of old wine in new bottles? There are indications that the new label is changing things. For a start, its use has furthered work in cognitive science in its own right, rather than as something which emerges piecemeal across different disciplines. Previously, research on aspects of mental life might be carried out independently in separate university and college departments of psychology, computer science and linguistics. Now, there is much more obvious interdepartmental cooperation so that the same problems are not only being jointly tackled from different perspectives, but the people doing the research are now working with each other and publishing together in the new cognitive science journals. Developments like these at the research level have had a number of wider academic and professional spin-offs. The 1980s have witnessed the growth of new courses in cognitive science designed to inform the next generation of scientists of the most up-to-date advances. These courses, and the opportunities afforded by certain university reorganizations, have in turn led to the creation of new departments specifically devoted to cognitive science. Large computer firms are also now funding cognitive science research.

On the whole, these developments have strengthened cognitive science's two core areas, though as we explain below, there are some reservations among cognitive psychologists that a biased picture of human nature may emerge if the pure cognitive science approach is unchecked by biological, ecological and other considerations. This aside, concepts from cognitive science are now affecting practically all areas of research on human cognition, including those such as attention, consciousness and awareness, which previously have been relatively unaffected (Hampson, 1989), and the profile of both cognitive psychology and AI is probably higher now than at any time in the past 20 years.

Problems with AI and cognitive science

Despite these important developments, there are some problems with the approach of AI in particular and cognitive science in general and we could be accused of presenting too rosy a picture if we did not at least mention these. Several commentators have criticized cognitive science, some claiming that it offers too restricted a view (e.g. Norman, 1981), others that it fails to provide any real explanation of the fundamental issues in psychology (e.g. Skinner, 1985).

There are indeed difficulties with the range and nature of explanations furnished by cognitive science, some of which are quite serious. Several of the issues for cognitive science enumerated by Norman (1981), for instance, still pose problems for the discipline. Take, as an example, his first issue, the relationship between knowledge and belief. Cognitive science could be defined as the study of the representation and use of knowledge by intelligent systems, but humans also possess beliefs acquired over a lifetime's experience. These beliefs, about themselves, the world around them, and each other, affect people's interactions with their surroundings often more powerfully than knowledge. Someone may know, intellectually, that there is little truth in the notion that different nationalities have characteristic personalities, but may still believe and treat Italians as if they were all irascible, impulsive and highly emotional. Some beliefs, of course, are grounded in scientifically testable knowledge, but many others depend on shared social and cultural assumptions. Members of one political party often believe members of all others to be either knaves or fools, and political leaders, in times of war, generally manage to convince their own citizens that their country is in the right. Cognitive science may have to broaden its scope and learn from sociologists and anthropologists if it is to paint a coherent picture of natural information processing sufficiently wide to encompass beliefs.

Or take the second of Norman's (1981) issues, consciousness. It is often argued that cognitive science has not really grasped the nettle of consciousness. One could be forgiven for thinking that the ideal organism, as far as cognitive science is concerned, processes information non-consciously and automatically. Consciousness raises issues of personal experience, intentionality and subjectivity, as well as cognitive control, which go far beyond many of our current cognitive models. Current AI programs lack intentionality and anything resembling a subjective state. At present, what they do is relevant only to their creator and users.

A third set of problems, isolated by Norman (1981), involves development and learning or, more generally, the study of changing systems. More often than not, AI researchers have tried to model stable, adult, cognitive systems. The fact that cognition develops and changes has received less attention, though, as we shall see in chapter 13, there are signs that this is now changing in other areas of cognitive science.

There has also been a tendency to study what Norman (1981) calls the pure cognitive system and for researchers to assume that its operations are both of the highest importance to the organism and are uncontaminated by emotion or motivation. Hence, a fifth issue for Norman is that more consideration should be given to emotion and its relation with cognition. Once again, there are now signs that this is happening, though many studies still examine the effect of emotion on cognition, rather than the reverse, and treat emotion as if it were some form of unwanted noise or contaminant in an otherwise pure system. Common experience suggests that the primary function of certain thought patterns may actually be to produce or sustain certain emotional states, and that these cognitions are further reinforced by the resulting emotion (Martin and Williams, 1990). Cognition may, at times, be less important, or primary, than the emotional and ultimately biological states which it serves.

Finally, as Norman (1981) points out, people interact with each other and with their surroundings and transmit knowledge through cultures. Interactions depend on the person having an appropriate model or representation of the system with which they are interacting. Such models and their social transmission have, according to Norman, received inadequate attention by cognitive science. The situation has changed somewhat since Norman wrote his article. For instance, as we stated earlier, the study of dialogue and other interactions now occupies a central position in language computation. Also, work in human–computer interaction is examining this issue to some extent. Nevertheless, as a general rule, cognitive science has concerned itself with the individual in isolation, not in interaction.

We see this problem as part of a deeper issue affecting cognitive science. There has lately been a growing, healthy trend in cognitive psychology to examine human cognition in its natural, everyday or 'ecological' setting (see chapter 7, also Neisser, 1976; Harris and Morris, 1984; Neisser and Winograd, 1988). This has had several important effects. Cognitive psychologists are now more likely to consider the ecological nature of the information which people process, as well as the information-processing mechanisms themselves. They are more likely to view cognition in a more dynamic, interactive fashion than previously. They are more aware of the wider evolutionary significance of cognitive processes. Areas affected by the ecological approach include perception, memory, language and attention, and not only have new phenomena been discovered, but broader theoretical perspectives have been realized. Cognitive science has yet to heed fully the lessons learned from the everyday approach, but it will need to do so if these simulations of intelligence are to become more natural and less artificial.

These difficulties apart, we are more optimistic about the future of cognitive science than some commentators, since we know, from talking to our colleagues, that cognitive psychologists at least are alert to all these issues. Moreover, as long as cognitive psychology still continues to maintain its influence within cognitive science, it will not be possible for cognitive science to retreat into a remote rationalism. To remain strong and influential, cognitive psychology should not, in our opinion, restrict its research to a small set of problems dictated by what are often short-term, technological interests, but should maintain its broad commitment to the study of human cognition across as wide a range of situations as possible. Otherwise, artificial intelligence will no longer effectively model natural man and will become weaker and more sterile as a result.

Further reading

A good, recent introduction to various aspects of artificial intelligence including further guidance on the AI literature can be found in A. Garnham 1988: *Artificial Intelligence*. London: Routledge; see also, M. Boden 1988: *Artificial Intelligence and Natural Man*. Sussex: Harvester. Readers interested in some of the general programming techniques used in AI might like to consult A. Bundy (ed.) 1978: *Artificial Intelligence: An Introductory Course*. Edinburgh: Edinburgh University Press; or P.H. Winston and B.K.P. Horn 1984: *LISP*, 2nd edn. Reading, Mass: Addison-Wesley for details of the LISP programming language. However, probably the most readable summary of recent AI and cognitive science is to be found in P.N. Johnson-Laird 1993: *The Computer and the Mind*. London: Fontana.

Discussion points

I   Psychology, like other sciences, makes extensive use of models in its theories and explanations. Does psychology always have to wait for advances in technology for new models of man? Would cognitive psychology have emerged if computers had not been invented?

2   Can machines think?

3   Will it ever be possible to simulate creativity on a computer?

4   Discuss the general problems involved in designing a machine that could play golf.

5   Was it a mistake to design programs which dealt with simplified environments like the BLOCKSWORLD or which, in general, only accepted simplified input?

Practical exercises

1   Find an example of a simple and a more complex (cryptic) crossword. Attempt to solve them. While doing so, think aloud and tape record your protocol. Play back the account of your solutions and try to note the major steps in working out the clues. How much can you learn about the mental processes in crossword solving from protocol analysis alone? For which task does protocol analysis appear to be the most revealing, the simple or complex crossword?

2   Three missionaries and three cannibals are standing at the side of a river together with a canoe with which they are attempting to cross. The canoe can only hold two people at a time, but must contain at least one person. If the cannibals on either bank outnumber the missionaries they will devour them. What is the most efficient way of getting everyone safely across the river?

This is a classic problem set for early AI programs. First of all, solve this problem yourself and note the major steps involved. Next, try to work out the space of all possible moves (some of which will lead to incorrect solutions) and having done so, work out ways in which a computer might search through the solution space to find the correct answer. Hint: think of the search space as a tree with alternative branches for each move.

3   Construct a short questionnaire consisting of several straightforward questions to sample public opinion as to the scope and nature of current AI programs. Try to avoid too many general questions such as whether computers can recognize everyday objects or whether computers understand language and so on. If possible, give out your questionnaire to at least two groups of people from different walks of life such as school-teachers, students, computer programmers, musicians, members of the clergy, shopkeepers, old people or young people. How well informed are most people regarding AI? Do people think computers can do more or less than they actually do?

Box 11.1
A general architecture for cognition

The working assumption behind the SOAR project is that tasks as diverse as playing simple games on the one hand and medical diagnoses on the other can be performed by one common cognitive system, using essentially the same methods of learning and problem solving. The aim is to create such a general architecture and to test its performance on as many problems as possible. SOAR 4, outlined by Laird et al. (1987), is an intermediate stage of the project, but was deemed sufficiently powerful by its authors to be introduced to a wider audience.

SOAR is a part of a long tradition of similar work in AI which has tried to create common architectures. In 1956, this work began with a program known as the Logic Theorist. Later, Newell and colleagues created the General

Problem Solver (GPS), which was moderately successful on certain problems, but unwieldy to use. Subsequent work on production systems also forms part of SOAR's ancestry, and has strongly influenced its shape. More recently, the series of programs leading up to ACT* (see text) have family resemblances to SOAR.

Here, following Laird et al., we briefly sketch SOAR's basic architecture, give some indication of the tasks to which it has been applied and draw attention to one of its important characteristics: its ability to learn from experience. We conclude with a brief comment on SOAR's limitations as a simulation of human cognition.

The architecture

The major components of SOAR are shown in box figure 11.1.1. As in ACT*, there is an important distinction between the production and working memories. Production memory embodies the procedures which SOAR uses to solve its problems by operating on representations (objects) in working memory and those procedures which it creates during the solution process. (Unlike ACT*, SOAR's long-term memory does not have a separate declarative component, though declarative-type representations can be formed within the production system.) Working memory holds the complete state that processing has reached on a particular problem, is operated on by the production memory, and feeds some of its results back to production memory.

A key feature of SOAR is that it is a tailor-made, problem-solving architecture, not merely a system for manipulating symbols. In practice this means that all the tasks which it performs are represented as problem spaces, and are solved by application of search procedures to attain the desired goal state. Problem spaces may already exist, and if so they are retrieved directly from production memory, or they may need to be created as required. To move through these spaces, working memory contains, at

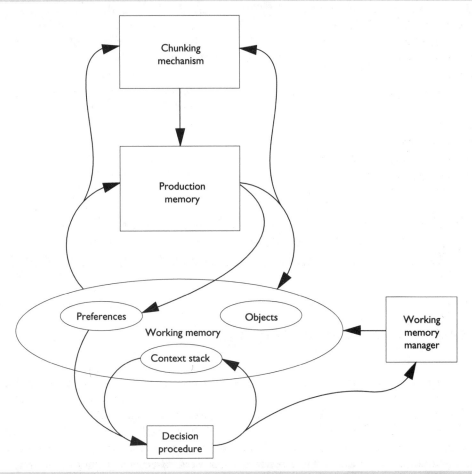

Box figure 11.1.1   The major components of SOAR. (Based on figure 5, Laird et al., 1987)

any given time, the following: a set of objects, consisting of the goals, subgoals and states of the problem; the context stack, which is a hierarchial ordering of these same goals, states, procedures and problem spaces; and a set of preferences for what to do next.

The other major systems components are: the decision procedure, which examines the preferences and goal hierarchy in working memory; the working memory manager, which as its name suggests oversees the operations of the working memory, by regulating its internal workings and its interactions with the decision procedure; and the production memory and the chunking mechanism, whose important role in learning is outlined below.

SOAR solutions proceed by moving from the initial state of the problem, through subgoals to the solution. This simple statement masks a complex set of operations, which fall into two major categories: task implementation and search control. Briefly, task implementation refers to the generation or retrieval of problem spaces, states of the problem, and ways of moving from one state to the next, while search control refers to the selection of problem spaces, states and operators. The key to SOAR's success lies in the efficient interaction of task-implementation and search-control aspects of the problem.

Applications of SOAR

Since its inception, SOAR has been applied across a range of tasks. Some idea of this range can be gathered from the list below (based on figure 1, Laird et al., 1987). The list shows the major categories of tasks to which SOAR has been exposed and gives instances of each category on which SOAR has performed satisfactorily. These range from typical AI tasks of the so-called knowledge-lean variety to high-level knowledge-intensive simulations of other expert systems, as well as various sorts of learning effects. This broad scope is very impressive.

Small, knowledge-lean tasks: Blocks world, Eight puzzle, eight queens, labelling line drawings, magic squares, missionaries and cannibals, monkey and bananas, picnic problem, robot location finding, three wizards problem, tic-tac-toe, Tower of Hanoi, water jug task.

Small, routine tasks: Expression unification, root finding, sequence extrapolation, syllogisms, Wason verification task.

Knowledge-intensive expert system tasks: RI-SOAR: Industrial expert system (25% simulated); NEOMYCIN: Revision of MYCIN.

Miscellaneous AI tasks: DYPAR-SOAR: Natural language parsing;
Version spaces: Concept formation;
Resolution theorem prover.

Search techniques and other AI methods: Generate and test, AND/OR search, hill climbing, means–ends analysis, operator subgoaling, hypothesize and match, breadth-first search, depth-first search, heuristic search, best-first search, A*, progressive deepening, B* (progressive depending), minimax, alpha-beta, iterative deepening, B*.

Types of learning: From a detailed examination on Eight puzzle, RI-SOAR, tic-tac-toe and Korf's macro-operators, SOAR demonstrates: Improvement with practice, within-task transfer, across-task transfer, strategy acquisition, operator implementation, macro operators, explanation-based generalization.

There are a number of tasks which SOAR could not do at the time that Laird et al. wrote their article. These include deliberate planning, the automatic acquisition of new tasks (learning what to do, as well as how to do it), creating new representations of tasks, dealing with other types of learning (by reading or instruction etc.), recovering from serious errors and interacting with the external environment of the task. However, as Laird et al. point out, the reason for drawing attention to these is 'not just to indicate the present limitations on SOAR, but to establish the intended scope of the system. SOAR is to operate through the entire spectrum of cognitive tasks' (1987, p. 4), and work is continuing on several of these 'limitations' at present.

Learning in SOAR

SOAR's power, as we stated earlier, lies in the fact that it can learn as well as solve problems. It does this by using a method known as chunking which resembles the human skill in some respects at least. Chunking, in general terms, involves organizing together several small pieces of information and replacing them with a more economical piece. So, when humans remember information, they frequently group, or 'chunk', units together rather than spelling everything out. Thus 'the seasons' stands for 'spring, summer, autumn and winter' and telephone numbers are remembered as groups of digits such 025 804 411 rather than 025804411.

In SOAR, chunking occurs when a successful decision has been made between several possible moves from a particular problem position. Instead of working through and selecting between the moves each time it solves the problem, if SOAR's chunking mechanism is turned on, the system remembers which is the best move to make at a particular impasse and stores this as a new procedure for use in the future.

Comments

SOAR's performance is very impressive but it has not yet been completely fleshed out as a full cognitive theory, in the way that, say, ACT* has been. At present its status is really that of a good piece of pure AI. It still needs, for example, to be evaluated against a wide set of behavioural data and, if possible, its performance to be contrasted with other similar models. One notable aspect of SOAR is that it 'thinks' using only one type of symbolic representation, its object structures, unlike the propositions, images and strings of ACT*. There are reasons to believe, from other areas of cognitive psychology, that humans use a variety of representational types too. By its use of one representation, SOAR might, therefore, be too limited to be a full simulation of human thinking. Another aspect of SOAR which allows it to perform efficiently, but which may not resemble human cognition, is its undifferentiated long-term memory. Moreover, as we mentioned earlier, there is still a range of tasks which SOAR cannot do, though this is being treated as an indication of what remains to be done rather than as an inherent limitation of the system.

Based on J.L. Laird, A. Newell and P.S. Rosenbloom 1987: SOAR: An architecture for general intelligence. *Artificial Intelligence*, 33, 1–64.

Box 11.2
An example of an expert system: PROSPECTOR in action

During the past few years, there has been increasing interest in the idea that computers can perform in the role of a human expert, highly skilled in a particular area and capable of answering complex questions on the domain in question.

In this box, we outline the capabilities and characteristics of one such expert, knowledge-based system, PROSPEC-TOR. This is a classic example of an expert system developed over the period 1974–83 at the Stanford Research Institute and designed to help exploration geologists in their search for ore deposits. PROSPECTOR illustrates some of the key features, strengths and limitations of a typical expert system.

What does PROSPECTOR do?
The basic abilities of PROSPECTOR are as follows:

1   It interacts with geology experts using terms with which the expert is familiar.
2   It then selects a hypothesis about ore deposits and, by asking the user further questions, tries to prove or disprove the hypothesis.
3   It permits the user to offer more information at any time during the session.
4   It is able to reword questions if the user fails to understand them.
5   It abandons hypotheses and chooses new ones when relevant evidence is supplied by the user.

6   It can explain why it needs a particular question to be answered.
7   It looks for and points out inconsistencies in the user's answers and allows the user to alter them.
8   It presents its conclusions together with its reasons for drawing them.

Some of these skills are illustrated in the following excerpts from an interaction between a user and PROS-PECTOR. PROSPECTOR's responses are in capital letters. At the beginning of the interaction, PROSPECTOR is taking in information about different forms of rocks and assigning the information a certainty value, on a scale from –5 to +5.

1   . . .
2   There is probably syendiorite
     SYENDIORITE 3
     . . .
     . . .
4   There might be some quartz monzonite
     QUARTZ MONZONITE 2
     . . .
     . . .
13   Done

This ends the first phase of data input. PROSPECTOR then forms a first hypothesis.

I AM CONSIDERING THE POSSIBILITY OF A KUROKO-TYPE MASSIVE SULPHIDE DEPOSIT IN THE TARGET AREA.

...

...

Later in the sequence, the user responds with a negative rating (–5) to a question that is crucial to this hypothesis.

16 TO WHAT DEGREE DO YOU BELIEVE THAT: (GALENA, SHALERITE, OR CHALCOPYRITE FILLED CRACKS IN RHILOTE OR DACTITE OR ANDESITE)?
    –5

This causes PROSPECTOR to abandon the first hypothesis and to select an alternative:

I AM CONSIDERING THE POSSIBILITY OF A TYPE-A PORPHYRY COPPER DEPOSIT IN THE TARGET AREA

...

...

28 TO WHAT DEGREE DO YOU BELIEVE THAT: (THERE ARE VOLCANIC ROCKS IN THE REGION CONTEMPORANEOUS WITH THE INTRUSIVE SYSTEM, I.E. COEVAL VOLCANIC ROCKS)?
    Why?

The user here wants more information. PROSPECTOR replies:

I AM TRYING TO ESTABLISH THE DEPTH ENVIRONMENT IN YOUR AREA. THE PRESENCE OF COEVAL VOLCANIC ROCKS IS GOOD EVIDENCE FOR THE RIGHT LEVEL OF EXPOSURE. THE TARGET WOULD LIE BELOW THE LEVEL OF (AT A GREATER DEPTH THAN) A COEVAL VOLCANIC PILE.

...

...

An inconsistency is later detected and clarified:

32 TO WHAT DEGREE DO YOU BELIEVE THAT: (THERE IS A QUARTZ-MONZONITE IN THE INTRUSIVE SYSTEM)?
    4
THIS ANSWER SEEMS TO BE INCONSISTENT WITH YOUR PREVIOUS ANSWERS TO THE FOLLOWING QUESTIONS:
4 QUARTZ-MONZONITE 2
DO YOU WANT TO CHANGE YOUR ANSWER TO QUESTION 32
    No

Finally, after asking several more questions PROSPECTOR eventually concludes, with certainty of 1.683 on a scale from –5 to +5, that there is evidence of porphyry copper deposits and provides, in detail if required, its reasons for doing so.

How does PROSPECTOR work?

Essentially, PROSPECTOR uses rules which link evidence (E) provided by the user with hypotheses (H) in the form of if ... then statements, expressed by terms of their certainty (LS, LN):

If E then H to degree, LS, LN

LS indicates how encouraging it is to find the evidence present, and LN how discouraging it is to find it absent. Various logical combinations of evidence can also be handled, such as

If E1 and E2 then H1
If E3 or E4 then H2

Hypotheses can, in turn, imply further hypotheses:

If H1 then H2 (LS1, LN1)

All the evidence and the hypotheses are thus interconnected in a large network known as the inference net. The certainty values, LS and LN, for the linking rules were built into the system when it was constructed, but the probabilities for the evidence and the hypotheses themselves are supplied and revised as the user interacts with the system, as we illustrated in the transcript. The fact that these probabilities can be changed allows PROSPECTOR to build up support or refutation for selected hypotheses. Thus, consider the following rules which are all assumed to have high linking probabilities (LS):

1 If E1 then H1
2 If E2 then H2
3 If H1 then H3
4 If H2 then H4
5 If E3 then H4

Suppose the likelihood that E1 is present is high and that E2 is present is low; PROSPECTOR will then assign a correspondingly high probability to H1 and a low probability to H2 (rules 1 and 2). These probabilities will then be automatically propagated up through the system and will result in H3 having a high probability and being selected as the current working hypothesis, while H4 is rejected (rules 3 and 4). If, however, the probabilities of E1 and E2 are reversed, so that E1 now is very unlikely and E2 very likely, the system will automatically reject H3 and select H4. In the actual system, the chains of evidence and hypotheses are longer than this simple example, but the idea of probability propagation is the same. Since the system is moving from the 'if' to the 'then' parts of the rules as it does this, the process is referred to as forward chaining.

Propagation and hypothesis selection obviously depend on new information coming into the system from the user. So, to get the system moving, PROSPECTOR must ask the user appropriate questions. It does this by inspecting the rules that support the current hypothesis and by asking the questions which have the most chance of changing the probability associated with the hypothesis. To illustrate this: suppose the current hypothesis is H4. In the above rules, H4 is suggested by H2 (rule 4) and by E3 (rule 5). PROSPECTOR examines both rules 4 and 5 to see whether knowledge of H2 or E3 would most affect H4, that is, make it more or less likely. If it turns out that E3 provides more information, then a direct question is asked about the particular piece of evidence, specified by E3. If, on the other hand, H2 proves to be more informative, then this is treated as a subsidiary hypothesis and the system back-tracks to find the question which when answered would most alter the probability of H2. The question selection mechanism, therefore, works backwards through the rules, and so is said to engage in backward chaining.

To sum up, the system as a whole works by an integrated network of rules, forward-chained probability propagation and backward-chained question selection.

How successful is PROSPECTOR?

As a working system, PROSPECTOR is extremely successful. Waterman points out that it demonstrates how rule and network knowledge-based systems can be combined to provide a powerful inference system. In addition, PROS-PECTOR was tested by analysing information from sites where there were already known to be certain mineral deposits, and proved to be highly accurate in predicting their location. A more impressive test, however, was carried out in 1980 when PROSPECTOR predicted the existence of molybdenum at a previously partially explored location. A mining company then drilled and found molybdenum in the specific places where PROSPECTOR had said that it would be found, and no molybdenum in those locations where PROSPECTOR claimed that it would not be found. As Waterman concludes: 'one could hardly ask for a better confirmation of the system's expertise' (1987, p. 58).

As a psychological model, PROSPECTOR is far less impressive. It is, of course, an interesting demonstration that a network of procedures could be used to support hypothesis testing, but it seems most unlikely that all human cognition uses such a representational system. More fatally, however, the system is limited by its initial scientific knowledge. The crucial probabilities linking the components of the rules are programmed in from the start. Human experts would easily adjust these probabilities as new discoveries are made by the science of geology. The only way to change PROSPECTOR'S scientific knowledge is to reprogram it. It is also interesting to compare PROSPEC-TOR with SOAR, see box 11.1. SOAR is intended to become a fully developed cognitive theory, though it does not yet have that status, and, as we saw, SOAR can not only simulate a range of cognitive tasks, but can also mimic the performance of several expert systems too. On a continuum stretching from pure AI, designed to produce immediate technological benefits, to more exploratory simulations, designed to advance our general knowledge of computation and cognition, PROSPECTOR is close to pure AI, while SOAR is a classic, cognitive science simulation.

Based on D.A. Waterman 1986: *A Guide to Expert Systems*, ch. 6. Reading, Mass: Addison-Wesley.

12 Cognitive Neuropsychology

A patient is introduced to a doctor. The doctor leaves the room and returns five minutes later. The patient then has to be reintroduced. He has forgotten who the doctor is. A keen musician, the same patient is taken to King's College Cambridge, where he conducts the choir with verve and great skill. Later, when shown a video tape of the episode, not only has he no conscious recollection of the event but he claims to have no musical skill at all and thinks he was hypnotized at the time.

A woman has lost all sensation of touch and pain down the right side of her body. Her problems are so severe that she frequently cuts or burns herself on that side without noticing that she has done so. She is blindfolded and her right arm is lightly pressed. Still denying that she is able to feel anything, the woman indicates accurately where her arm was touched.

A man retires to bed after an exhausting business trip. When he wakes up, everyday objects look unfamiliar. He thinks that a picture on the wall is a box and searches in it for missing things. He mistakes his jacket for a pair of trousers and fails to recognize the cutlery on the table. His normal surroundings appear strange and peculiar.

These people have all suffered some form of brain damage and are having to deal with its mental consequences. The brain is the organ of the mind and, like any other organ of the body, when its physical structure is damaged its function suffers too. How then are we to explain, or model, the mental changes which follow brain injury?

An exciting, and rapidly developing new branch of cognitive psychology, cognitive neuropsychology, is now trying to find out. Cognitive neuropsychology uses standard explanations of cognition to account for the mental activity and behaviour of brain-injured people. Many psychologists are now convinced that these explanations, formed originally by studying normal, healthy people, can be applied more widely and can be used successfully to account for cognitive impairment. After all, a person who takes his car to a garage because of a knocking engine expects the mechanic to use her knowledge of the workings of a normal, 'healthy' engine to understand what has gone wrong. The good mechanic does not need two theories, one for knocking engines and the other for normal ones! Brains and minds are far more complicated than car engines and the injured brain may behave in unexpected ways, but the same principle should apply. An understanding of normal performance should shed light on the abnormal.

As well as studying the impaired abilities of brain-injured patients, cognitive neuropsychologists also examine what the brain-injured are still able to do. Once again, they use normal cognitive theories and models to do this. Understanding normal cognition thus helps us to explain what brain-injured patients fail to do but also accounts for what they are still able to do.

Cognitive neuropsychology has a further benefit. By examining the brain-injured, it exposes standard theories to a wider range of data, and explores them more fully. This often shows up problems in the original theory which might not have been discovered simply from testing normal, healthy volunteers. The study of the brain-injured can thus increase our knowledge of normal as well as abnormal cognition.

These aims of cognitive neuropsychology have been clearly stated by Ellis and Young (1988). The first aim is 'to explain the patterns of impaired and intact cognitive performance seen in brain-injured patients in terms of damage to one or more of the components of a theory or model of normal cognitive functioning' (1988, p. 4). The second aim is 'to draw conclusions about normal, intact cognitive processes from the patterns of intact and impaired capabilities seen in brain-injured patients' (ibid.).

Like artificial intelligence, cognitive neuropsychology involves modelling cognition. However, it is also an empirical area, which means that it deals with data, not just theories. By constantly shuttling back and forth between brain damage and its resulting mental impairment, cognitive neuropsychology reminds us that cognitive processes depend on brain activity and are severely constrained by it. If a cognitive model does not cope properly with what real people with real brains, damaged or undamaged, can do, then such a model must be wrong or incomplete. This brings cognitive psychology right down to earth and prevents models being suggested which are neurologically implausible or just plain silly, a danger from which pure artificial intelligence and mainstream cognitive psychology are not so well protected.

In this chapter we will discuss the methods, techniques and research style of cognitive neuropsychology, provide some examples of the approach in action and finish by examining its broader implications and future prospects.

Methods and Techniques in Cognitive Neuropsychology

Cognitive neuropsychology uses accounts of normal cognition to explain mental activity following brain damage. This means that the cognitive neuropsychologist needs a working account of the relationship between the mind and the brain, some way of describing cognitive models in general, and some way of using cognitive models to explain what can go wrong as a result of brain injury. We will discuss all of these in this section and end with a brief comment on the distinctive research style of cognitive neuropsychology.

Mind and brain

The mind–brain problem has, of course, kept generations of philosophers busy. We do not want to get involved in the details of this philosophical debate here; instead we will state what we believe are three fairly simple but important assumptions about the mind–brain relationship which guide contemporary cognitive neuropsychology.

First of all it is taken for granted that the living brain is essential for mental activity. 'No brain, no mind' is a succinct way of putting this. Second, the brain is assumed to be a complex system consisting of many interacting parts. Third, different areas of the brain are thought to be responsible for different aspects of mental activity, but no single localized area of the brain is thought to support a whole cognitive function such as language, memory or perception.

Assuming the reader agrees with the first assumption we can now discuss the others in more detail. Studies of the intact and damaged brain show that the brain is composed of different interconnected parts and regions which have different jobs to do. Over many years, neuroanatomists, neurophysiologists and traditional neuropsychologists have tried to work out what these various parts are and what functions they serve. The cortex, or outermost part of the brain, for instance, seems to be heavily involved in many cognitive activities, with some specialization of function between its left and right halves, though other deeper areas of the brain are responsible for these too. The cortex has been divided into four main areas or lobes (see figure 12.1). These are the frontal, temporal, parietal and occipital lobes. Another important area, the motor cortex, runs just in front of the major fold or the Rolandic fissure.

At a gross level, some fairly simple statements can be made about the effects of damage to these different brain areas. For instance, damage to an area known as the pre-frontal, motor cortex, or Broca's area, can cause severe problems with speech, while injury to the temporal lobes often severely disrupts memory. Blindness may follow extensive damage of the occipital areas, and the ability to think, to plan, or to deal with new tasks can be hampered by frontal lobe injury. These facts led some of the first neuropsychologists to believe that entire cognitive functions were to be found in quite distinct and small regions of the brain. According to this view, language, memory, vision, thinking and other mental faculties are

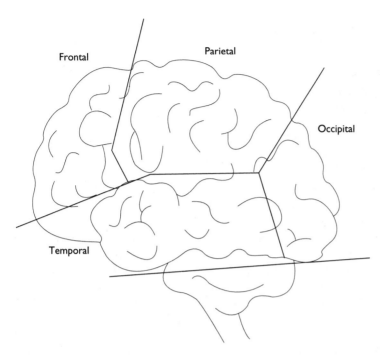

Figure 12.1   The four lobes of the human cerebral cortex seen from the left

each located in separate brain areas. This strict 'localization' view of mind was carried to an extreme by the phrenologists in the nineteenth century who even suggested that one special part of the brain was needed for doing business and another for dealing with domestic issues! Phrenologists produced detailed charts, based on bumps on the head, to indicate which of a person's brain regions, and hence mental faculties, were well developed.

Reasons why this view is almost certainly wrong, or at least far too simple, are now clear. To begin with, the brain is not merely a set of separate parts. It is a complex, functional system. To understand what this means, consider a car engine again. Imagine that an engine is stripped down and all its separate pieces are spread out on a garage floor. It would be extremely difficult for someone who has never encountered an engine before to discover what each part does in the engine as a whole merely by examining it in isolation. The way in which the parts interact dynamically reveals the principles of internal combustion. Similarly, it is the way the parts of the brain cooperate and work together which allows mental activity to take place.

A second reason why strict localization of entire functions is wrong is that unless brain damage is massive, entire cognitive functions are rarely lost completely. Usually brain damage affects aspects or parts of cognitive functions, not the functions as a whole. Also, in certain cases, there is an unexpected relationship between the amount of neural tissue supporting cognitive abilities. People with quite thin cortices, relative to the rest of the population, have been discovered who have no intellectual impairment, and in certain brain operations, removal of more cortical tissue can sometimes lead to less, not more, functional impairment.

A radical alternative to localization is the idea that distinct regions of the brain do not have different jobs to do at all, but that various amounts of brain tissue are needed for different cognitive activities. Lashley (1951), who popularized this 'equipotentiality' view, claimed that behaviour was disrupted to a great or lesser extent by the quantity, not the type, of tissue removed from an animal's brain. The view of the brain as a complex functional system shows why this cannot be correct either. Various parts of the brain have different architectures, or structures, indicating that they do have different jobs to do. Electrophysiological and other direct brain-imaging techniques such as Magnetic Resonance Imaging (MRI) and Positron Emission Tomography (PET scans) show that different regions are active during different mental activities and brain damage to specific areas does have quite specific cognitive effects. On the whole, evidence suggests that different parts of the brain do different things.

A happy medium between the two extremes of localization and equipotentiality is the notion that parts or subcomponents of cognitive activities are localized in the brain. To understand more fully what is implied by the term 'subcomponents' it helps to consider what is meant by models of the mind.

Models of the mind

In the course of this book we have introduced several theories and models of mental processes. These often apply to quite small and detailed aspects of cognition, and, as Eysenck (1984) has stated, seem to multiply like rabbits in a hutch. What, if anything, do all these models have in common?

One common property might be that models of the mind represent the arrangement of mental structures or processing components needed to perceive, speak, think or remember. The view that memory can be divided into distinct stores used for short- and long-term remembering is a good example of this approach (see chapter 2 for details). The structural view of mind suggests an interesting possibility as far as brain injury is concerned. Perhaps individual processing components or structures depend on specific brain areas and can therefore be separately damaged. As we shall see later, the fact that some patients can be found with long-term memory difficulties and others with impairments of immediate memory was once thought to support the structural view of memory, though it challenged certain aspects of it as well.

A different view, to which many psychologists now subscribe, is that cognitive psychology should account for the activities of thinking, perceiving, speaking, acting and remembering, not the underlying structures which support them. Cognitive activities, such as reading or remembering, are then assumed to involve several interacting but potentially independent processes. Reading, for example, requires processes for letter analysis, word identification, grammatical analysis, comprehension and so on. According to this approach, models of the mind should refer to mental processes, not mental structures, and the task of the cognitive psychologist (and neuro-psychologist) is to work out how such mental processes work and how they are organized.

One theory of the mental organization of processes, expressed strongly by Fodor (1983) but also by Marr (1982), is that mental processes are arranged into independent, but interacting modules. Everyday examples of modular systems include kitchens containing fitted units, the courses which make up Open University degrees, and hi-fi rack systems. The parts of a modular system all fit and work neatly together, but they can work independently, and can often be separated out without damage to the rest of the system.

Modular systems are easy to sort out when they are damaged, but more important still, they continue working, after a fashion, even when one of their modules is badly damaged. This has clear survival value. The man who could not recognize everyday objects could still see that something was there. The woman who could not feel down her right side could still feel on the left. Another important property is that single modules can be improved without needing to improve all the others. If you want a better amplifier for your rack system you can unplug the old and put in a new one. People cannot unplug bits of their minds, but they may be able to improve the operation of their cognitive modules by practice or even acquire new ones, such as when they learn to read or write. For these reasons, evolution may well favour modular designs.

The modularity idea interests many cognitive neuropsychologists. Combined with a functional approach to the brain's workings, it can neatly explain cognitive impairment. All we need to do is to assume that processing modules, not entire cognitive activities, are located in particular brain areas. Damage to these brain areas will then result in disruption of the modules they support. Moreover, because only some modules, not all, are damaged by brain injury, it is possible to work out what is impaired as well as what is unimpaired by a suitable selection of tasks which tap the modules in question. Ellis and Young (1988) use the rack system analogy to illustrate this in more detail. Modern hi-fi systems are highly modular in that their components such as the tape deck, record player, amplifier, speakers and headphones can be plugged in and unplugged as required. If, as they put it, 'the record you are playing sounds dreadful, you can decide whether the fault lies in the deck, amplifier or speakers by trying a cassette, listening through headphones instead of through speakers and so on' (1988, p. 11).

Another and in some ways better example of a simple modular system would be a robot in a car assembly plant able to sense and operate on various car components. Such a device is likely to have separate modules concerned with the visual (or sensory) and action components of the task. The operation of these modules corresponds naturally to the two basic functions of the task, perceiving and acting, and each of these in turn is likely to be composed of further, more specialized modules. Thus, the essence of a modular system is an arrangement of components which mirrors the functional structure of the tasks which the system is meant to perform. Form is related to function.

The possible link between functional modules and brain areas is interesting but most cognitive neuropsychologists tread warily here. Modularity is primarily a theory of cognitive processes, and the issues of where specific modules are located in the brain is really quite separate. While most neuropsychologists would accept that such localization does occur, their main concern is with cognitive impairment.

Explaining cognitive impairment

As we have just suggested, to work out which components or parts of a cognitive model are damaged, the performance of the brain-injured is examined on carefully selected tasks. One important cognitive neuropsychological method tries to find a dissociation between performance on two tasks (Shallice, 1988). Suppose a patient complains of difficulty in reading. Her problem might indeed be specific to reading, or she might have some general difficulty with other types of visual stimuli, not just with written material. Suppose then that we asked our patient to read some words and to name objects in a picture. If we found that the patient did in fact have difficulties with reading, but not with picture naming, we would have found a dissociation in performance on the two tasks. The patient performs poorly on one task but well on another.

We might then conclude that the damaged modules or processes underlying reading were not required for picture naming. While tempting, this is not the only logical conclusion. Reading and picture naming might use similar processes but reading could simply be more difficult than picture naming. If this is the case, even slight damage to some crucial modules might affect reading, but leave picture naming unimpaired. Suppose, however, we were to discover another patient who, this time, can read perfectly well but cannot name pictures at all. Together with the data from our first patient we now have a double dissociation in performance. Patient one succeeds on task A but fails on task B, patient two fails on task A but succeeds on task B.

Double dissociations are better indicators of the independence of cognitive processes than single dissociations, but they are not the end of the story. The specific nature of the disorder still has to be explained. In the above example we may feel more confident that our first patient has a specific reading problem, but the precise character of her difficulty must now be worked out. Further dissociations between separate aspects of reading must be uncovered before we can pinpoint her problem.

Far less useful, though perhaps easier to find, are associations between performance. Here, a person is impaired on task A, but also, say, on tasks B, C and D. This could mean that the same set of damaged modules is needed for all four tasks. Or, it could just as easily mean that different modules are involved, but, since these are located in neighbouring areas of the brain, they have all suffered some damage. While less conclusive than dissociations, associations can be of some help in unravelling the nature of impairment when used in conjunction with other data from cognitive psychology.

Although their internal processing is insulated from each other, modules do not usually work in isolation. They accept output from and provide input to other modules. To do so, they need to be interconnected. This suggests another way in which cognitive impairment can arise. Two or more modules can become disconnected or separated from each other. Each module, on its own, may still be capable of carrying out its job, but it is now unable to communicate with its neighbours.

Disconnection explanations can be understood at the brain level too. Different brain areas are interlinked and severing of these neural connections can occur, though, as in the problem of where modules themselves are localized, cognitive neuropsychologists would be cautious here in claiming a particular physical basis for cognitive disconnections. At times, however, the anatomical disconnection is patently obvious. The two major halves of the brain, or cerebral hemispheres, are joined by an important band of fibres called the corpus callosum. Several patients with severe epilepsy, an electrical disturbance of the brain, have had their corpus callosum surgically severed in an attempt to contain the epileptic seizure to one hemisphere. These 'split-brain' patients were then extensively studied by Sperry and colleagues (e.g. Sperry et al., 1969) and others. Sperry was able to show that visual information could be separately processed by either hemisphere but named overtly only by the left.

Participants and syndromes

It should be clear by now that cognitive neuropsychologists try to provide detailed accounts of mental impairment following brain injury. This means that the descriptions they use are much more detailed than those employed by traditional neuropsychologists or by the medical profession. The standard literature on neuropsychology is full of labels such as amnesia (literally: without memory), agnosia (literally: lack of knowledge), aphasia (literally: loss of language) and so on. These are then often subdivided into finer categories such as visual agnosia or expressive aphasia. Labels like these are supposed to refer to syndromes or groups of symptoms which are thought to recur in patients with one or other of these problems. Just as someone with influenza has aching muscles, a high temperature, mild depression, but no rash, so someone with expressive aphasia has difficulties with speaking but not with listening. There are three problems with this approach. The first is that it can easily convey the impression that the disorder, once labelled, is fully understood, whereas the full implications of the brain injury still need to be uncovered. The second difficulty is that the categories are often too broad to explain the problem precisely. Finally, the ideal set of symptoms, suggested by the traditional labels, is rarely found in practice. Brain damage does not respect our convenient categories. Because of these problems, many, though not all, cognitive neuropsychologists completely reject the classical categories as explanations of patients' problems and prefer to treat each case on its merits. In this way, they are able to explain patients' problems in more detail. It is also quite common for cognitive neuropsychologists to do experiments on one participant or patient at a time. Because of the variability of brain damage, group studies can blur important distinctions which in-depth studies of single cases can reveal.

The variable nature of brain injury and the use of single case studies give cognitive neuropsychology quite a distinctive research style, rather unlike the incremental process by which theories are proposed and tested in normal science. In some ways, doing cognitive neuropsychology is more like detective work. A patient presents with a problem, and using the often skimpy and informal descriptions available at the start of the investigation, the psychologist establishes a rough picture of what has gone wrong. How did the disorder arise? Was there a closed or open head injury? Did the individual have a stroke? Is the patient a chronic alcoholic? Broadly speaking, which cognitive functions are impaired? Does the patient have memory problems? Is memory intact but perception impaired? Are there some particular types of stimuli, such as faces, with which the patient has difficulty, and so on?

Many of these questions can be answered quite quickly. Medical knowledge and techniques are now so advanced that information on the neurological basis of disorders is readily available. Modern techniques such as MRI scans can usually establish accurately the nature, extent and location of any brain damage, so that the previous role of clinical neuropsychologists, to pinpoint brain damage, is less important than it was. Also, the gross behavioural and cognitive consequences of the disorder can be rapidly established, using standardized psychometric tests developed over the years, and, less formally, simply by interviewing the patient and his relatives. Rather like routine police work, then, where the nature and immediate circumstances surrounding a crime are quickly established, this phase of the investigation can be thought of as narrowing the range of possibilities for later phases.

These later phases are rather different. Here the cognitive aspects of neuropsychology come to the fore. The specification of the disorder in terms of damage to one or more components of a theory of normal cognitive functioning, and revision of this theory in the light of the findings, is rather more like the creative work that goes into tracking down suspects, checking out alibis and catching a criminal. There is, however, an important difference between detection and cognitive neuropsychology. Whereas the detective may only have the vaguest of theories at the start as to who might be a potential criminal, the neuropsychologist often has the more explicit support of a detailed model of the cognitive function in question. Useful though this is, the neuropsychologist must still proceed cautiously, since as Humphreys and Riddoch (1987a) put it using a different analogy:

> One is presented with a conundrum, a jigsaw puzzle comprising a great number of pieces. These pieces are made up of the tasks the patient is able to do as well as the tasks he or she is unable to do. One's initial hunch about where the pieces should go represents one's starting conceptions . . . Clearly, one needs to be careful not to force the pieces together simply on the basis of this hunch. (1987, p. 32)

We have tried to illustrate the distinctive, extended nature of cognitive neuropsychological work in box 12.1 which will also be referred to later in this chapter.

Cognitive Neuropsychology in Action

In this section we provide examples of cognitive neuropsychology in action by describing important work on impairments of perception, memory and language. These three areas contain some of the best and most intriguing examples of cognitive neuropsychology and show how it can enrich the rest of cognitive psychology as well as explain the mental effects of brain damage.

Perceptual impairments

In chapter 3, it was pointed out that two major jobs for the visual system are to decide what and where things are, and that, in effect, there are two visual systems, one for dealing with the visual appearance and nature of objects, the other for positions, movement and spatial information processing.

If two separate visual systems exist, perhaps they can be separately damaged. Studies of brain-damaged patients indicate that this is so. There are patients who find it hard to recognize or even detect objects but who are unimpaired in perceiving the positions of objects or noting that objects are moving, and there are patients who have no difficulty in recognizing objects but who have severe problems with a variety of other aspects of vision such as spatial location, spatial attention and movement.

Perceptual disorders also often have consequences for patients' ability to form and use visual images. We will only refer to this in passing here, but it is interesting to note that recent neuropsychological investigations of mental imagery suggest that the distinction between visual and spatial processing may apply here too and may be separately disrupted in imagery as well as perception (e.g. Farah et al., 1988; see also Baddeley, 1990, for a discussion).

Disorders of object recognition and detection   At the beginning of this chapter we described a man who, on waking up, found that everyday objects looked unfamiliar. This person, to whom we will refer by his initials, GL, is one of several cases of object recognition disorders discussed by Ellis and Young (1988). The clinical term for disorders of object recognition is agnosia, which literally means 'without knowledge', but like many classical neuropsychological labels, agnosia is rather broad and covers a variety of different problems which are only now being interpreted using theories of normal visual perception. GL, unfortunately, lived in the nineteenth century, too early to be studied with the new methods.

The theory of David Marr (1982) has helped to explain the perceptual disorders of more contemporary patients than GL. Marr claimed that object recognition begins with the input of sensory information, which is then transformed by cells in the retina into a spatial pattern depicting the various levels of brightness in the scene or object. From this 'grey level description', perceptual processes then extract and group together information about lines, edges, blobs and other visual features to form a rough, two-dimensional representation of the object, known as the 'primal sketch'. With only a primal sketch, a person might be able to draw an object, or possibly match one picture with another, but could do very little else. The primal sketch contains no information about depth or orientation of the object. Further interpretation is needed to perceive the angle and relative distance from the viewer of the object's various surfaces. This interpretation produces the 'viewer-centred representation' or '2-D sketch', which represents the structure of the object more clearly, but still only from one viewpoint. To achieve full object recognition, a three-dimensional 'object-centred representation' must be formed and then identified using previously stored information about the object's structure. An object-centred representation, independent of any particular viewpoint, is crucial to recognize objects which are viewed from unusual angles. Marr's theory is modular in that independent systems construct different aspects of the various representations, and largely data driven in that there is a processing sequence from grey level, to primal sketch, to viewer-centred, to object-centred representation (see chapters 2 and 11 for more detailed accounts of Marr's theory).

Because it is sequential and modular, it is possible to use this theory to interpret the visual problems of agnosic patients (Ratcliff and Newcombe, 1982; Ellis and Young, 1988). Suppose a person claims to have difficulty seeing objects and, after testing, is found to have problems naming visually presented objects, cannot draw them or trace their outlines with his finger, but has no difficulty saying where things are, nor in identifying objects by touch or by sound. A patient with these difficulties, RC, has been studied by Campion and Latto (1985). RC suffered accidental poisoning from carbon monoxide which has apparently severely damaged his visual cortex, and resulted in a large number of blind spots across the whole of his visual field. RC is unaware of the blind spots themselves, but they obscure details and outlines of objects rather as fog or a dirty window pane might. In terms of Marr's theory, the degradation caused to his visual input seriously interferes with the formation of the initial representation or primal sketch from which all subsequent visual representations are derived.

A rather different type of patient, however, with damage to the right posterior part of the brain, usually the parietal lobe, has been examined by Warrington and colleagues (e.g. Warrington and Taylor, 1978; Warrington, 1982). Warrington's patients can name or match objects easily, provided the object, or picture of it, is seen from a usual viewpoint, but experience severe difficulties when presented with an unusual view. In general, as Warrington explains, these patients find it hard to cope with the problem of object constancy. (Object constancy, as we explained in chapter 2, refers to people's ability to perceive objects as the same despite changes in lighting, distance from viewer or orientation.) Using Marr's theory, Ellis and Young (1988) offer a more detailed interpretation. They point out that in Marr's account, the object-centred representation is formed by working out where the parts of the object lie relative to the object's principal axis. One characteristic of many unusual views is that the principal axis is obscured or foreshortened, making it harder for patients who might already be experiencing some problems here.

Recent work by Humphreys and Riddoch (1984) supports but also slightly challenges this account. Humphreys and Riddoch point out that unusual views can not only shorten an object's principal axis, but can sometimes obscure an important part or feature which might be used to identify the object. For instance, if an elephant can be identified because it has a long trunk, then a view of an elephant from above, which obscures the trunk, might make recognition more difficult even though the principal axis is still clear. Like Warrington, Humphreys and Riddoch have found that many patients with damage to the right side of the brain are frequently handicapped when an object's principal axis is shortened. But one patient, HJA, whom they have tested in great detail, is more affected by loss of an object's distinctive feature than by foreshortening its axis. HJA's disorder is very important in that it shows how other factors as well as those mentioned by Marr may be involved in object recognition. For instance, HJA has problems in linking an object's overall shape with its features. This and other important aspects of HJA's case are described in more detail in box 12.1.

So far we have discussed difficulties which arise at the initial and object-centred stages of visual analysis. Working out the visual structure of an object does not, on its own, indicate what the object is nor what it is for. A full, semantic analysis is needed to recognize the object completely. Other perceptual problems, therefore, have been found which are more to do with understanding the meaning of a stimulus than with analysing its appearance. Some patients can see, match, draw and cope with unusual views of an object but cannot describe its functions. These patients seem to have disorders of the semantic system itself, since they arise when no obvious visual problems are present and also when they are tested with verbal stimuli. Quite often their problems are highly specific. Some patients, for instance, have difficulty in identifying pieces of furniture, while others may have problems with living things (Warrington and Shallice, 1984). The specificity of these disorders is good evidence that semantic memory is organized into separate categories (Shallice, 1988).

It is a tribute to Marr that his theory accounts so well for disorders of object recognition, but, as we have seen, neuropsychological data, such as Humphreys and Riddoch's, can also extend and qualify existing models as well as simply supporting them. Another example of this benefit of cognitive neuropsychology is the unusual condition known as blindsight. Patients afflicted with blindsight report no visual experience whatsoever, but still know where certain visual stimuli are located (e.g. Weiskrantz, 1986). These patients have intact spatial abilities in the absence of any reported visual experience and their problems dramatically demonstrate how one set of abilities, spatial in this case, may be preserved while others are lost. It now looks like conditions comparable to blindsight can occur in other sensory modalities. The woman described at the beginning of the chapter who could not feel on one side of her body but could accurately indicate where she had been touched seems to have a tactual equivalent. Blindsight and associated conditions raise important issues for theories of cognition in general. One possibility is that only the conscious or subjective experience of perception is lost, while underlying processing mechanisms remain intact (cf. Marcel, 1983a, 1983b). If this is true it means that we need to be even more cautious than ever in using subjective reports as evidence that processing systems themselves are damaged.

Spatial disorders   Although the structure of spatial processing is far less well understood than object perception, a number of distinct conditions have been recorded. Pure examples of these disorders are quite rare, but careful examination of patients shows that difficulties can be experienced in dealing with the locations of objects, perceiving movement and in visual attention.

Some of the best descriptions of disorders of spatial location were reported by neurologists who studied soldiers injured in the First World War (e.g. Holmes, 1919). Some of Holmes' patients were strikingly impaired in their ability to cope with the positions of objects, but were quite able to perceive the objects themselves, and were also able to detect movement. Reading Holmes' descriptions shows just how incapacitating it can be to lose the ability to locate objects. One of his patients, for example, had great difficulty feeding himself. Whenever he reached for bread or tried to pick up a cup his hand would move in a totally inappropriate direction. As Ellis and Young (1988) point out, these problems contrast markedly with blindsight where the patient has completely lost the ability to see objects, but can still accurately detect the location of simple visual stimuli.

The world is not merely composed of static objects in different positions. Things move. As with disorders of spatial location, some early work on this was done on soldiers suffering from gunshot wounds in the First World War. Specific disorders of movement perception are, however, extremely uncommon, and only very recently has a pure case been reported by Zihl et al. (1983). Their patient, LM, apparently sees the world as a series of static pictures, but is able to perceive objects themselves and can detect their locations accurately.

A third set of spatial problems concerns our ability to attend to different aspects of the world around us. One way to focus attention is to move our eyes towards an object and hold our gaze steady on it. A disease of the nervous system known as supranuclear palsy can severely disrupt this ability by affecting voluntary eye movements. Generally speaking, people attend to what they are looking at directly, but we have all had the experience of looking at one thing and concentrating on another out of 'the corner of our eye'. Perhaps the overt and covert dimensions of attention are controlled by separate mechanisms. Detailed work by Posner and colleagues supports this idea and shows that supranuclear patients, who have difficulties with overt eye movements, can still covertly shift their attention, while other patients with damage to the parietal cortex are severely impaired in their covert attention (Posner et al., 1982; Posner et al., 1984).

One the of the most dramatic disorders of spatial processing, however, is the condition known as unilateral neglect. Patients with this problem completely ignore one half of space and sometimes half of their own body. The neglected half is always opposite (contralateral) to the damaged side of the brain, usually the right side. Unilateral neglect is not merely a perceptual disorder. Italian neuropsychologists have tested the mental imagery of patients with quite a clever technique and shown that this can be affected too (Bisiach and Luzatti, 1978). Patients with neglect of the left-hand side are asked to imagine themselves in the cathedral square in Milan and to describe what they see. When they imagine the square from one perspective, they successfully describe the buildings on the right but ignore those on the left. When asked to imagine the square from the opposite side, the previously neglected buildings are now reported and the previously described buildings are neglected.

Describing neglect is reasonably straightforward, explaining it is more difficult. The fact that imagery as well as perception has been implicated in neglect suggests that the disorder may be to do with the internal representation of information and not simply attention (for a thorough coverage of the issues surrounding neglect and some new experiments see Sunderland, 1990; see also Halligan and Marshall, 1988; Marshall and Halligan, 1988).

Memory disorders

Perceptual difficulties can be extremely incapacitating but imagine what it must be like to suffer memory loss as severe as that as the man described at the beginning of the chapter. For some reason you are in hospital though you feel quite well. A new doctor is suddenly introduced to you, but she claims to have seen you five minutes ago. She seems genuine enough, but is she lying? Are you losing your mind? The doctor gives you some words to look at and asks whether you remember her showing them to you. You do not recognize any of them, but then why should you? After all, you think you have never seen the doctor before. You try to keep a diary but all you can write in it is that you have now really come awake after a long deep sleep. You read the previous ten entries and are puzzled to see that they say exactly the same thing. Your wife leaves the room and returns. You greet her and claim that you have not seen her for months. Discussing this case, Baddeley (1990) writes: 'Experienced once, such an event could be intriguing and touching, but when it happens repeatedly, day in, day out, it rapidly loses its charms' (1990, p. 5).

Memory disorders not only cause people to forget things but also interfere with their view of themselves as someone with a past, a meaningful present and a future. The person described at the beginning of the chapter now lives his life as a succession of brief time capsules in which events occur, are noted, but are not explicitly remembered. With an impaired long-term memory, the past contracts and the ability to sustain and carry out future plans is disrupted.

Despite these severe problems, he, and other amnesic patients (patients with such memory problems), can still remember and do a great deal. They can perform old skills and learn new ones, they can remember the meaning of words, they know a great many facts about the world. Two questions, then, interest researchers who study memory disorders: what aspects of memory are impaired and what aspects are undamaged or preserved?

Amnesia and other memory disorders: what is impaired There are several different types of memory disorders. Some of these are quite specific and result in memory loss for particular types of stimuli such as faces. Others, which we will discuss here, are more general and affect memory for stimuli of various kinds.

Amnesia, the most extensively studied memory problem, can be caused in several ways. Brain surgery, chronic alcoholism, open and closed head injury and encephalitis are just some of the conditions which can produce amnesia following damage to the temporal lobes, hippocampus and other brain areas. The classical amnesic patient has difficulties with the long-term remembering of information about specific events, and the chances of full recovery are often slight. Memory is particularly poor for information acquired after the onset of the injury or trauma (anterograde amnesia), but, almost invariably, events which occurred before the onset can be difficult to remember too (retrograde amnesia). Amnesics, however, are usually still able to retain information for brief periods of time. Short-term remembering, measured by tasks such as digit span, is more or less within normal limits.

When amnesics were first studied in detail using cognitive techniques, it was thought that their impairment reflected a damaged long-term store combined with an intact short-term store (e.g. Baddeley and Warrington, 1970). Amnesics' performance on tasks like list learning was used to support this idea. As we explained in chapter 2, the beginning and the end of a list of words are generally better remembered than the middle portions. The first few items remembered from a list were assumed to have been transferred to long-term store while the last few were thought to come from short-term store. Amnesic patients have most difficulty remembering the initial items of a list, indicating problems with long-term store.

At about the same time, another type of memory disorder was discovered. Warrington and Shallice (1969) reported a patient, KF, with apparently intact long-term memory, but a severely limited immediate memory capacity. Asked to repeat back a simple list of digits, KF could often remember only one of them. KF also had a grossly impaired recency effect, that is, he found it hard to remember the last few items in a list, though his memory for the first few items was normal. KF's problems, therefore, were thought to stem from a damaged short-term store.

When combined, these two sets of data, KF's and the amnesics', looked like good evidence for dividing the memory system into separate stores, but the reader may have spotted a problem here. In the original structural model, information could only reach the long-term store by first passing through short-term store. How then was it possible for a patient like KF to have a normal long-term memory for new material if his short-term store was so damaged? To cope with this problem Shallice and Warrington (1970) suggested that the structural model needed to be rearranged to allow separate access into long- and short-term stores.

However, as we explained in chapter 2, the initial structural theory of memory has been largely replaced by theories about memory dynamics. It is the active processes of encoding, retention and retrieval of information, and the operation of subsystems such as working memory, which now tend to interest psychologists, rather than simply the size and arrangement of storage systems. Within this newer framework, data from amnesics, and patients like KF, can be interpreted as the result of a double dissociation between immediate and long-term remembering rather than as evidence for two memory stores. The challenge now is to explain what aspects of short- and long-term remembering are impaired.

Difficulties in creating and retaining new traces in memory account quite well for certain types of amnesia. One famous patient who has severe problems in this regard is HM. HM, an epileptic, had an operation in 1953 to relieve his condition. The operation involved the cutting of the temporal lobes of the cortex and removal of parts of his hippocampus and amygdala (mid-brain structures). HM has been incapable of consciously remembering, for more than a few minutes, anything that has happened since then, but has reasonably clear, though not perfect, memories of events which occurred prior to the operation.

Not all types of amnesia can be explained simply in terms of the difficulty in learning new material. Logically speaking, long-term memory impairment could arise at any or all of the three major stages of remembering: encoding, retention and retrieval. Prolonged alcohol abuse can lead to Korsakoff's syndrome, a type of amnesia where the patient suffers from retrograde as well as anterograde amnesia. If encoding and retaining new material is the only problem, these patients should be quite able to remember events prior to their illness. The fact that they often cannot means that other factors must be involved.

In practice, it has been difficult to relate Korsakoff amnesia to any one stage of memory, though one encouraging development suggests that Korsakoff patients may have difficulties in using the context in which material is learned to reinstate their memories (see Parkin, 1987 and Baddeley, 1990 for good discussions). The importance of context in remembering was described in chapter 2. The study of Korsakoff's syndrome is further complicated by the fact that researchers have often studied groups of patients rather than single cases. The danger here is that subtle differences between patients can be overlooked and a rather general picture of the condition results.

In some ways, rather better progress has been made in understanding deficits in short-term than long-term remembering. The working memory model, developed by Baddeley and colleagues, has been useful here (Baddeley and Hitch, 1974; Baddeley, 1986, 1990). Working memory, as we explained earlier (in chapter 2), provides a more detailed account of how immediate memory operates than the old structural model. As we explained in chapter 2, the system itself is comprised of three major parts: a coordinating component or central executive, a verbal, articulatory loop and a visuo-spatial sketch pad. A number of patients, similar to KF, have now been studied from the perspective of this model. Briefly, their problems seem to arise because of damage to part of the articulatory loop, the phonological store, which retains, for a short time, a record of the sound of the incoming information (e.g. Vallar and Baddeley, 1984a, 1984b). Together with patients who show selective deficits in imagery and others who seem to have problems on tasks thought to reflect the functions of the central executive, good evidence is now emerging for the dissociability of the various components of working memory (Baddeley, 1990).

What do amnesics remember? Amnesics forget a great deal, but they can also learn and remember things too; they can learn new skills as well as remember old ones. These skills can be mental as well as perceptual–motor, though the patient rarely remembers the circumstances in which the skill was learned. For instance, Wood et al. (1982) taught amnesic patients to use a mathematical rule in which numbers in a series are generated by adding the two previous ones together, giving the numbers 1, 2, 3, 5, 8, 13 . . . and so on. Patients learned this rule within a few trials, but, what is more important, they took far fewer trials to relearn it when tested again some 17 weeks later, despite having no conscious recollection of ever having seen the rule or the experimenter before. Some of the many other tasks which amnesics can still perform and learn anew include doing jigsaws, negotiating mazes, learning a new tune on a musical instrument and solving anagrams (see Moscovitch, 1982 for a full list).

These undamaged or 'preserved' abilities imply that the procedural memory system, needed to perform skills, is unaffected by amnesia. Another view is that both semantic and procedural memory systems are unimpaired. Amnesic patients can still use and define words normally and know many facts about the world, which means that their use and understanding of previously learned semantic categories is relatively intact. But can they acquire new semantic memories? Some commentators argue that this has not yet been demonstrated (Ellis and Young, 1988), though at least one study strongly suggests that new semantic memories can be formed. Another patient studied by Wood et al. (1982) was a young girl who contracted encephalitis at age nine. Encephalitis can badly damage the brain and one of its side-effects is often a severe amnesia. The girl's schooling was disrupted by her illness, but, after a while, she was taught by a home teacher, and eventually returned to her normal school. Still densely amnesic, every time she returned to school after a holiday she had to relearn her way around and be reintroduced to her teachers. Nevertheless, she continued to make progress through the American grade school system, passing the various tests appropriate to her age. To do this she had to acquire and retain a large number of facts, as well as skills, indicating that she was increasing the content of her semantic memory, though as Parkin (1987) points out, she 'continued to show poor performance on vocabulary tests and the Wechsler Intelligence Scale for Children (WISC), both of which could indicate impaired semantic memory' (1987, p. 97). However, Glisky et al. (1986) have shown that amnesics can acquire and remember new computer terminology, and Tulving et al. (1988) investigated a densely amnesic, closed-head injury patient who has acquired new factual knowledge from episodes that he cannot consciously remember. Both of these studies suggest that amnesics can form new semantic memories.

Other recent discoveries, however, and some old observations, indicate that a broader explanation of amnesics' preserved abilities may be needed. There are now many demonstrations that amnesics can retain information about quite specific events, not just general knowledge and skills. Around the turn of the twentieth century, Claparede (1911), a French neuropsychologist who worked with amnesics, shook hands with a Korsakoff patient with a drawing pin concealed in his hand. Later, the patient had to be reintroduced, having forgotten who Claparede was, but refused to shake hands. When asked for an explanation he replied that 'sometimes drawing pins are hidden in people's hands!' More recently (and ethically!) Jacoby and Witherspoon (1982) verbally presented amnesic participants with questions which contained homophones (words with the same sound but different meanings) such as 'What instrument do you play with a reed?'. (Here, 'reed' is the homophone.) Some time later, they gave their participants a spelling test which included the homophones from the previous questions. The amnesics were now far more likely to give the less frequent spelling 'r–e–e–d' than the more frequent 'r–e–a–d' even though, unlike normal participants, they had no conscious recollection of having heard 'reed' in the recent past. This experiment is described in more detail in box 12.2. Since Jacoby and Witherspoon's study there have been several other demonstrations of similar effects. All show that amnesics can retrieve quite specific information, given sufficiently sensitive testing conditions, but without any awareness that they are using memory to do so.

What is happening here? In one sense, amnesic patients are using their episodic memories in that they are remembering details about particular events, but they do so without any conscious recollection. As we explained in chapter 2, situations where people retrieve information without any conscious experience of remembering are examples of implicit memory (Schacter, 1987). So, perhaps it is implicit rather than explicit memory which is preserved in amnesia. Redefining the problem in this way may advance our understanding of amnesia, since it emphasizes other dimensions of remembering such as the subjective experiences which accompany it, rather than the amount or type of information retrieved (Tulving, 1989). But the question still remains as to how implicit memory works and this will need to be explained before the abilities of amnesics are fully understood. Memory research in the 1990s will, we expect, examine this issue thoroughly, partly because of pressure from cognitive neuropsychology. In addition, memory research in the next ten years is likely to be far more concerned with the neurophysiological details of remembering, forgetting and amnesia than it has hitherto (e.g. Cohen and Eichenbaum, 1993).

Language problems

To be an otherwise intelligent person but to be unable to communicate properly or understand what others are saying to you must be extremely frustrating.

The neuropsychological study of language disorders has made dramatic progress in the past 20 years. A large variety of different disorders have been studied and explained; these include problems with reading (dyslexia) and writing (dysgraphia) as well as with speaking (aphasia) and difficulties in comprehending as well as producing language. Some of the many types of dyslexias have already been discussed in chapter 9, and so here, instead, we will concentrate on four problems in perceiving and producing speech. Before doing so it is worth noting that many of the errors which brain-injured patients make resemble in an exaggerated fashion the speech errors which all normal people make from time to time (see chapter 4). This shows all the more clearly that models of normal cognition must, at some point, be capable of explaining how things can go wrong.

To help us to explain language disorders we will use part of a more complex model of language perception and production outlined by Ellis and Young (1988), whose account of these problems we follow here. The model describes some of the processes involved in taking in, analysing and understanding speech and in going from the intention to speak to producing actual words (see figure 12.2).

Understanding speech begins with the intake of information in the form of sound. The physical characteristics of this must first be analysed. The sound has to be detected, distinguished from other competing noises and its acoustic pattern determined, despite differences in accent, voice or speed of speech. These are some of the jobs of the 'auditory analysis system'. Next, the system has to decide whether the speech sound corresponds to a known word. To do this it tries to match the analysed sound with a set of stored representations of words. These word recognition units in the 'auditory input lexicon' simply tell the person that the sound is a word that they have encountered before or not, they do not reveal what the word means. To find out what it means the word's entry in the input lexicon is

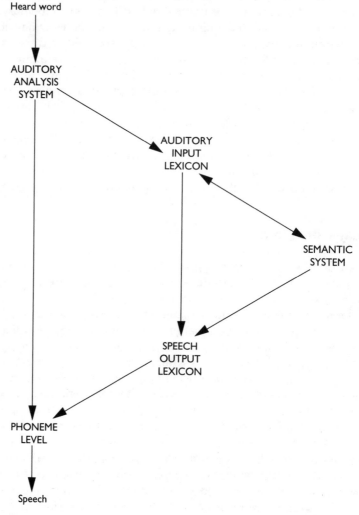

Figure 12.2 A simple model for analysing and producing single words and other lexical items. (Based on figure 6.1, Ellis and Young, 1988)

used to activate the corresponding meaning in the 'semantic system'. (In fact, the relationship between the word recognition units and the semantic system is very similar to that between the object recognition units and the semantic system as described in the section on perceptual disorders.)

Speaking, in some ways, is the reverse of listening. The speaker begins with the intention to say something, expressed as meaning in the semantic system. To clothe this meaning in words, appropriate items have to be chosen from the speech output lexicons. Everyday experience as well as experimental work shows that high frequency rather than low frequency words tend to be selected more easily at this stage. Finally, the pronunciation pattern for the word is worked out using the 'phonetic representation' of the word which is used to guide the articulation and control the speech output.

The reader may now find it helpful to refer to figure 12.2 while following our account of language disorders. The model we have just described is modular and sequential, and it is clear that damage could occur to any of its various components or to the links between them.

Damage to the auditory analysis system is the most likely explanation of a condition known as pure word deafness (e.g. Goldstein, 1974; Auerbach et al., 1982). Patients with this difficulty experience problems in understanding speech, though they are able to speak, read and write perfectly well, and testing shows their hearing and perceptual discrimination of tones and other sounds to be within normal limits. Words, however, cause them great problems. One afflicted patient described speech as 'sounding like foreign folk speaking in the distance'. What is it about words which makes them so difficult to perceive? The answer is that speech involves a very rapidly changing sound pattern or acoustic signal and it is the rapidity with which it changes that seems to cause problems. Some parts of the acoustic signal, corresponding to consonants, change very rapidly indeed, while other parts, corresponding to vowels, change more slowly. Not surprisingly, patients with pure word deafness often complain that words come too quickly, have more difficulty dealing with consonants than vowels and can be helped by speaking v..e..r..y slowly.

Patients with pure word deafness, then, appear to have difficulty with the analysis of speech sounds, but not with word meanings. A contrasting condition has been described as 'word-meaning deafness'. Here, as before, patients cannot understand spoken words but, unlike patients with pure word deafness, they are quite able to repeat words or non-words which are spoken to them. Given this impairment in understanding combined with intact word perception, it is tempting to explain word-meaning deafness as the result of damage to the semantic system itself. This would be reasonable were it not that word-meaning deafness patients can usually understand written words. Another possibility is that the auditory input lexicon is damaged. This again seems unlikely since patients can often write to dictation words which they do not immediately understand. To write a spoken word down implies that the speech signal is recognized as a word and its component letters (graphemic code) deduced. Recognizing words is the job of the auditory input lexicon. A third and more likely possibility suggested by Ellis and Young (1988), which the reader may already have spotted, is that the link between the auditory input lexicon and the semantic system could be broken. This would leave both components intact but disconnected and would make it impossible for the patient to get from word recognition to meaning.

Word-meaning deafness can be partially explained by our simple model, but the model would need to be expanded to cope with it in full. If the link into the semantic system is cut, how are patients ever able to repeat or write down spoken input? To account for these abilities, additional links (see figure 12.2) which short-circuit the semantic system are needed and directly join input with output systems.

Semantic damage is the problem in the aptly named 'semantic anomia' (anomia = without words). Several patients with semantic anomia, studied in detail by Warrington and Shallice (1984), have particular problems in referring to specific semantic categories such as 'living things', while others have more general semantic impairment. We mentioned above that these patients find it difficult to name objects in particular categories, but their problems do not end there. They are also unable to comprehend spoken words when these refer to the troublesome categories, they find it hard to use the damaged categories to sort items, and have great difficulty producing words relating to the categories in question. The strikingly selective impairment of semantic categories observed in semantic anomia testifies to the organized nature of semantic memory.

Non-semantic anomia is another word-finding problem. This time, patients' speech is fluent and grammatical though still quite short on object names. When they are unable to find a particular word, patients with non-semantic anomia will frequently find a passable alternative or circumlocute. A patient with this condition, EST, has been described by Kay and Ellis (1987). EST is quite capable of identifying named pictures and other tests involving semantic knowledge, but has difficulty with the spontaneous production of object and action words. When Kay and Ellis examined EST's performance, they discovered that he had most difficulty retrieving low frequency items, but when prompted with the initial phoneme of the word, he was able to produce several of these too. EST would also sometimes produce a word on a subsequent occasion that he had been unable to find on a previous one. Kay and Ellis suggest that EST's difficulties lie at the stage of the auditory output lexicon, but they reject the idea that the system itself is damaged, on the grounds that prompting helps EST and that he shows sporadic recovery. They prefer, instead, the idea that the contents of his output lexicon are inaccessible because the amount of activation reaching it from the semantic system is reduced. As Ellis and Young explain, 'the reduced activation is still enough to boost up to full activation entries whose resting levels are already high (i.e. entries for frequently used words), but entries for infrequently used words whose resting levels are low, can no longer be boosted sufficiently to allow all their phonemes to be activated and articulated' (1988, p. 122).

These four disorders illustrate but by no means exhaust the many different ways in which language can go wrong, and show how many complex processes are involved even in the simple repetition of words. Language, of course, entails more than the perception and production of single words; words have to be arranged into grammatical sequences and used to convey complex meanings. Damage can arise at these levels too, and traditional category labels such as Broca's and Wernicke's aphasia are often used to describe these disorders. However, it is now clear that these clinical categories are far too broad and that more detailed analysis is required to understand these problems in full. Fortunately, detailed work is now being done by cognitive neuropsychologists and, although we cannot cover it here, extensive reviews can be found in Ellis (1984), Ellis and Young (1988), Coltheart et al. (1987) and MacCarthy and Warrington (1990).

Conclusions: Future Trends and Implications of Cognitive Neuropsychology

Cognitive neuropsychology is a new venture, barely 20 years old, though important work was done along similar lines in the nineteenth century which is only now being rediscovered. As this chapter has shown, its approach differs from traditional neuropsychology in several ways. It is less concerned with localization of function, it has a distinctive research style, and it uses purpose-made tasks rather than standardized tests and describes individual patients' problems with finer categories, based on cognitive theory. Because it provides a functional explanation of cognitive impairment it is better able to suggest how the cognitive effects of brain injury might be 'repaired' or, at least, how best to mitigate the worst effects of brain damage.

Two questions remain: first, how extensively can cognitive neuropsychology be applied? In particular, can all types of mental impairment following brain injury or other intervention be explained using cognitive neuropsychological techniques? Second, what path is its future development likely to take?

As we have seen, the idea that cognitive functions can be divided into discrete entities or modules has been very helpful in neuropsychology, but the modularity idea has caught on more strongly in some areas of cognition than others. Perception and language, for example, have been described with highly modular models, and the cognitive neuropsychology of these areas is now quite well developed. Memory, on the other hand, has been described in a rather less detailed way and this would be why current understanding of certain memory disorders is still sketchy. To be fair, some memory models, such as Baddeley's working memory system, are quite modular, and good progress has been made in understanding disorders of immediate memory. But other approaches have simply described memory in terms of broad frameworks, such as levels of processing, or systems such as episodic, semantic and procedural memory. This might simply reflect the different degrees of progress in memory research compared with perception and language, or it might mean that memory cannot be split up in such a detailed fashion. Fodor (1983) himself claims that higher mental processes are not modular. Although he would probably not describe memory as a higher cognitive function, memory does often involve high-level, conscious processes such as effortful recollection as well as more automatic processes such as cued recall, and these non-automatic aspects of remembering may simply not be describable in a modular way. Is an effective neuropsychology possible for non-modular systems? Ellis and Young (1988) put it thus.

Dealing with a modular process is, they state, like carving a chicken at its joints, but, if Fodor is right and higher cognitive processes are not modular, then trying to develop a neuropsychology of higher cognition will be like trying to carve a meat loaf at its joints. It does not have any. It will be interesting in this respect to see whether, for example, the central executive, in Baddeley's model, can be split up into smaller components each of which can be separately disrupted, or whether higher functions involving consciousness are, in the end, unitary and indivisible.

These problems aside, the future of cognitive neuropsychology looks good. Closer links with cognitive psychology are sure to develop and closer cooperation with AI and cognitive science looks likely. The use of AI models is already apparent in applications of Marr's work, but also in studies by Shallice (1982) and others. Also, as we shall show in the next chapter, it is now possible not only to use existing models of normality to explain pathology, but, by selectively 'damaging' components of working models of the mind, the cognitive activity of the brain-injured can be simulated directly. This, in turn, is likely to have a more immediate effect on the construction of cognitive models. At present, models are formed from a knowledge of normal data, then tested against abnormal as well as normal populations. If we are right, a new generation of cognitive models could emerge which are constructed from the beginning to explain abnormal as well as normal performance and which incorporate more explicit theories about the effects of brain injury than our present accounts.

◄ Further reading ▶ ▶ ▶

Probably still the most comprehensive, recent account of cognitive neuro-psychology, which covers most of the issues raised in this chapter in great detail, is A. Ellis and A. Young 1988: *Human Cognitive Neuropsychology*. Hove: Lawrence Erlbaum Associates. Excellent accounts of memory and its impairments are to be found in A. Parkin 1987: *Memory and Amnesia*. Oxford: Blackwell, and A. Baddeley 1990: *Human Memory: Theory and Practice*. Hove: Lawrence Erlbaum Associates, see also A. Parkin 1993: *Memory: Phenomena, Experiment and Theory*. Oxford: Blackwell. Detailed examinations of different types of language impairments are presented in M. Coltheart, G. Sartori and R. Job (eds) 1987: *The Cognitive Neuropsychology of Language*. Hillsdale, NJ: Lawrence Erlbaum Associates. For an in-depth study of the problems of object recognition experienced by HJA, the reader is recommended to consult G.W. Humphreys and M.J. Riddoch 1987: *To See But Not to See: A Case Study of Visual Agnosia*. Hove: Lawrence Erlbaum Associates, which is both readable and informative. G.W. Humphreys and M.J. Riddoch (eds) 1987: *Visual Object Processing*. Hove: Lawrence Erlbaum Associates, provides more background on other object recognition problems. Ideas about modularity are forcibly expressed in J. Fodor 1983: *The Modularity of Mind*. Cambridge, Mass: MIT Press. Also, see R. MacCarthy and E. Warrington 1990: *Cognitive Neuropsychology: A Clinical Introduction*. London: Academic Press and T. Shallice 1988: *From Neuropsychology to Mental Structure*. New York: Cambridge University Press. Both provide further thorough reviews, though the latter might prove hard going for newcomers to the area.

Discussion points ▷ ▷ ▷

1   What is new about cognitive neuropsychology?
2   What are the benefits of modular systems? How and why might evolution have produced a modular mind? Are all cognitive functions modular?
3   Many cognitive neuropsychologists now prefer to study individual brain-injured participants in detail rather than groups of participants together. Why do you think this is? What are the benefits of single participant studies? What are their weaknesses?
4   Why is it important to find out which cognitive abilities are left intact as well as which are impaired by brain injury? What do amnesics remember?
5   Discuss ways in which cognitive neuropsychology is currently influencing cognitive psychology.

Practical exercises

1   One way to mimic certain working memory impairments is to tie up part of the working memory system using a technique known as articulatory suppression. Simply repeating a word such as 'the' over and over again engages the articulatory loop of working memory and prevents it being used in other situations. Examine the effects of articulatory suppression on tasks such as mental arithmetic, reading for comprehension, and listening to speech. Compare the effects of suppression on verbally based tasks such as these with its effects on visual ones such as picture matching or solving a maze. What predictions would you make from this about the effects of damage to the articulatory loop?

2   List as many incidents as you can which happened to you before the age of three and which you remember in detail; now list the things which you must have learned and still know from before that age. Can you remember the specific circumstances in which you learned all these facts and skills? Compare your data on childhood amnesia with the discussion of acquired amnesia in the chapter. How are the two similar and how do they differ?

3   (a)   Suppose you were examining a patient who claimed to have difficulty seeing faces. Design tasks which would allow you to discover whether his problem was specific to faces or was more general, and whether his problem lay in perceiving the appearance of a face or in remembering whose face it is.

   (b)   Show several people pictures of 20 faces and 20 objects for around five seconds each. Make sure the stimuli are all roughly the same size and that the faces do not have distinctive features such as scars or jewellery. Now add 20 new faces and 20 new objects to the original set, mix the two sets together, and, after 15 minutes has elapsed, show the pictures upside down to your participants. Ask your participants to pick out the objects and faces they saw originally. Count how many faces and how many objects they correctly recognize. Which suffers more from inversion, picture or face recognition? What does this indicate about face memory? How might face memory be impaired?

Box 12.1
A disorder of visual perception

The flavour of an extended neuropsychological investigation of one patient, John (referred to as HJA in the text and
in journal articles), is well illustrated by Humphreys and
Riddoch's (1987a) book. Here, we briefly outline the nature
of John's disorder, agnosia, describe some of Humphreys
and Riddoch's investigations, and show how aspects of
perceptual theory have been modified as a result of their
work.

The patient

In 1981, following an operation for a perforated appendix,
John had a stroke which damaged the artery leading to the
occipital lobes, parts of the rear of the brain which support
vision. It was apparent as soon as he awakened from the
anaesthetic that he had problems, though these were
initially attributed, by the medical staff in the hospital, to
transient post-operative difficulties. John's problems included being unable to recognize his wife, being unable to
read properly and getting lost in the immediate vicinity of
his hospital ward. On returning home, things did not 'click
into place' and 'he was unable to recognize familiar faces,
the familiar objects around his home, he got lost when he
ventured outside, he could only read slowly and with great
effort, and, though he could write he could not read back
what he had written; he had also lost the ability to perceive
colour. The world had become black, white and shades of
grey' (1987, p. 29). Upset by his condition, John tended to
become angry at the slightest provocation and, on one
occasion, stormed out of the house onto a nearby hillside
only to discover, as he puts it,

> ... that I had no idea how to go home again; it was no
> good looking back; I knew there was a gate from the
> grassed area into the road where the house stood, but
> I could not recognize it. My hot temper cooled very
> rapidly as I had to work out from memory that as long
> as I travelled down-hill and followed the line of trees
> and undergrowth ... I could reach the wicket-gate into
> our road. Fortunately, though, I didn't have to make
> the journey alone as my better half had already set off
> to rescue me! (ibid., p. 29)

Assessment by a clinical psychologist indicated that John
had severe difficulties with a range of visual tasks, but had
unimpaired verbal abilities and was otherwise of high

intelligence. His visual problems indicated that brain damage had occurred, despite the negative findings of a CAT
scan.

Three years later, however, clear evidence of brain injury
was apparent when another CAT scan was performed. It
seemed that the area of dead brain tissue had not taken on
its distinctive appearance in time to be picked up by the
first scan, which was performed soon after the stroke.

Informal interviews by Humphreys and Riddoch bore out
these preliminary findings. Among other things, John reported severe difficulties in recognizing common objects,
recognizing familiar faces and finding his way around. John's
reading was also severely impaired and could only proceed
laboriously, one letter at a time. To get some feel for how
hard reading in this way is, try the following message
embedded in xxxxxs:

```
xixxtxx  xixxsx  xvxxexxrxxyx  xdxxixxfxxfxxixxcx-
xuxxlxxtx   xtxxox   xrxxexxaxxdx   xtxxhxxixxsx
xbxxexxcxxaxxuxxsxxex          xexxaxxcxxhx  xwx-
xoxxrxxdx  xixxsx  xsxxpxxrxxexxaxxdx  xoxxuxxtx
xaxxnxxdx     xexxaxxcxxhx     xlxxexxtxxtxxexxrx
xmxxuxxsxxtxx       xbxxex       xdxxexxaxxlxxtx
xwxxixxtxxhx xsxxexxpxxaxxrxxaxxtxxexxlxxyx
```

The conclusion at the end of the first phase was clear
enough: John was suffering from agnosia; but the important
question still remained: precisely which visual processes
were impaired?

The investigations

It was quickly established that most of John's problems
were specific to visual recognition. John had extreme
difficulty in naming everyday things whether these were
presented in line drawings, pictures or as real objects,
though his erroneous responses were often from the
correct category; animals were misnamed as other animals,
for example. Admittedly, he did perform much better with
real objects than with drawings, recognizing 67 per cent of
the former compared with 42 per cent of the latter when
first tested, but this is still a lot lower than 100 per cent
which is what one would expect with such common
objects. Despite these poor visual recognition scores, John
scored much better when blindfolded and presented with
objects to touch, but his problems in the visual modality

included faces as well as objects. He mistook Humphreys and Riddoch for distant relatives, and when shown photographs of famous faces he classified Prince Charles and the Queen as politicians and Edward Heath and Harold Wilson as royalty!

Perhaps John's problem was that he could not find the name of visually presented objects which he could otherwise see satisfactorily. If no naming was required would John be able to perform normally on visual recognition tasks? After all, as Humphreys and Riddoch point out, 'we have all been in situations where we know we can recognize an object or person, but just can't think of the name' (1987a, p. 62). To explore this possibility Humphreys and Riddoch used two different sorts of matching tasks. In one, John was given three photographs, two of which depicted different examples of the same type of object, such as different types of clock. In the other, he was asked to match photographs of the identical object taken from different angles. John performed very poorly on the first of these, but much better on the second. However, he apparently matched the objects presented at different angles, not by first recognizing what they were, but by matching salient features, such as the spout of a teapot. If one of the objects was pictured at such an angle as to obscure the salient feature his performance deteriorated. 'Thus he can do certain types of matching task – in particular, he can match visual features in two photographs. He is only impaired when the task requires him to recognize the objects' (ibid., p. 63). Given that John failed to match visually dissimilar objects but did better with visually identical ones, it is possible that he simply does not know what objects are but can still see them. Perhaps he has lost all general knowledge about objects. Humphreys and Riddoch easily discounted this possibility by asking him to describe named objects which he failed to recognize from pictures. Here is John's verbal definition of the word CARROT:

A carrot is a root vegetable cultivated and eaten as human consumption worldwide. Grown from seed as an annual crop, the carrot produces long thin leaves

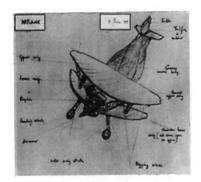
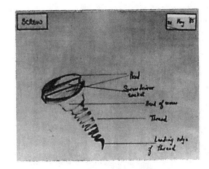

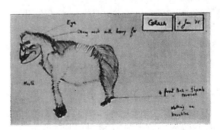

Box figure 12.1.1 Examples of John's drawings from memory, along with his notes on the salient parts of each object. (Figure 4.3, Humphreys and Riddoch, 1987a, reprinted with permission)

growing from a root head; this is deep growing and large in comparison with the leaf growth, sometimes gaining a length of 12 inches under a leaf top of similar height when grown in good soil. Carrots may be eaten raw or cooked and can be harvested during any size or state of growth. The general shape of a carrot root is an elongated cone and its colour ranges between red and yellow. (ibid., p. 64).

It is fascinating to compare this description with his response when shown a picture of a carrot: 'a brush'. At other times, or if pressed, John might be able to give a feature-by-feature description of an object from a picture but could still not recognize it.

Many people's definitions, John's included, tend to stress what objects are for rather than how they appear, though some definitions, like the example above, do include visual descriptions. A possibility, therefore, is that John still has general knowledge about objects' functions but lacks the specific visual knowledge of appearance to interpret what he sees. Humphreys and Riddoch were able to eliminate this possibility too by showing that John had sufficiently rich visual knowledge to draw objects from memory and to complete incomplete drawings when told what they were (see box figure 12.1.1).

So, assuming this is a problem of visual recognition, can John's disorder be specified more precisely still? The results of a number of ingenious studies and observations carried out by Humphreys and Riddoch suggest that it can. One important clue came from watching John copy drawings of objects. This he was able to do slavishly and with much effort by painstakingly copying line by line, a strategy similar to the feature-by-feature descriptions he gave when trying to identify objects.

The fact that John can detect perceptual features raises the question as to whether he is also able to detect overall form. Intriguingly, he does seem to have the ability to deal with some aspects of global perception. He does not for instance bump into objects, he can reach appropriately for objects and on a number of objective tests he is as fast at detecting overall shape as control participants.

So what then is his problem? John's disorder, while quite subtle, is nevertheless quite clear-cut. He seems to have difficulty in integrating local feature information with global feature information. The whole and the parts simply do not cohere when he looks at objects, and knowledge from one level cannot be brought to bear on the other. A simple illustration of this can be seen in box figure 12.1.2.

The task is to find a target shape among a set of distractors. In box figure 12.1.2(a) the target is a sloping line, while in box figure 12.1.2(b) the target is an inverted letter T. When looking for a sloping line John's performance was normal. He was as fast as a group of control participants and, like the control participants, his reaction times were not affected by increasing the number of distractors. This indicates that he was able to take in single features, such as straight lines, simultaneously. By contrast, his performance when searching for the inverted letter T was much poorer than the control group's. In this case it is the conjunction of two features, a horizontal and a vertical

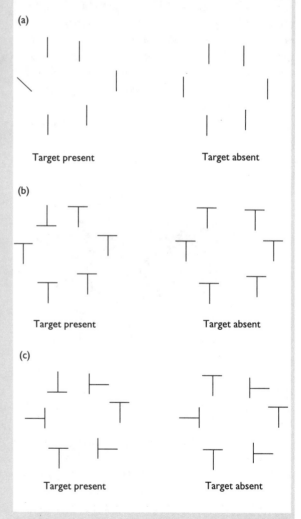

(a)

Target present   Target absent

(b)

Target present   Target absent

(c)

Target present   Target absent

Box figure 12.1.2 Examples of visual search tasks presented to John: (a) sloping line target, (b) inverted T, (c) inverted T with heterogeneous distractors. (Based on figure 4.9, Humphreys and Riddoch, 1987a)

line, which distinguishes the target from the distractors, rather than a single feature as in the case of the sloping lines, and it is this that proves difficult for John. Humphreys and Riddoch summarize John's performance on this and other related tasks as follows:

> These studies ... showed that he could derive 'global' information about the overall shape of objects but, unlike normal subjects, his global descriptions of objects are not elaborated by detailed coding of the 'parts'. We may conclude from this that such global shape descriptions can be derived independently of

the processes involved in 'binding' the parts together. (1987a, p. 103)

The fact that whole and part information are dissociable in this way clarifies issues about which earlier theories of perception, such as the Gestalt approach, were vague and adds to our knowledge of normal as well as abnormal perception.

Based on G.W. Humphreys and M.J. Riddoch 1987a: *To See But Not to See: A Case Study of Visual Agnosia*, chs 2, 4 and 6. London: Lawrence Erlbaum Associates.

Box 12.2
Remembering without awareness

The idea that remembering can occur without conscious recollection of the learning episode is important and has shaped our views not only on normal memory, but also on the memory abilities of amnesics. Jacoby and Witherspoon (1982) were among the first, in recent years, to draw our attention to this possibility. They reported a number of effects and demonstrations in their paper to support their argument that memory need not involve conscious recollection, including the frequently cited experiment which we describe here.

The experiment used as participants five Korsakoff patients classified as amnesic on standardized tests and five university students (controls).

The procedure was straightforward. In phase one, all participants were asked a series of verbally presented questions. Half of the questions included a homophone (a word which has two possible spellings corresponding to different meanings). For instance, in the sentence 'Name a musical instrument which can be played with a reed', the homophone is 'reed', and has an alternative spelling, READ, corresponding to its other meaning. In every case the meaning of the homophones used in the questions corresponded to their least frequent spelling. The remaining questions contained no homophones, as in 'What is your favourite sport?'. In this first phase of the experiment, participants were merely asked to answer the questions and Jacoby and Witherspoon report that few difficulties were experienced with this.

The second phase, presented soon after the first, involved a spelling test. Participants were asked to spell the (old) homophones and (old) non-homophones from the previous questions and some (new) homophones and (new) non-homophones which had not been previously presented. This phase of the experiment was designed to test whether the previous questions had biased the interpretation of the homophones and whether this bias had lasted sufficiently long to affect subsequent spelling. Thus, if someone still retains the effects of having heard the word reed, they should be more likely to spell it REED than READ. New homophones were also included in this phase to check that only the spelling of the old homophones had been biased. The non-homophones allowed the investigators to check further that general spelling performance was otherwise unaffected by the procedure.

In phase three of the experiment, all participants were given a recognition test in which they were asked to pick out the old homophones and non-homophones from a set which included them, together with some new homophones and new non-homophones which had not been presented in either phases one or two. The results were intriguing and can be seen in box table 12.2.1.

Columns one and two show the probability with which the controls and the amnesics spelled the old and new homophones in the less frequent way. Notice that both groups show clear effects of the previous biasing. The likelihood of spelling the new homophones in the less frequent way was only around 0.20 whereas the old

Box table 12.2.1 Low frequency spelling and recognition performance of amnesics and controls, and recognition given previous low frequency spelling – p (rec/sp)

| | Spelling | | Recognition | p (rec/sp) |
	Old homophone	New homophone		
Normal	0.40	0.20	0.76	0.82
Amnesics	0.63	0.21	0.25	0.29

Source: Based on table 11, Jacoby and Witherspoon, 1982

homophones were much more likely to be spelled in line with the previous question (0.63 and 0.49). In fact, the Korsakoff patients actually displayed rather more effects of memory (0.63) than the controls (0.49), a difference which, as Jacoby and Witherspoon (1982) suggest, may reflect the response perseveration characteristics of Korsakoff patients, possibly due to frontal lobe damage.

A contrasting picture emerged on the recognition test. Here the performance of the Korsakoff patients was very poor indeed, while that of the controls was at normal levels. So, whereas both groups showed effects of memory on the spelling task, only the controls recognized the words to any degree. Amnesics remembered, but failed to recollect seeing the words before.

Jacoby and Witherspoon then considered the important question of how the two sets of data, spelling and recognition, related, in order to make it clear that 'a person need not be aware of remembering for past experience to influence his/her interpretation of a word' (1982, p. 305). They examined, for both controls and amnesics, whether words that had been spelled in the least frequent way were more likely to be recognized. To do this they first created a contingency table, see box table 12.2.2, and divided the data up into numbers of low frequency (LF) spellings recognized, number of high frequency (HF) spellings recognized, numbers of low frequency spellings not recognized and numbers of high frequency spellings not recognized. Using a simple statistical test, known as the Chi-square test, they were able to see whether there was any pattern in these numbers. The test did not give a significant result, which indicated that spelling and recognition performance were independent in normals as well as amnesics.

To check on this independence in a slightly different way, Jacoby and Witherspoon (1982) then compared the data in column three and four of box table 12.2.1. Column three simply shows the overall probability for correct recognition

for the controls and the amnesics. Column four, on the other hand, shows the probability of correctly recognizing a word given that it has already been spelled in the least frequent way. If the numbers in column four are significantly greater than in column three, then previous spelling and subsequent recognition are related. Again, despite the apparent difference between the two sets of numbers, there was no statistically significant difference between them in either normals or amnesics, indicating the independence between spelling and recognition.

A number of criticisms can be made of the study. To begin with, a rather small number of participants was used, though the clarity and consistency of the results makes this a minor problem. More serious is the fact that no real attempt was made to match the controls and the amnesics on age or other possibly relevant factors. Although unlikely, it might be that the poor performance of the amnesics on, say, the recognition task was more a function of their age or intelligence than their medical condition. A third problem is the duration of the effects reported. In their 1982 article, Jacoby and Witherspoon did not give any clear indication of what interval transpired between the questions and the subsequent memory tests. Perhaps these effects only last over very short intervals, though later

Box table 12.2.2 Contingency table for spelling and recognition

| | | Old homophones | |
		LF spelling	HF spelling
Old homophones	Recognized	X	X
	Not recognized	X	X

work has shown that they can be quite durable (e.g. Schacter, 1987). Finally, there are a number of minor statistical and procedural details missing from the report. This reflects, in part, the nature of the article, which was designed as a general review of the area, but in a more formal experimental report a fuller report of the methods and results is the norm.

Based on L.L. Jacoby and D. Witherspoon 1982: Remembering without awareness. *Canadian Journal of Psychology*, 36, 300–24.

13 Connectionism

The two approaches to modelling mental functions examined so far, cognitive neuropsychology and artificial intelligence (AI), lead to rather different views of how mind should be studied. Neuropsychology shows how closely mind and brain are linked. Damage to particular brain areas often has specific mental consequences which cognitive neuropsychologists then interpret in terms of disruption of one or more parts in a cognitive model (see chapter 12). Not all areas of the brain work in the same way nor serve the same mental functions. Workers in artificial intelligence, as we saw in chapter 11, approach the problem of modelling mental functions rather differently. With some notable exceptions (e.g. Marr, 1982), they assume that brains, like computers, are general purpose symbol-processors, and have argued that mind can be studied independently from brain, just as programs can be written without worrying too much about the details of the computer on which they are to run. The result is a pure, functional, symbol-based view of mind, which generally ignores the underlying structure of the brain.

An important way of modelling cognition has recently re-emerged which blends certain aspects of AI with neuropsychology, though it differs from both in important ways too. Connectionism, the name of the approach, offers a powerful, new way of explaining human cognitive activity. Like AI, its primary aim is to simulate aspects of normal cognitive activity, and so, unlike neuropsychology, it does not dwell too much on the mental effects of brain injury. But connectionism is sometimes also known as neural modelling. Unlike AI, therefore, it rejects the idea that mind can be understood, separately from the brain, as a pure, symbol-processing system. Like neuropsychology, it recognizes that neural mechanisms not only support mental life but that their arrangement and structure contribute to its very shape.

Rather than using rules or symbols to explain mind, connectionists suggest that mental activity depends on the combined activity of thousands of simple, interlinked, neurone-like, processing units. Connectionists try to work out the number, pattern and strength of the links between such units used to perform various mental tasks. This basic contrast between connectionism and symbol processing is illustrated in diagrammatic form in figure 13.1.

The aim of this chapter is to introduce the general themes and principles of connectionism, to show how some of its important models work, and to discuss the strengths and limits of the approach. We hope that we adequately convey some of the reasons why connectionism is currently attracting such interest in psychology, biology and computer science.

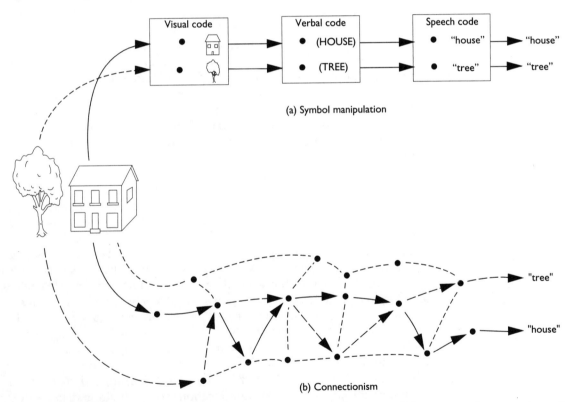

Figure 13.1 Two ways of naming objects using (a) symbols and (b) links between simple processing units. Symbol manipulation uses internal representations such as visual or verbal codes; connectionism merely assumes that there is some pattern or link between input and output

Introduction to Connectionism

Connectionism and standard AI

Connectionism re-emerged in the 1980s, but its roots go back at least 40 years. Soon after the Second World War, when interest in thinking machines began to develop, it was generally thought that simulations of intelligence would require the modelling of neural, not mental processes. People used to talk a lot, then, about the coming of 'electronic brains', not artificial intelligence as they do now. This was probably because the first computer programmers did not have at their disposal the wide range of computer languages that exist today. Knowing how to program a computer, in those early days, was not so obviously separate from understanding the computer itself as it is now. Clever programs were simply taken to mean clever machines. Later on, the distinction between the computer's program, or software, and its machinery, or hardware, became apparent as high-level computer languages developed. Programming then became possible for people who knew little if anything about the computer's inner workings. Only then did the analogy really emerge between the brain and a computer, and between the mind and a computer program (Miller et al., 1960).

Several neurologically plausible models of cognition appeared in psychology and computer science in the 1940s and 1950s, and many themes from this initial work still persist in the new connectionism. The psychologist D.O. Hebb, for instance, described how patterns of neural (brain) activity could be sustained when outside stimulation ceased (Hebb, 1949). Hebb's ideas about 'reverberating circuits' initially had a large influence on theories of memory consolidation. More recently, the idea that networks can be dynamically self-sustaining has been revived by the new connectionism. Hebb also argued that learning involves some change or strengthening of the connections between elements in a neural network. Taken as a literal description of what was going on in the brain, this led to a detailed study of how electrochemical impulses were passed across the gap, or synapse, between individual neurones. Modified versions of Hebb's ideas have since been incorporated into the general theory of connectionism. This relates learning to changes in the connection strengths between a large number of simple processing units, which are not necessarily equated with individual neurones. The new work shows how changing connection strengths affect the pattern of activity in the system as a whole, in a way that detailed neurophysiological study of a simple synapse can never do.

At much the same time as Hebb, Lashley (1950) argued that separate memories do not occupy separate locations in the brain and in so doing anticipated one of the main ideas of many recent connectionist models, namely that representations are distributed rather than localized. Distributed representations have some powerful properties that localized ones lack, as we shall see later. Other important developments occurred in computer science when Rosenblatt (1962) offered a general theory for neural computing, or what he called 'neurodynamics', and described a class of simple parallel processing, learning mechanisms which he called 'perceptrons'. Rosenblatt continued to work in this field until his death, despite theoretical criticisms of his views by Minsky and Papert (1969).

One of the first pattern recognition systems was also inspired by the neural metaphor. 'Pandemonium', a program written by Selfridge (1959), attempted to recognize letters by combining the activity of several, interacting, processing units. Pandemonium's legacy was twofold. First, it showed how quite simple, and essentially stupid, processing elements could cooperate to produce quite complex and apparently intelligent behaviour. Second, as it worked by analysing separate features of a given letter at the same time, it showed how simple processing units can be arranged to operate in parallel. Both ideas remain with us today.

What happened to all this early enthusiasm for neural models? Despite their initial promise, neural approaches to cognition suffered some severe setbacks in the 1960s. For one thing, there was little by way of an accepted general theory for neural computing, following Minsky and Papert's proof that Rosenblatt's perceptrons failed to deal with certain logical problems, and even some simple pattern classification problems. This left a series of isolated models which were easily picked off one by one. For instance, it soon became clear that Pandemonium was limited in some crucial ways. Apart from the fact that it got very confused if shown more than one letter at a time, the model could only cope with well-defined, complete characters. Humans, on the other hand, are able to read a variety of styles of lettering of varying quality, as teachers and the designers of advertising logos can testify. Finally, as in other areas of science, a more popular approach, or paradigm, simply achieved pre-eminence. Symbol processing emerged as the major philosophy dominating both AI and cognitive psychology and was largely unchallenged for 30 years.

Adoption of the symbol-processing approach had another effect. Somewhat ironically, although the computer metaphor implies that mind can be studied independently from brain, many of its models were influenced, tacitly or otherwise, by the serial processing architecture of standard computers (see chapter 11). Highly successful simulations were also produced of game playing and other situations where thought might be reasonably expected to proceed in a step-by-step fashion. Simulations of apparently lower or more basic functions such as memory or perception, where parallel processing was likely to be used by humans, were rather less successful. Not surprisingly, interest in parallel processing waned as a result.

Connectionism re-emerges

Renewed interest in parallel processing in the 1970s seems to have brought about the renaissance of connectionism in the 1980s. There are three main reasons for this.

Simple but powerful arguments were revived to show why brains use parallel processing. These arguments emphasize the short time in which human actions can be performed, and the comparatively slow rates at which neurones transmit impulses. Many seemingly simple everyday actions, such as hitting a ball, typing, or playing notes on a musical instrument, are carried out in fractions of a second, but must involve considerable amounts of mental activity. Actions such as these rely on the combination of several even simpler behaviours, each of which can be broken down further into basic processing decisions. Consider hitting a ball in a game of squash. The player sees the current position of the ball, works out its likely trajectory, positions her arm and hand so that the racquet makes good contact with the ball, decides on the force and direction needed to place the ball, keeps her balance, and, perhaps, carries on a somewhat laconic conversation with her adversary. All of this may have to be done in less than a second. Each of the subtasks in turn, such as positioning the arm or tracking the ball, entails many separate decisions such as the exact angles needed for shoulder, upper arm, elbow, wrist and other body parts or how to move the head and eyes to keep the ball in view. So, a simple stroke in a squash game involves hundreds, possibly thousands of computational steps (see chapter 6 for a further discussion of skills and actions). The problem is that neurones, unlike modern microprocessors, transmit information quite slowly, at speeds of the order of a few milliseconds. At these neuronal rates of transmission there is only time to perform about a hundred computations every second. If actions involving several hundred computational steps can be carried out in less than a second, then lots of the elementary processing operations, which make up actions, must be performed simultaneously. Another psychological argument for parallel processing is that many everyday activities, such as interpreting language or keeping one's balance, are performed best when information from several sources is dealt with at once. Language, for instance, relies on the mutual interplay of sound, meaning, grammar and context. These interactions are so fast that they allow you to assign one grammatical interpretation to 'flying' in *I saw the Alps flying to Italy* and another to 'grazing' in *I saw the sheep grazing on the hill*. Decisions like these are made so adeptly that grammar and meaning are either dealt with extremely rapidly, or, more plausibly, they are dealt with at the same time.

Developments in computer hardware have also renewed interest in parallel processing. Improvements in the manufacture of microchips and innovations in chip design mean that the construction of a truly parallel processing computer is now a real possibility. Even now, before fully parallel hardware has arrived, the storage capacity and processing speed of modern machines is such that simulations using large numbers of interacting processing elements are possible. Hardware and software suitable for connectionist experiments are currently available for desktop microcomputers.

A third reason for taking parallel processing seriously is that there is now a good framework for connectionist models. This framework, largely though not solely the work of the Parallel Distributed Processing (PDP) research group led by Jay McClelland and David Rumelhart, has not only addressed some of the earlier criticisms of specific connectionist models, but is working toward a general theory of all neural networks. One goal of the PDP group is to explain the behaviour of interconnected nets in rigorous, mathematical terms. Impressive progress has been made in this respect, and explanations from the physical and mathematical sciences have already been applied to dynamic networks. These range from applications of the branch of physics concerned with the behaviour of fluids and gases, thermodynamics, to recent interest in the application of the mathematics of complex, non-linear systems, known as 'chaos theory'.

Despite the importance of the PDP team's work, we would not like to convey the mistaken impression that parallel processing, or distributed processing for that matter, is synonymous with connectionism. There are connectionist models which do not involve fully distributed representations, as we shall see shortly. Also, it is possible to envisage symbolic parallel processing systems. Nevertheless, connectionism offers a more accommodating framework for both parallel and distributed models, and so its fortunes have risen together with theirs.

A simple connectionist model

Parallel processing and other important aspects of connectionism are simply illustrated by a recent memory model proposed by McClelland (1981). The model represents information about a number of general concepts and specific instances. In the original, the information described some rather infamous people with dubious occupations who were members of either the 'Jets' gang or the 'Sharks' gang. To simplify the model and to show that it applies outside the torrid world of New York gangland, our example deals with some internationally more famous, and considerably more attractive, animals!

The information which the model uses is shown in table 13.1. Each named animal is a member of a particular species, is small, medium or large, hails from America or Britain and is either a character in a book, features in a TV cartoon or cartoon strip or is a film star. In a standard model of semantic memory, information about each animal would most likely be grouped closely around its name, either as a list of features, or as closely situated points or nodes in a network. Models such as these are not particularly flexible, one of their major problems being that they are not content addressable. Content addressability refers to the way in which people can quickly access information based on almost any attribute of a concept. For instance, if asked, people can readily supply the names of famous animals which have starred in films, or give examples of small, American cartoon characters. If information is stored under name headings, the name of each animal would have to be found first before the properties of the animal could be inspected in detail. Such a search process is clearly inefficient, since several animals' entries might be searched before even one was found with the desired attributes.

Table 13.1   Some famous animals and their characteristics

Name	Animal	Size	Origin	Country
Mickey	mouse	small	film	US
Bambi	deer	medium	film	US
Toad	toad	small	book	UK
Eeyore	donkey	large	book	UK
Woodstock	bird	small	strip cartoon	US

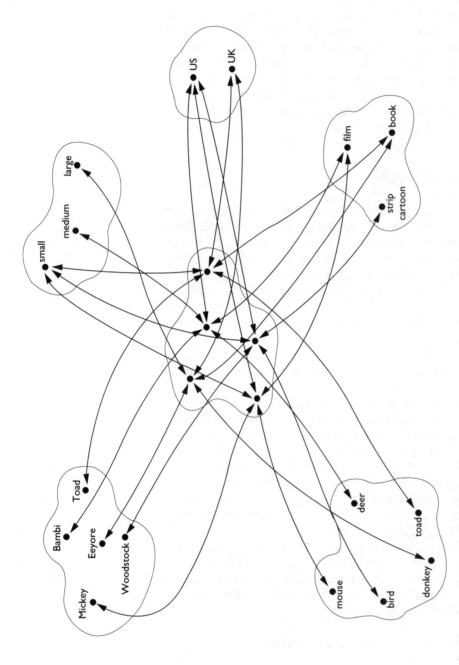

Figure 13.2 A connectionist model of memory

Figure 13.2 shows a connectionist scheme for some of this information. Each animal's name in the list is linked to an 'instance node', shown as a dark circle, which in turn is linked to nodes which specify each of the animal's properties. There are in fact two general types of connections or links in the model, inhibitory and excitatory. Items within each cloud or region are mutually inhibitory. So, if the 'film' node is active it will try to shut off the 'cartoon' and 'book' nodes. Items in different regions linked by arrows excite one another. So, the node labelled 'small' sends excitation to 'book' and other nodes via its instance node. For clarity, only the excitatory links are shown in the diagram.

This simple model has a number of important properties. To begin with, it is highly content addressable. For instance, all and only the names of animals hailing from the US are automatically and simultaneously activated by probing the 'US' node. As nodes for 'Bambi', 'Mickey' and 'Woodstock' become active they inhibit nodes 'Eeyore' and 'Toad', animals from the UK, which share the same region. The power of content addressability is even more apparent when the effects of activating two nodes are examined. What happens if 'US' and 'small' are probed at once? The 'US' node, as we have just stated, sends activation to several nodes including 'Bambi', 'Mickey' and 'Woodstock'. The node labelled 'small' sends additional excitation to 'Mickey' and 'Woodstock' and also activates 'Toad'. Because of their extra activation, 'Mickey' and 'Woodstock' now have the edge on both 'Toad', a small but non-American creature, and 'Bambi', a medium sized American creature, which they inhibit, but are each too active to be suppressed by the other. Thus, activating 'small' and 'American' produces the class of small, American creatures and their properties.

What are the general properties of American media animals? The model quickly returns the answer that typical American animals are small and appear in films. Both 'small' and 'medium' are activated by US, but 'small' achieves more activation and becomes dominant. Similarly, 'film' with its three inputs is able to suppress 'strip cartoon' which has only one, and 'book' which has none. British media creatures are shown by the model to have a more book-based background than their American cousins. Probing the 'UK' node activates the instance nodes for 'Toad' and 'Eeyore' and their literary pedigree is quickly revealed. However, the typical bookish, British animal, in our example at least, is of indeterminate size: both 'large' and 'small' nodes are excited to some extent, when the 'UK' node is activated.

The model's ability to produce general properties from a set of particular instances like this is most impressive. It mimics an important skill which humans are known to possess but which has been extremely hard to explain. We will discuss a more powerful model which has similar properties later in the chapter.

In common with most subsequent connectionist theories, McClelland's memory model uses parallel processing, but unlike many later models, its representations are not fully distributed. As you can see, the model stores individual concepts such as 'deer', 'large' or 'cartoon' at specific nodes in the network. Destruction of any one of these nodes would result in complete loss of information about the identity of a concept, while cutting the connections to them would leave them in splendid isolation from their neighbours. In a fully distributed model, information about each concept, and not just about how it links with others, would be spread out as a pattern of connections throughout the network. Distributed models are far more resistant to damage than schemes which use local representations. Damage to a particular location, or the severing of a link, does not eliminate or disconnect information in so complete or final a way in a distributed model as it does in a localized one.

Making Connections ▶ ▶

McClelland's memory model illustrates some but not all properties of recent connectionist accounts. What then are the key features of connectionist models? How are connections made in general? In this section we answer these questions using the framework outlined by the PDP research group and then apply this to an important connectionist model known as a pattern associator.

General properties of PDP models

Building on earlier work by Feldman and Ballard (1982), the PDP group have described the formal properties of all connectionist models using a branch of mathematics known as linear or matrix algebra. While the mathematically inclined would doubtless appreciate their account, we reassure readers who are less interested in mathematics that our description of the principles of connectionism is less technical than theirs.

All connectionist models include a set of interconnected simple processing elements, or 'units', see figure 13.3. There are three types of unit: input, output and hidden. Input units take in information, either through the normal sensory channels or from other parts of the network of connections. Output units put out information and either control actual responses directly or send information to other parts of the network. Hidden units, which feature in some but not all models, communicate with both input and output units but not with the external environment in which the model operates. They are said to be 'hidden' because their behaviour cannot be directly observed from outside the system. In certain models, like the memory one above, the units represent words, instances, concepts or other meaningful representations. In distributed models, the units do not represent whole meaningful entities such as words or images. In a distributed system, a unit may stand for a part, feature, attribute or even more abstract element. The whole entity – be it a word, image, concept, schema or whatever – emerges in distributed systems when units interact; it is not a property of any one unit in isolation.

Units, and their connections, are where most of the important work goes on in a connectionist model. There is no central executive, controller or separate processor. This means that the processing as well as the representation of information is devolved or spread across the entire network. In fact, the clear separation between representations and processes present in many AI models is blurred by connectionism: the representation of information in

Connectionism 335

connected units and its processing is one and the same thing. Neural nets are dynamic processing systems.

All units have some level of activity denoted by their 'activation value'. This is very important as it determines how much activation or output a unit passes on to its connected neighbours. In some simple models the output of a unit equals its activation value, but in many systems, the unit must reach some minimum level of activity before it produces an output, or 'fires', rather like a neurone, in fact.

Units are interconnected in various ways. Different patterns of connectivity are suitable for different cognitive activities and affect the flow or 'propagation' of activity through the system. The properties of several activity patterns are now well understood. Two important connection schemes, for instance, are those which support data-driven and concept-driven processing. In data-driven processing the flow of information moves from relatively raw or unprocessed levels of input to more highly interpreted ones. For example, when looking at an object in good viewing conditions, information flows from the object up through the system and

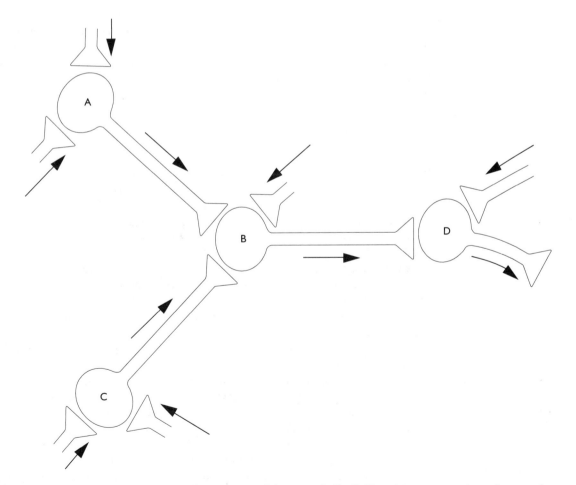

Figure 13.3 A connectionist model consisting of the units A, B, C, D and interconnections. Arrows denote the direction of flow of activation

allows the observer to work out what is being seen. Concept-driven processing works the other way and uses high-level general knowledge to interpret incoming data. For example, when walking on a foggy day people use their knowledge of the locality to avoid getting lost (see chapter 3 for a more detailed discussion of both types of processing). Connection schemes for both processing modes, therefore, rely on groups of units arranged in levels from lower to higher. Data-driven systems are so arranged that lower levels affect only higher levels, while top-down schemes use the reverse arrangement. A third scheme, of which the interactive letter recognition model of McClelland and Rumelhart (1981) is a good example (see chapter 9), allows for mutual interaction between high and low levels of units.

There is another vital ingredient in all connectionist schemes which, together with the activation levels and connection pattern, controls the way that activation and hence information is spread through the network. When an output from one unit arrives at another neighbouring unit its effect is often modified by multiplying it by a 'connection weight'. Connection weights do two important things. First, they alter the size of the input into the receiving unit. For example, if the output sent from unit A to unit B, in figure 13.3, is 2 and the connection weight is 3 then the resulting input into B from A is $3 \times 2 = 6$. By simple arithmetic, connection weights greater than one increase the strength of a link, while connection weights less than one but greater than zero decrease the strength of a link. Second, connection weights can alter the type of input from excitatory to inhibitory or vice versa. Excitatory inputs increase the activation level of their recipient, inhibitory ones diminish it. If, in the example above, the connection weight is –1, the new input from A to B is now given by $-1 \times 3 = -3$. The weight has the effect of changing a previously positive, excitatory input into a negative, inhibitory one of the same size. Similarly, outputs that are themselves negative can be changed into positive ones. So an output from A of –2 and a connection weight of –2 gives an input into B of $-2 \times -2 = 4$, in this case changing both the magnitude and the direction of the effect.

The reader should now be starting to realize that as each input converges on a unit it either adds to, reduces or leaves unaffected the activation value of the receiving unit. Usually, a unit's final activation value is worked out by adding together all its inputs, taking due account of whether they are positive or negative, and combining the result with the existing activation value. Then, the new activation value, if large enough, produces a further output which is sent on to other units, and so the pattern continues. The final pattern of activation occurs when all the units are in a dynamic equilibrium, or a stable energy state, mutually exciting and inhibiting each other's activities.

Connectionist models do not usually stay in a steady state for ever; just like human cognitive processes, many of them continually change or learn. Learning occurs whenever the overall pattern of activation alters in response to the input. This can happen in one of three ways: by forming new connections, by removing old connections or by changing the connection weights. Although nature may grow new physical connections during development or lose existing ones in old age, during brain surgery or following injury, most connectionist models in psychology learn by varying their connection weights. This is not as limiting as it seems. The effect of growing a new connection can be easily mimicked by changing a weight from zero to non-zero. This releases previously blocked input into a unit. The same method in reverse can also be used to disconnect a link. Similarly, setting a previously non-zero weight to zero prevents input from using the link in question, and results in the connectionist equivalent of a brain lesion.

Various learning rules have been worked out which allow networks to modify their behaviour. Many of these depend on a simple idea originally suggested by Hebb (1949) who argued that the link between two units should be strengthened if both were highly active at the same time. Using Hebb's rule, connection weights are altered in proportion to the product of the output of the sending unit and the activation of the recipient. If both are high the link is strengthened.

When people learn, they often do so with the help of a teacher or friend. A commonly used connectionist learning scheme, therefore, measures the behaviour of the system against some standard or 'teacher' to see how much more it has to learn. A technique known as the delta rule, and its more general form, 'backward error propagation', is used to do this. The delta rule changes connection weights in proportion to the product of the output of the sending unit and the difference between the receiving unit's current activation and the activation level desired. When the difference between the current and target activation of the recipient unit is large, a large change is made in the connection weight. When the difference between the existing and the target activation is small, the change made in the weight becomes correspondingly smaller. The delta rule allows the model to home in steadily on the correct solution. Yet another learning scheme, competitive learning, does not rely on an external teacher but simply allows units to compete with each other in the battle for activation.

Pattern associators

Connectionist models known as pattern associators put many of these abstract principles into practice.

Pattern associators show how people might link two patterns together. For instance, the word 'sunset' readily summons up a mental image of a beautiful scene, the sight of a glass of wine reminds us of its bouquet, the mention of onions brings a peculiar taste to mind, and the image of a dog makes us think of its name. How does one pattern produce another so rapidly and correctly? How do we avoid thinking of the smell of bacon when we see a rose?

The simple pattern associator, illustrated in figure 13.4, deals with these problems. Pattern associators not only link two sets of stimuli, or two sets of ideas, they can be used to join any two patterns such as one memory with another or stimuli with responses. Also, just as a person many think of the taste of coffee when they see several different types of coffee jar in a supermarket, so too, pattern associators respond in similar ways to similar patterns; they exhibit what is known as stimulus generalization. Like many other connectionist models, and again, like people, pattern associators can

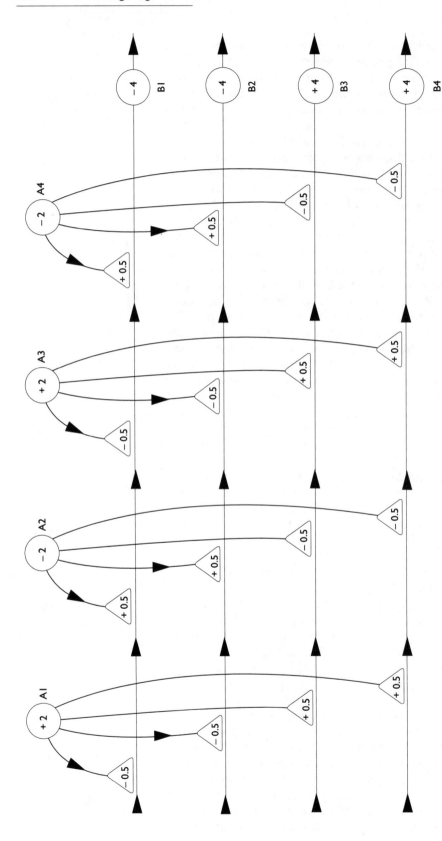

Figure 13.4 A simple pattern associator. The activation on the B units results from multiplying the activation pattern on the A units by the connection weights. For example, B1's activation = $(-0.5 \times 2) + (0.5 \times -2) + (-0.5 \times 2) + (0.5 \times -2)$

deal with poor or degraded patterns. They still link patterns when one is weak or has parts missing. A further property is that they can associate lots of patterns with the very same set of units, as long as the patterns are all different. Whether people match different sets of patterns with the same machinery is not known, but if they do use something like a pattern associator, the matching can be done very efficiently and without any confusion.

The details of how pattern associators work are a little technical, but some understanding of this gives further insight into the general principles of connectionism, and the reader is advised to read through the following paragraphs carefully to get a good feel for connectionism in action.

The pattern associator is called a one-layer network since it consists only of input (A) units and output (B) units, with no hidden units (see figure 13.4). Each unit is shown with a particular activation value. The two patterns of activation on the input and output units are abstract ways of representing the situations that are associated. So, the pattern (+2, –2, +2, –2) on the input units might represent the image of a rose, while the pattern on the output units (–4, –4, +4, +4) might represent its smell. Each input unit connects with each output unit, and the connection weights, in triangles in the diagram, are arranged so that the pattern on the A units produces the pattern on the B units. Multiplying the input activation by the connection weights gives the output activation. (The connection weights are learned in the first place by applying the Hebb rule described above.)

It was stated above that similar input patterns on a pattern associator produce similar outputs. Two special cases where this occurs are when an input pattern has a part missing or when the overall input is feeble. For instance, suppose you are trying to read a poor quality photocopy, or maybe a document written on a typewriter with damaged letters. You are able to do so, though with some difficulty. Similarly the weak or incomplete input patterns presented to a pattern associator produce essentially the same pattern of output as the clear, original pattern but at reduced strength. If, for example, unit A1 is damaged and its activation falls to zero, the same general pattern of activation arrives at the B units but at a slightly weaker level (–3, –3, +3, +3). The reader might like to check that this is so by multiplying the new input pattern (0, –2, +2, –2) by the connection weight to obtain the new pattern on the B units.

It was also stated that patterns with nothing in common can be processed by the very same processing network without any confusion arising between their outputs. To do this, the associator must acquire suitable connection weights. Figure 13.5 illustrates this remarkable property. In figure 13.5(a) and (b) two distinct sets of patterns are shown together with their connection weights in the form of an array or matrix. The connection matrix in figure 13.5(c) is obtained by simply adding the corresponding entries in the two matrices (a) and (b). The new set of weights then allows either pattern on the A units to elicit its associated B pattern without affecting the other. Figure 13.5 (c) shows this happening for the first set of patterns. This means that the same computational structure can support two or more distinct mental operations, though whether the complete independence of patterns needed to allow this is ever found in real life is debatable. Elephants are quite unlike mice in many ways, but in other ways they are similar: both have four legs, tails, eyes and so on. True pattern independence might be a mathematical rather than a psychological reality.

Simple pattern associators are powerful but they do have some limitations. As we have just explained, whenever two patterns are similar they elicit a similar response. This means, then, that when two patterns are quite different they cannot be made to produce similar or identical responses. One logical problem which requires this and which therefore cannot be solved by a simple pattern associator is the XOR or the 'exclusive or' problem. An example of the XOR problem in real life is the way in which we define a half-sister or half-brother. If either one of your parents has a female child with another partner who is not one of your parents, then the child is your half-sister. If the child is the product of the union of either both of your parents or of neither of them she cannot be your half-sister. The

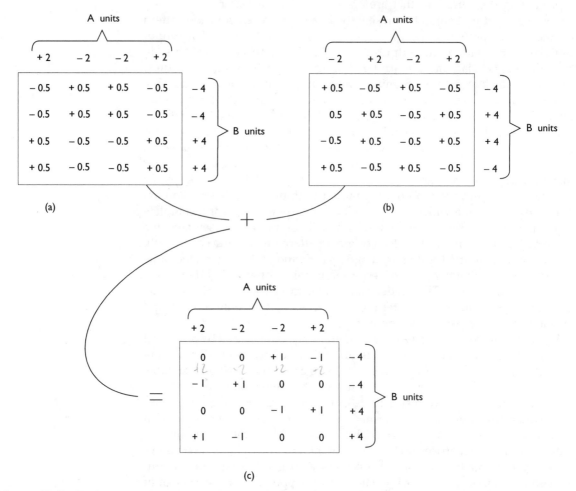

(a)

(b)

(c)

Figure 13.5   The connection weights and activation values for two dissimilar sets of patterns (a) and (b), and (c) the combined connection weights obtained by adding weights from (a) and (b) which allow each pattern on the A units to elicit its associated pattern on the B units without interference (see text for full explanation)

Input (parents)

your father	woman	present
man	your mother	present
man	woman	absent
your father	your mother	absent

Output (half-sister)

(a)

Input
(Presence of my biological parent)

1 = presence

1	0
0	1
0	0
1	1

Output
(Presence of half-sister)

1 = presence

1
1
0
0

(b)

Figure 13.6 The XOR problem: (a) real-life version, (b) abstract version

(input) patterns of parents which define the (output) pattern of a half-sister involve quite different individuals as do the patterns which define the absence of a half-sister. Figure 13.6(a) shows the verbal version of the problem described here, and figure 13.6(b) a more general, abstract version. The similarity between the two is easy to grasp if 1 is allowed to stand for the presence and 0 for the absence of an individual.

A connectionist network which can deal with the XOR problem is shown in figure 13.7. The obvious difference between this and the simple pattern associator is that it contains hidden units.

Hidden units are used by the extended associator to evaluate the relationship between the pattern elements. If the input to any unit is greater than 0.1 the unit produces an output as shown on the links in the diagram. Examine what happens if the pattern 1,0 (your father, another woman) is presented to input units A and B respectively. Unit A receives an input of +1 and so fires, unit B receives an input of 0 and does not fire. Hidden unit C then receives net input of +1 from A and fires, hidden unit D receives net input of –1 from A, and so does not fire. The output unit, E, then receives 1 unit from C and puts out a response of 1 (a half-sister). The mirror image of this occurs if the input is 0,1 (another man, your mother) with the same result. Now, C receives –1 input from B, and D receives +1 from B. The same response of +1 (a half-sister) is then output from unit E but has been produced via a different route. If, however, an input of 1,1 (your father, your mother) is received, neither unit C nor unit D fires as their excitation from one input is exactly cancelled by the inhibition from the other. No input is received by E and the system produces an output of zero (not a half-sister). Finally, an input of 0,0 is not strong enough to fire either input unit and no response at all results (not a half-sister).

Whether extended pattern associators like this are actually used by humans to solve XOR problems is a moot point. Such problems, though they exist, are quite rare in real life and even then might be simplified to involve some similarity or matching. For you to have a half-sister only one of your parents is involved, and you might use this fact, rather than the various possible combinations of parents, to define a half-sister. Also, people are notoriously bad at dealing with XOR problems, unless they are given special instructions and have memory cued in the right way. This might indicate that multi-layer networks are not used in exactly this way when dealing with such problems.

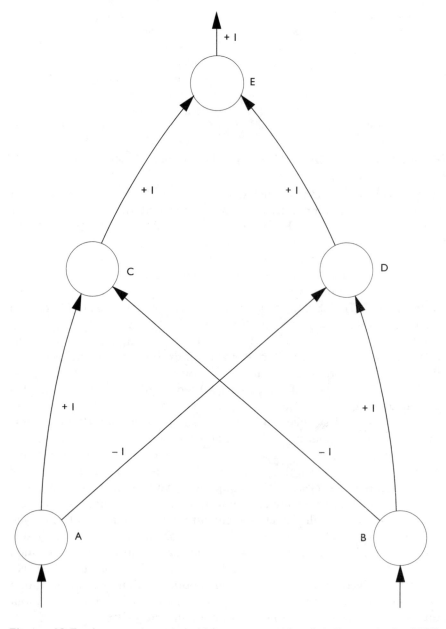

Figure 13.7 A network, with hidden units, capable of dealing with the XOR problem. The threshold of each unit is 0.1, potential outputs from each unit are shown on the connecting links. See text for further explanation

Whatever the psychological validity of the XOR problem, multi-layer networks do have other advantages. Hidden units allow pattern associators to process any possible pattern match. This is a clear point in their favour. The computational basis for multi-layer networks is not yet fully worked out, though progress is being steadily made (Bechtel and Abrahemsen, 1991, provide a thorough review.)

Connectionism in Action

As well as representing factual knowledge and associating patterns, there are now several other psychological applications of connectionism. Many of these are simulations of perceptual and memory processes and their conspicuous success contrasts with other less impressive simulations which have used standard AI techniques. Connectionist models of language, for example, display many of the characteristics of the use and acquisition of language as a natural consequence of the way they work. These characteristics do not have to be specially built into them as sets of rules or procedures. Memory models too have properties which human memories exhibit but which have been hard to simulate on computers up to now. We introduce and discuss some of these models in this section.

There are also indications that connectionism can be applied to some aspects of higher as well as to more basic cognitive functions. Some of this work is covered here briefly too.

Language: comprehension, production and acquisition

Language is an excellent domain to test connectionist principles, since it involves the simultaneous analysis of information at various levels. Language is grammatically organized and is used to convey meaning within shared contexts. In addition, speech has acoustic and phonological dimensions and print has various visual characteristics. All these aspects, and their mutual constraints, need to be taken into account when interpreting an utterance or reading a sentence, and imply that parallel, or at least highly interactive, processing is needed for linguistic information, as we intimated in chapters 4 and 9. Also, linguistic input is often rather varied. No two speakers produce the same word in quite the same way and various styles of print and handwriting differ around some prototype or standard. Connectionism ought to be well suited to dealing with problems like these. Finally, language is comprehended, spoken or written and acquired. Perception, responding and learning are all issues which any full simulation of language will have to face. Connectionism has made some inroads into these problems but a complete model of language processing is still a long way off. Nevertheless, progress to date has been quite impressive.

An early connectionist model of language is the letter and word identification model of McClelland and Rumelhart (1981). Letter and word recognition are, of course, essential components of reading. We discussed this model in some detail in chapter 9, so we will merely remind the reader here of its chief characteristics. The model copes with letter and word recognition by combining information about the features of individual letters, letters-as-wholes and the words in which they appear. If evidence from these three levels fits together, mutual excitation occurs. If evidence is contradictory either between levels or within a level, mutual inhibition results. Evidence for words accumulates as evidence for their separate letters comes in. The word whose unit has the highest level of final activation is perceived. An important property of the model is that it shows what is known as the word superiority effect. This means that letters forming real words are perceived faster than those which are part of random letter strings. So, the letter 's' in 'measure' is perceived faster than the 's' in 'atbskhu', though see Mewhort and Johns (1988) for some limitations of the model in this respect. Also, letters that are partially obscured and ambiguous can still be identified providing they are part of real words or even part of pronounceable non-words. The model copes with ambiguous or degraded stimuli by using the dominant interpretation from the word level to constrain its choice at the letter level.

There is, of course, far more to reading than identifying letters or even single words. Reading involves the perception and integration of organized groups of words arranged into sentences and paragraphs. Even if we ignore grammar, meaning and other aspects of reading, any model of reading must be able to cope with more than one word at a time. Perhaps something like the McClelland and Rumelhart model of letter recognition could be enlarged to deal with extended text. The difficulty here is that an embarrassingly large number of units is then needed to read even a few simple words. In the original model, a separate set of feature and letter units and their connections is required for the position of every letter in a word. So, every four-letter word demands four complete sets of feature and letter units. Adding another word to the display would immediately double the number of units required. Think of the computational requirements for all the words of different lengths in different positions in this book. Large though its information capacity is, the brain would probably be unable to devote so much machinery to word identification alone. A solution to the problem of duplicating feature and letter units might be to have one set of connection machinery in some central location in the brain and to present to it one word, or even one letter, at a time. While this might work, it would not be very realistic since skilled readers appear to take in several words at once. Also, it would remove one of the chief benefits of the original model, namely its ability to perform rapid, parallel processing.

McClelland (1986) has offered an interesting way round the problem with two models of reading. The first, CID, deals with simple two-word displays, the second PABLO, an extension of CID, copes with a vocabulary of 92 words and lines of text 20 characters long. McClelland's approach combines the advantages of centralized knowledge with the speed and flexibility of parallel processing and uses two general types of connection machinery: a central knowledge store and a set of programmable modules. All information relating to word and letter recognition is economically contained in one fixed set of connections in the central knowledge store. The incoming words themselves, however, do not make direct contact with this. Instead, they are picked up by two or more programmable networks operating in parallel. The programmable networks consist of interconnected letter and word units as in the original McClelland and Rumelhart model, but with one essential difference: their connection weights are not fixed or tuned to any particular combination of letters and words. Rather, they can be programmed and reprogrammed, as many times as required, by the central knowledge store, which resets their connection weights as determined by the incoming information. Knowledge in the central store is triggered by the information passed up by the programmable modules as required. The idea that one party of a complete connectionist system can reprogram another in this way represents an important advance in connectionist theory, though whether human reading mechanisms are quite like this is as yet unclear. However, when models like PABLO are applied to text they can take in more than one word at a time without needing too much cumbersome machinery. PABLO can actually make a series of 'saccades', or shifts of gaze direction, and 'fixations' like human eye movements when reading, and like a human reader, information in the periphery of its 'vision' can affect processing at the centre of its 'attention'.

The most complete connectionist reading model to date, however, is probably the one described by Seidenberg and McClelland (1989; see also Sejnowski and Rosenberg, 1986 for a similar model). The model is complete in the sense that it works right through from print to pronunciation and, while learning to say words, passes through stages remarkably like those of a child learning to read. Recently, the model has been subjected to the sort of treatment that causes severe reading problems if it happens accidentally to human brains. Patterson et al. (1989) have lesioned the model or effectively cut some of its connections. The result is that the model now exhibits reading difficulties which resemble those of patients with surface dyslexia (see box 13.1 for a fuller account of this work, and chapter 9 for a discussion of surface dyslexia).

Connectionist accounts of language acquisition are also starting to appear. Language acquisition is an important domain to model since it looks as if the child learns all sorts of linguistic rules during development whereas, of course, connectionist models do not use rules at all. For instance, when learning the past tense of English verbs, children discover that many verbs in English can be made into the past tense by adding '-ed' to the verb stem, as in 'play + ed' or 'start + ed'. Other verbs, however, have irregular past tenses, 'think' becomes 'thought' and 'swing' becomes 'swung'. Rumelhart and McClelland (1986) have constructed a connectionist model which learns past tenses and acts as if it is a rule user, but actually uses no rules at all. Instead, the model learns to associate correct endings with verb stems by measuring its own performance against some ideal standard, just as a child might modify its own speech with the help of a parent or teacher.

A most intriguing aspect of the model, however, is that at a certain point in its learning it behaves as if all verbs can be changed into their past tense by adding '-ed'. It overgeneralizes, as children do, and makes mistakes such as 'swinged' and 'teached'. Later, as it is exposed to more and more irregular words it manages to sort out which verbs take '-ed' and which have their own special endings. See box 13.2 for more details.

All the models of language we have discussed in this section have involved reading or dealing with individual words. Other recent accounts have attempted to model aspects of sentence production. These models are attempting to deal with various aspects of language, such as grammar and meaning, that critics of such as Fodor and Pylyshyn (1988) claim will be difficult to simulate with connectionism. For instance, Reilly (1992) has shown how representations of sentences might be captured by connectionist networks, and Cullinan et al. (1993, 1994) have simulated some basic aspects of the transition from two- to three-word utterances in language development. Many of these simulations are quite technical, but the interested reader is referred to Orchard (1993) for more examples.

Memory and prototypes

We introduced a simple model of memory earlier in this chapter which, though more powerful than many, was still limited. For one thing its representations were not fully distributed. Damage to the one of the nodes in the model or the severing of one of its connections could remove information or leave information isolated. Yet, apart from extreme cases, human memory rarely fails in so specific a way. A second problem was that it did not show how material arrives in memory through perception in the first place. Suppose you have a memory for what you did on holiday last year. The stored information which forms part of this memory must have resulted in part from actual perceptual experiences when you saw the lakes and mountains in Cumbria. How does perception give rise to memory? Nor did the simple model account for how the cognitive system is able to reproduce perceptual input when the input is no longer present. You are no longer in the Lake District, but you can still revive images of your stay.

McClelland and Rumelhart (1986) have dealt with these problems in a fully distributed model of memory. Their model is composed of a number of interacting, but potentially autonomous, processing modules, each of which consists of a number of simple, processing units. The units are interconnected in such a way that they can either fire in response to external input, or they can fire by reactivating each other with feedback when very little external information is present. Thus they can respond and record perceptual input, laying down memories, and they can be revived with very sparse memory cues, just as the words 'last year's holiday' might do in the above example.

The fact that the model uses distributed representations means that it is far more resistant to damage and deals with poor data far better than a localized system. Even a small part of the original pattern can often elicit or 'cue' the remainder.

The model also copes well with a number of problems which plague many other theories of conceptual memory. These difficulties depend on whether memory relies on general or specific information. People seem to be able to make generalizations and extract common features from sets of instances but they also appear to make liberal use of particular, named examples when thinking. Evidence for both abilities is easy to find. Posner and Keele (1968), for example, showed participants a set of patterns which were all variations of some average pattern or prototype. Later on, participants claimed to have seen the prototype and were better at recognizing it than actual specific patterns which had been presented (see also Rosch, 1975). But extensive use of specific instances also occurs. Experts interviewed during the construction of expert systems, for example, often describe their expertise by reference to specific cases, while the knowledge engineer dealing with them would much prefer a neat set of general rules to plumb into the computer (see also Jacoby, 1983). Which type of information, then, specific or general, forms the true basis of memory?

One answer is that perhaps people use both sorts of information and keep two independent sets of records, one general, the other specific. Unfortunately, this raises another set of problems. Specific instances require general categories for their interpretation in the first place. How can you remember the appearance of a particular tree in your garden without a general concept of 'tree' to start you off, and what is that general concept like if you cannot use your memory of specific trees to think about it? Also, how do you ever set up rules for abstracting the general from the specific if you do not know what general category you want to abstract before you start? The specific and the general, it seems, must somehow interact.

Readers with some familiarity with philosophy should recognize these as old and thorny but important issues in the theory of knowledge.

McClelland and Rumelhart's model cuts a neat swathe through these conceptual brambles. The model automatically extracts a prototype if it is given a series of specific patterns to deal with which vary about some common denominator. An analogy might help to explain how it does this. Suppose you take a number of sheets of clear plastic material and draw a different face of roughly the same size on each one. Then imagine what would happen if you stuck the pieces of plastic together and projected light through them onto a screen. No one single face would appear on the screen, but rather a blend or composite of all the faces. Notice how this prototypical face emerges without any need for rules which tell you how to work out the common pattern. The general is simply the superposition or blending together of the specific. In the model the connection weights for the specific instances combine in a similar way to create those for the prototype.

Although it extracts prototypes with such ease, the model is also capable of retaining specific instances, a necessary feature if it is to mimic human cognition. After all, people can retain particular details, especially when a stimulus or event is repeated several times. A child, for example, re-members its mother's face which it sees on many occasions, but forgets the details of faces which it sees only once. To extend the plastic sheet analogy, suppose that among a set of 100 faces one face is repeated and appears 50 times. Now, half of the 100 patterns are different and half are the same. If this happens, the repeated face establishes its own image in the set and can be seen on the screen together with the more general prototype of the remainder. Likewise, in the model, repeated stimuli establish their own strong connections and their specific patterns are retained together with the general prototype.

A final advantage of the distributed memory model is that it can account for how general knowledge, or semantic memories, can be acquired from a number of different situations. Suppose a child learns that 'Dublin is the capital of Ireland'. This information may be learned across a series of separate contexts, such as in school, at home, by watching television, or by reading books. The fact is constant but the events where it is learned vary. Repeated exposure to the same fact in different situations, therefore, leads to a strengthening of the connections concerned with the fact, but a weakening of the links between the fact and any one specific context. The semantic core remains, while the episodic context washes out.

Thought, schemata and large-scale knowledge

How widely can connectionism be applied? It appears to have a great deal to offer the simulation of memory, perception and language but what about thinking and other higher cognitive functions? Could a connectionist model understand how everyday things like houses, railway stations and shopping centres are structured?

One important theme in higher cognition is that people seem to use large packets of knowledge or schemata to interpret and think about everyday situations (see especially chapters 7, 8 and 9). Unfortunately, the schema concept has been so vaguely defined throughout most of the history of psychology as to be of very little use. In the past 20 years or so, however, attempts have been made to tighten up the idea. Minsky (1975), for example, has suggested that large knowledge systems, or frames, are used to interpret common situations. A frame consists of fixed aspects of the general situation and variables which are specified by the situation itself. A frame for a room might have fixed the knowledge that rooms have floors, walls, ceilings and usually windows, but leave unspecified the nature of the floor covering, the colour of the wallpaper or the number of windows.

A problem with these standard schema theories is that it is difficult to know how much fixed knowledge to write into a schema and how much to leave variable. Do all rooms have windows? Must a room have a door in a wall? This problem is solved in a connectionist schema model of Rumelhart et al. (1986) which has no fixed information at all, and indeed, no single, separate representation or scheme. Their model deals with the general attributes of rooms in a house and typical objects found therein. So, kitchens have walls, ceilings and floors, but also sinks, cupboards, kettles, coffee grinders, and, sometimes, cats. Studies have walls, floors and ceilings, desks, chairs, books, coffee mugs, computers and, less frequently, cats. Bedrooms have floors, walls and ceilings, beds and, thankfully, hardly ever any cats. How is all this and more information combined to form schemata for kitchens, studies and bedrooms?

The model uses a database formed by asking two human participants to decide whether each one of 40 entities such as a ceiling, wall, picture, coffee cup or ashtray would be likely to be found in a kitchen, a living room, a bathroom, a bedroom or an office. Participants' ratings allowed an assessment of the probability with which pairs of entities would be likely to be active or inactive together, that is, found in the same room. The model was then permitted to interconnect the items with one another, and suitably weight the connections so that their joint probabilities of occurrence in the various rooms were preserved.

To use the model, one of the properties is 'clamped' or given a precise activation value and held at that value. The rest of the model is then allowed to run free. The result is that entities that are highly linked to the one that is fixed turn on, and those that are negatively linked with it turn off. For instance, if 'fridge' which is assumed to be a typical kitchen object is clamped, all the other entities found in kitchens become automatically active too. The system produces a kitchen schema on demand. The same applies for the other four types of room.

The model contains no pre-programmed schemata for any of the rooms. These are constructed afresh as required. As Rumelhart et al. point out, although there are in principle 2^{40} possible states into which the machine could settle, in practice it settles into only five possible states, which correspond to the five room types, if one property is clamped. Other states are possible if more than one property is clamped and the exact form of the schema then depends closely on the units that are fixed. The model therefore responds in a flexible and sensitive fashion to different inputs.

Strengths and Limits of Connectionism ▶ ▶ ▶

It should be clear by now that connectionism has many strengths. Its models permit parallel and distributed processing; they are resistant to disruption and damage; they cope well with poor or degraded stimuli; they learn and develop. The workings of many connectionist simulations do not merely resemble human cognition in a general sense but are quite like it in detail. They display properties such as automatic generalization, prototype extraction and pattern matching which are hallmarks of human thinking. Other benefits of connectionism are its detailed accounts of cognition, its emphasis on the close links between processing structures and processing functions and its use of mathematical models to describe mental activities.

But . . . the reader will have guessed that there was one! Is connectionism as powerful as it appears? Are there any limits at all to connectionist explanations, or will we all be connectionists soon? Can the idea that people use mental rules and represent external reality with symbols, which has been at the heart of cognitive psychology for the past 30 years, finally be laid to rest? Do all the traditional theories in cognitive psychology now need to be overhauled?

The answers to these questions are right now being hotly debated by the scientific community. In this final section of the book we can only provide the flavour of a discussion that is likely to go on for some time.

Connections and associations

As we suggested earlier, Fodor and Pylyshyn (1988) presented an extensive analysis and critique of connectionism. Among their many arguments, one important claim was that connectionist models merely acknowledge what they call the 'causal connectedness' between nodes as a basic relationship. Such models, they argue, contain no intrinsic information about the nature of the structural relationships between nodes. In other words, connectionism fails, in the way that earlier associationist theories failed, to cope adequately with issues of meaning and logical relationships, which standard information processing takes in its stride. Fodor and Pylyshyn's criticism can be applied to situations where information must be integrated across a series of representations. For example, when looking around a room, information about several eye fixations must be integrated into one unambiguous percept, or when listening to extended speech, inferences and links often between quite distant sentences must be made.

Fodor and Pylyshyn's (1988) criticisms may now be less compelling than was at first thought. For one thing, it can be argued that symbol processing, the other computational approach to cognition, has problems with issues of meaning, inference and intentionality too, and that to single out connectionism for special treatment is misguided (Casey and Moran, 1989). Or, as Reilly (1989) has indicated, there are now successful connectionist models which deal with the very issues of temporal and logical connectedness which trouble Fodor and Pylyshyn. Either way, it seems that these complaints alone are not going to halt connectionist research, and there are now various simulations designed to deal with some of the issues that Fodor and Pylyshyn find troublesome (e.g. Barnes and Hampson, 1993a, 1993b; Cullinan et al., 1993).

Levels of explanation

Another complaint made by some psychologists is that connectionism offers explanations at the wrong level, or at least at too detailed a level to indicate properly what mental life is all about. According to this argument, talk about units, weights and connections may be fascinating for the neurophysiologist or computer scientist but it does not really explain how people do real tasks, such as navigating through cities or solving maths problems. Surely, to understand cognition in life-sized chunks, more meaningful talk about ideas, concepts and other sorts of symbols is needed.

Answers to this criticism take several forms. One reply is that connectionism is more fundamental than symbol-based explanations and in that sense is more correct. In physics, classical explanations dating from the time of Newton explain the behaviour of reasonably large bodies moving at average speeds rather well, but other, more specialized, quite different accounts such as quantum mechanics are needed to explain what is really happening at the subatomic or micro level. Connectionism might be more like quantum mechanics, the more correct level of explanation and one which indicates what is really going on. After all, at some point we will need to have quite detailed models of even large-scale mental processes.

However, although Newtonian physics is not so accurate as the quantum theory, it is much more convenient to use in many situations. Perhaps symbol processing also provides a less precise but far more understandable and human account of mental life. Perhaps also, people believe that they themselves are symbol-processors. Maybe certain mental operations, such as introspection, only make sense if the person doing the introspecting believes that all their mental activity is meaningful and refers to something, as symbols do. Asked to describe their mental imagery, people normally do just that, they do not tell us about their connection weights! Even if the mind is not ultimately a symbol-processor, it may be more plausible and sometimes necessary to describe some mental activities as if it were.

Connectionism and the brain

Supposing, for the sake of argument, we accept that connectionism is not the only or even the best level to understand mental processes. How does connectionism relate to the brain? Are connectionist models really models of neural not mental activities?

Most connectionist schemes are not meant as explicit brain models but they are often neurologically plausible, and so they can be used as hypotheses to guide neurophysiological and neuroanatomical research. At the moment, some features of connectionist models are known to occur in the brain while others have not been found. This might mean that models that possess these features are simply on the wrong track, or it might be that as neurophysiologists look harder they will find that these features were there all the time.

Whatever their details, it is interesting to speculate how patterns of connectivity arise in the brain. Some must be reasonably well formed at birth to allow the newly born to perform rudimentary actions, but others apparently grow and become more complex during development under the control of genetic and environmental factors. Obviously, connections for activities such as reading, recognizing new objects, or learning to type could only be laid down and modified after birth!

In addition, studies of brain-injured children suggest that networks can re-establish themselves in other brain regions if they are damaged at an early age. Language functions, for example, can sometimes be re-established if damage to the relevant brain regions occurs in the early years of life. Research indicates that other areas of the cortex are able to specialize and take over the job of the injured areas. How is this restructuring controlled? Connectionism may well have a lot to offer those who study the plasticity of neural tissue, but the reverse is also likely to be true.

Basic and higher cognition

Another frequently heard complaint is that connectionism explains basic cognitive functions such as memory and perception rather well, but provides poor accounts of thinking, reasoning, problem solving and other higher activities. Higher functions often involve advance planning, not automatic responding, and an apparently sequential flow of information. Perhaps connectionism applies well to lower functions, which use a lot of parallel processing, and where symbol theories have been less successful, and symbol processing provides a better account of higher cognition where connectionism fails.

Current attitudes toward the application of connectionism to higher cognition can be summed up as 'nothing ventured nothing gained', 'why can't we have both connectionism and symbol processing?' and 'over my dead body!'. Some psychologists, especially those of the PDP group, are trying to apply connectionism to as many mental functions as possible. We applaud these attempts since the only way that we will discover to our satisfaction whether connectionism works or not is to try it out. Others are less optimistic or downright pessimistic about its application. Still others think that a marriage of symbol processing and connectionism is likely to be needed, but none are sure how much each partner will need to contribute. We sympathize with this last view. As this chapter has shown, some higher functions have been simulated, especially those involving automatic use of schemata. Flexible and novel processes, however, have been harder to deal with.

Consciousness

Consciousness is a problem for all psychology, not just connectionism, but it could be argued that connectionism works better for non-conscious than for conscious mental activity. Of course, conscious activity is often associated with high-level cognition so the above arguments could apply here too. However, not all higher functions are conscious nor lower ones non-conscious. Consciousness has its own special properties which might cause problems for connectionism. For one thing, it is associated with awareness and intention. For another, it seems to be involved in important matters of cognitive control.

Some symbol-based accounts have suggested that consciousness is associated with the management of the rest of the cognitive system. As we explained in chapter 8, Morris and Hampson (1983) proposed that conscious mental operations were rather like the actions of the controller or boss of a large organization who receives summaries of the firm's activities from lower-level employees and who guides and monitors the overall progress of the firm, and the idea of a 'central executive' or 'supervisory system' appears in other theories (Baddeley, 1986; Norman and Shallice, 1986). These notions may indicate one way in which symbol and connectionist models can be reconciled. Norman (1986), for example, has argued that one weakness in many connectionist models is that they need someone or some system to change the connection weights. Connectionist modules need a programmer or controller. Norman goes on to suggest that two types of control system might be needed: one, the DCC system, which relies on what he calls deliberate conscious control, the other a PDP (Parallel Distributed Processing) mechanism which involves a pre-programmed set of procedures. One role for DCC is to monitor overall progress and to see when things are going smoothly. Another of its jobs is to program activation values of PDP modules that are not yet properly set. DCC would be especially used for novel and unskilled mental activity and the PDP mechanisms would take full charge when learning was complete.

So, a central, possibly symbol-based, conscious control system and a large number of lower-level connectionist modules controlled in a routine way may be the sort of arrangement needed to support human mental life.

Conclusions

In this chapter we have introduced the new and expanding area of connectionism, contrasted the approach with symbol processing and explained some of its basic aspects. Various connectionist models of language, memory and higher cognition have been described and some criticisms of the connectionist approach considered.

One question which currently troubles cognitive psychologists is whether connectionism is merely an intellectual fashion whose limitations will soon become apparent, or whether we now have a sound basis on which to construct psychological models, guide neurophysiological enquiry and build effective computer simulations. Fashionable ideas, like fashionable clothes, are not always very durable nor very practical, but our impression is that connectionism is made from strong and useful stuff. Its basic fabric, the neural network, is formed by what the great neurophysiologist, Sir Charles Sherrington, called 'the enchanted loom', the human brain, and brains are here to stay.

But whether connectionism can accommodate all of cognition is another matter. Our own suspicion is that connectionism will provide the right language for dealing with basic, largely automatic functions but that as human cognition is complex, takes place at many levels and includes activities which are conscious as well as non-conscious, no single type or level of explanation will cover its entire range. Maybe some effective combination of connectionism and symbol processing will emerge and provide a powerful framework for cognitive psychology in the first part of the twenty-first century, in the way that symbol processing alone has done in the latter half of the twentieth (see Johnson-Laird, 1988 for a similar view), or maybe interest in connectionism will once again decline.

But really, at this point, we are no wiser than the reader, since only time will tell.

Further reading

Because connectionism is so new there are not many easy to assimilate sources of information about the approach as yet. However, W. Bechtel and A. Abrahemsen 1991: *Connectionism and the Mind*. Oxford: Blackwell, is an outstanding general introduction. Similar material is covered in P. Quinlan 1991: *Connectionism and Psychology: A Psychological Perspective on New Connectionist Research*. London: Harvester, though some sections may be tough for the beginner. The reader interested in some feel for the emergence of connectionism in the 1980s is recommended to consult the important texts such as those edited by D. Rumelhart and J. McClelland (eds) 1986: *Parallel Distributed Processing*, vol. 1. Cambridge, Mass: MIT Press, and J. McClelland and D. Rumelhart (eds) 1986: *Parallel Distributed Processing*, vol. 2. Cambridge, Mass: MIT Press. Volume 1 covers the background to the approach and volume 2 provides details of several connectionist models from psychology and biology. Both are quite tough going, but you should be able to understand the earlier parts of volume 1 and various chapters in volume 2 after reading our chapter.

A good account of the possible future development of cognitive science and the relation between connectionism and symbol processing can be found in P.N. Johnson-Laird 1993: *The Computer and the Mind*. London: Fontana. See also R.G.M. Morris (ed.) 1989: *Parallel Distributed Processing: Implications for Psychology and Neuroscience*. Oxford: Oxford University Press, for reports of some recent work.

Also, *Cognitive Science, Cognition, Connection Science* and other leading cognitive psychological journals now regularly feature articles on connectionism.

Discussion points

1   Compare and contrast connectionism and more standard information-processing accounts.
2   Discuss the evolutionary advantages of parallel and distributed processing.
3   What sorts of problems would be encountered in constructing a connectionist model that could read aloud and understand sentences and paragraphs?
4   Is connectionism primarily a psychological, neurological or computational approach or is it all three?
5   Why might connectionism be said to account better for non-conscious than conscious mental activity?

Practical exercises

1   The content addressability of human memory is illustrated by the way in which we can be reminded of past events and previously acquired knowledge by chance occurrences or cues in the world around us.

Keep a diary, for two or three days, of the various incidents in which you are reminded of something, someone or some event. If possible note the incident itself, the event or stimulus which triggered the reminding, and the other thoughts and feelings that this evoked. Note the number of different cues in a particular sensory modality. Are most of the cues visual or auditory or what? How complete or fragmentary are the cues? Are remindings accompanied by strong emotions? What general form would a connectionist model take that simulated human remindings?

2   Draw a diagram of a pattern associator which will take up to eight elements in the input and output patterns. Equip your associator with suitable connection weights and try out a pattern input and see what output it produces. Vary the input pattern slightly and

check to see how this affects the output. Leave out one or two parts of the input pattern. What effect does this have on the output?

3 In the chapter, we discussed a model for solving the XOR problem which used two hidden units (see figure 13.7). The same problem can also be solved with only one hidden unit arranged as shown in figure 13.8. The diagram shows the various thresholds at which the units fire (in the circles) and the outputs of all but one of the units when their firing threshold is exceeded (next to the arrows). What size would the output from unit C to unit D have to be for this system to solve the XOR problem? (Hint: outputs can be inhibitory as well as excitatory.) Try out other arrangements of outputs and thresholds which will solve the XOR problem.

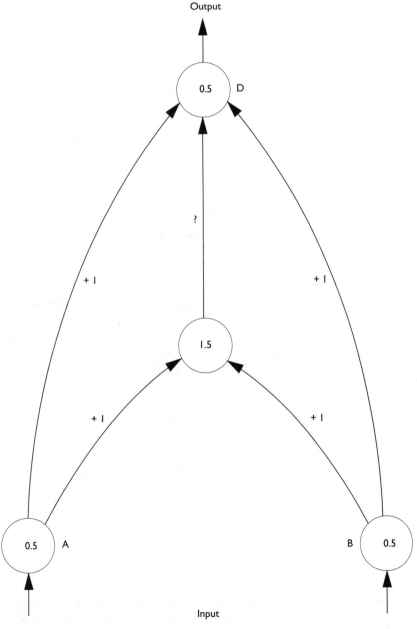

Figure 13.8 An alternative model for solving the XOR problem. Work out the output from C to D

Box 13.1
Reading impairments and connectionism

One of the advantages of connectionist models is that they do not stop working completely when some of their units or connections are damaged. They exhibit what is known as the principle of graceful degradation. In this respect, their behaviour resembles the after-effects of many types of injury to the human brain. Performance deteriorates but is not completely destroyed.

With these ideas in mind, Patterson et al. (1989) investigated the effects of giving a connectionist model of reading the equivalent of brain damage by setting some of its connection weights and activation levels to zero. How would this affect its reading ability? Would its performance resemble that of human participants suffering from reading disability? For instance, in one type of reading disorder, surface dyslexia, patients have particular difficulty with words with irregular pronunciations, tending to regularize pronunciations to make, say, PINT rhyme with HINT, MINT or LINT. Would the damaged model behave like a surface dyslexic or in some other less predictable way?

The model itself, developed by Seidenberg and McClelland (1989), was designed to link print with pronunciation. As box figure 13.1.1 shows, it consists of input units which deal with the orthography (spelling patterns) of words, output units which deal with phonology (pronunciation) and a set of hidden units between input and output. Connections link the orthographic with the hidden units and the hidden units with the phonological units. There is also a feedback loop back from the hidden units to the orthographic units. Presenting a string of letters to the model results in a pattern of activation across the orthographic units. This activation, sustained by the feedback loop from the hidden units, represents the spelling pattern of the word. Activation is also produced across the phonological units when a letter string is presented. This activation represents the sound of the word.

The model is taught to pronounce words using a supervised learning system. Activation patterns on the orthographic units are checked against predetermined codes for print and pronunciation and the model's connection weights are gradually adjusted to ensure that the activation patterns are correct.

Patterson et al. first trained the model on 2,897 words including all the single syllable words in the Kucera and Francis (1967) norms. Based on word counts of written material, these norms provide estimates of word frequency, or how often each word is used in the language. Patterson et al. were able to use word frequency to determine how many times a word should be presented during training. Over 250 training sessions, a word was presented with a probability determined by its Kucera and Francis frequency. So a frequent word like 'the' was presented around 230 times while an infrequent one might be presented as little as 12 times. The 2,897 items included words with regular pronunciations like CAVE and SAVE and also irregular ones like HAVE. Regular words are often assumed to involve pronunciation rules in English whereas irregular words are not.

The effects of training were then evaluated by comparing the model's performance with experiments on human participants. Behavioural data show that high frequency words are invariably named faster than low frequency words and that there is a bigger difference between naming speeds of regular versus irregular low frequency words than there is between regular versus irregular high frequency words. Both of these effects were mimicked in a simulation which used the same words as previous experiments with human participants, indicating that at least in these respects the model behaves like a normal human reader. Stronger connections are made for high frequency words, and both regular and irregular words are efficiently dealt with, while the weaker links for low frequency words mean that irregular words tend to be poorly learned, slowly read and error-prone.

Following training and evaluation, the model was first damaged or 'lesioned' and then tested on various words. Damage of varying severity was inflicted at three locations: the weights on the links between the orthographic units and the hidden units, the hidden units themselves and the weights on the links between the hidden units and the phonological units. Damage entailed setting the weights or activation levels to zero. Patterson et al. describe four experiments where the effects of damage were evaluated, though we only discuss aspects of experiment 1 here.

After damage, in experiment 1, the model was tested on 16 regular and 16 irregular words and a small part of a very

Box table 13.1.1 Reversal rates following damage to connectionist model

	Proportion damaged			
	0.1	0.2	0.4	0.6
Damage to hidden units (%)				
Regular words	0	0	2.5	7.5
Irregular words	1.3	2.5	16.3	23.8
Damage to links between hidden and output units (%)				
Regular words	0	0	0	0
Irregular words	0	0	1.3	8.3

Source: Based on Table 3, Patterson el al., 1989

large set of observations can be seen in box table 13.1.1. The table shows how four different levels of damage inflicted either on the hidden units or the links between hidden and output units affected the model's performance. The scores represent 'reversals'. These show how likely the model was to produce an alternative pronunciation following damage. In the case of irregular words, reversals were regularized pronunciations and occurred quite frequently, especially after extensive damage. In the case of regular words, reversals tended to be some other pronunciation. In short, the damaged models behaved very like a surface dyslexic patient: irregular words were pronounced more like regular ones. The other experiments conducted by Patterson et al. confirmed and extended these basic findings.

Although these attempts to simulate brain damage on a computer are very impressive, one criticism of this work could be that it is restricted in scope in that only one of the many varieties of dyslexia has been mimicked. However, we feel that this is an unfair criticism in that research has to start somewhere, and, in any case, attempts are now under

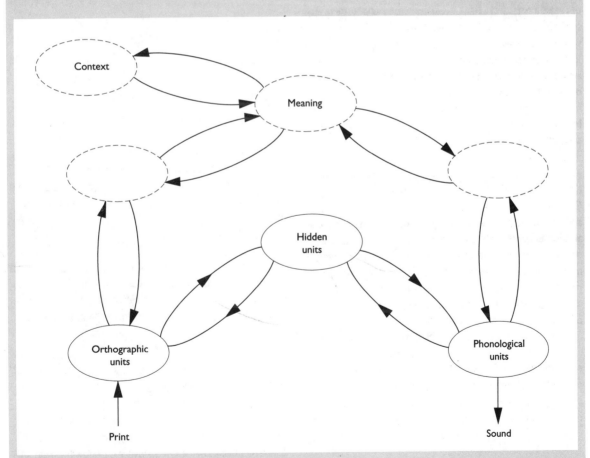

Box figure 13.1.1 The Seidenberg and McClelland (1988) model of reading; the dotted areas have not yet been implemented. (Based on figure 1, Patterson et al., 1989)

way to try to simulate other types of reading disorder. A more serious criticism concerns the adequacy of the model itself. Although the system does pronounce printed words, it does not understand what they mean. The model is meant to form part of a larger system in which meaning as well as sounds are extracted from print, but until the rest of it is implemented any final judgement must be suspended.

Finally, one impressive aspect of this research is that it sheds light on theories of normal as well as impaired reading. Several accounts of normal reading suggest that two routes are needed to get from print to sound. The first, sub-lexical route, which can be used for regular words and non-words, assumes that the reader has a number of rules relating letter groups to pronunciation (spelling-to-sound correspondence rules) which are used to construct the sound of the word. In the case of irregular words and non-words, where spelling rules are inapplicable, a second route is required to link the whole word pattern with its pronunciation. The present model manages to read both types of word using only one route from print to sound and, of course, no 'rules' whatsoever.

Based on K. Patterson, M.S. Seidenberg and J.L. McClelland 1989: Connections and disconnections: acquired dyslexia in a computational model of reading processes. In R.G.M. Morris (ed.) *Parallel Distributed Processing: Implications for Psychology and Neuroscience*. Oxford: Oxford University Press.

Box 13.2
Supervised learning: an example

In a study which has already become a classic, Rumelhart and McClelland (1986) have constructed a connectionist model which learns to form the past tense of English verbs from their present tense. This choice of topic may seem a little unusual, but it does demonstrate several important properties of connectionist learning.

Learning the past tense of English verbs

Before describing the model, we must first describe the phenomenon of verb learning in humans. If you have ever observed young children you will know that learning a language is an impressive skill. Within a few short years, children master quite complicated grammatical structures and progress from a vocabulary of just a few words at 12–15 months to sophisticated language use at age four or five. Learning verbs is part of this process.

The past tenses of English verbs are either regular or irregular. The past tense of a regular verb is formed by adding '-ed' to the verb stem. For example:

lift + ed → lifted
kick + ed → kicked
wipe + ed → wiped

Irregular verbs, on the other hand, have a variety of forms, such as:

come → came
get → got
go → went

Studies of children learning verbs show that they pass through three major stages. In stage 1, they use a small number of verbs in the past tense and they tend to do so correctly. The verbs used at this stage are generally ones which occur frequently in the language and are often irregular. A typical set of verbs used in stage 1 would be:

came, got, gave, needed, took, went

Later, in stage 2 the child learns many more verbs, some of which are irregular, but the majority of which turn out to be regular. Evidence that the child is using a linguistic rule seems to emerge; the rule is 'to form the past tense, add "-ed" to verb stems'.

Two observations are important here:

1   In stage 2, the child is able to supply regular endings for invented verbs, thus

    plick → plicked
    grend → grended

2   The child now begins to overgeneralize the rule and begins to add '-ed' to irregular verbs which she correctly used in stage 1.

In stage 3, the child sorts out these problems and begins to use regular and irregular verbs correctly.

The model

Rumelhart and McClelland have simulated this learning process using a simple connectionist model (see box figure 13.2.1). The model is basically a pattern associator, linked to an encoding and a decoding network, which links the stem or base form of the verb (input pattern) with its past tense form (output pattern). The input and output patterns are coded versions of the phonological or sound structure of the word. Because the sounds of part of a word are affected by other parts of the word (contrast the 'c' in 'cereal' and 'castle'), each sound component was coded together with a key feature of its immediate neighbours. So, roughly speaking, the coding for LIFT would be based on:

Li lIf iFt fT

This method of coding is efficient and sensitive to quite subtle sound variations, and the resulting elements are known as Wickelfeatures after their inventor Wickelgren.

The model was then trained by giving it pairs of patterns consisting of the base form as input and a teaching pattern of the past tense as output. The model derived internal representations based on Wickelfeatures then adjusted its connection strengths, using a version of the delta rule, so that it became more likely to produce the correct output when given the input.

The simulation

Rumelhart and McClelland's simulation of human verb learning involved a set of 506 verbs made up of:

10 high frequency verbs (8 regular and 2 irregular)
410 medium frequency verbs (334 regular and 76 irregular)
86 low frequency verbs (72 regular and 14 irregular).

They then exposed their model to the sort of training produce that a child learning the language might receive. This involved:

Phase 1: ten training cycles on the ten high frequency verbs,
Phase 2: adding the medium frequency verbs to the set and providing another 190 learning cycles,
Phase 3: testing on the low frequency verbs.

The most important findings were as follows:

- Performance of the model on phase 1 closely resembled the performance of a child in stage 1; both

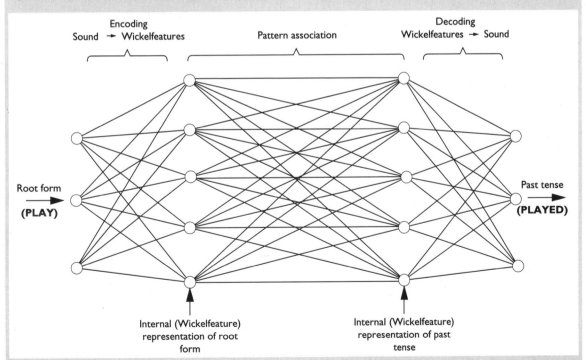

Box figure 13.2.1   A model for learning the past tense of English verbs. (Based on figure 1, Rumelhart and McClelland, 1986)

types of verb endings were quickly learned after only ten training cycles.

- On cycle 11, the first cycle of stage 2, the medium frequency verbs were introduced. This had quite a dramatic effect (see box figure 13.2.2). Over the first ten learning cycles, during stage 1, there was no difference in performance on the regular and irregular verbs; the model got around 80 per cent correct. After cycle 11, regular verbs continue to improve, but there was an immediate drop in performance on the irregular verbs. Eventually, however, these recovered, so that by the end of 200 learning cycles, the model performed almost perfectly on both types of verb. In other words, early in phase 2 of the training procedure, the model began to make the same sort of mistakes with irregular verbs as those made by a child at stage 2. It overgeneralized and treated irregular verbs as if they had '-ed' endings in the past tense. At the end of phase 2, when the model was performing correctly on both types of verb, it resembled a stage 3 child.

A number of criticisms can be made about this procedure. To begin with, it could be suggested that it is inappropriate to offer a perfect copy of the verb on each learning cycle. On the other hand, it is probably a fair assumption that children are provided with a reasonably correct copy of the language by their parents, even if not on every learning trial, and that they gradually refine their output to match this. A second criticism is one of scope. The model simply links two phonological patterns together. It knows nothing about the meaning of the verbs it deals with, nor how they could be used in actual sentences. This criticism, however, misses the point in that the model is not meant to cover these wider aspects of language. Another criticism, acknowledged by Rumelhart and McClelland, is that the model does not behave perfectly. Their own reply to this is 'that people – or at least children, even in the early grade school years – are not perfect rule-applying machines either … Thus we see little reason to believe that our model's "deficiencies" are significantly greater than those of native speakers of comparable experience' (1986, p. 266). Perfect or not, the model is impressive. For example, once

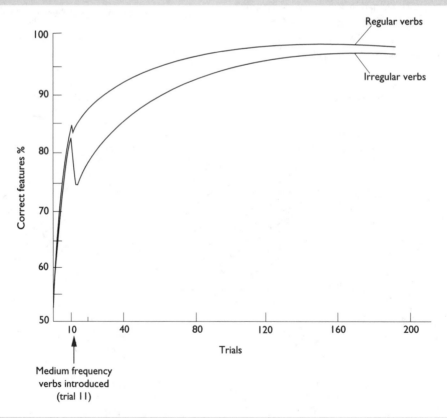

Box figure 13.2.2 Percentage correct features of regular and irregular verbs. Note the drop in performance for irregular verbs on trial 11. (Based on figure 4, Rumelhart and McClelland, 1986)

trained, it is not restricted to generating the past tenses of the verbs in the training set. To see how well it would perform on new verbs, Rumelhart and McClelland presented a fresh set of 86 low frequency verbs, 72 regular and 14 irregular. The model managed to produce the correct versions for over 90 per cent of these verbs without any previous experience with them.

Finally, we stated earlier that it looks as if children have acquired a linguistic rule when they are learning verbs. However, it is clear that the model has not formed or stored any rule at all. It simply associates verb stems and their endings, even though, to an outside observer, the behaviour may look rule-like. Perhaps children behave like this too when learning language, or perhaps children do form internal rules and thus the model is merely mimicking their performance by a different means.

Based on D.E. Rumelhart, and J.L. McClelland 1986: On learning the past tenses of English verbs. In J.L. McClelland and D.E. Rumelhart (eds) *Parallel Distributed Processing*, Volume 2: *Psychological and Biological Models*. Cambridge, Mass: MIT Press.

References

Aaronson, D. and Scarborough, H.S. 1977: Performance theories for sentence coding: Some quantitative models. *Journal of Verbal Learning and Verbal Behavior,* 16, 277–303.

Adams, J.A. 1971: A closed-loop theory of motor learning. In G.E. Stelmach (ed.), *Motor Control: Issues and Trends.* New York: Academic Press.

Alba, J.W. and Hasher, L. 1983: Is memory schematic? *Psychological Bulletin,* 93, 203–31.

Allport, D.A. 1980: Attention and performance. In G. Claxton (ed.), *Cognitive Psychology: New Directions.* London: Routledge and Kegan Paul.

Allport, D.A., Antonis, B. and Reynolds, P. 1972: On the division of attention: A disproof of the single channel hypothesis. *Quarterly Journal of Experimental Psychology,* 24, 225–35.

Allport, D.A. and Funnell, E. 1981: Components of the mental lexicon. *Philosophical Transactions of the Royal Society of London,* B, 295, 397–410.

Anderson, J.R. 1983: *The Architecture of Cognition.* Cambridge: Mass: Harvard University Press.

Anderson, J.R. 1985: *Cognitive Psychology and its Implications.* New York: W.H. Freeman.

Anderson, J.R. and Bower, G.H. 1973: *Human Associative Memory.* Washington, D.C.: Winston.

Anderson, J.R. and Thompson, R. 1988: Use of analogy in a production system architecture. In S. Vosniado and A. Ortony (eds), *Similarity and Analogical Reasoning.* New York: Cambridge University Press.

Appleyard, D.A. 1976: *Planning a Pluralistic City.* Cambridge, Mass: MIT Press.

Atkinson, R.C. and Shiffrin, R.M. 1968: Human memory: A proposed system and its control processes. In K.W. Spence (ed.), *The Psychology of Learning and Motivation: Advances in Research and Theory.* New York: Academic Press.

Attneave, F. 1954: Some informational aspects of visual perception. *Psychological Review,* 61, 183–93.

Atwood, M.E. and Polson, P.G. 1976: A process model for water jug problems. *Cognitive Psychology,* 8, 191–216.

Auerbach, S.H., Allard, T., Naeser, M., Alexander, M.P. and Albert, M.L. 1982: Pure word deafness: An analysis of a case with bilateral lesions and a defect at the prephonemic level. *Brain,* 105, 271–300.

Baddeley, A.D. 1966: Short term memory for word sequences as a function of acoustic, semantic and formal similarity. *Quarterly Journal of Experimental Psychology,* 18, 362–65.

Baddeley, A.D. 1976: *The Psychology of Memory.* New York: Basic Books Inc.

Baddeley, A.D. 1982: Domains of recollection. *Psychological Review,* 89, 708–29.

Baddeley, A.D. 1983: *Your Memory: A User's Guide.* Harmondsworth: Penguin.

Baddeley, A.D. 1986: *Working Memory.* Oxford: Oxford University Press.

Baddeley, A.D. 1990: *Human Memory: Theory and Practice.* London: Lawrence Erlbaum Associates.

Baddeley, A.D. and Hitch, G. 1974: Working memory. In G.A. Bower (ed.), *Recent Advances in Learning and Motivation,* vol. 8. New York: Academic Press.

Baddeley, A.D., Lewis, V.J. and Nimmo-Smith, I. 1978: When did you last . . . ? In M.M. Gruneberg, P.E. Morris and R.N. Sykes (eds), *Practical Aspects of Memory.* London: Academic Press.

Baddeley, A.D. and Lieberman, K. 1980: Spatial working memory. In R. Nickerson (ed.), *Attention and Performance.* Hillsdale, NJ: Lawrence Erlbaum Associates.

Baddeley, A.D. and Longman, D.J.A. 1978: The influence of length and frequency of training sessions on the rate of learning to type. *Ergonomics,* 21, 627–35.

Baddeley, A.D., Thomson, N. and Buchanan, M. 1975: Word length and the structure of short term memory. *Journal of Verbal Learning and Verbal Behavior,* 9, 176–89.

Baddeley, A.D. and Warrington, E.K. 1970: Amnesia and the distinction between long and short-term memory. *Journal of Verbal Learning and Verbal Behaviour,* 9, 176–89.

Bahrick, H.P. 1984a: Semantic memory content in permastore: Fifty years of memory for Spanish learned at school. *Journal of Experimental Psychology: General,* 113, 1–29.

Bahrick, H.P. 1984b: Memory for people. In J.E. Harris and P.E. Morris (eds), *Everyday Memory, Actions and Absent-Mindedness.* London: Academic Press.

Barclay, J.R., Bransford, J.D., Franks, J.J., McCarell, N.S. and Nitsch, K. 1974: Comprehension and semantic flexibility. *Journal of Verbal Learning and Verbal Behavior,* 13, 471–81.

Barkowitz, P. and Brigham, J.C. 1982: Recognition of faces: Own-race bias, incentive and time-delay. *Journal of Applied Social Psychology*, 12, 255–68.

Barnes, D.P. and Hampson, P.J. 1993a: Learning to learn: The contribution of behaviour analysis to connectionist models of inferential skill in humans. In G. Orchard (ed.), *Neural Computing: Research and Applications*. London: Adam Hilger.

Barnes, D.P. and Hampson, P.J. 1993b: Stimulus equivalence and connectionism: Implications for behaviour analysis and cognitive science. *Psychological Record*, 43, 617–38.

Barnes, J.M. and Underwood, B.J. 1959: 'Fate' of first-list associations in transfer theory. *Journal of Experimental Psychology*, 58, 97–105.

Baron, J. 1979: Orthographic and word-specific mechanisms in children's reading of words. *Child Development*, 50, 60–72.

Bartlett, Sir F.C. 1932: *Remembering*. Cambridge: Cambridge University Press.

Beattie, G.W. and Butterworth, B. 1979: Contextual probability of word frequency as determinants of pauses and errors in spontaneous speech. *Language and Speech*, 22, 201–11.

Beattie, G.W., Cutler, A. and Pearson, M. 1982: Why is Mrs Thatcher interrupted so often? *Nature*, 300, 744–7.

Bekerian, D.A. and Bowers, J.M. 1983: Eyewitness testimony: Were we misled? *Journal of Experimental Psychology: Learning and Cognition*, 9, 139–45.

Bechtel, W. and Abrahamsen, H. 1991: *Connectionism and the Mind*. Oxford: Blackwell.

Biederman, L. 1987: Recognition by components: A theory of human image understanding. *Psychological Review*, 94, 115–45.

Bigelow, E.B. 1934: School progress of under age children. *Elementary School Journal*, 35, 186–92.

Birch, H.G. and Rabinowitz, H.S. 1951: The negative effect of previous experience on productive thinking. *Journal of Experimental Psychology*, 41, 121–5.

Bisiach, E. and Luzatti, C. 1978: Unilateral neglect of representational space. *Cortex*, 14, 129–33.

Boden, M. 1988: *Artificial Intelligence and Natural Man* (2nd edn). Sussex: Harvester.

Boomer, D. 1965: Hesitation and grammatical encoding. *Language and Speech*, 8, 145–58.

Bothwell, R.K., Deffenbacher, K.A. and Brigham, J.C. 1987: Correlation of eye-witness accuracy and confidence: Optimality hypothesis revisited. *Journal of Applied Psychology*, 72, 691–5.

Bower, G.H. 1981: Mood and memory. *American Psychologist*, 36, 129–48.

Bower, G.H., Black, J.B. and Turner, T.J. 1979: Scripts in memory for text. *Cognitive Psychology*, 11, 177–220.

Bowers, J. and Bekerian, D.A. 1984: When will post-event information distort eyewitness testimony? *Journal of Applied Psychology*, 69, 461–72.

Braddick, O.J. 1980: Low level and high level processes in apparent motion. *Philosophical Transactions of the Royal Society of London*, Series B, 209, 137–51.

Brewer, W.F. 1988: A qualitative analysis of the recalls of randomly sampled autobiographical events. In M.M. Gruneberg, P.E. Morris and R.N. Sykes (eds), *Practical Aspects of Memory: Memory in Everyday Life*. Chichester: John Wiley and Sons.

Brewer, W.F. and Lichtenstein, E.H. 1981: Event schemas, story schemas and story grammars. In J. Long and A.D. Baddeley (eds), *Attention and Performance*. Hillsdale, NJ: Lawrence Erlbaum Associates.

Brewer, W.F. and Treyens, J.C. 1981: Role of schemata in memory for places. *Cognitive Psychology*, 13, 207–30.

Broadbent, D.E. 1954: The role of auditory localization in attention and memory span. *Journal of Experimental Psychology*, 47, 191–6.

Broadbent, D.E. 1958: *Perception and Communication*. London: Pergamon Press.

Broadbent, D.E. 1977: Levels, hierarchies and the locus of control. *Quarterly Journal of Experimental Psychology*, 29, 181–201.

Broadbent, D.E. 1987: Simple models for experimentable situations. In P.E. Morris (ed.), *Modelling Cognition*. London: Wiley.

Brown, E.L., Deffenbacher, K.A. and Sturgill, W. 1977: Memory for faces and the circumstances of encounter. *Journal of Applied Psychology*, 62, 311–18.

Brown, G.D. and Watson, F.L. 1987: First in, first out: Word learning age and spoken word frequency as predictors of word familiarity and word naming latency. *Memory and Cognition*, 15, 208–16.

Brown, R. and Kulik, J. 1977: Flashbulb memories. *Cognition*, 5, 73–99.

Brown, R. and McNeill, D. 1966: The 'tip of the tongue' phenomenon. *Journal of Verbal Learning and Verbal Behavior*, 5, 325–37.

Bruce, V. and Green, P. 1985: *Visual Perception: Physiology, Psychology, and Ecology*. London: Lawrence Erlbaum Associates.

Bryan, W.L. and Harter, N. 1899: Studies on the telegraphic language: The acquisition of a hierarchy of habits. *Psychological Review*, 6, 345–75.

Buckhout, R. 1974: Eyewitness testimony. *Scientific American*, 231(6), 23–31.

Buckhout, R. and Regan, S. 1988: Explorations in research on the other-race effect in face recognition. In M.M. Gruneberg, P.E. Morris and R.N. Sykes (eds), *Practical Aspects of Memory*. Chichester: Wiley.

Bundy, A. 1978: *Artificial Intelligence: An Introductory Course*. Edinburgh: Edinburgh University Press.

Burton, A.M., Shadbolt, N.R., Hedgecock, A.P. and Rugg, G. 1988: A formal evaluation of knowledge elicitation techniques for expert systems. In D.S. Moralee (ed.), *Research and Development in Expert Systems IV*. Cambridge: Cambridge University Press.

Butterworth, B. 1975: Hesitation and semantic planning in speech. *Journal of Psycholinguistic Research*, 4, 75–87.

Butterworth, B. 1980: Evidence from pauses. In B. Butterworth (ed.), *Language Production*. London: Academic Press.

Byrne, R. 1979: Memory for urban geography. *Quarterly Journal of Experimental Psychology*, 31, 147–54.

Campion, J. and Latto, R. 1985: Apperceptive agnosia due to carbon poisoning: An interpretation based on critical band masking from disseminated lesions. *Behavioural Brain Research*, 15, 227–40.

Carbonell, J.G. 1982: Metaphor: An inescapable phemonemon in natural language comprehension. In W.G. Lehnert and M.H. Ringle (eds), *Strategies for Natural Language Processing*. Hillsdale, NJ: Lawrence Erlbaum Associates.

Carr, T.H., Brown, J.S. and Charalambous, A. 1989: Repetition and reading: Perceptual encoding mechanisms are very abstract but not very interactive. *Journal of Experimental Psychology: Learning, Memory and Cognition*, 15, 763–78.

Carson, L.M. and Wiegand, R.L. 1979: Motor schema formation and retention in young children: A test of Schmidt's schema theory. *Journal of Motor Behavior*, 11, 247–51.

Casey, G. and Moran, A. 1989: The computational metaphor and cognitive psychology. *Irish Journal of Psychology*, 10, 143–61.

Ceci, S.J., Baker, J.E. and Bronfenbrenner, U. 1988: Prospective remembering, temporal calibration and context. In M.M. Gruneberg, P.E. Morris and R.N. Sykes (eds), *Practical Aspects of Memory: Current Research and Issues*. Chichester: Wiley.

Ceci, S.J. and Bronfenbrenner, U. 1985: Don't forget to take the cup-cakes out of the oven; Prospective memory, strategic time-monitoring and context. *Child Development*, 56, 152–64.

Chall, J. 1967: *Learning to Read: The Great Debate*. New York: McGraw Hill.

Chase, W.G. and Simon, H.A. 1973: Perception in chess. *Journal of Experimental Psychology: Human Perception and Performance*, 7, 1019–30.

Cherry, E.C. 1953: Some experiments on the recognition of speech with one and two ears. *Journal of the Acoustical Society of America*, 25, 975–9.

Chi, M.T.H. 1978: Knowledge structures and memory development. In R.S. Siegler (ed.), *Children's Thinking: What Develops?* Hillsdale, NJ: Lawrence Erlbaum.

Chomsky, N. 1957: *Syntactic Structures*. The Hague: Mouton.

Chomsky, N. 1959: Review of Skinner's *Verbal Behavior. Language*, 35, 26–58.

Chomsky, N. 1965: *Aspects of the Theory of Syntax*. Cambridge, Mass: MIT Press.

Chomsky, N. 1970: Phonology and reading. In H. Levin and J.R. Williams (eds), *Basic Studies in Reading*. New York: Basic Books.

Christie, D.F. and Ellis, H.D. 1981: Photofit constructions versus verbal descriptions of faces. *Journal of Applied Psychology*, 66, 358–63.

Christina, R.W. 1970: Minimum visual feedback processing time for amendment of incorrect movement. *Perceptual and Motor Skills*, 31, 991–4.

Claparede, E. 1911: Recognition and moiite. *Archives de Psychologie Geneve*, 11, 79–90.

Clarke, A.C. 1983: *2010: Odyssey Two*. London: Grafton Books.

Clocksin, W.F. 1980: Perception of surface slant and edge labels from optical flow: A computational approach. *Perception*, 9, 253–71.

Cofer, C.N. 1951: Verbal behavior in relation to reasoning and values. In H. Guetzkow (ed.), *Group Leadership and Men*. Pittsburgh, PA: Carnegie Press.

Cohen, G. 1989: *Memory in the Real World*. Hove, England: Lawrence Erlbaum Associates.

Cohen, G. and Freeman, R. 1978: Individual differences in reading strategies in relation to handedness and cerebral asymmetry. In J. Requin (ed.), *Attention and Performance VII*. Hillsdale, NJ: Lawrence Erlbaum Associates.

Cohen, N.J. and Eichenbaum, H. 1993: *Memory, Amnesia, and the Hippocampal System*. Cambridge, Mass: MIT Press.

Colegrove, F.W. 1899: Individual memories. *American Journal of Psychology*, 10, 228–55.

Collins, A.M. and Loftus, E.F. 1975: A spreading activation theory of semantic processing. *Psychological Review*, 82, 407–28.

Collins, A.M. and Quillian, M.R. 1969: Retrieval time from semantic memory. *Journal of Verbal Learning and Verbal Behavior*, 8, 240–7.

Coltheart, M. 1978: Lexical access in simple reading tasks. In G. Underwood (ed.), *Strategies of Information Processing*. London: Academic Press.

Coltheart, M. 1979: When can children learn to read and what should they be taught? In T.G. Waller and G.E. MacKinnon (eds), *Reading Research: Advances in Theory and Practice*, vol.1. New York: Academic Press.

Coltheart, M. 1981: Disorders of reading and their implications for models of normal reading. *Visible Language*, 15, 245–86.

Coltheart, M. 1983: Iconic memory. *Philosophical Transactions of the Royal Society of London, B*, 302, 283–94.

Coltheart, M., Besner, D., Jonasson, J.T. and Davelaar, E. 1979: Phonological encoding in the lexical decision task. *Quarterly Journal of Experimental Psychology*, 31(3), 489–507.

Coltheart, M., Sartori, G. and Job, R. (eds), 1987: *The Cognitive Neuropsychology of Language*. London: Lawrence Erlbaum Associates.

Combs, B. and Slovic, P. 1978: Causes of death: Biased newspaper coverage and biased judgements. *Journalism Quarterly*, 56, 837–43.

Conrad, R. and Hull, A.J. 1964: Information, acoustic confusion and memory span. *British Journal of Psychology*, 55, 429–32.

Conway, M.A. 1988: Images in autobiographical memory. In M. Denis, J. Engelkamp and J.T.E. Richardson (eds), *Cognitive and Neuropsychological Approaches to Mental Imagery*. Dordrecht, Netherlands: Martinus Nijhoff.

Conway, M.A. 1990: *Autobiographical Memory: An Introduction*. Milton Keynes: Open University Press.

Conway, M.A. and Bekerian, D.A. 1988: Characteristics of vivid memories. In M.M. Gruneberg, P.E. Morris and R.N. Sykes (eds), *Practical Aspects of Memory*. Chichester: Wiley.

Cooper, L.A. and Shepard, R. 1973: Chronometric studies of the rotation of mental images. In W.G. Chase (ed.), *Visual Information Processing*. London and New York: Academic Press.

Cosky, M.J. 1976: The role of letter recognition in word recognition. *Memory and Cognition*, 4(2), 207–14.

Costello, F. and Keane, M. 1992: Conceptual combination: A theoretical review. *Irish Journal of Psychology*, 13, 125–40.

Craik, F.I.M. and Lockhart, R.S. 1972: Levels of processing: A framework for memory research. *Journal of Verbal Learning and Verbal Behavior*, 11, 671–84.

Craik, F.I.M. and Tulving, E. 1975: Depth of processing and the retention of words in episodic memory. *Journal of Experimental Psychology: General*, 104, 268–94.

Craik, F.I.M. and Watkins, M.J. 1973: The role of rehearsal in short-term memory. *Journal of Verbal Learning and Verbal Behavior*, 12, 599–607.

Craik, K. 1943: *The Nature of Explanation*. Cambridge: Cambridge University Press.

Craik, K.J.W. 1966: *The Nature of Psychology*. Cambridge: Cambridge University Press.

Crossman, E.R.F.W. 1959: A theory of the acquisition of speed skill. *Ergonomics*, 2, 153–66.

Crouse, J.H. 1971: Retroactive interference in reading prose materials. *Journal of Educational Psychology*, 62, 39–44.

Crovitz, H.F. and Schiffman, H. 1974: Frequency of episodic memories as a function of their age. *Bulletin of the Psychonomic Society*, 4, 517–18.

Crovitz, H.F. and Quina-Holland, K. 1976: Proportion of episodic memories from early childhood by years of age. *Bulletin of the Psychonomic Society*, 7(1), 61–2.

Cullinan, V., Barnes, D.P., Hampson, P.J. and Lyddy, F. 1993: Combining new response sequences through equivalence relations: An experimental demonstration and a connectionist model. Paper presented at the Annual Meeting of the Experimental Analysis of Behaviour Group, University College London.

Cullinan, V., Barnes, D.P., Hampson, P.J. and Lyddy, F. 1994: A transfer of explicitly and nonexplicitly trained sequence responses through equivalence relations: An experimental demonstration and a connectionist model. *Psychological Record*, 44, 559–85.

Darwin, C.J., Turvey, W.T. and Crowder, R.G. 1972: An auditory analogue of the Sperling partial report procedure: Evidence for brief auditory storage. *Cognitive Psychology*, 3, 255–67.

Davies, G. 1979: Face and Places: Laboratory research on context and face recognition. In G.M. Davies and D.M. Thomson (eds), *Memory in Context: Context in Memory*. Chichester: Wiley.

Dawson, M.E. and Schell, A.M. 1983: Lateral asymmetries in electrodermal responses to nonattended stimuli: A reply to Walker and Ceci. *Journal of Experimental Psychology: Human Perception and Performance*, 9, 148–50.

Deese, J. 1978: Thought into speech. *American Psychologist*, 66, 314–21.

Deese, J. 1980: *Thought into Speech*. Englewood Cliffs, NJ: Prentice-Hall.

Deffenbacher, K.A. 1988: Eyewitness testimony: The next ten years. In M.M. Gruneberg, P.E. Morris and R.N. Sykes (eds), *Practical Aspects of Memory: Current Research and Issues*. vol. 1: *Memory in Everyday Life*. Chichester: Wiley.

De Groot, A.D. 1965: *Thought and Choice in Chess*. The Hague: Mouton.

Deutsch, J.A. and Deutsch, D. 1963: Attention: Some theoretical considerations. *Psychological Review*, 70, 80–90.

Diringer, D. 1962: *Writing*. London: Thames and Hudson.

Done, D.J. and Miles, T.R. 1978: Learning, memory and dyslexia. In M.M. Gruneberg, P.E. Morris and R.N. Sykes (eds), *Practical Aspects of Memory*. London: Academic Press.

Downing, C.J. and Pinker, S. 1985: The spatial structure of visual attention.

In M.L. Posner and O.S.M. Marin (eds), *Attention and Performance, XI*. Hillsdale, NJ: Lawrence Erlbaum Associates.

Downing, J. and Leong, C.K. 1982: *The Psychology of Reading*. New York: Macmillan.

Drew, G.C. 1940: An experimental study of mental fatigue. British Air Ministry Flying Personnel Research Committee, paper no. 277. reprinted in E.J. Dearnaley and P.J. Warr (eds), 1979: *Aircrew Stress in Wartime Operations*. London: Academic Press.

Duncker, K. 1945: On problem solving. *Psychological Monographs*, 58, 270.

Ebbinghaus, H. 1885: *Uber das Gedachtnis*. Leipzig: Dunker. (Trans. by H. Ruyer and C.E. Bussenius 1913: *Memory*. New York: Teachers' College, Columbia University).

Eich, J.E. 1980: The cue dependent nature of state dependent retrieval. *Memory and Cognition*, 8, 157–73.

Eich, J.E. 1984: Memory for unattended events: Remembering with and without awareness. *Memory and Cognition*, 12, 105–11.

Einstein, G.O. and McDaniel, M.A. 1990: Normal aging and prospective memory. *Journal of Experimental Psychology: Learning, Memory and Cognition*, 16, 717–26.

Ellis, A.W. 1984: *Reading, Writing and Dyslexia: A Cognitive Analysis*. London: Lawrence Erlbaum Associates.

Ellis, A.W. 1993: *Reading, Writing and Dyslexia: A Cognitive Analysis* (2nd edn). London: Lawrence Erlbaum Associates.

Ellis, A.W. and Beattie, G. 1986: *The Psychology of Language and Communication*. London: Weidenfeld and Nicolson.

Ellis, A.W., Miller, D. and Sin, G. 1983: Wernicke's aphasia and normal language processing: A case study in cognitive neuropsychology. *Cognition*, 15, 111–44.

Ellis, A.W. and Young A.W. 1988: *Human Cognitive Neuropsychology*. London: Lawrence Erlbaum Associates.

Ellis, H.D., Shephard, J.W. and Davies, G.M. 1975: An investigation of the use of the photofit technique for recalling faces. *British Journal of Psychology*, 66, 29–37.

Ericsson, K.A., Chase, W.G. and Faloon, S. 1980: Acquisition of a memory skill. *Science*, 208, 1181–2.

Ericsson, K.A. and Simon, H.A. 1980: Verbal reports as data. *Psychological Review*, 87, 215–51.

Eriksen, B.A. and Eriksen, C.W. 1974: Effects of noise letters upon the identification of a target letter in a nonsearch task. *Perception and Psychophysics*, 16, 143–9.

Eriksen, C.W. and Murphy, T.D. 1987: Movement of attentional focus across the visual field: A critical look at the evidence. *Perception and Psychophysics*, 14, 299–305.

Eriksen, C.W. and Yey, Y.Y. 1985: Allocation of attention in the visual field. *Journal of Experimental Psychology: Human Perception and Performance*, 11, 583–97.

Erman, L.D. and Lesser, V.R. 1980: The HEARSAY–II speech understanding system. In W.A. Lea (ed.), *Trends in Speech Recognition*. Englewood Cliffs, NJ: Prentice-Hall.

Eysenck, M.W. 1984: *A Handbook of Cognitive Psychology*. London: Lawrence Erlbaum Associates.

Eysenck, M.W. and Keane, M.T. 1990: *Cognitive Psychology: A Student's Handbook*. Hove: Lawrence Erlbaum.

Farah, M.J., Hammond, K.M., Levine, D.N. and Calviano, R. 1988: Visual and spatial mental imagery: Dissociable systems of representation. *Cognitive Psychology*, 20, 439–62.

Feldman, J.A. and Ballard, D.H. 1982: Connectionist models and their properties. *Cognitive Science*, 6, 205–54.

Fell, M. 1992: Encoding, retrieval and age effects on recollective experience. *Irish Journal of Psychology*, 13, 62–78.

Fischhoff, B., Slovic, P. and Lichtenstein, S. 1978: Fault trees: Sensitivity of estimated failure probabilities to problem representation. *Journal of Experimental Psychology: Human Perception and Performance*, 4, 330–4.

Fischler, I. and Bloom, P.A. 1979: Automatic and attentional processes in the effects of sentence contexts on word recognition. *Journal of Verbal Learning and Verbal Behavior*, 18, 1–20.

Fisher, R.P. and Geiselman, R.E. 1988: Enhancing eyewitness memory with the cognitive interview. In M.M. Gruneberg, P.E. Morris and R.N. Sykes (eds), *Practical Aspects of Memory*. Chichester: Wiley.

Fitts, P.M. 1954: The information capacity of the human motor system in controlling the amplitude of movement. *Journal of Experimental Psychology*, 47, 381–91.

Fitts, P.M. 1964: Perceptual motor skill learning. In A.W. Melton (ed.), *Categories of Human Learning*. New York: Academic Press.

Fitts, P.M. and Posner, M.I. 1967: *Human Performance*. Monterey, CA: Brooks Cole.

Fodor, J. 1983: *The Modularity of Mind*. Cambridge, Mass: MIT Press.

Fodor, J. and Pylyshyn, Z.W. 1988: Connectionism and cognitive architecture. *Cognition*, 28, 3–71.

Frederikson, J.R. and Kroll, J.F. 1976: Spelling and sound: Approaches to the internal lexicon. *Journal of Experimental Psychology: Human Perception and Performance*, 2, 361–79.

Friedman, A. and Polson, M.C. 1981: The hemispheres as independent resource systems: Limited capacity processing and cerebral specialisation. *Journal of Experimental Psychology: Human Perception and Performance*, 7, 1031–58.

Frith, U. 1985: The usefulness of the concept of unexpected reading failure: Comments on 'Reading retardation revisited'. *British Journal of Developmental Psychology*, 3(1), 15–17.

Funnell, E. 1983: Phonological processes in reading: New evidence from acquired dyslexia. *British Journal of Psychology*, 74, 159–80.

Gagne, R.M. 1973: Observations of school learning. *Educational Psychologist*, 10(3), 112–16.

Gallistel, C.R. 1980: From muscles to motivation. *American Scientist*, 68(4), 398–409.

Galton, F. 1883: *Inquiries into Human Faculty and its Development*. London: Dent.

Gardiner, J.M. 1988: Functional aspects of recollective experience. *Memory and Cognition*, 16, 309–13.

Gardiner, J.M. and Java, R.I. 1990: Recollective experience in word and nonword recognition. *Memory and Cognition*, 18, 23–30.

Gardiner, J.M. and Java, R.I. 1993: Recognising and remembering. In A.F. Collins, S.E. Gathercole, M.A. Conway and P.E. Morris (eds), *Theories of Memory*. Hove: Lawrence Erlbaum Associates.

Garman, M. 1990: *Psycholinguistics*. Cambridge: Cambridge University Press.

Garnham, A. 1988: *Artificial Intelligence: An Introduction*. London: Routledge and Kegan Paul.

Garrett, M.F. 1975: The analysis of sentence production. In G.H. Bower (ed.), *The Psychology of Learning and Motivation*. New York: Academic Press.

Garrett, M.F. 1976: Syntactic processes in sentence production. In R. Wales and E. Walker (eds), *New Approaches to Language Mechanisms*. Amsterdam: New Holland.

Gathercole, S.E. and Baddeley, A.D. 1989: Development of vocabulary in children and short term phonological memory. *Journal of Memory and Language*, 28, 200–13.

Gathercole, S.E. and Baddeley, A.D. 1990: Phonological memory deficits in language disordered children: Is there a causal connection? *Journal of Memory and Language*, 29, 336–60.

Geiselman, R.E. 1988: Improving eyewitness memory through mental reinstatement of context. In G.M. Davies and D.M. Thomson (eds), *Memory in Context: Context in Memory*. Chichester: Wiley.

Gibson, E.J., Pick, A.D., Osser, H.T. and Hammond, M. 1962: The role of grapheme–phoneme correspondences in the perception of words. *American Journal of Psychology*, 75, 554–70.

Gibson, J.J. 1966: *The Senses Considered as Perceptual Systems*. Boston: Houghton Mifflin.

Gibson, J.J. 1979: *The Ecological Approach to Visual Perception*. Boston: Houghton Mifflin.

Gick, M.L. and Holyoak, K.J. 1980: Analogical problem solving. *Cognitive Psychology*, 12, 306–55.

Glanzer, M. and Ehrenreich, S.L. 1979: Structure and search of the internal lexicon. *Journal of Verbal Learning and Verbal Behavior*, 18(4), 381–98.

Glisky, E.L., Schacter, D.L. and Tulving, E. 1986: Computer learning by memory impaired patients: Acquisition and retention of complex knowledge. *Neuropsychologia*, 24, 313–28.

Glucksberg, S. and Cowan, G.N. 1970: Memory for nonattended auditory material. *Cognitive Psychology*, 1, 149–56.

Glushko, R.J. 1979: The organisation and activation of orthographic knowledge in reading aloud. *Journal of Experimental Psychology: Human Perception and Performance*, 5(4), 674–91.

Goldman-Eisler, F. 1961: The predictability of words in context and the length of pauses in speech. *Journal of Communication*, 11, 95–9.

Goldman-Eisler, F. 1968: *Psycholinguistics: Experiments in Spontaneous Speech*. London: Academic Press.

Goldstein, M.N. 1974: Auditory agnosia for speech ('pure word deafness'): A historical review with current implications. *Brain and Language*, 1, 195–204.

Goswami, U. 1991: Learning about spelling sequences: The role of onsets and rimes in analagies in reading. *Child Development*, 62, 1110–23.

Gough, P.B. 1972: One second of reading. In J.P. Kavanagh and I.G. Mattingley (eds), *Language by Ear and by Eye*. Cambridge, Mass: MIT Press.

Graf, R. and Torrey, J.W. 1966: Perception of phrase structure in written language. *Proceedings of the 74th Annual Convention of the American Psychological Association*, 83–4.

Gray, J.A. and Wedderburn, A.A. 1960: Grouping stratagies with simultaneous stimuli. *Quarterly Journal of Experimental Psychology*, 12, 180–4.

Gregg, V.H. and Gardiner, J.M. 1991: Components of conscious awareness in a long term modality effect. *British Journal of Psychology*, 82, 153–62.

Gregory, R. 1972: *Eye and Brain* (2nd edn). London: World University Library.

Gregory, R. and Wallace, J.G. 1963: *Recovery from Early Blindness: A Case Study*. Cambridge: Cambridge University Press.

Grice, H.P. 1975: Logic and conversation. In P. Cole and J.L. Morgan (eds), *Studies in Syntax*, vol. III: *Speech Acts*. New York: Seminar Press.

Griggs, R.A. and Cox, J.R. 1982: The elusive thematic-material effect in Wason's selection task. *British Journal of Psychology*, 73, 407–20.

Gross, C.G., Rocha-Miranda, E.E. and Bender, D.B. 1972: Visual properties of neurons in the inferotemporal cortex of the macaque. *Journal of Neurophysiology*, 35, 96–111.

Grosz, B., Pollack. M.E. and Sidner, C.L. 1989: Discourse. In M.L. Posner (ed.), *Foundations of Cognitive Science*. Cambridge, Mass: MIT Press.

Gruneberg, M.M. 1987: *Linkword French, German, Spanish, Italian*. London: Corgi.

Gruneberg, M.M. 1992: The practical application of memory aids: Knowing how, knowing when, and knowing when not. In M.M. Gruneberg and P.E. Morris (eds), *Aspects of Memory*, vol 1: *The Practical Aspects*. London: Routledge.

Guzman, A. 1969: Decomposition of a visual field into three-dimensional bodies. In A. Grasselli (ed.), *Automatic Interpretation and Classification of Images*. New York: Academic Press.

Haber, R.N. 1983: The impending demise of the icon: A critique of the concept of iconic storage in visual information processing. *Behavioral and Brain Sciences*, 6, 1–11.

Haberlandt, K. and Bingham, G. 1978: Verbs contribute to the coherence of brief narrative passages: Reading related and unrelated sentence triplets. *Journal of Verbal Learning and Verbal Behavior*, 17, 419–25.

Halligan, P.W. and Marshall, J.C. 1988: How long is a piece of string? A study of line bisection in a case of virtual neglect. *Cortex*, 24(2), 321–8.

Hampson, P.J. 1989: Aspects of attention and cognitive science. *Irish Journal of Psychology*, 10, 261–75.

Hampson, P.J., Marks, D.T. and Richardson, J.T.E. 1989: *Imagery: Current Developments*. London: Routledge.

Hampson, P.J. and Morris, P.E. 1989: Imagery, consciousness and cognitive control: The BOSS model reviewed. In P.J. Hampson, D.F. Marks and J.T.E. Richardson (eds), *Imagery: Current Developments*. London: Routledge.

Harré, R., Clarke, D. and DeCarlo, N. 1985: *Motives and Mechanisms: An Introduction to the Psychology of Action*. London: Methuen.

Harris, J.E. 1980: Memory aids people use: Two interview studies. *Memory and Cognition*, 8, 31–8.

Harris, J.E. and Morris, P.E. (eds) 1984: *Everyday Memory, Actions and Absentmindedness*. London and New York: Academic Press.

Harris, J.E. and Wilkins, A.J. 1982: Remembering to do things: A theoretical framework and illustrative experiment. *Human Learning*, 1, 1–14.

Haviland, S.E. and Clark, H.H. 1974: What's new? Acquiring new information as a process in comprehension. *Journal of Verbal Learning and Verbal Behavior*, 13, 512–21.

Hay, D.C. and Young, A.W. 1982: The human face. In A.W. Ellis (ed.) *Normality and Pathology in Cognitive Functions*. London: Academic Press.

Healy, A.F. 1976: Detection errors on the word 'the': Evidence for reading units larger than letters. *Journal of Experimental Psychology: Human Perception and Performance*, 2(2), 235–42.

Hebb, D.O. 1949: *The Organisation of Behavior*. New York: Wiley.

Held, R. 1965: Plasticity in sensory motor systems. *Scientific American*, 213, 84–94.

Held, R. and Hein, A. 1963: Movement produced stimulation in the development of visually guided behaviour. *Journal of Comparative and Physiological Psychology*, 56, 872–6.

Henderson, L. 1982: *Orthography and Word Recognition*. New York: Academic Press.

Henderson, S.E. 1975: Predicting the accuracy of a throw without visual feedback. *Journal of Human Movement Studies*, 1, 183–9.

Higbee, K.L. 1988: Practical aspects of mnemonics. In M.M. Gruneberg, P.E. Morris and R.N. Sykes (eds), *Practical Aspects of Memory: Current Research and Issues*. Chichester: Wiley.

Hildreth, E.C. and Ullman, S. 1989: The computational study of vision. In M.L. Posner (ed.), *Foundations of Cognitive Science*. Cambridge, Mass: MIT Press.

Hirst, W., Spelke, E.S., Reaves, C.C., Caharaak, G. and Neisser, U. 1980: Dividing attention without alternation or automaticity. *Journal of Experimental Psychology: General*, 109, 98–117.

Holmes, G. 1919: Disturbances of visual space perception. *British Medical Journal*, 2, 230–3.

Holmes, M.C. 1928: Investigation of reading readiness of first grade entrants. *Childhood Education*, 3, 215–21.

Hubel, D.H. and Weisel, T.N. 1962: Receptive fields, binocular interaction and functional architecture in the cat's visual cortex. *Journal of Physiology*, 160, 106–54.

Humphreys, G.W. and Bruce, V. 1989: *Visual Cognition: Computational, Experimental and Neuropsychological Perspectives*. London: Lawrence Erlbaum Associates.

Humphreys, G.W. and Riddoch, M.J. 1984: Routes to object constancy: Implications from neurological impairments of object constancy. *Quarterly Journal of Experimental Psychology*, 36A, 385–415.

Humphreys, G.W. and Riddoch, M.J. 1987a: *To See But Not To See: A Case Study of Visual Agnosia*. London: Lawrence Erlbaum Associates.

Humphreys, G.W. and Riddoch, M.J. (eds), 1987b: *Visual Object Processing*. London: Lawrence Erlbaum Associates.

Jacobs, J. 1887: Experiments on 'prehension'. *Mind*, 12, 75–9.

Jacoby, L.L. 1983: Perceptual enhancement: Persistent effects of an experience. *Journal of Experimental Psychology: Learning, Memory and Cognition*, 9, 21–38.

Jacoby, L.L. and Dallas, M. 1981: On the relationship between autobiographical memory and perceptual learning. *Journal of Experimental Psychology: General*, 110, 306–40.

Jacoby, L.L., Kelley, C., Brown, J. and Jasechko, J. 1989: Becoming famous overnight: Limits on the ability to avoid unconscious influences of the past. *Journal of Personality and Social Psychology*, 56, 326–38.

Jacoby, L.L. and Witherspoon, D. 1982: Remembering without awareness. *Canadian Journal of Psychology*, 36, 300–24.

James, W. 1890: *Principles of Psychology*. New York: Holt.

Jarvella, R.J. 1971: Syntactic processing of connected speech. *Journal of Verbal Learning and Verbal Behavior*, 10, 409–16.

Johansson, G. 1973: Visual perception of biological motion and a model for its analysis. *Perception and Psychophysics*, 14, 201–11.

Johnson, M.K., Kim, J.K. and Risse, G. 1985: Do alcoholic Korsakoff's syndrome patients acquire affective reactions? *Journal of Experimental Psychology: Learning, Memory and Cognition*, 11, 22–36.

Johnson-Laird, P.N. 1977: Procedural semantics. *Cognition*, 5, 189–214.

Johnson-Laird, P.N. 1983: *Mental Models*. Cambridge: Cambridge University Press.

Johnson-Laird, P.N. 1988: *The Computer and the Mind*. London: Fontana.

Johnson-Laird, P.N. 1989: Human experts and expert systems. In L.A. Murray and J.T.E. Richardson (eds), *Intelligent Systems in a Human Context*. Oxford: Oxford University Press.

Johnson-Laird, P.N. and Byrne, R.M.J. 1991: *Deduction*. Hove: Lawrence Erlbaum Associates.

Johnson-Laird, P.N., Herrmann, D.J. and Chaffin, R. 1984: Only connections: A critique of semantic networks. *Psychological Bulletin*, 96 (2), 292–315.

Johnson-Laird, P.N., Legrenzi, P. and Sorino-Legrenzi, M. 1972: Reasoning and sense of reality. *British Journal of Psychology*, 63, 395–400.

Just, M.A. and Carpenter, P.A. 1980: A theory of reading: From eye fixations to comprehension. *Psychological Review*, 87, 329–54.

Kahneman, D. 1973: *Attention and Effort*. New Jersey: Prentice-Hall.

Kahneman, D. and Tversky, A. 1973: On the psychology of prediction. *Psychological Review*, 80, 237–51.

Kahneman, D. and Tversky, A. 1974: Subjective provability: A judgement of representativeness. In C-A.S. Stael Von Holstein (ed.), *The Concept of Probability in Psychological Experiments*. New York: Academic Press.

Kamon, E. and Gormley, J. 1968: Muscular activity pattern for skilled performance and during learning of a horizontal bar exercise. *Ergonomics*, 11, 345–57.

Kay, J. and Ellis, A.W. 1987: A cognitive neuropsychological case study of anomia: Implications for psychological models of word retrieval. *Brain*, 110, 613–29.

Keane, M.T. 1988: *Analogical Problem Solving*. Chichester: Wiley.

Keele, S.W. 1981: Behavioural analysis of motor control. In V. Brookes (ed.), *Handbook of Physiology*, vol. 2: *Motor Control*. Bethesda, MD: American Physiological Society.

Keppel, G., Postman, L. and Zavortink, B. 1968: Studies of learning to learn: VIII. The influence of massive amounts of training upon the learning and retention of paired-associate lists. *Journal of Verbal Learning and Verbal Behavior*, 7, 790–6.

Klapp, S.T. 1975: Feedback versus motor programming in the control of aimed movements. *Journal of Experimental Psychology: Human Perception and Performance*, 104, 147–53.

Koestler, A. 1975: *The Act of Creation*. London: Picador. (First published 1964).

Kolodner, J.L. 1983: Reconstructive memory: A computer model. *Cognitive Science*, 7, 281–328.

Krueger, W.C.F. 1929: The effect of overlearning on retention. *Journal of Experimental Psychology*, 12, 71–8.

Kucera, H. and Francis, W.N. 1967: *Computational Analysis of Present Day American English*. Providence: Brown University Press.

Kvavilashvili, L.J. 1987: Remembering intention as a distinct form of memory. *British Journal of Psychology*, 78, 507–18.

Laird, J.E., Newell, A. and Rosenbloom, P.S. 1987: SOAR: An architecture for general intelligence. *Artificial Intelligence*, 33, 1–64.

Lashley, K.S. 1950: In search of the engram. In *Society of Experimental Biology Symposium No.4: Psychological Mechanisms in Animal Behavior*. London: Cambridge University Press.

Lashley, K.S. 1951: The problem of serial order in behaviour. In L.A. Jeffress (ed.), *Cerebral Mechanisms in Behavior*. New York: Wiley.

Latour, P.L. 1962: Visual threshold during eye movements. *Vision Research*, 2, 261–2.

Lee, D.N. 1976: A theory of visual control of braking based on time to collision. *Perception*, 5, 437–59.

Lee, D.N. 1980: The optic flow field: The foundation of vision. *Philosophical Transactions of the Royal Society of London*, Series B, 290, 169–79.

Lee, D.N. and Aronson, E. 1974: Visual proprioceptive control of standing in infants. *Perception and Psychophysics*, 15, 529–32.

Lee, D.N. and Lishman, J.R. 1975: Visual proprioceptive control of stance. *Journal of Human Movement Studies*, 1, 87–95.

Lee, D.N., Lishman, J.R. and Thomson, J.A. 1982: Regulation of gait in long-jumping. *Journal of Experimental Psychology: Human Perception and Performance*, 8, 448–59.

Lenat, D.B. 1977: The ubiquity of discovery. *Artificial Intelligence*, 9, 257–85.

Levy, R.L. and Loftus, G.R. 1984: Compliance and memory. In J.E. Harris and P.E. Morris (eds), *Everyday Memory, Actions and Absentmindedness*. New York: Academic Press.

Levy, R.L., Yamashita, D. and Pow, G. 1979: Relationships of an overt commitment to the frequency and speed of compliance with decision making. *Medical Care*, 17, 281–4.

Lichtenstein, S., Slovic, P., Fischhoff, B., Layman, M. and Combs, B. 1978: Judged frequency of lethal events. *Journal of Experimental Psychology: Human Learning and Memory*, 4, 551–78.

Lieberman, P. 1963: Some effects of semantic and grammatical context on the production and perception of speech. *Language and Speech*, 6, 172–87.

Light, L.L. and Carter-Sobell, L. 1970: The effects of changed semantic context on recognition memory. *Journal of Verbal Learning and Verbal Behavior*, 9, 1–11.

Lindsay, P.H. and Norman, D.A. 1977: *Human Information Processing*. New York: Academic Press.

Linton, M. 1982: Transformations of memory in everyday life. In U. Neisser (ed.), *Memory Observed*. San Francisco: W.H. Freeman & Co.

Lishman, J.R. and Lee, D.N. 1973: The autonomy of visual kinaesthesis. *Perception*, 2, 287–94.

Loftus, E.F. 1979: *Eyewitness Testimony*. Cambridge, Mass: Harvard University Press.

Loftus, E.F. and Loftus, G.R. 1980: On the permanence of stored information in the human brain. *American Psychologist*, 35, 585–9.

Loftus, E.F. and Marburger, W. 1983: Since the eruption of Mount St. Helens, has anyone beaten you up? Improving the accuracy of retrospective reports with landmark events. *Memory and Cognition*, 11, 114–20.

Loftus, E.F. and Palmer, J.C. 1974: Reconstruction of automobile destruction: An example of the interaction between language and memory. *Journal of Verbal Learning and Verbal Behavior*, 13, 585–9.

Logie, R.H. and Baddeley, A.D. 1990: Imagery and working memory. In P.J. Hampson, D.F. Marks and J.T.E. Richardson (eds), *Imagery: Current Developments*. London: Routledge.

Lorayne, H. 1958: *How to Develop a Super-Power Memory*. Preston: A. Thomas & Co.

Lorayne, H. 1990: *Memory Makes Money: How to Get Rich Using the Power of your Mind*. Wellingborough: Thorsons.

Luchins, A.S. 1942: Mechanisation in problem solving: The effect of Einstellung. *Psychological Monographs*, 54, 248.

MacCarthy, R. and Warrington, E. 1990: *Cognitive Neuropsychology: A Clinical Introduction*. London: Academic Press.

MacKay, D.G. 1973: Aspects of the theory of comprehension, memory and attention. *Quarterly Journal of Experimental Psychology*, 25, 22–40.

Macken, W.T. and Hampson, P.J. 1993: Integration, elaboration and recollective experience. *Irish Journal of Psychology*, 14, 270–85.

Maier, N.R.F. 1931: Reasoning in humans II: The solution of a problem and its appearance in consciousness. *Journal of Comparitive Psychology*, 12, 181–94.

Maier, N.R.F. 1945: Reasoning in humans III: The mechanisms of equivalent stimuli and of reasoning. *Journal of Experimental Psychology*, 35, 349–60.

Malpass, R.S. and Devine, G. 1981: Guided memory in eyewitness identification. *Journal of Applied Psychology*, 66, 343–50.

Mandler, G. 1975: *Mind and Emotion*. New York: Wiley.

Manelis, L. 1974: The effect of meaningfulness in tachistoscopic word recognition. *Perception and Psychophysics*, 16, 183–92.

Mantelow, K.I. and Evans, J. St. B.T. 1979: Facilitation of reasoning by realism: Effect or non effect. *British Journal of Psychology*, 70, 477–88.

Marcel, A.J. 1983a: Conscious and unconscious perception: Experiments on visual masking. *Cognitive Psychology*, 15, 197–237.

Marcel, A.J. 1983b: Conscious and unconscious perception: An approach to the relations between phenomenal experience and perceptual processes. *Cognitive Psychology*, 15, 238–300.

Marr, D. 1982: *Vision*. San Francisco: Freeman.

Marr, D. and Hildreth, E. 1980: Theory of edge detection. *Philosophical Transactions of the Royal Society of London*, Series B, 207, 187–217.

Marr, D. and Nishihara, H.K. 1978: Representation and recognition of the spatial organisation of three-dimensional shapes. *Philosophical Transactions of the Royal Society of London*, Series B, 290, 269–94.

Marr, D. and Poggio, T. 1976: A computational theory of human stereo vision. *Philosophical Transactions of the Royal Society of London*, Series B, 301–28.

Marsh, G., Friedman, M. Welch, V. and Desberg, P. 1981: A cognitive-developmental theory of reading acquisition. In G.E. MacKinnon and T.G. Waller (eds), *Reading Research: Advances in Theory and Practice*. New York: Academic Press.

Marshall, J.C. and Fryer, D.M. 1978: Speak, memory! An introduction to some historic studies of remembering and forgetting. In M.M. Gruneberg and P.E. Morris (eds), *Aspects of Memory*. London: Methuen.

Marshall, J.C. and Halligan, P.W. 1988: Blindsight and insight in visuo-spatial neglect. *Nature*, 336, 766–7.

Marshall, J.C. and Newcombe, F. 1973: Patterns of paralexia: A psycholinguistic approach. *Journal of Psycholinguistic Research*, 2, 175–99.

Martin, M. and Williams, R. 1990: Imagery and emotion: Clinical and experimental approaches. In P.J. Hampson, D.E. Marks and J.T.E. Richardson (eds), *Imagery: Current Developments*. London: Routledge.

Masters, R.S.W. 1992: Knowledge, nerves and know-how: The role of explicit versus implicit knowledge in the breakdown of a complex skill under pressure. *British Journal of Psychology*, 83, 343–58.

Mathieson, C.M., Sainsbury, R.S. and Fitzgerald, L.K. 1990: Attentional set in pure versus mixed lists in a dichotic listening paradigm. *Brain and Cognition*, 13, 30–45.

Maylor, E.A. 1990: Recognizing and naming faces: Aging, memory retrieval and the tip of the tongue state. *Journal of Gerontology*, 45, 215–26.

McCann, R.S. and Besnor, D. 1987: Reading pseudohomophones: Implications for models of pronunciation assembly and the locus of word frequency effects in naming. *Journal of Experimental Psychology: Human Perception and Performance*, 13, 14–24.

McClelland, J.L. 1976: Preliminary letter identification in the perception of words and nonwords. *Journal of Experimental Psychology: Human Perception and Performance*, 2, 80–91.

McClelland, J.L. 1981: Retrieving general and specific information from stored knowledge of specifics. *Proceedings of the Third Annual Meeting of the Cognitive Science Society*, 170–2.

McClelland, J.L. 1986: The programmable blackboard model of reading. In J.L. McClelland and D.E. Rumelhart (eds), *Parallel Distributed Processing: Explorations in the Microstructure of Cognition,* vol. 2: *Psychological and Biological Models.* Cambridge, Mass: MIT Press.

McClelland, J.L. and Johnston, J.C. 1977: The role of familiar units in perception of words and nonwords. *Perception and Psychophysics,* 22(3), 249–61.

McClelland, J.L. and Rumelhart, D.E. 1981: An interactive activation model of context effects in letter perception: Part 1. An account of basic findings. *Psychological Review,* 88, 375–407.

McClelland, J.L. and Rumelhart, D.E. 1986: A distributed model of human learning and memory. In J.L. McClelland and D.E. Rumelhart (eds.) *Parallel Distributed Processing: Explorations in the Microstructure of Cognition,* vol. 2: *Psychological and Biological Models.* Cambridge, Mass: MIT Press.

McCloskey, M., Wible, C.G. and Cohen, N.J. 1988: Is there a special flashbulb memory mechanism? *Journal of Experimental Psychology: General,* 117, 171–81.

McGeogh, J.A. and MacDonald, W.T. 1931: Meaningful relation and retroactive inhibition. *American Journal of Psychology,* 43, 579–88.

McGurk, H. and MacDonald, J. 1976: Hearing lips and seeing voices. *Nature,* 264, 746–8.

McKeithen, K.B., Reitman, J.S., Rueter, H.H. and Hirtle, S.C. 1981: Knowledge representation and skill differences in computer programmers. *Cognitive Psychology,* 13, 307–25.

Meacham, J.A. and Leiman, B. 1975: Remembering to perform future actions. Paper presented at the APA, Chicago. Also in U. Neisser (ed.), 1982: *Memory Observed: Remembering in Natural Contexts.* San Francisco: W.H. Freeman.

Melton, A.W. and Irwin, J.M. 1940: The influence of degree of interpolated learning on retroactive inhibition and the overt transfer of specific responses. *American Journal of Psychology,* 53, 173–203.

Metzger, W. 1930: Optische Untersuchungen in Ganzfeld II. *Psychologische Forschung,* 13, 6–29.

Mewhort, D.J.K. and Johns, E.E. 1988: Some tests of the interactive-activation model for word identification. *Psychological Research,* 50, 135–47.

Miller, G.A. 1956: The magic number 7 plus or minus two: Some limits on our capacity for processing information. *Psychological Review,* 63, 81–97.

Miller, G.A., Galanter, E. and Pribram, K.H. 1960: *Plans and the Structure of Behavior.* New York: Holt, Rinehart and Winston.

Miller, G.A. and Johnson-Laird, P.N. 1976: *Language and Perception.* Cambridge: Cambridge University Press.

Miller, G.A. and McKean, K.O. 1964: A chronometric study of some relations between sentences. *Quarterly Journal of Experimental Psychology,* 16, 297–308.

Minsky, M. 1975: A framework for representing knowledge. In P.H. Winston (ed.), *The Psychology of Computer Vision.* New York: McGraw–Hill.

Minsky, M. and Papert, S. 1969: *Perceptions.* Cambridge, Mass: MIT Press.

Mitchell, D.C. 1982: *The Process of Reading.* Chichester: J. Wiley.

Monsell, S. 1991: The nature and locus of word frequency effects in reading. In D. Besner and G.W. Humphreys (eds), *Basic Processes in Reading: Visual Word Recognition*. Hillsdale, NJ: Lawrence Erlbaum Associates.

Moray, N. 1959: Attention in dichotic listening: Affective cues and the influence of instructions. *Quarterly Journal of Experimental Psychology*, 11, 26–30.

Morgan, M.J. 1984: Computational theories of vision (A critical notice of 'Vision' by D. Marr). *Quarterly Journal of Experimental Psychology*, 36A, 157–65.

Morphett, M.V. and Washburne, C. 1931: When should children begin to read? *Elementary School Journal*, 31, 496–503.

Morris, C.D., Bransfold, J.D. and Franks, J.J. 1977: Levels of processing versus transfer appropriate processing. *Journal of Verbal Learning and Verbal Behavior*, 16, 519–33.

Morris, P.E. 1977: On the importance of acoustic encoding in short-term memory: The error of studying errors. *Bulletin of the British Psychological Society*, 30, 380.

Morris, P.E. 1979: Strategies for learning and recall. In M.M. Gruneberg and P.E. Morris (eds), *Applied Problems in Memory*. London: Academic Press.

Morris, P.E. 1981: The cognitive psychology of self-reports. In C. Antaki (ed.), *The Psychology of Ordinary Explanations of Social Behaviour*. London and New York: Academic Press.

Morris, P.E. 1984: The validity of subjective reports on memory. In J. Harris and P.E. Morris (eds), *Everyday Memory and Absentmindedness*. London: Academic Press.

Morris, P.E. 1986: Memory images. In D.G. Russell and D.F. Marks (eds), *Proceedings of the Second Imagery Conference*.

Morris, P.E. 1988: Expertise and everyday memory. In M.M. Gruneberg, P.E. Morris and R.N. Sykes (eds), *Practical Aspects of Memory: Current Research and Issues*. Chichester: Wiley.

Morris, P.E. 1992a: Cognition and consciousness: Presidential address to the British Psychological Society. *The Psychologist*, 5, 3–8.

Morris, P.E. 1992b: Prospective memory. In M.M. Gruneberg and P.E. Morris (eds), *Aspects of Memory*, vol. 1: *The Practical Aspects* (2nd edn). London: Routledge.

Morris, P.E. and Greer, P.J. 1984: The effectiveness of the phonetic mnemonic system. *Human Learning*, 3, 137–42.

Morris, P.E. and Hampson, P.J. 1983: *Imagery and Consciousness*. London and New York: Academic Press.

Morris, P.E., Jones, S. and Hampson, P.J. 1978: An imagery mnemonic for the learning of people's names. *British Journal of Psychology*, 69, 335–6.

Morris, P.E. and Reid, R.L. 1970: The repeated use of mnemonic imagery. *Psychonomic Science*, 20, 337–8.

Morris, P.E. and Reid, R.L. 1973: Recognition and recall: latency and recurrence of images. *British Journal of Psychology*, 64, 161–7.

Morris, P.E. and Stevens, R.A. 1974: Linking images and free recall. *Journal of Verbal Learning and Verbal Behavior*, 13, 310–15.

Morris, P.E., Tweedy, M. and Gruneberg, M.M. 1985: Interest, knowledge and the memorizing of soccer scores. *British Journal of Psychology*, 76, 415–25.

Morris, R.G.M. (ed.), 1989: *Parallel Distributed Processing: Implications for Psychology and Neuroscience*. Oxford: Oxford University Press.

Morris, V. and Morris, P.E. 1985: The influence of question order on eyewitness accuracy. *British Journal of Psychology*, 76, 365–71.

Morton, J. 1969: Interaction of information in word recognition. *Psychological Review*, 76, 165–78.

Morton, J. 1970: A functional model for memory. In D.A. Norman (ed.), *Models of Human Memory*. New York: Academic Press.

Morton, J. 1979: Facilitation in word recognition: Experiments causing change in the logogen model. In P.A. Kolers, M. Wrolstad and H. Bouma (eds), *Processing of Visible Language*, vol. 1. New York: Plenum Press.

Moscovitch, M. 1982: Multiple dissociations of function in amnesia. In L.S. Cermak (ed.), *Human Memory and Amnesia*. Hillsdale, NJ: Lawrence Erlbaum Associates.

Naveh-Benjamin, M. and Ayres, T.J. 1986: Digit span, reading rate and linguistic relativity. *Quarterly Journal of Experimental Psychology*, 38, 739–51.

Naveh-Benjamin, M. and Jonides, J. 1984a: Maintenance rehearsal: A two-component analysis. *Journal of Experimental Psychology: Learning, Memory and Cognition*, 10, 369–85.

Naveh-Benjamin, M. and Jonides, J. 1984b: Cognitive load and maintenance rehearsal. *Journal of Verbal Learning and Verbal Behaviour*, 23, 494–507.

Navon, D. 1985: Attention division or attention sharing. In M.I. Posner and O.S.M. Marin (eds), *Attention and Performance*, vol. 11, Hillsdale NJ: Lawrence Erlbaum.

Nazarian, L.F., Machuber, J., Charnay, E. and Coulter, M.D. 1976: Effects of a mailed appointment reminder on appointment keeping. *Pediatrics*, 53, 349–51.

Neisser, U. 1976: *Cognition and Reality*. San Francisco: Freeman.

Neisser, U. 1978: Memory: What are the important questions? In M.M. Gruneberg, P.E. Morris and R.N. Sykes (eds), *Practical Aspects of Memory*. London: Academic Press.

Neisser, U. 1981: John Dean's memory: A case study. *Cognition*, 9, 1–22.

Neisser, U. 1982: *Memory Observed*. San Francisco: W.H. Freeman & Co.

Neisser, U. and Winograd, E. (eds) 1988: *Remembering Reconsidered: Ecological and Traditional Approaches to the Study of Memory*. Cambridge: Cambridge University Press.

Nelson, T.O. 1977: Repetition and depth of processing. *Journal of Verbal Learning and Verbal Behavior*, 16, 151–71.

Newell, A. 1981: Reasoning, problem solving and decision processes. In R.S. Nickerson (ed.), *Attention and Performance VIII*. Hillsdale, NJ: Lawrence Erlbaum Associates.

Newell, A. and Rosenbloom, P. 1981: Mechanisms of skill acquisition and the law of practice. In J.R. Anderson (ed.), *Cognitive Skills and their Acquisition*. Hillsdale, NJ: Lawrence Erlbaum Associates.

Newell, A. and Simon, H.A. 1963: GPS, a program that simulates human thought. In E.A. Feigenbaum and J. Feldman (eds), *Computers and Thought*. New York: McGraw-Hill.

Newell, A. and Simon, H.A. 1972: *Human Problem Solving*. Englewood Cliffs, NJ: Prentice-Hall.

Newstead, S.E. and Dennis, J. 1979: Lexical and grammatical processing of unshadowed messages: A reexamination of the MacKay effect. *Quarterly Journal of Experimental Psychology*, 31(3), 477–88.

Nickerson, R.S. and Adams, M.J. 1979: Long term memory for a common object. *Cognitive Psychology*, 11, 287–307.

Nigro, G. and Neisser, U. 1983: Point of view in personal memories. *Cognitive Psychology*, 15, 467–82.

Nisbett, R.E. and Wilson, T.D. 1977: Telling more than we can know: Verbal reports on mental processes. *Psychological Review*, 84, 231–59.

Norman, D.A. 1968: Toward a theory of memory and attention. *Psychological Review*, 75, 522–36.

Norman, D.A. 1980: Twelve issues for cognitive science. *Cognitive Science*, 4, 1–32.

Norman, D.A. 1981: Categorisation of action slips. *Psychological Review*, 88, 1–15.

Norman, D.A. 1986: Reflections on cognition and parallel distributed processing. In J.L McClelland and D.E. Rumelhart (eds), *Parallel Distributed Processing: Explorations in the Microstructure of Cognition*, vol. 2: *Psychological and Biological Models*. Cambridge, Mass: MIT Press.

Norman, D.A. and Bobrow, D.T. 1975: On data-limited and resource-limited processes. *Cognitive Psychology*, 7, 44–64.

Norman, D.A. and Shallice, T. 1986: Attention to action: Willed and automatic control of behavior. In R.J. Davidson, D.E. Schwartz and Shapiro, D. (eds), *Consciousness and Self-Regulation: Advances in Research and Theory*, vol. 4. New York: Plenum Press.

Oatley, K. and Johnson-Laird, P.N. 1987: Towards a cognitive theory of emotions. *Cognition and Emotion*, 1, 29–50.

Orchard, G. (ed.) 1993: *Neural Computing: Research and Applications*. London: Adam Hilger.

Orne, M.T., Soskis, D.A., Dinges, D.F. and Orne, E.C. 1984: Hypnotically-induced testimony. In Well, G.L. and Loftus, E.F. (eds), *Eyewitness Testimony: Psychological Perspectives*. New York: Cambridge University Press.

Ortony, A., Clore, G.L. and Collins, A. 1988: *The Cognitive Structure of Emotions*. New York: Cambridge University Press.

Parkin, A.J. 1979: Specifying levels of processing. *Quarterly Journal of Experimental Psychology*, 31, 175–95.

Parkin, A.J. 1987: *Memory and Amnesia*. Oxford: Blackwell.

Parkin, A.J. 1993: *Memory: Phenomena, Experiment and Theory*. Oxford: Blackwell.

Patterson, K.E. 1981: Neuropsychological approaches to the study of reading. *British Journal of Psychology*, 72, 151–74.

Patterson, K.E. 1982: The relation between reading and phonological coding: Further neuropsychological observations. In A.W. Ellis (ed.), *Normality and Pathology in Cognitive Functions*. London: Academic Press.

Patterson, K., Seidenberg, M.S. and McClelland, J.L. 1989: Connections and disconnections: Acquired dyslexia in a computational model of the reading process. In R.G.M. Morris (ed.), *Parallel Distributed Processing:*

Implications for Psychology and Neurobiology. Oxford: Oxford University Press.

Pavilidis, G.T. 1981: Do eye movements hold the key to dyslexia? *Neuropsychologia*, 19(1), 57–64.

Pavlidis, G.T. 1983: Erratic sequential eye-movements in dyslexics: Comments and reply to Stanley et al. *British Journal of Psychology*, 74(2), 189–93.

Penfield, W. 1958: Some mechanisms of consciousness discovered during electrical stimulation of the brain. *Proceedings of the National Academy of Sciences*, 44, 51–66.

Pentland, A. 1986: Perceptual organisation and the representation of natural form. *Artificial Intelligence*, 28, 293–331.

Perrett, D.I., Mistlin, A.J., Chitty, A.J., Harries, M.H., Newcombe, F. and DeHaan, E. 1988: Neuronal mechanisms of face perception and their pathology. In C. Kennard and F. Clifford Rose (eds), *Physiological Aspects of Clinical Neuro-Ophthalmology.* London: Chapman and Hall.

Peterson, L.R. and Peterson, M.J. 1959: Short-term retention of individual verbal items. *Journal of Experimental Psychology*, 58, 193–8.

Pillsbury, W.B. 1897: A study in apperception. *American Journal of Psychology*, 8, 315–93.

Polanyi, M. 1964. *Personal Knowledge.* New York: Harper and Row.

Pollatsek, A., Bolozky, S., Well, A.D. and Rayner, K. 1981: Asymmetries in the perceptual span for Israeli readers. *Brain and Language*, 14, 174–80.

Pople, H.E. 1982: Heuristic methods for imposing structure on ill-structured problems: The structuring of medical diagnosis. In P. Svlovits (ed.), *Artificial Intelligence in Medicine.* Boulder, Colorado: Westview Press.

Posner, M.I. 1978: *Chronometric Explorations of Mind.* Hillsdale, NJ: Lawrence Erlbaum Associates.

Posner, M.I. 1980: Orienting of attention. *Quarterly Journal of Experimental Psychology*, 32, 3–25.

Posner, M.I., Cohen, Y. and Rafal, R.D. 1982: Neural systems control of spatial orienting. *Philosophical Transactions of the Royal Society of London*, Series B, 298, 187–98.

Posner, M.I. and Keele, S.W. 1968: On the genesis of abstract ideas. *Journal of Experimental Psychology*, 77, 353–63.

Posner, M.I., Walker, J.A., Friedrich, F.J. and Rafal, R.D. 1984: Effects of parietal injury on covert orienting of visual attention. *Journal of Neuroscience*, 4, 1863–74.

Pritchard, R.M. 1961: Stabilised images on the retina. *Scientific American*, 204, 72–8.

Rasmussen, J. 1986: *Information Processing and Human–Machine Interaction.* Amsterdam: North Holland.

Ratcliff, J. and Newcombe, F. 1982: Object recognition: Some deductions from the clinical evidence. In A.W. Ellis (ed.), *Normality and Pathology in Cognitive Functions.* London and New York: Academic Press.

Rayner, K. 1978: Eye movements in reading and information processing. *Psychological Bulletin*, 85, 618–60.

Rayner, K. 1983: Eye movements, perceptual span and reading disability. *Annals of Dyslexia*, 33, 163–73.

Rayner, K., Well, A.D. and Pollatsek, A. 1980: Asymmetry of the effective visual field in reading. *Perception and Psychophysics*, 27, 537–44.

Reason, J.T. 1977: Skill and error in everyday life. In M. Howe (ed.), *Adult Learning: Psychological Research and Applications*. London: Wiley.

Reason, J.T. 1979: Actions as not planned. In G. Underwood and R. Stevens (eds), *Aspects of Consciousness*. London: Academic Press.

Reason, J.T. 1984: Absentmindedness and cognitive control. In J.E. Harris and P.E. Morris (eds), *Everyday Memory: Actions and Absentmindedness*. New York: Academic Press.

Reason, J.T. 1990: *Human Error*. Cambridge, Mass: Cambridge University Press.

Reason, J.T. and Mycielska, K. 1982: *Absentmindedness: The Psychology of Mental Lapses and Everyday Errors*. Englewood Cliffs, NJ: Prentice-Hall.

Reicher, G.M. 1969: Perceptual recognition as a function of meaningfulness of stimulus material. *Journal of Experimental Psychology*, 81, 274–80.

Reilly, R. 1989: On the relationship between connectionism and cognitive science. *Irish Journal of Psychology*, 10, 162–87.

Reilly, R. 1992: The psychological reality of connectionist language representations. Paper presented at Trinity College, University of Dublin.

Reitman, J.S. 1976: Skilled perception in GO: Deducing memory structures from inter-response times. *Cognitive Psychology*, 8, 336–56.

Roberts, L.G. 1965: Machine perception of three-dimensional solids. In J.T. Tippet, D.A. Berkowitz, L.C. Clapp, C.J. Koester and A. Vanderburgh (eds), *Optical and Electro-Optical Information Processing*. Cambridge, Mass: MIT Press.

Roediger, M.L. 1990: Implicit memory: Retention without remembering. *American Psychologist*, 45(9), 1043–56.

Roediger, M.L., Weldon, M.S. and Challis, B.H. 1989: Explaining dissociations between implicit and explicit measures of retention: A processing account. In M.L. Roediger and F.I.M. Craik (eds), *Varieties of Memory and Consciousness: Essays in Honour of Endel Tulving*. London: Lawrence Erlbaum.

Rosch, E. 1973a: Natural categories. *Cognitive Psychology*, 4, 328–49.

Rosch, E. 1973b: On the internal structure of perceptual and semantic categories. In T.E. Moore (ed.), *Cognitive Development and the Acquisition of Language*. London and New York: Academic Press.

Rosch, E. 1975: Cognitive representations of semantic categories. *Journal of Experimental Psychology: General*, 104, 192–233.

Rosch, E. 1978: Principles of categorisation. In E. Rosch and B.B. Lloyd (eds), *Cognition and Categorisation*. Hillsdale, NJ: Lawrence Erlbaum Associates.

Rosch, E., Mervis, C.B., Gray, W., Johnson, D. and Boyes-Braem, P. 1976: Basic objects in natural categories. *Cognitive Psychology*, 8, 382–439.

Rosenbaum, D.A. 1991: *Human Motor Control*. San Diego: Academic Press.

Rosenblatt, F. 1962: *Principles of Neurodynamics*. New York: Spartan.

Rubenstein, H.R., Garfield, L. and Millikan, J.A. 1970: Evidence for phonemic recoding in visual word recognition. *Journal of Verbal Learning and Verbal Behavior*, 10, 645–57.

Rubenstein, H.R., Lewis, S.S. and Rubenstein, M.A. 1971: Homographic entries in the internal lexicon. *Journal of Verbal Learning and Verbal Behavior*, 9, 487–94.

Rubin, D.C. 1982: On the retention function for autobiographical memory. *Journal of Verbal Learning and Verbal Behavior*, 21, 21–38.

Rubin, D.C. and Kozin, M. 1984: Vivid memories. *Cognition*, 16, 81–95.

Rubin, D.C., Wetzler, S.E. and Nebes, R.D. 1986: Autobiographical memory across the lifespan. In D.C. Rubin (ed.), *Autobiographical Memory*. Cambridge: Cambridge University Press.

Rumelhart, D.E. 1975: Notes on a schema for stories. In D.G. Bobrow and A.M. Collins (eds), *Representation and Understanding*. New York: Academic Press.

Rumelhart, D.E. and McClelland, J.L. 1981: Interactive processing through spreading activation. In A.M. Lesgold and C.A. Perfetti (eds), *Interactive Processes in Reading*. Hillsdale, NJ: Lawrence Erlbaum.

Rumelhart, D.E. and McClelland. J.L. 1982: An interactive activation model of context effect in letter perception. Part 2: The contextual enhancement effect and some tests and extensions of the model. *Psychological Review*, 89, 60–94.

Rumelhart, D.E. and McClelland, J.L. 1986: On learning the past tenses of English verbs. In J.L. McClelland and D.E. Rumelhart (eds), *Parallel Distributed Processing: Explorations in the Microstructure of Cognition*, vol. 2: *Psychological and Biological Models*. Cambridge, Mass: MIT Press.

Rumelhart, D.E. and Norman, D.A. 1981: Analogical processes in learning. In J.R. Anderson (ed.), *Cognitive Skills and their Acquisition*. Hillsdale, NJ: Lawrence Erlbaum Associates.

Rumelhart, D.E., Smolensky, P., McClelland, J.L. and Hinton, G.E. 1986: Schemata and sequential thought processes in PDP models. In J.L. McClelland and D.E. Rumelhart (eds), *Parallel Distributed Processing: Explorations in the Microstructure of Cognition*, vol. 2: *Psychological and Biological Models*. Cambridge, Mass: MIT Press.

Saffran, E.M., Schwartz, M.F. and Marin, O.S.M. 1980: The word order problem in agrammatism. II: Production. *Brain and Language*, 10, 249–62.

Sapir, E. 1929: The status of linguistics as a science. *Language*, 5, 207–14.

Schacter, D.L. 1987: Implicit memory: History and current status. *Journal of Experimental Psychology: Learning, Memory and Cognition*, 13, 501–18.

Schaeffer, B. and Wallace, R. 1969: Semantic similarity and the comparison of word meanings. *Journal of Experimental Psychology*, 82, 343–6.

Schaffer, H.R. 1975: Concordance of visual and manipulative responses to novel and familiar stimuli: A reply to Rubenstein (1974). *Child Development*, 46, 290–1.

Schank, R.C. 1975: *Conceptual Information Processing*. Amsterdam: North Holland.

Schank, R.C. 1982: *Dynamic Memory*. Cambridge: Cambridge University Press.

Schank, R.C. and Abelson, R. 1977: *Scripts, Plans, Goals and Understanding*. Hillsdale, NJ: Lawrence Erlbaum Associates.

Scherer, K.R. 1984: On the nature and the function of emotion: A component process approach. In K.R. Scherer and P. Ekman (eds), *Approaches to Emotion*. Hillsdale NJ: Lawrence Erlbaum Associates.

Schmidt, R.A. 1975: A schema theory of discrete motor skill learning. *Psychological Review*, 82, 225–60.

Schneider, W. and Shiffrin, R.M. 1977: Controlled and automatic information processing I: Detection, search and attention. *Psychological Review*, 84, 1–66.

Segal, S.J. and Fusella, V. 1970: Influence of imaged pictures and sounds on detection of visual and auditory signals. *Journal of Experimental Psychology*, 83, 458–64.

Seibel, R. 1963: Discrimination reaction time for a 1,023 alternative task. *Journal of Experimental Psychology*, 66(3), 215–26.

Seidenberg, M.S. and McClelland, J.L. 1989: A distributed developmental model of visual word recognition and pronunciation: Acquisition, skilled performance and dyslexia. In A.M. Galaburda (ed.), *From Reading to Neurons: Toward Theory and Methods for Research on Developmental Dyslexia*. Cambridge, Mass: MIT Press.

Sejnowski, T.J. and Rosenberg, C.R. 1986: NETtalk: A parallel network that learns to read aloud. Baltimore: John Hopkins University, *EE and CS Technical Report JHU/EE CS–86/01*.

Selfridge, O. 1959: Pandemonium: A paradigm for learning. In *Symposium on the Mechanisation of Thought Processes*. London: HM Stationery Office.

Senden, M.V. 1960: *Space and Sight*. New York: Free Press.

Sewall, L.P., Reeve, T.G. and Day, R.A. 1988: Effect of concurrent visual feedback on acquisition of a weight-lifting skill. *Perceptual and Motor Skills*, 67, 715–18.

Shaffer, L.H. 1975: Multiple attention in continuous verbal tasks. In P.M.A. Rabbitt and S. Dornic (eds), *Attention and Performance*, vol. 5. London: Academic Press.

Shallice, T. 1982: Specific impairments of planning. *Philosophical Transactions of the Royal Society of London*, Series B, 298, 199–209.

Shallice, T. 1988: Specialisation within the semantic system. *Cognitive Neuropsychology*, 5, 133–42.

Shallice, T. and Warrington, E.K. 1970: Independent functioning of verbal memory stores: A neuropsychological study. *Quarterly Journal of Experimental Psychology*, 22, 261–73.

Shiffrin, R.M. and Schneider, W. 1977: Controlled and automatic human information processes: Perceptual learning, automatic attending and a general theory. *Psychological Review*, 84, 127–90.

Shortliffe, E.H. 1976: *MYCIN: Computer Based Medical Consultations*. New York: Elsevier.

Simon, H.A. 1981: *The Sciences of the Artificial* (2nd edn). Cambridge, Mass: MIT Press.

Skinner, B.F. 1957: *Verbal Behavior*. New York: Appleton-Century-Crofts.

Skinner, B.F. 1985: Cognitive science and behaviourism. *British Journal of Psychology*, 76, 291–301.

Slobin, D.I. 1966: Grammatical transformations and sentence comprehension in children and adults. *Journal of Verbal Learning and Verbal Behavior*, 5, 219–27.

Smith, E.E. and Collins, A.M. 1981: Use of goal-plan knowledge in understanding stories. *Proceedings of the third Annual Conference of the Cognitive Science Society, Berkeley: California*, 115–16.

Smith, E.E., Shoben, E.J. and Rips, L.J. 1974: Structure and process in semantic memory: A feature model of semantic decisions. *Psychological Review*, 81, 214–41.

Smith, M.C. 1983: Hypnotic memory enhancement of witnesses: Does it work? *Psychological Review*, 94, 387–407.

Smith, S.M. 1979: Remebering in and out of context. *Journal of Experimental Psychology: Human Learning and Memory*, 5, 460–71.

Smith, W.M. and Bowen, K.F. 1980: The effects of delayed and displaced visual feedback on motor control. *Journal of Motor Behavior*, 12, 91–101.

Smyth, M.M., Morris, P.E., Levy, P.M. and Ellis, A.W. 1987: *Cognition in Action*. London: Lawrence Erlbaum Associates.

Smyth, M.M., Collins, A.F., Morris, P.E. and Levy, P. 1994: *Cognition in Action* (2nd edn). Hove: Lawrence Erlbaum Associates.

Spelke, E.S., Hirst, W. and Neisser, U. 1976: Skills of divided attention. *Cognition*, 4, 215–30.

Sperber, D. and Wilson, D. 1986: *Relevance, Communication and Cognition*. Oxford: Basil Blackwell.

Sperling, G. 1960: The information available in brief visual presentations. *Psychological Monographs: General and Applied*, 74, 1–29.

Sperry, R.W., Gazzaniga, M.S. and Bogen, J.E. 1969: Interhemispheric relations: The neocortical commisures; syndromes of hemispheric disconnection. In P.J. Vinken and G.W. Bruyn (eds), *Handbook of Clinical Neurology*, vol. 4. Amsterdam: North Holland.

Spilich, G.J., Vesonder, G.T., Chiesi, H.L. and Voss, J.F. 1979: Text processing of domain related information for individuals with high and low domain knowledge. *Journal of Verbal Learning and Verbal Behavior*, 18, 275–90.

Stanley, G. 1978: Eye movements in dyslexic children. In G. Stanley and K.W. Walsh (eds), *Brain Impairment: Proceedings of the 1977 Brain Impairment Workshop*. Victoria: The Dominian Press.

Stanley, G., Smith, G.A. and Howell, E.A. 1983: Eye movements and sequential tracking in dyslexic and control children. *British Journal of Psychology*, 74, 181–7.

Stanovich, K.E. 1980: Toward an interactive-compensatory model of individual differences in the development of reading fluency. *Reading Research Quarterly*, 16, 32–71.

Stevens, A. and Coupe, P. 1978: Distortions in judged spatial relations. *Cognitive Psychology*, 10, 422–37.

Stillings, N.A., Feinstein, M.H., Garfield, J.L., Rissland, E.L., Rosenbaum, D.A., Weisler, S.E. and Baker-Ward, L. 1987: *Cognitive Science: An Introduction*. Cambridge, Mass: MIT Press.

Stratton, G.M. 1897: Vision without inversion of the retinal image. *Psychological Review*, 4, 341–60.

Strongman, K.T. 1987: *The Psychology of Emotion*. Chichester: Wiley.

Stubbs, M. 1980: *Language and Literacy: The Sociolinguistics of Reading and Writing*. London: Routledge and Kegan Paul.

Summers, J.J. 1975: The role of timing in motor program representation. *Journal of Motor Behavior*, 7, 229–41.

Sunderland, A. 1990: The bisected image? Visual memory in patients with visual neglect. In P.J. Hampson, J.T.E. Richardson and D.F. Marks (eds), *Imagery: Current Developments*. London: Routledge.

Swinney, D.A. 1979: Lexical access during sentence comprehension: (Re)-consideration of context effects. *Journal of Verbal Learning and Verbal Behavior*, 18, 645–59.

Taft, M. 1991: *Reading and the Mental Lexicon*. Hove, England: Lawrence Erlbaum.

Teasdale, J.D. 1983: Negative thinking in depression: Cause, effect or reciprocal relationships. *Advances in Behaviour Research and Therapy*, 5, 3–25.

Thompson, C.P. 1982: Memory for unique personal events: The roommate study. *Memory and Cognition*, 10, 324–32.

Thorndyke, P.W. 1977: Cognitive structures in comprehension and memory of narrative discourse. *Cognitive Psychology*, 9, 77–110.

Thorndyke, P.W. 1984: Applications of schema theory in cognitive research. In J.R. Anderson and S.M. Kosslyn (eds), *Tutorials in Learning and Memory*. New York: W.H. Freeman.

Tinker, M.A. 1946: The study of eye movements in reading. *Psychological Bulletin*, 43, 93–120.

Tinker, M.A. 1958: Recent studies of eye movements in reading. *Psychological Bulletin*, 55, 215–31.

Tipper, S.P. and Driver, J. 1988: Negative priming between pictures and words in a selective attention task: Evidence for semantic processing of ignored stimuli. *Memory and Cognition*, 16, 64–70.

Treisman, A. 1960: Contextual cues in selective listening. *Quarterly Journal of Experimental Psychology*, 12, 242–8.

Treisman, A. 1964: Monitoring and storage of irrelevant messages in selective attention. *Journal of Verbal Learning and Verbal Behavior*, 3, 449–59.

Treisman, A. 1964: Verbal cues, language and meaning in selective attention. *American Journal of Psychology*, 77, 206–19.

Treisman, A. 1988: Features and objects: The fourteenth Bartlett Memorial Lecture. *Quarterly Journal of Experimental Psychology*, 40A, 201–37.

Treisman, A. and Davies, A. 1973: Divided attention to ear and eye. In S. Kornblum (ed.), *Attention and Performance IV*. London: Academic Press.

Treisman, A. and Gelade, G. 1980: A feature integration theory of attention. *Cognitive Psychology*, 12, 97–136.

Treisman, A. and Riley, J.G.A. 1969: Is selective attention selective perception or selective response: A further test. *Journal of Experimental Psychology*, 79, 27–34.

Treisman, A. and Schmidt, H. 1982: Illusory conjunctions in the perception of objects. *Cognitive Psychology*, 14, 107–41.

Treisman, A. and Souther, J. 1985: Search assymetry: A diagnostic for preattentive processing of separable features. *Journal of Experimental Psychology: General*, 114, 285–310.

Tulving, E. 1979: Relation between encoding specificity and levels of processing. In L.S. Cermak and F.I.M. Craik (eds), *Levels of Processing in Human Memory*. Hillsdale, NJ: Lawrence Erlbaum Associates.

Tulving, E. 1983: *Elements of Episodic Memory*. Oxford: Oxford University Press.

Tulving, E. 1985: Memory and consciousness. *Canadian Psychology*, 26, 1–12.

Tulving, E. 1989: Memory, performance, knowledge and experience. *European Journal of Cognitive Psychology*, 1, 3–26.

Tulving, E. and Gold, C. 1963: Stimulus information and contextual information as determinants of tachistoscopic recognition of words. *Journal of Experimental Psychology*, 66, 319–27.

Tulving, E. and Schacter, D.L. 1990: Priming and human memory systems. *Science*, 247, 301–6.

Tulving, E., Schacter, D.L., McClachlan, D.R. and Moscovitch, M. 1988: Priming of semantic autobiographical knowledge: A case study of retrograde amnesia. *Brain and Cognition*, 8, 3–20.

Tulving, E., Schacter, D.L., and Stark, H.A. 1982: Priming effects in word-fragment completion are independent of recognition memory. *Journal of Experimental Psychology: Learning, Memory and Cognition*, 8, 336–42.

Turvey, M.T. 1973: On peripheral and central processes in vision: Inferences from an information processing analysis of masking with patterned stimuli. *Psychological Review*, 80, 1–52.

Tversky, A. and Kahneman, D. 1982: Judgemants of and by representativeness. In D. Kahneman, P. Slovic and A. Tversky (eds), *Judgements Under Uncertainty: Heuristics and Biases*. Cambridge, UK: Cambridge University Press.

Tversky, B. 1981: Distortions in memory for maps. *Cognitive Psychology*, 13, 407–33.

Tversky, B. and Kahneman, D. 1974: Judgement under uncertainty: Heuristics and biases. *Science*, 185, 1124–31.

Underwood, B.J. 1957: Interference and forgetting. *Psychological Review*, 64, 49–60.

Vallar, G. and Baddeley, A.D. 1984a: Fractionation of working memory: Neuropsychological evidence for a phonological short-term store. *Journal of Verbal Learning and Verbal Behaviour*, 23, 151–62.

Vallar, G. and Baddeley, A.D. 1984b: Phonological short-term store, phonological processing and sentence comprehension: A neuropsychological case study. *Cognitive Neuropsychology*, 1, 121–41.

Valvo, A. 1971: *Sight Restoration after Long-Term Blindness: The Problems and Behavior Patterns of Visual Rehabilitation*. New York: American Foundation for the Blind.

Vellutino, F.R., Stager, J.A. DeSetto, L. and Phillips, F. 1975: Immediate and delayed recognition of visual stimuli in poor and normal readers. *Journal of Experimental Child Psychology*, 19, 223–32.

Verfaellie, M., Bauer, R.M. and Bowers, D. 1991: Autonomic and behavioral memory and amnesia. *Brain and Cognition*, 15, 10–25.

Von Cranach, M. and Harré, R. (eds) 1982: *The Analysis of Action*. Cambridge: Cambridge University Press.

Wagenaar, W.A. 1986: My memory: A study of autobiographical memory over six years. *Cognitive Psychology*, 18, 225–52.

Wagenaar, W.A. 1988: People and places in my memory: A study on cue specificity and retrieval from autobiographical memory. In M.M. Gruneberg, P.E. Morris and R.N. Sykes (eds), *Practical Aspects of Memory:*

Current Research and Issues, vol.1: *Memory in Everyday Life*. Chichester: Wiley.

Waldfogel, S. 1948: The frequency and affective character of childhood memories. *Psychological Monographs*, 62, 1–34.

Walker, D. 1978: *Understanding Spoken Language*. New York: Elsevier North Holland.

Warr, P.B. 1964: The relative importance of proactive inhibition and degree of learning in retention of paired associate items. *British Journal of Psychology*, 55, 19–30.

Warrington, E.K. 1982: Neuropsychological studies of object recognition. *Philosophical Transactions of the Royal Society of London*, Series B, 298, 15–33.

Warrington, E.K. and Shallice, T. 1969: The selective impairment of auditory verbal short-term memory. *Brain*, 92, 885–96.

Warrington, E.K. and Shallice, T. 1984: Category-specific semantic impairments. *Brain*, 107, 829–54.

Warrington, E.K. and Taylor, A.M. 1978: Two categorical stages of object recognition. *Perception*, 7, 695–705.

Warrington, E.K. and Weiskrantz, L. 1970: Amnesic syndrome: Consolidation or retrieval. *Nature*, 228, 628–30.

Wason, P.C. 1965: The contexts of plausible denial. *Journal of Verbal Learning and Verbal Behavior*, 4, 7–11.

Wason, P.C. 1966: Reasoning. In B.M. Foss (ed.), *New Horizons in Psychology*. Harmondsworth: Penguin.

Waterman, D.A. 1986: *A Guide to Expert Systems*. Reading, Mass: Addison-Wesley.

Watt, R.J. 1988: *Visual Processing: Computational, Psychophysical and Cognitive Research*. London: Lawrence Erlbaum Associates.

Weiskrantz, L. 1986: *Blindsight: A Case Study and Implications*. Oxford: Oxford University Press.

Weizenbaum, J. 1966: ELIZA – a computer program for the study of natural language communication between man and machine. *Communications of the Association for Computing Machine*, 9, 36–45.

Welch, J. 1898: On the measurement of mental activity and the determination of a constant of attention. *American Journal of Physiology*, 1, 228–306.

Welford, A.T. 1968: *Fundamentals of a Skill*. London: Methuen.

Wertheimer, M. 1912: Experimentalle Studien uber das Sehen von Bewegung. *Zeitschrift fur Psychologie*, 61, 161–265. Translated in T. Shipley (ed.), 1961: *Classics in Psychology*. New York: Philosophical Library.

White, P.A. 1988: Knowing more about what we can tell: Introspective access and causal report accuracy 10 years later. *British Journal of Psychology*, 79, 13–45.

Whorf, B.L. 1956: *Language, Thought and Reality*. Cambridge, Mass: MIT Press.

Wickens, C.D. 1984: Processing resources in attention. In R. Parasuraman and D. Davies (eds), *Varieties of Attention*. New York: Academic Press.

Wilkins, A.J. and Baddeley, A.D. 1978: Remembering to recall in everyday life: An approach to absentmindedness. In M.M. Gruneberg, P.E. Morris and R.N. Sykes (eds), *Practical Aspects of Memory*. London: Academic Press.

Winograd, T. 1972: *Understanding Natural Language*. New York: Academic Press.

Winstein, C.J. and Schmidt, R.A. 1990: Reduced frequency of knowledge of results enhances motor skill learning. *Journal of Experimental Psychology: Learning, Memory and Cognition*, 16, 677–91.

Winston, P.H. and Horn, B.K.P. 1984: *LISP* (2nd edn). Reading, Mass: Addison-Wesley.

Wittgenstein, L. 1953: *Philosophical Investigations*. (Translation by G.E.M. Anscombe). Oxford: Blackwell.

Wood, F., Ebert, V. and Kinsbourne, M. 1982: The episodic–semantic memory distinction in memory and amnesia: Clinical and experimental observations. In L.S. Cermak (ed.), *Human Memory and Amnesia*. Hillsdale, NJ: Lawrence Erlbaum Associates.

Woodworth, R.S. 1938: *Experimental Psychology*. London: Methuen.

Woodworth, R.S. and Schlosberg, H. 1954: *Experimental Psychology*. New York: Holt.

Woodworth, R.S. and Sells, S.B. 1935: An atmosphere effect in formal syllogistic reasoning. *Journal of Experimental Psychology*, 18, 451–60.

Young, A.W., Hay, D.C. and Ellis, A.W. 1985: The faces that launched a thousand slips: Everyday difficulties and errors in recognising people. *British Journal of Psychology*, 76, 495–523.

Young, R.M. 1989: Human interface aspects of expert systems. In L.A. Murray and J.T.E. Richardson (eds), *Intelligent Systems in a Human Context*. Oxford: Oxford University Press.

Zajonc, R.B. 1980: Feeling and thinking: Preferences need no inferences. *American Psychologist*, 35, 151–75.

Zihl, J., Von Cramon, D. and Mai, N. 1983: Selective disturbance of movement vision after bilateral brain damage. *Brain*, 106, 313–40.

Author Index

Subject Index